Imagined Enemies

Imagined Enemies

CHINA PREPARES FOR
UNCERTAIN WAR

John Wilson Lewis and Xue Litai

STANFORD UNIVERSITY
STANFORD, CALIFORNIA
2006

Stanford University Press
Stanford, California

Printed in the United States of America on acid-free, archival-quality paper

Library of Congress Cataloging-in-Publication Data

Lewis, John Wilson, 1930–
  Imagined enemies : China prepares for uncertain war / John Wilson Lewis and Xue Litai.
    p.   cm.
  Includes bibliographical references and index.
  ISBN-13: 978-0-8047-5391-3 (cloth : alk. paper)
    1. China—Military policy.   2. China—Armed Forces.   3. Military planning—China.   4. China—Relations—Taiwan.   5. Taiwan—Relations—China.   I. Xue, Litai, 1947–   II. Title.
UA835.L428   2006
355'.033551—dc22

2006009400

Typeset by G & S Typesetters, Inc. in 11/14 Adobe Garamond

Original Printing 2006

Last figure below indicates year of this printing:
15   14   13   12   11   10   09   08   07   06

For Mildred Taylor and Yuying Gao

Contents

Charts

Preface

Since the publication of *China Builds the Bomb* in 1988, we have continued our research on the Chinese military. Our main theme then and in most of our subsequent work has dealt with the impact of large military-technical programs on the Chinese political system and broader national development. What continued to elude us was a clear understanding of the process of decisionmaking and operations in the People's Liberation Army as it made the transition from a huge conventional force to a more modern military armed with advanced strategic weapons and electronic systems, and facing a more limited range of imagined enemies.

We wondered whether it would be possible to identify the principal benchmarks in the evolution of Chinese military culture and its incorporation of lessons traceable to ancient wisdom, revolutionary principles, and the legacy of repeated conflicts. Taken together, national culture and battlefield lessons, while permanent residents in the Chinese psyche, seemed to fade, and it became important to weigh the past against the dramatic shift in domestic priorities and the awesome demonstrations of modern weaponry and warfare in faraway lands.

With astonishing speed, China under Deng Xiaoping, its leader for almost two decades after the death of Mao Zedong in 1976, resolved or set aside historic boundary disputes and the bitter hostilities with the United States and the Soviet Union. Yet, as the prospect of a nuclear showdown with the two superpowers slowly retreated, the legacy of the civil war remained and grew more threatening. Could a future unwanted struggle against Taiwan and its principal supporter warrant a gradual movement toward increased defense budgets and equipment imports? How would that movement drive the transformation of the national command authority in peace and war and the strengthening of the PLA's command-and-control systems?

Not surprisingly, our labors to answer these and a long list of other questions proved far more daunting and time consuming than we had first estimated. Part of the problem, of course, was that we found ourselves in the middle of a mystery with no clear understanding of the plot or the characters. In the China of Deng Xiaoping, Jiang Zemin, and Hu Jintao, publications proliferated, and it became virtually impossible using established analytical paradigms to sift the informed from the idiotic. Where once the story line of postrevolutionary China was relatively clear cut, now stories blossomed within stories. Who were the experts? Who were the imposters? How gullible were foreigners, when even the best and brightest in China could not discern the reality from imported jargon, promising plans from Party hyperbole? As difficult as our earlier investigations had been into some of the most sensitive security issues, this challenge was new, a mixture of exciting discovery and maddening puzzlement.

More than knowledge and the honing of analytical tools is at stake in the study of war and peace in Asia. So staggering is the potential human cost of conflict that those who study it do so in the hope that we can make a difference in preventing it. One of the authors joined the navy within days after the outbreak of the Korean War, and during much of his career, he has dealt with the threat of a war that could engulf the Korean Peninsula and the Taiwan Strait. The other author lived in China through the tumultuous decade of the Cultural Revolution and the violence it inflicted on so many millions. There are, of course, things worth fighting for and expending national treasure to protect, but so much of what we have learned in our own lives is that all too often the path to war is marked by amazing stupidity and stubbornness. All too often, war is not the last resort, and the high values of sovereignty and national interest it allegedly protects are lost in far less lofty political purposes.

More than a decade has passed since we began the research on this book. During these years we have made more than fifty trips to mainland China, Taiwan, and Hong Kong. We have met several hundred officials and security specialists and used every possible opportunity to develop and test our analysis. The last trip took place just after Chinese New Year 2005, the cutoff date for our manuscript, and several conversations during this visit brought us up short on conclusions that we were certain had stood the test of time.

In completing the research for this book, we received extensive assistance from colleagues here and abroad. Rather than a long list of names, the references to their writings found in the bibliography at the end of this volume will attest to our gratitude for their contributions to this study and the field as a whole. We do wish to acknowledge the contributions made by two anonymous reviewers, one of whom went far beyond a reviewer's ordinary charge and whose many suggestions, including the addition of the Introduction, have been readily accepted. Kenneth Allen, William J. Perry, and Dean Wilkening helped us rethink Chapter 7 when it was still an article for *International Security*. We wish to thank the holders of the copyright to that article, the President and Fellows of Harvard College and the Massachusetts Institute of Technology, for granting us permission to use a revised and expanded version of that article for this book. We also thank the Stanford University Press for its permission to use a section from *China's Strategic Seapower*, chapter 9, in this volume's final chapter.

The photographs in this book came from several Chinese sources, which we acknowledge with thanks. Pictures were purchased from *Junshi Wenzhai* (Military Digest) and Zhongguo Xinwen She (China News Agency) and are used with their permission. Other pictures were generously provided by officers at one of China's military academies, and a confidential copy of their permission is on file at the Stanford University Press. Finally, we wish to acknowledge the generosity of Richard "Rick" Fisher, Jr., for providing selected pictures from his remarkable collection and for identifying the equipment and technologies in many of the photos that we have used.

There is no way of adequately thanking the librarians, editors, proofreaders, and manuscript preparers who have made this book possible. We put a heavy burden on the staffs of the Stanford University East Asia Library, the Universities Service Centre of the Chinese University of Hong Kong, and the Stanford University Press. We particularly wish to thank Muriel Bell, Judith Hibbard, and Harold Moorehead at the Press, and our copyeditor, Richard Gunde. In our Asian project at the Center for International Security and Cooperation, Carole Hyde significantly helped us complete this book, and our wives, Jacquelyn Lewis and Yuying Gao, unfailingly provided encouragement and support over these many years.

Additional generous backing for our research and writing came from a number of important sources. We wish to thank Dr. Marjorie Kiewit, the John D. and Catherine T. MacArthur Foundation, and the Freeman Spogli Institute for International Studies under the leadership of David Holloway and Coit Blacker.

When we finished our book *China's Strategic Seapower*, we wrote that it represented the last in a series of books and articles intended to understand the scope and evolution of Chinese security policy. Each of our earlier books on the military built on those that had come before, even though the chronology of their publication did not follow the order of Chinese history. Our study of the origins of the Korean War helped provide the context for our study of the Chinese nuclear program, and the findings from that study helped introduce the development of China's nuclear-powered submarine and its ballistic missile. The latter two studies concentrated on the evolution of the military-industrial system and on the interactions among politics, technology, and security policy during the first forty-four years of the People's Republic.

In the decade that has passed since the *Seapower* book went to press, those interactions have accelerated and have been extensively chronicled. Their extraordinary significance in the rise of China warrants, we believe, the publication of this fourth volume in our study of the Chinese People's Liberation Army.

We bring this effort to a close during a period of great uncertainty. The crises in the Taiwan Strait and on the Korean Peninsula could still threaten the peace in East Asia, and conflicts in either place could erupt in a war that could escalate and involve the United States. Haunted by imagined enemies nearby and across the Pacific, the Chinese nation reluctantly prepares for uncertain war. Decades from now we will know whether the imagined became real or statesmen could finally reclaim the promise of peace.

J.W.L.
X.L.T.
Chinese New Year's Day, 2005

Imagined Enemies

ONE

Introduction

Should China survive the trials of the coming decades, history may record this as the time it crossed the threshold to become a global power. In a twinkling it seems, the world's most populous nation has become the dominant manufacturer and exporter. While many Chinese remain impoverished, the sheer number of those relentlessly pressing into the middle and even upper classes is staggering. We have examined elsewhere the unique challenges of Chinese economic successes, and despite the many unresolved regional, social, and environmental contradictions that plague this land, China has a reasonable chance to regain its historical stature.[1]

One reason for this opportunity is the grit and endurance of a talented people, but power is relative, and lest it be forgotten, over the past century several once-powerful states have lost vast amounts of their national treasure in warfare and from military or other unproductive programs in comparison to China. Comparatively speaking, these states may now face near-irreversible decline. While many current powers can still boast an edge in such critical areas as science and technology, China is working to lessen that advantage through favorable business deals, strategic technology acquisitions, and targeted scientific programs. Should that effort continue unimpeded, China's race to greatness could succeed within the next twenty years.

To increase the odds for that success, China has dramatically reversed direction from the combative rule of Mao Zedong and even Deng Xiaoping. It has resolved virtually all its contested boundaries—the glaring exception being the Sino-Indian border—and in the case of the South China Sea and several disputed islands it has shelved the most contentious disputes indefinitely. Over the last decade or so, China has increasingly made its voice heard in the United Nations, joined multilateral organizations in East Asia, created the Shanghai Cooperation Organization jointly with Russia and four Central Asian states, moved aggressively in the common struggle against terrorism, and pursued a negotiated solution to the Korean nuclear crisis.

Standing outside the inner sanctum of Beijing's political-military high command, we cannot accurately determine whether this striking redirection toward growth and diplomacy stems from real choices and the political acumen of Mao's successors or from a more intelligent expression of the Machiavellian opportunism that underlay much of his strategy. Whatever the causes, China's path to greatness seems ever wider and smoother. Its current and potential rivals lack the fierce resolve of China's leadership, its near-universal appeal for investors, and the global dispersion of its people.

The Chinese know well that the past is littered with cases of nations with high promise missing or sacrificing their time of greatness. Their leaders in the new millennium have been acutely aware of the possible dangers for China, having so recently witnessed the rise and fall of the Soviet state. Still, they, too, cannot escape their own legacy with its false dreams and hidden perils. The very nationalism that mixed so uncomfortably with imported Marxism and revolutionary Maoism helped propel them to victory but then dogged them for the first thirty years of the People's Republic. Marxism and Maoism receded, it seems clear, but Chinese nationalism did not. It replaced discredited ideology and reinforced popular visions of grandeur, and it became the creed of the nation's youth and undercut strict economic rationalism. It came in the guise of "one China," and the fear of losing Taiwan gripped the Chinese soul.

It is Taiwan's moves toward de jure statehood that pose the most-dangerous threat to China's long-term ambitions. In an important interview in November 2004, President Hu Jintao told an overseas Chinese audience that Beijing's priorities are development first and reunification second, but he then said, "We absolutely do not allow anyone to separate Taiwan from China in whatever form."[2]

A war to prevent the island from becoming a sovereign state would slash the odds that China could become a great power within a generation, if ever. Though they profess to grasp the danger and thus to be acting with caution, all Chinese leaders feel compelled to advance toward an endgame that could ruin their fondest aspirations. Also in November 2004, President Hu told President George W. Bush that Taiwan's independence would "wreck the peace in the Taiwan Strait and seriously disrupt peace, stability, and prosperity in the entire Asia-Pacific region."[3] Even so, China's leaders would once more prepare for deadly warfare, though this time the enemy would resemble the images in their mirrors. Hence this study's focus on China, war, and the coming confrontation with Taiwan, a confrontation that could doom China's long-sought promise.

Just as Mao's anti-American and anti-Soviet pronouncements blithely dismissed the consequences of a nuclear war for his nation, his heirs would now willingly mortgage the nation's destiny in order to preserve Taiwan as a province of China despite the huge losses that the effort could inflict.[4] One need only speak to a Shanghai college student or a Guangdong merchant to appreciate the depth of that commitment, its hold on the national psyche. China's defense White Paper for 2004 called the cross-strait situation "grim," and declared: "We will never allow anyone to split Taiwan from China through whatever means. Should the Taiwan authorities go so far as to make a reckless attempt that constitutes a major incident of 'Taiwan independence,' the Chinese people and armed forces will resolutely and thoroughly crush it at any cost."[5]

This is a book about conflicts waged since the 1960s and preparations for a renewed, but more deadly civil war that no one wants but all see coming. Facing any large conflict in the nuclear age is sometimes said to clear the mind and simplify the available alternatives, though considerable evidence exists to the contrary. In the decades encompassed in this study, moreover, the old rationales for going to war, at least in East Asia, have come into conflict with the compelling forces of economic globalism and regional cooperation. Were it not for the specter of terrorism, the notion of inevitable conflict between states, let alone civilizations, could well have been relegated to historical annals and fading memories.

Military intentions and capabilities have constantly shifted, to be sure, but for the Chinese people the possibility of war in this nuclear era, though low, has not disappeared, nor have they made a clear choice between national development and imposed unification. At the same time, thoughtful Chinese appear to understand that when the flames of war have finally died out, no one would be able to distinguish victor from vanquished among those they once called brothers.

ORGANIZATION OF THE STUDY

This book begins in the Middle Kingdom's ancient but hardly forgotten past and moves quickly to events only a few decades old. It thereby acknowledges what all current military leaders in China assume: They are at heart a product of both proud tradition and events within their own memories or that of their immediate forebears. That tradition and those events, future historians will correctly hold, help justify otherwise prudent Chinese and their commanders embracing policies that could lead to national disaster.

For two centuries, war has gone hand in hand with China's quest for survival, independence, and unity. Born in 1949 after decades of chaos and devastating violence, the People's Republic of China applied the lessons and culture of the revolutionary years to the next three decades of near-perpetual hostilities and repeated warfare. Korea, America, India, Russia, and Vietnam came one after the other in the parade of enemies.

While inherited dogma dictated the primacy of Party rule over the nation's powerful armed forces, the recurrent warfare and constant external tensions in those thirty years reinforced military traditions and gave license to imposing military solutions on political problems, thereby shaping economic plans and social institutions. Nevertheless, Mao's China was never a typical military dictatorship, though People's Liberation Army (PLA) commanders did temporarily hold state power in the aftermath of their victory in 1949 and did grab it again for a few fleeting months during the Cultural Revolution in the late 1960s. Moreover, the unrelenting quest for nuclear weapons and the means to deliver them in those years dominated the nation's industrial policies, and each nuclear explosion or missile launch was heralded as great-power symbols as well as agents of retaliation or deterrence.[6] For

Mao, political power grew out of the barrel of a gun, and in later days the gun enforced the authority of his Party and state.[7]

Although those symbols and their architects held sway during the first decade or so after the Korean War and then again in the 1980s to restart China's industrial programs, the leaders after Mao Zedong's death in 1976 always had more in mind than just raw military power.[8] They saw beyond the swords to the plowshares. During the 1980s, under the guidance of Deng Xiaoping, economic and social priorities came dramatically to the fore, and with the end of the Cold War and the country's opening to the West, many senior cadres and educated youth were motivated to demonstrate for more rapid political reforms and personal freedoms in defiance of traditional Party values. The resultant crisis in 1989 forced the Party elders to choose, and they opted to use force to suppress those incipient reforms and freedoms at the showdown in Beijing that June. The appreciation of the social limits of politically induced change came slowly and at significant additional cost to the Party's legitimacy and mystique.

Nevertheless, the momentum of national modernization had its own logic over the next decade as China moved to become a powerful economic engine, and the grip of the People's Liberation Army on the national consciousness and state's purse strings was steadily diminished. Only the threat of Taiwan "separatism" and the far lesser danger of widespread domestic turmoil seemed to justify spending much on advanced armaments or a multimillion-man army, and when Party leader Deng Xiaoping ordered the slowdown of military modernization and then the end of military-run businesses in the 1990s, the army lost most of its autonomous economic base. The recurrent debate over whether the Party would control the army seemed ever more dated and far removed from other high-profile concerns. Since Jiang Zemin became chairman of the Central Military Commission (CMC) in 1989, its leadership has been held by men with no modern military experience and who have viewed the armed forces as contributing little to China's "peaceful rise," though vital to preserving national sovereignty and territorial integrity.

Nevertheless, the PLA elite judged these transitions in a very different light, though generational changes, career advancement, and infrastructure requirements made some of them more sympathetic to the new domestic priorities than others. Recognizing these variations and the problems in integrating them in a coherent study, this book attempts to reveal and analyze the full range of security decisionmaking from the national command authority to operations in the field, from planning and research centers to weapons procurement and war preparations.

We first probe the traditional Chinese approaches to military power and how they have been transformed in response to lessons of the battlefield and the revolution in weaponry and information technology. High-performance weapons and technology have radically altered how militaries act and widened the gap between the leading military powers and all others. For the last forty or more years, on an extraordinarily slim budget and slowly evolving technology base, the Central Military Commission has sought to leave "all others" behind and join the first rank of military powers.

This volume builds on our earlier studies that focused on the making of China's atomic bomb, ballistic missiles, and nuclear-powered submarines and summarized the decades-long development of China's strategic nuclear forces and their influence on PLA plans and objectives. Our purpose here is to go beyond these advanced military technologies and to examine the underlying decision processes and operations of a Chinese military on the move, the People's Liberation Army in action.

As we explore the intellectual and operational world of the Chinese military and security establishment, we touch on but do not deal with the raging academic dispute in the West about China's long-term goals. The questions often posed in that debate are: Is China a status quo or dissatisfied power?[9] Is China a potential or an unlikely threat in the future? These are important questions for the Chinese state and those who must deal with it in this century, but they are not the most compelling questions for the military. They do what they are told, and there is no doubt that senior generals are unhappy with the status quo not because they are seized of the question of China's ultimate status but because the PLA has been tasked to deal with threats on budgets that would seem ludicrously small in Washington's terms.

As we shall see, especially in the final chapter, many of the modernization campaigns within the command, weapons procurement, and strategic planning systems over the past decade have concentrated on a possible war with Taiwan. Given the history of the Taiwan crisis, the high command has concluded that should the order come to attack or militarily contain Taiwan, the United States undoubtedly would intervene on the side of Taipei and the war could easily become regional and even nuclear.

While this potential conflict poses great dangers and uncertainties, it also has focused the Chinese military on a single mission, the forceful preservation of one China. That mission has given Beijing's military planning what might be termed mission coherence. Such coherence in turn has structured national security decisionmaking and operational command and control. It has given direction to acquisitions, deployments, and logistics and helped refine doctrine and strategy. To a remarkable degree, the steady but reasonably low-budget growth of the PLA's capability has depended on the mission's objective requirements, and those requirements have collided with and reshaped the security establishment's thinking about war.

To reach the point in our story on a potential future conflict, we have chosen to divide this study into four parts. The first deals with the traditional military mind-set or culture reaching back over the centuries to the writings of Sun Tzu. In Chapter 2, we attempt to trace the evolution of tensions between Chinese and Western military philosophies and between old and new concepts. The search for understanding then leads us to consider what in Chinese planning for war has changed and why and to examine the post-1989 reappraisals about what wars might come.

Still within this first part of the book, Chapter 3 revisits the pivotal decade of the 1960s, the years of internal political struggle and a two-front confrontation with the United States and the Soviet Union during the Cold War struggle for Indochina. We examine the tortuous path that led Party chairman Mao Zedong in these tumultuous years to move closer to Washington and to define Moscow as his main enemy.

The conflicts along the Soviet border toward the end of the decade coincided with the meteoric rise of Marshal Lin Biao, a figure whose position in Chinese history is only now coming into balance. The moment of truth arrived in October 1969, during the showdown with the Soviets and the apparent triumph of Lin, then Mao's anointed successor, when Beijing's missile forces were put on a war footing apparently without Mao's prior approval. The results of this episode came just as China was deploying the missile delivery systems for its first-generation nuclear warheads. Its lessons then shaped China's national command authority and the PLA's command-and-control system, the Second Artillery, and the air force, each the subject of the chapters that follow.

The second part of the book deals with how those lessons were applied over the coming thirty-five years. Chapter 4 details the structure and operations of the national command authority (NCA), primarily as it functions in peacetime. Like almost everything else in China, the origins of the central Party and state systems can be traced to the pre-1949 revolution and its powerful legacy. That experience proved the efficacy of authoritarian rule and the necessity of a small core within the Party Politburo having supreme command. The terminology and organizational details affecting that core—whether Standing Committee or Central Secretariat—would change over time under the rule of Chairman Mao Zedong, but the principle of Party dominance of the state and army remained constant.

While it is generally known how Communist systems such as China's work, we concluded that a comprehensive treatment of the NCA's history and its structural and operational peculiarities were essential to a full understanding of the overall political-military system. So, while much of the initial treatment of the subject may seem formalistic, it should quickly become obvious that the very bureaucratic formalism was having a crippling effect on a leadership faced with fast-paced, complex political-military crises.

Deng Xiaoping also recognized that effect and revived an interagency institution introduced by Mao in the 1950s, the leading group, to counteract it. We review the further development of leading groups as their number increased in the 1990s, and suggest that those dealing with security, foreign policy, Taiwan affairs, and counterterrorism might be merged and streamlined. This could well constitute an interim solution whose final form could resemble the U.S. National Security Council, as the Chinese understand the present-day NSC. As the number of leading groups and their composition changes, however, the central Party and military decision, reporting, and enforcement structures remain in place. We end this examination of the NCA with our analysis of the likely institutional transformations that lie ahead.

This fourth chapter highlights the war-making authority of the Party supreme leader and the Politburo Standing Committee prior to the outbreak of a conflict and the transfer of responsibility to the Party's military leaders under the Central Military Commission when war begins. The discussion that follows in Chapter 5 deals with that commission and its subordinate organizations for command and control (C^2) of the entire PLA. It was in the military domain after 1949 that Maoist ideology and political skills could be most quickly and directly applied, but the crises since 1969 and the growing understanding of American power in a unipolar world energized the leadership to modernize both the NCA and the PLA's C^2 mechanisms. Here we provide a detailed examination of the improvement and current status of those mechanisms and stress the functions of the General Staff and its Operations Department system.

The first real test of those C^2 functions came in the brief but broad-scope war against Vietnam in February 1979, and to highlight the problems, we examine the lead-up to that war within the planning and operations commands. Responding to the many command-control-communications-and-intelligence (C^3I) failures in that conflict, some more capable PLA officers understood the need for basic changes and began to press hard for them. But, no serious enemies loomed on the horizon thereafter, and in any case Deng Xiaoping's economic and foreign policy priorities in the 1980s did not permit an accelerated military reorganization or a fundamental reallocation of scarce resources. For many PLA soldiers who had faced the battle-hardened Vietnamese, moreover, the war had become a bitter memory that none wanted to deal with truthfully or openly. For these and other reasons, the story of that conflict has yet to be fully told, and few Chinese who were not there grasp the full import of China's "last war" for the present-day PLA.

When the United States unleashed its most sophisticated weaponry and made the world aware of its information and surveillance technologies in the wars of the 1990s, however, Beijing quickly decided that well-overdue changes could no longer be avoided. Even so, the improved relations with Taiwan, the United States, and its neighbors early in the decade drained the imperatives from plans for revamping the C^3I system and applying the lessons of Vietnam and the Gulf War of 1991. We will examine the rethinking that occurred later in the 1990s, but our assessment at the end of Chapter 5 suggests that the process of change in that system is far from completion.

A series of events in the mid-1990s fundamentally transformed and drove the PLA's strategic priorities. This was the mounting crisis in the Taiwan Strait from 1995 to 1996, which has been widely analyzed and discussed.[10] Until then, the rule of the Nationalist Party (Kuomintang or KMT) on the island seemed safe against the vocal but hardly threatening independence-minded parties composed mostly of native Taiwanese. Within the KMT, however, key leaders, including Party chairman Lee Teng-hui, were planning to undo earlier agreements that had endorsed the enduring unity of Taiwan and the mainland and began advancing toward nationhood. Lee's moves split the Kuomintang, energized the Taiwanese opposition, and caused a fierce reaction from Beijing.

That reaction led to the confrontations of 1995 and 1996, when Chinese threats and missile firings provoked a direct American intervention. As fate would have it, these Chinese and American actions almost immediately followed the completion of the CMC's detailed assessments of the U.S.-led Gulf War and the comparative status of China's combat forces. Comparable evaluations of Chinese military readiness after the disastrous invasion of Vietnam in February 1979 had led to a concentration on the modernization of command and control just as the 1969 alert of the Second Artillery and the entire army had caused enhancements to be made in the national command authority. The coincidence of Taiwan's defiance and the intervention of U.S. naval forces further confirmed the systemic weaknesses that remained uncorrected and caused the highest priority to be placed on strengthening and retrofitting the strategic rocket forces and the PLA Air Force.

The high command, finally recognizing the absolute centrality of a survivable missile deterrent and modern air power for national defense and in any future attack on Taiwan, abandoned the desultory attempts to modernize the air force on a self-reliant basis. For years thereafter CMC representatives would negotiate deals with Russian, other European, and Israeli arms manufacturers to purchase advanced aircraft, avionics and other electronics, and air defense arms. The new national strategy called for air dominance over the Taiwan Strait and protection of the missile units, part of which would now carry conventional warheads. The ultimate logic of that strategy, as we shall see in the final chapter, would lead to a debate within the PLA on the use of nuclear weapons not just as a last resort.

The third part of the book thus deals with the primary weapons systems that have changed the most in line with the growing concerns about Taiwan "separatism" and American "interventionism." Chapter 6 provides the most complete description in any unofficial source of the evolution, organization, and operations of the Second Artillery and builds on the discussion in Chapter 3 of the 1969 missile alert. Chapter 7 updates our earlier publication on "China's search for a modern air force" and expands that work to include air defense. This does not mean that the other services are unimportant. They are critical to any complete evaluation of China's military capabilities. We and others have dealt with programs for the navy, and we analyze key components of the other general purpose forces in the context of command and control in Chapter 5 and the 2001 Dongshan exercise in Chapter 8.[11]

We justify the focus on the Second Artillery and the PLA Air Force because they have taken center stage in China's strategic plans and they constitute the most relevant case studies of the direction, obstacles, and successes in restructuring the entire military. Throughout much of the last fifty years only the program to build the nuclear-powered submarine had the same urgency as the strategic nuclear programs and the PLA Air Force, and the PLA Navy was what one retired U.S. admiral has called "the step-child of the Chinese armed forces." [12] Only after Jiang Zemin's call in October 1995 for the "construction of a modern navy with comprehensive combat capabilities" did Chinese military budgets allow for the purchases of Russian ships and naval aircraft and the placing of the Naval Air Force in "an important strategic position." The modernization of the navy has just begun even though a decade ago Jiang had made it responsible for the security of China's territorial waters and possible moves against Taiwan. [13]

Within the military, it is painfully obvious that the CMC "shift of the focal point of weapon systems development to conventional weapons" in 1977 was almost solely limited to antitank and antiaircraft weapons, suppression weapons (foreign advanced artillery and rocket launchers), and modifications of existing tanks and naval vessels. [14] PLA officers we have interviewed made no secret of the rivalry between the General Staff's Equipment Department (conventional weapons procurement) and the Commission of Science, Technology, and Industry for National Defense (COSTIND) (weapons R&D with special emphasis on strategic weapons). The 1998 merger of the department and COSTIND into the General Armament Department under the leadership of General Cao Gangchuan was supposed to have rekindled the long-delayed effort to rebuild the conventional ground forces, but that did not happen except in the area of C^3I.

Part Four then summarizes Beijing's national strategy and it preparations for war. Chapter 8 begins by posing questions that a latter-day Sun Tzu or Mao Zedong might have asked themselves were they members of today's CMC. It examines the growing complexity and nuanced realism of Chinese foreign policy as it leaves well in the past simplistic friend-or-foe dichotomies that no longer apply. The leadership of the Politburo Standing Committee can now foresee a coming historic shift in global power within the next few decades, with China the chief beneficiary.

This final chapter treats the military consequences of this transformation by looking first at the reevaluation of the traditional "active defense" doctrine over the past fifty years. The Chinese language has several words that can be translated as "doctrine" or "thought," and most often Chinese texts refer to the "active defense strategic doctrine" (*jiji fangyu zhanlüe sixiang*). Military writers differentiate the "active defense strategy" (*jiji fangyu zhanlüe*) from the doctrine, though that distinction is often blurred by explanations that make the strategy "the essence" of the doctrine. In this study, we will discuss "active defense" doctrine with quotation marks but active defense strategy without them.

We argue that the content of the doctrine has repeatedly changed, though the term "active defense" has remained constant. The earlier chapters will have shown how the doctrine's fluid content has reflected new military realities and international challenges. The strategy gives the appearance of continuity but provides a political cover for agile decisionmaking and the modernization of PLA forces for both offensive and defensive missions.

The subsequent section in the chapter pursues these doctrinal changes into the practical world of military exercises, especially the mammoth Dongshan exercise of 2001. Designed to test the recently introduced command-and-control systems and active defense strategies as applied to Taiwan, these exercises help explain the reasoning behind the precedence given to the Second Artillery and PLA Air Force. At the same time they revealed the high command's thinking about the progression of a conflict with Taiwan from a preemptive information war to a land invasion and a probable confrontation with the United States Navy.

Finally, the chapter shows how the current mainland-Taiwan impasse is slowly becoming a major crisis and reveals how U.S. military doctrine and actions from the Gulf War of 1991 to the Iraq War of 2003–4 have led the CMC to reappraise that progression. In appearance, U.S.-China relations have steadily improved despite recurrent ups and downs, but hidden from view, the Chinese military has concluded that should a cross-strait military showdown occur on President Bush's watch, the Americans would probably intervene and have signaled in the U.S. *Nuclear Posture Review* that they would use nuclear weapons. At the same time, Taiwan also would resort to measures that Beijing would regard as the use of weapons of mass destruction. Thus China could foresee a narrow use-it-or-lose-it window for their missile units and the planes that would be defending them and providing air cover for an invasion of the island. In 2004, a few in the Chinese military issued a signal of their own: they would now contemplate the preemptive use of tactical nuclear weapons, thereby meeting strategy for strategy. While that signal was quickly silenced, it served as a warning that nuclear threats against China could have disastrous consequences.

The logic of this book then links past, present, and future in the arenas of Chinese military power that would be brought to bear in any future conflict. The past helps explain the operational Chinese military culture and the impact of the violent revolutionary heritage on how that power is conceived, unleashed, directed, and employed. The chapters on the Second Artillery and the air force illuminate how competing priorities and the larger political context have affected that culture and weakened the efficacy of the power system in building a modern military force. It is our hope that by the end of Chapter 8 the reader will have a much better understanding of how Beijing views crises, reacts to them, and may deal with the most intractable of them, the crisis in the Taiwan Strait.

THE SOURCES

In developing the story of the People's Liberation Army in action, we have stayed close to the sources at hand. Not all sources in China are equal, of course, and no single source rarely if ever gives the full picture on even limited subjects. Key elements of military programs are either highly confidential or known to only a select few. We have used hundreds of written sources and drawn on three decades of interviews in the People's Republic, but many of these sources are contradictory, not just incomplete, and with changes ongoing, many sources are time-bound without a clear dating of the evidence. Moreover, how can we fairly distinguish fact from fiction when the goal so frequently is to obscure, not inform?

We know that Beijing wants outsiders to answer such questions on its terms or not at all. Although numerous publications and insiders do go beyond the established line, their information is often hard to verify. Dealing with military questions is a difficult undertaking in any society, but China has put a secret or confidential stamp on a large array of military documents, and even when this is not the case it has declared unclassified or widely available materials to be off-limits to foreigners. Our own experience with a gifted colleague now in prison for "leaking state secrets" has painfully sensitized us to the problem of foreigners dealing with open materials on our own library shelves. So, it is that the references section painstakingly lists all of the sources we have cited. In addition to protecting other Chinese colleagues from similar unfounded charges, we hope that this listing will help guide the reader to what is the opportunity and yet the problem of dealing with a vast array of documentary collections, articles, memoirs, and official histories.

Based almost exclusively on Chinese sources, this study examines the operations of China's military forces and central aspects of their development required to cope with the onslaught of advanced technologies, global political changes, and demands driven by old rivalries and rising nationalism. It thus touches on a vast literature dealing with the modernization and evolution of those forces. We have drawn heavily on this secondary literature, but have cited only those publications that we have used directly in the study, which gives credit to only a small percentage of what is available. Fortunately, within the past several years several bibliographical compilations and assessments have been published, and we see no need to duplicate them here.[15]

Although we might claim to have used "original" Chinese materials, most historians would dismiss most of them as not truly original but merely Chinese-language sources, notwithstanding the fact that many are written by well-placed Chinese officials and military officers and are published in the official media. They are correct. That is the lot of those faced with a staggering number of published materials and interview opportunities that not only are derivative, strictly speaking, but also must be presumed to be biased. Historians bearing these caveats in mind can use focused questions and relevant knowledge of Chinese history and culture to sift through so much information, to identify possible nuggets of potentially useful evidence, and to subject that evidence to extensive reliability tests, including multiple sourcing, which can never be perfect.

Zhou Enlai once quipped to a senior U.S. official about the quaintness of Americans who had no historical memory, and it is clear that for Chinese officials history, distorted and ethnocentric though it may be, critically determines their current mind-set. But, as a colleague of ours once remarked, "for Marxists, history is always changing, only the future is certain." One need only have visited the Historical Museum on Tiananmen Square over several decades to recognize the truth of his observation—the constantly changing selection of historical displays all too often reflect the political correctness of the moment. This, too, is the case with many Chinese memoirs, however useful, and with official compilations of documents that purport to be accurate and representative. Especially on such politically sensitive topics as leadership disputes or unsuccessful military operations of the past, meeting objective standards for the selection and dissemination of information is seldom a main concern.

There is another problem in the matter of sources that is not unique to the People's Liberation Army. For shorthand identification, we call those who advocate armed might in the solution of political problems "hard-liners," and for them, the military power that must be available to the state must equal or exceed that of China's potential foes. Yet, as is so often the case in any military service, mid-rank officers (majors through senior colonels) have tended to espouse a less moderate line to prove their mettle as trusted warriors, only to become more seasoned and realistic about the efficacy of military force as they rise through the ranks. Over the years, we have witnessed this transformation as officers move up the promotion ladder with a secondary phenomenon of reversion to their earlier, hard-line views that occurs as senior flag officers touch the uncompromising world of high politics.

Yet, even the most self-serving memoirs and propagandistic articles can provide significant data and insights. These data and insights, it would seem, have been introduced by their authors to prove their works' authenticity to hostile critics and knowledgeable peers, though often with incomplete or altered texts and without acknowledging that deletions or modifications have been made. Selectivity and bias are not unknown even in official U.S. compilations, but eventually archives are opened and the true record is revealed. To date in China, no Party, military, or state contemporary security-related archives have been opened to the general citizenry, let alone foreign scholars.

Save for their retirement memoirs, senior officers typically write less for open publications and are more circumspect in their public statements in order to protect themselves and their reputations. Perhaps for this reason, a large number of published sources on the Chinese military have come to display a toughness and opaqueness. The same holds true for research papers, both open and classified. The toughness will be seen in the articles on the possible uses of nuclear weapons in an invasion of Taiwan, and opaqueness will be repeatedly evident in Party pronouncements and general calls for modernization. Only careful mining of non-obvious writings and interviews with senior officers can help right the balance in assessing the leadership's actual intentions, but even with these we have tried never to forget the necessary cautions in dealing with Chinese military documents and specialists.

Those cautions apply with special force to the Internet. Much has been made recently of the extensive and highly useful Internet-based PLA sources that often reveal important but hard-to-verify military information, including data in private homepages, discussion forums, and so-called enthusiast sites.[16] Beginning in late 2001, some of the most productive sites, such as the homepage for the Academy of Military Science (www.ams.ac.cn), were removed from public access and transferred to the PLA's own restricted-access intranet or taken offline. As our citations will show, we, too, have used many of these troves of Internet materials, while recognizing and attempting to deal with their selectivity and potential distortions.

The art of writing on military history and operations never gets much easier with practice. It always requires extraordinary patience and discrimination while wading through oceans of materials often obscured by politically inspired generalizations and, taken together, conflicting testimony. Many other scholars have also found themselves caught up in the tasks of trying to understand China's military programs and security dilemmas, and we owe them a great debt. The fields of Chinese studies and security research have become so large and complex that it could not be otherwise, and as we look to the next generation of scholars our hope is that we collectively have done our job in providing them the intellectual tools and knowledge base to continue the building process.

PART ONE

History, Memory, and Experience
in Chinese Military Thinking

The Threat of War,
the Necessity of Peace

Chinese views on war combine strong beliefs and great uncertainty. Mao Zedong, Beijing's leader for the first twenty-seven years of the People's Republic, considered the global struggle for dominance a constant and major war an inevitability. His successor, Deng Xiaoping, reached much the same conclusion but believed the showdown with China's imagined foes lay sometime in the distant future.

In 1989, Jiang Zemin came next in the succession, and the coincidence of an ascendant America following the collapse of the Soviet Union in the early 1990s and the steady rise of independence forces on Taiwan made armed conflict both unthinkable and yet loom closer. For more than fifty years, the likelihood of war has weighed on Beijing's leaders even as they reduced their armed forces and military budgets, stretched out weapons procurements, and dedicated themselves to national economic progress. This is a story of a nation torn between the fear of war and the leadership's determination to protect and reunify the country even if that could mean war.

The central thesis of this book is that the priority given to domestic modernization and economic growth narrowed the scope for military development and planning and that, within that more limited scope, the changing risks and nature of the ultimate battle have shaped and reshaped Chinese military doctrines, strategies, and preparations.

By probing China's conception of a future conflict, we seek to explain the nation's security actions over the past several decades. How has Beijing's high command, the national command authority, been structured, and how has it operated? What changes have been made to strengthen command and control? How have the strategic rocket forces, the Second Artillery, responded to the remote threat of nuclear war and the near-term possibility of a local conventional war that might become nuclear? Has the air force been able to keep pace with the revolution in military affairs and the ever more acute problem of air defense? Does Chinese strategy reflect military realities or just the compromises of balancing immediate priorities and the long-term specter of violent conflict?

Our goal is to understand how and why the central elements of military power in China have changed and where they appear to be headed in the coming decades. This is a study of China's preparations for war on the path to peace.

COMPARATIVE STUDIES
OF MILITARY PHILOSOPHIES

The place to begin this task is China's military culture. What are the deeply held "Chinese" qualities—if one may say so—that hold sway in the highest level decisionmaking bodies and armed forces, the People's Liberation Army (PLA)? The modern Chinese state was born in war, barely survived its infancy because of the Korean War, engaged in a bitter contest with its erstwhile Soviet partner, waged a proxy war with the United States in Vietnam and border clashes with India and Vietnam, and then moved into an era of low-intensity struggle with Taiwan and its American protector. The enduring climate of tensions and unresolved disputes shaped the country's industrial plans and guided its diplomacy, even as Beijing pressed forward to rebuild the society and economy and restore the nation's great power status.

Forestalling violence and managing foreign tensions over the decades became almost second nature to the Communist leadership and triggered policies and values that the Chinese believe are special to their history and modern outlook. When they speak of the "Chinese characteristics" of their ideology, economic policies, and military doctrines, the Chinese dig deep into the reservoirs of their past, and it is those traditional reservoirs with which we begin.

The Origins of Chinese Strategic Thinking

For the past three millennia, the Chinese have looked inward, presumed and cherished their moral superiority, and disdained but feared outside marauders and invaders. Here, of course, one has to distinguish ethnic Han emperors from the Khitan, Mongol, and Manchu rulers who imposed their dominion on the Middle Kingdom for many centuries. Yet even non-Han emperors embraced the Middle Kingdom's security assumptions and fear of collapse wrought by "inside disorder and outside calamity." They saw no need to conquer "barbarian" territories beyond the empire but only to manage nearby neighbors as subservient vassals against more powerful, distant foes.[1] Except when directly menaced by non-Han "barbarians," Chinese rulers regarded these neighbors as a part of the nation's security belt. In exchange for exacting loyalty and tribute from vassal states, the emperors pledged to protect them. Over many centuries, Chinese emperors typically regarded the use of force as the last resort.[2]

At the strategic level, the dominant Chinese philosophy created a culture characterized by "strong secularism, weak religiousness," "strong inclusiveness, weak exclusiveness," and "strong conservativeness, weak aggressiveness."[3] These features wax and wane in a twentieth-century China wracked by war, revolution, and globalization, but the Chinese now appear to believe they are in the ascendancy and in the recent past have given primacy to diplomacy in resolving disputes. In today's China, leaders draw on the traditional code of conduct that "peace claims precedence" (*he wei gui*). From Mao to Deng, Jiang Zemin, and now Hu Jintao, he wei gui is invoked to justify diplomatic negotiations and the avoidance of war.[4] In the tradition, peace and stability ensured progress and heaven's blessing, while war could unleash decades of strife and usher in centuries of foreign rule. That tradition finds an echo in modern Beijing's political and military councils, and we shall encounter it again at the end of our inquiry.

The dangers of war and the opportunities wrought by enduring tranquility required skilled statesmen and prudent policies, and the Chinese held that the writings of ancient, revered sages were must-read texts for all aspiring leaders and youthful cadets in training. Those steeped in the wisdom of treasured ancestors would be best equipped to guide the ship of state away from impending disasters and toward a common ideal.[5] Whether one speaks of the Mandate of Heaven or the authority of Party cadres, the subject always begins with learning from the past and heeding its supposed lessons.

For those charged with guarding the nation against foreign incursions and internal strife, the place to begin was Sun Tzu, the Middle Kingdom's renowned military strategist. His *Art of War*, written about 500 B.C., during the Spring and Autumn years of the Zhou dynasty, summarizes the classical notion that the best prepared for war either will win without fighting or will fight and win. War must be studied. Its basic rules and principles are universal and, taken together, are an art that can and must be learned. Sun Tzu urges leaders to think boldly but to act with extreme caution because war is "a matter of life and death, a road to safety or ruin."[6] As Confucius later declared, "The cautious seldom err."[7]

In essence, the art of war is a battle of wits, and those who master the art have the best hope of winning without fighting. That mind-against-mind struggle is characterized by brilliant stratagems, active diplomacy and deception, and judicious intimidation. Yet, armed struggle sometimes cannot be prevented, and Sun Tzu's guidance for generations of generals stipulated the priorities for achieving victory or avoiding defeat when war occurs: "What is of supreme importance in war is to attack the enemy's strategy. Next best is to disrupt his alliances by diplomacy. The next best is to attack his army. And the worst policy is to attack cities. . . . Those skilled in war subdue the enemy's army without battle. . . . Therefore, I say: Know the enemy and know yourself; in a hundred battles, you will never be defeated."[8]

The art of war blends the skills of statesmanship and generalship, though Sun Tzu warned, "He whose generals are able and not interfered with by the sovereign will be victorious."[9] Historians also record stories of the ruthless side of Sun Tzu that transcend this warning. One story illustrates his fierce insistence on submission to command. When challenged by the king of the state of Wu to demonstrate his skills by drilling the palace concubines, Sun

Tzu divided the women into two groups and explained his demand for absolute obedience and the penalties for failure. When his new recruits merely giggled and ignored him, Sun Tzu selected the king's two favorites and had them beheaded.[10] The giggling ended. "In the tumult and uproar, the battle seems chaotic, but there must be no disorder in one's own troops," Sun Tzu wrote.[11] From empire to revolution to the Korean War, Chinese soldiers have fought in the certain knowledge that iron obedience is their only option.

Sun Tzu's dictums are echoed in the texts of Confucius. Wise leaders, Confucius held, must constantly reflect on war and prepare for it. The most consequential national security decision comes when selecting a military commander. A nation's leader must pick as his generals or members of his national security team, as Washington would put it, those who understand the right mix of political and military preparations for war, approach the coming battles prudently, and act with caution. Overconfident generals or ineffectual security advisors can bring ruin to the strongest state. For Confucius, a qualified commander "must be afraid of the assignment he is going to undertake" and must be able to win by prudently planned strategies that outmaneuver and outthink an adversary.[12]

Chinese traditionally deemed the symbols of force—swords, guns, trophies, and war medals—inauspicious.[13] A Chinese maxim says, "Those good at war do not speak about war" (*shan zhan zhe bu yan zhan*). For generations, the best generals shunned boasting about their military skills and did their utmost to avoid an armed struggle. Should war break out, they would pursue and bring victory because they had so diligently made ready for it politically, psychologically, and militarily.[14] In modern times, they typically denigrated the West's "stress on military force" (*shangwu*) and adopted a "force avoidance" (*rouwu* or "soft military") or low-posture stance. Veiled threats and brief-strike military "lessons" reflect this classical legacy in modern-day China. The culture disparaged the race to war and lauded its avoidance as marks of wisdom and moral strength.[15]

The Contrast of American and Chinese Military Philosophies

Chinese strategists draw on these classical perspectives to study and assess potential adversaries, extrapolating military philosophies from their conduct on the battlefield. The didactic process of comparison and assessment of perceived differences has helped chart the equation of liabilities and assets underlying each side's doctrines and set the stage for pitting strategy against strategy. This constitutes an exercise in the great tradition of Sun Tzu and a prelude to directing the complex process from national command decision to battlefield tactics.[16]

Lodged in military academies and command-and-staff colleges, these comparative studies start with the basics, sometimes exhibiting considerable insight and often simplistic and biased distillations. They begin with assertions about concepts of basic human nature, and though they speak somewhat grandly of the "West," they most often mean the United States or their characterization of its beliefs and biases. For the West, so these uniformed academics say, human nature is deemed to be evil, causing its citizens to exaggerate the importance of the law and to rely on courts for punishments and redress of wrongs to individuals. Chinese in the mainstream Confucian tradition, by contrast, hold that human nature is good or perhaps just neutral and can profit from education and the collective wisdom of the past. For Chinese, court-imposed enforcement, except to protect the state, is a last resort or a foreign artifact to be scorned. Translated to the level of strategic culture, Western strategists rely on power politics, stress individual as opposed to social misbehavior, and threaten forceful retaliation to back up negotiating demands. Chinese, generally speaking, prefer recurring rounds of diplomacy, insist on consensus building especially on matters of general principle, and consider harmony reached through negotiations and compromise to be the epitome of diplomatic skill.[17]

This presumed or alleged contrast in worldviews applies to the exercise of military power as a means to accomplish political and economic aims. Compared to leaders in the West, the Chinese profess to place a higher strategic, even moral value on tranquility and peace, a condition long absent in their own modern history.[18] This difference, however, could help explain why the Chinese often yield to pressures from the outside world, especially in the early stages of a crisis, and only suddenly and unexpectedly resort to force as a crisis unfolds and a head-on conflict appears inevitable. According to Chinese military scholars, Westerners often prematurely terminate talks in favor of military action and, comparatively speaking, more often refuse to patiently explore promising areas of potential agreement.

Holding the view that "offense is the best defense," Westerners, so the Chinese argument goes, too readily have adopted an aggressive stance in order to seize the initiative, while Chinese traditionally "forsake offensive actions in favor of defensive postures" (*fei gong*), an approach underlying one of their basic strategic doctrines, "active defense" (*jiji fangyu*).[19] An oft-used Chinese character for "force" (*wu*) reflects the culture's ambivalence toward its use: the defining component or "radical" part of the character is *zhi*, meaning "stop," while the second component, *ge*, is the name for an ancient dagger-axe. Such contradictions flourish in the Chinese language and speak in subtle ways to what is sometimes interpreted as "inscrutable" Chinese behavior. As this study proceeds, however, we shall encounter signs of that behavior changing under the demands of military modernization and the complexities of the Taiwan and American challenges.

In the language of the war room, the Chinese stress intentions, while Westerners focus on capabilities. Sometimes this Chinese emphasis is phrased as a strategy of looking for an adversary's weaknesses as opposed to the West's fixation on an adversary's strengths.[20]

In recent decades, Westerners trumpet their prowess in science and technology—their hardware—though any disparities in this respect would seem to be rapidly eroding as the Chinese scramble to achieve scientific and technological excellence and seem to rely less on the wisdom of the ages. Still the distinction between a "hardware" orientation and one proclaiming the virtues of the intellect or "software" does reflect variations in national culture, not just in the stage of development. The tradition of Chinese intellectuals to "attach importance to self-cultivation but neglect technology" (*zhong dao qing qi*) may be waning, but the signs of its influence are far from disappearing.

Indeed, zhong dao qing qi figures in many current internal critiques of Chinese military thinking. Military leaders and planners tend to criticize the influence of the concept for their failures to forge the People's Liberation Army into a more capable fighting force and for the persistence of a bias that inhibits an uninterrupted concentration on advances in technology. Although technological inferiority purportedly causes PLA planners to adopt more creative strategies than their adversaries, that inferiority also reduces strategic options and magnifies the importance of strategic failures.[21]

Finally, the two cultures face in unlike directions. China looks inward, exhibiting a certain smugness, while the West looks outward and seems restless to expand and control. It would be hard to find an American whom the

Chinese have not called impatient or worse. In strategic terms, this also reflects a land-sea dichotomy, at least in modern times. For generations, Western strategists called for dominance of the seas and more recently of the air and outer space. Chinese strategists from Sun Tzu to Beijing's generals, by contrast, have been guardians of the land.[22] They have paid closer attention to domestic political challenges than to international crises.[23] Foreign conflicts and crises seldom take precedence over internal stability and the political power of the established rulers.

China's sea, air, and strategic missile units belong to the People's Liberation Army and have never achieved genuine equality with their brothers and sisters in the ground forces. Even in the age of long-range aircraft and missiles, China's large landmass is still thought to provide a strategic advantage even though the PLA abandoned the doctrine of "luring an enemy in deep" in the 1980s.[24] China is essentially a continental economy, its soldiers mostly hail from landlocked villages, and alien regimes one after the other have been swallowed up in China's vast territory. These become significant data points when explaining the Chinese military's strategies from People's War to "active defense under modern conditions."

Old Ideas Versus New Concepts

Today's Chinese strategists acknowledge and seek to modify a number of behaviors that accompany the traditional outlook. Three such unwanted behaviors stand out. First, these strategists have begun to reconsider the longheld article of faith that China has always been the innocent victim, the passive target of foreign aggression. Indeed, Mao Zedong interpreted all modern Chinese history in this light and called for the people to "stand up." Moreover, he perpetuated both the leadership's proclivity toward preparing for the worst when making policies in crises and its allergy to taking the initiative. In 1955, he admonished his associates, "[We] will not suffer losses if we always take into account the worst scenario," and subsequent generations were taught to take his admonition to heart.[25] Driven by repeated setbacks of the revolutionary years, worst-case planning carried over to the People's Republic and only in the Jiang Zemin era in the 1990s and beyond seemed to be dying out.[26]

From their stronger, more self-confident positions at least for the moment, Western leaders are said to be more inclined to consider a wider range of options and regard the worst case as only one of several possibilities. Where once the PLA belittled the West in this regard, it now privately admires it and increasingly strives to emulate it.

A second behavior is implicit in the first: extreme "cautiousness toward the first battle" (*shenzhong chuzhan*). Tradition teaches Chinese to fear that round one of the fighting could decisively influence the war's final outcome.[27] From their perspective, Western strategists by contrast are inclined to believe that a nation's military superiority can compensate for any initial strategic mistakes and that by seizing the initiative they can define the battlefield and determine the nature of the battles to come. This implies that the Chinese, comparatively speaking, may be less inclined to take risks before launching major undertakings or an armed conflict and could be less flexible after the outbreak of a war. Throughout China's nuclear test program, for example, getting it right the first time translated into far fewer tests. Some explain this by pointing to China's poverty, but the attitude, as we shall see in our later discussion of the Vietnam border war of 1979, reflects culture as well as money. As the Chinese come face to face with modern warfare, risk taking and seizing the initiative, we shall also suggest, may become mandatory, and rising domestic prosperity may well ease the change to a more "Western style" of military conduct.

The final unwanted behavior that we should note is one of methodology more than style. PLA strategists attach importance to macroanalysis, and believe that their counterparts in the West pay closer attention to microanalysis. The variations in approach to science and technology are deemed part of this behavioral disparity, as are outlooks toward human nature, matters of principle, and negotiating techniques. Nevertheless, Chinese hold that this methodological bias is based as much on necessity as on choice. Neither quantitative nor qualitative methods alone, they acknowledge, can yield a complete and adequate strategic picture, and achieving a balance between the two methodologies in today's world is not easy.[28]

For the moment, the Chinese military lacks sufficient sophisticated technical means for the real-time surveillance and reconnaissance needed for accurate quantitative judgments or the nuanced human intelligence for complete qualitative assessments. China's technological inferiority, military leaders have concluded, has crippled or delayed their plans for the nation's security. The PLA urgently seeks to acquire those means.[29]

In the traditional and revolutionary-era military cultures, the Chinese formulated strategic doctrines first and then determined the type, scope, and pace of weapons programs. Their lack of resources then narrowed the range of choices and the margins for error. To this day, antecedent strategic guidelines, always controversial and painful to formulate, tend to dictate the direction and scope of most arms programs and place a premium on weapons procured to match specific priorities. This approach limits the procurement of weapons optimized not only for immediate needs but also capable of flexible modification to deal with unexpected contingencies over the full lifespan of the weapon. It makes it more difficult to consider interrelated weapons systems and makes R&D on them depend principally on analyses of past Chinese and foreign conflicts, much less so on future unknowns.[30]

While "fighting the last war" and adopting technologies developed elsewhere are not unique to China, the People's Liberation Army only recently has begun to recognize that the profound post-Vietnam change in the U.S. military, which seeks to leapfrog over next-generation weapons and tactics, is made possible by an active synergy between imaginative battlefield theories and innovative technologies. Neither doctrines nor weapons programs necessarily comes first. Each can drive the other, a reality that has only recently been understood and embraced in the People's Republic.[31]

What we are seeing is that the cultural differences, so important in earlier years, have begun to narrow and their continued influence often disgusts younger, better-trained PLA officers. The reasons for this continuity, to be sure, may stem in some degree from shortages of resources as much as of vision, though examples such as the air force rejecting cheaper, more advanced satellite-based air traffic control systems in favor of outmoded radars in the 1990s suggest that the problem is one of mind-set as much as money.[32]

The evolution that is occurring in China's military hardware and doctrines has resulted largely from the direct application of military experience from Korea to Vietnam, from planning for a conflict in the Taiwan Strait, and from the dramatic lessons provided by the wars fought by the United States since the debacle of Vietnam. The worst-case planning, aversion to risk, and preference for qualitative or macroanalysis persist as do the artificial boundaries between military doctrine and weapons procurements, but as the chapters that follow will show, the Chinese are rectifying the problems born of rigid thinking and are steadily modifying their approach to war, making it more refined and flexible.

In the course of these changes, the critique of outmoded concepts has become more direct and open. In 2001, a senior PLA general echoed Sun Tzu's declaration that national strategy is a matter of "life and death" and a road to "safety or ruin." He castigated the nation's think tanks for their failure to devise that strategy for the new century.[33]

In response, senior military strategists began a systematic review of the "six domains" of strategy: politics, military affairs, economy, science and technology, culture, and society. They argued that China faces severe challenges in all six areas and outlined five strategic goals in the decades ahead: safeguard territorial sovereignty and "rights"; maintain domestic stability and a stable environment in the Asian-Pacific region; promote economic growth; oppose hegemony and power politics; and build a new international political and economic order.[34] The six domains and five goals have set the framework for the ongoing doctrinal changes that will be explored in the chapters that follow.

CHANGE AND THE PLANNING FOR WAR

Starting from the 1970s and continuing into the present, the transformation of Chinese views on war has accelerated and come to encompass a richer content. The shackles of Maoist dogma on People's War have been broken, and its legacy is slowly fading. That process now includes the classification of future threats, estimates on the likelihood of war and of the prevailing attitudes toward it, the determination of the type of the war that China might fight, the interpretation of "active defense," and the redefinition of strategic and operational concepts for fighting a war. We now turn to a consideration of this transformation.

The Changing Probability of War

Perhaps the most prominent change in the past two decades has been a reassessment of the probability of a future war. Until the mid-1970s, Mao and his generals held that an all-out war with the Soviet Union was likely and would happen soon. During the preceding decade, Mao had moved the nation's ordnance factories to the interior or "third-line" provinces and believed they would ride out Soviet and U.S. air strikes and survive to supply the wherewithal for the nation's recovery and eventual victory. After Mao's death and as Sino-American relations were steadily being normalized and tensions with Moscow eased, Deng Xiaoping in the mid-1980s became convinced that China could avert a collision with either superpower for several decades if not indefinitely.[35] Deng discarded the belief that war was inevitable and imminent. There would be no large-scale war for a "fairly long time to come." His view was steadily coming into consonance with the traditional Chinese idea that war need not be inevitable and that skilled leaders might delay or even prevent it.

That view lasted until the mid-1990s, when the overt backing by the United States for Taipei's defiance of Beijing and appraisals of U.S. air operations in the 1991 Persian Gulf War shattered the complacent belief that war lay in the misty future with victory assured. Within a few short months in 1995 and 1996, the prospect of a coming crisis loomed ever larger in the minds of Beijing's leaders, and became more urgent after a U.S. plane mistakenly destroyed the Chinese embassy in Belgrade in 1999. After a careful reevaluation of multiple and somewhat incongruous changes especially in Taiwan, Chinese security officials concluded that the nation might still forestall a full-scale war with the United States, but at the same time they raised the probability of a local war over Taiwan or another "high-tech local war."[36]

A noted Chinese scholar, for example, claimed that Washington ultimately wanted to slow China's advancement and that by supporting Taiwan, it sought to block China's access to the Pacific and the world's resources. In this view, America's policymakers were deliberately plotting to weaken a potential rival and to do so would use Taiwan to perpetuate hostilities. Thus defined, Washington leaves little, if any, room for lasting accommodation regardless of the convergence of broader strategic interests.[37] The same underlying concerns about America's supposedly hostile intent can be found throughout the community of Chinese strategists.[38]

Avoid Needless Conflicts, But Plan for War

Despite the uncertainties produced by the lingering distrust of Taiwanese and American intentions, the Chinese remain convinced that their future development depends on a tranquil international environment and that astute policies can preserve that environment far into the future. This is a significant change. Preoccupied by revolutionary illusions and aspirations, Mao and his Politburo comrades held the firm conviction that the essence of successful crisis management lay in the readiness to retaliate. He proclaimed, "If we are attacked, we will certainly counterattack" (*ren ruo fan wo, wo bi fan ren*), and he was prepared to do so in the face of suicidal odds. The world's chess game, the Chinese leader and his lieutenants held, required the will to engage in tit-for-tat struggle, and this view caused him to forsake the tradition of caution and compromise.[39] The global jungle had immutable rules: "Either kill the tiger, or be eaten by him."[40] That Hobbesian outlook, however, began to die out with Mao's successors and with the priority they have given to the economy and national progress.

In contrast to that outlook, Deng Xiaoping told his military brothers, "The forces of peace are growing faster than the forces for war. . . . So China's development represents the forces of peace and against war. . . . We can concentrate without fear on the drive for modernization."[41] In 1975, Deng quipped, "In the past, a company commander at the front could just hold up a Mauser and cry, 'Charge!' Today he must know much more. And this is even more true of officers above the company level."[42] For the next few years, to be sure, Deng mostly concentrated on his own survival and the revival of the nation's political soul. Yet, as a military man, he understood that the nature of war had changed and China must change with it. Only with the establishment of a good economic and technological foundation based on modern science and technology would "it be possible for us to modernize the army's equipment." Everything else would be subordinated to building that foundation.[43]

As the "forces of peace" gained stride, the requirements of sustained economic expansion undermined the self-reliant fortress mentality, though the explosive issue of Taiwan obstructed the path away from instant retaliation no matter what the cost. More and more Chinese strategists urged caution and cooperation and decreed that few security challenges warranted a military reaction. The language of Sun Tzu calling for appropriate responses and political skill to deflect the provocations of hegemonistic foes replaced the shrill slogans of the revolutionary years. China would not fight unless the nation's sovereignty should be seriously threatened, because lasting security required peace and stability. A PLA strategist even quoted a Chinese proverb to justify accepting temporary setbacks and galling concessions: "Suffering losses may lead to good fortune" (*chikui shi fu*). Premature military action, however justified in principle, might propel China into the adversary's hidden trap because endless provocations could be part of the adversary's grand conspiracy.[44] Moreover, any recklessness might bring unintended consequences that could slow or even reverse economic construction, and today's most immediate worries might be far less perilous than the ones yet to emerge.

By the fall of 1995, the Central Military Commission (CMC) had formulated the so-called *wen nan bao bei* policy, which, loosely translated, meant that the PLA would shift its planning priorities from the South China Sea to Taiwan and its "foreign supporters." Wen nan or "stabilize the south" was a call for China's diplomats to try to resolve its outstanding border or territorial disputes from the Philippines to India and Central Asia. The principal challenge, Beijing declared, was the danger to the nation's territorial integrity, and the time had come to guarantee the north (bao bei) and draw a line that the "separatists" in Taiwan must not cross.[45]

The question was: How to signal warnings and increase pressure that would influence the Taiwanese population and its leaders without triggering an unwanted or uncontrolled backlash or even conflict? Taipei would have to be forced to choose between the fragile status quo and escalating violence, and the Taiwanese would be put in a position of having to decide for themselves. A senior PLA officer told us at the time: "They will think twice before making a radical push."

So, when it comes to matters of war and peace, the Chinese tend to equivocate and hold a dual view of wars that may never come. On the one hand, their policies call for doing whatever possible to prevent a head-on collision with a more powerful adversary and simultaneously and judiciously preparing for a possible showdown that cannot be avoided.[46] The worst case is universally recognized: a simultaneous conflict with Taiwan and the United States. Current Party and state guidelines lead to coping with lesser crises in a piecemeal and almost feckless way, because who can say which ones truly matter and which might simply blow over and be forgotten?

Moreover, as China's modernization progresses and its stake in the status quo rises, the inhibitions against participating in or provoking foreign conflicts grow as well. Still, for the leaders in the nation's center of power, Zhongnanhai, preparations for war have moved inexorably forward even as the grounds for war seem to diminish by the year.

Homeland Security and International Crises

In the last two or more decades of rapid economic development, the shifting balance between international and domestic concerns has directly altered Beijing's policies toward war. During Mao's era, radical actions in one domain did exacerbate problems in the other, but each domain had its own dynamic and unconstrained momentum. Even in the Cultural Revolution (1966–76), social upheaval throughout the nation had often made little difference to Mao's approach to external crises, though a powerful interaction of domestic politics and military decisions repeatedly occurred as we shall see in the next chapter.

Then, starting in the latter half of the Deng Xiaoping era, social chaos markedly hampered Beijing's foreign standing and diplomacy. The most notorious example, of course, came during the complex aftermath of the suppressed pro-democracy movement on Tiananmen Square in 1989. For several years thereafter, internal order worsened and remained unstable. As protests and social unrest spread through the towns and villages among the poor, the unemployed, and demobilized soldiers, the legitimacy of the Party sharply declined, and ensuring the continuity of its power rose to the number one spot on its agenda. That agenda required the lowering of military budgets and manpower, the lessening of concern with many problems beyond China's borders, and a willingness to accommodate what would earlier have been regarded as intolerable offenses.[47]

Since 1989, the Chinese Communist Party leaders have proclaimed, "Stability claims precedence over all others" (*wending yadao yiqie*). They have calculated that stability at home and abroad would help ensure steady economic growth and political support, both essential for sustained Party rule. Recognizing that domestic upheaval, if unchecked, could lead to chaos and separatism, the Chinese government has typically acted to suppress protests and opposition movements despite foreign denunciations and a loss of face in some parts of the international community. Deng Xiaoping's belief that societal turmoil could even lead to civil war has unspoken currency in China today.[48] In escalating external crises, therefore, any temptation to take action by Beijing tends to be checked by the leadership's domestic priorities.

Unfortunately for the nation's leaders, the weight given to internal problems might become a double-edged sword. The fear of domestic instability could undermine Beijing's foreign policymaking and the culture of caution. To ensure stability, the Party has promoted nationalism, and the rise of nationalist sentiments within the youth and People's Liberation Army now molds popular attitudes especially toward the rising independence forces on Taiwan and American unilateralism. Increased nationalism could well weaken Beijing's commitment to stability and growth if that should result in vitiating the one-China principle as applied to Taiwan. It could force Chinese leaders to take drastic action toward Taiwan no matter what the cost.

Moreover, the twin commitments to stability and Party rule could come into conflict, and the dedication to stability could falter in the face of threats to that rule. A decision to use force in managing an international crisis might depend on whether such a decision could help assure the Party's continuation in power. Facing social upheaval, Party leaders might take advantage of a foreign crisis, throw caution to the winds, and manipulate the crisis in an attempt to neutralize political opposition. China would not be the first country to sacrifice principle and long-standing plans in order for its leaders to perpetuate their power. As students of the Party-led revolution and its repeated experience with factional struggle, the Communist leaders remember how united front compromises and conflicts in Korea and Vietnam and on their northern border saved or solidified the Party's power and helped preserve national unity. History does not predict future actions though it could show a certain disposition to situations in extremis.

WHAT WARS MAY COME

Although the possibility of war remains a constant in China's national plans, the kind of war to be fought has repeatedly changed, as we have already seen. In the early 1960s, for example, the military's high command, the Central Military Commission, told the PLA to "make preparations for fighting a local war" in an attempt to frustrate the alleged U.S. plot to "wage a small-scale war against Beijing," but from the middle of that decade until Mao Zedong's death in 1976, the Chinese adopted an apocalyptic outlook.[49] Mao ordered his generals to plan for "an early war, an all-out war, and a nuclear war," and the scope of the preparations—moving industrial complexes to China's interior, construction of massive tunnel complexes in many cities, crash programs to fight a nuclear conflict, and mass mobilization movements—was staggering.[50] After Mao's passing, the shifting relations with the superpowers and more sober assessments of the peril caused his successors to cancel his order and end his most dangerous policies.

It fell to Deng Xiaoping, who returned to power in 1977, to rethink the nation's security and reset its priorities. His first conclusions were that war, as we have noted, now deemed highly improbable, would not be global and was not imminent. The United States was pitted against the Soviet Union in a global stalemate, and a complex of forces had defeated American power in Vietnam. Whatever conflicts lay ahead would be "local," which he interpreted as small and conventional against largely inferior adversaries unless aided by an outside power. Consistent with this view, he could foresee a clash with Vietnam coming soon and one with India at some distant point. Conflicts with Japan or South Korea were possible but highly unlikely because of their alliances with the United States. By the mid-1980s, the Central Military Commission adopted a new strategic guideline to prepare for local wars and limited conflicts.[51] The steady evolution of that guideline is the subject of the section that follows.

Local War in a Nuclear-Armed Environment

In early 1993, following a prolonged review of the Gulf War's "lessons," the CMC announced two seminal changes: Change the military from dependence on manpower and People's War to greater reliance on science and technology; and switch plans for military preparedness from winning a conventional local war to winning a high-tech local war. The coming conventional struggle would still be waged within an environment of nuclear deterrence, but the nation would concentrate on acquiring the wherewithal for fighting a nonnuclear war. That focus would last at least until the U.S. missile defense program and stepped-up arms sales to Taiwan during the George W. Bush presidential years more seriously jeopardized the limited arsenal of China's retaliatory missiles and called into question its relatively small military budget.[52]

PLA theorists by no means have belittled the nuclear threat, but it is one that they—like military minds everywhere—have found difficult to comprehend and gauge with any realism. Since the dawning of the nuclear age, strategists have debated the impact of nuclear arms on the likelihood of wars, both conventional and nuclear.[53] Do those arms make a limited war more or less likely, and do they encourage compromise or obduracy? When a state intervenes in an external conflict, does the fact that it or its enemy possesses nuclear weapons measurably change the outcome? From the Korean War to the Cuban missile crisis and the 1999 Indian-Pakistani war in Kashmir, the debate rages about the role of nuclear weapons in ending or containing the crisis.

The near circular logic of deterrence and compellence is also the grist for strategic arguments in China, and PLA strategists, too, rely on conflicting theories drawn from the historical record. Though they are baffled by recent official American statements on the "immediate contingency" utility of nuclear weapons in "a military confrontation over the status of Taiwan," they remain convinced that the United States would not employ nuclear weapons against them in any conflict over the island. They officially have held that should Taiwan declare its independence China could successfully wage a high-tech conventional war even in the face of the nuclear sword.[54]

That official position, however, has come under considerable pressure for reasons that we will come to at the end of this study. America's increasing inclination to settle international crises militarily and its announced doctrinal shift from deterrence to preemption have prompted PLA leaders to reexamine the precise kind of war that China might have to fight in the future. They loosely define such a conflict as "a conventional war in nuclear, biological, and chemical environments," but leave the exact nature of those environments unspecified.[55] At the onset of the conflict, they appear to agree, China would most probably face "an information war under nuclear deterrence" imposed by a technologically more advanced adversary, meaning the United States, and in some circumstances the U.S military might deploy—though not necessarily employ—tactical nuclear weapons in conventional engagements.[56]

Furthermore, the PLA would have to confront a U.S.-led coalition that could include America's allies and a number of China's other potential adversaries.[57] The engagements could proceed through ever more violent and complex stages and might in the end involve direct confrontation with the United States and its full "conventional" arsenal, not excluding tactical nuclear weapons.[58] Thus, the Chinese have come to recognize that the United States might threaten to use or even launch low-yield nuclear weapons. Nevertheless, they appear to believe that the conflict would remain mostly conventional even though they must prepare for further escalation.

It is their conception of this last stage that most concerns PLA strategists and that has complicated the modernization of its strategic rocket forces. How can they evaluate the possible introduction of nuclear weapons in a limited war across the Taiwan Strait? Does this possibility and commensurate changes in U.S. strategic and nuclear doctrine alter Beijing's somewhat vague definition of a nuclear environment in a high-tech local war? Could these changes mean the end to robust nuclear deterrence and once more living on the edge of a nuclear holocaust?

While these and similar questions remain open and the subject of a spirited debate throughout the Chinese defense establishment, the dominant voices remain confident that the nuclear environment will translate into a nuclear standoff and that a local war involving Taiwan and the United States will stay purely conventional. Acknowledging the changing nature of future wars has not yet equated to conceding the U.S. claims that "nuclear capabilities possess unique properties that give the United States options to hold at risk classes of targets [that are] important to achieve strategic and political objectives."[59] They reject the American conclusions that such a war, should it occur, would be unlikely to escalate and, implicitly, that Beijing would be so traumatized that it would yield to American "blackmail" and tolerate the permanent loss of Taiwan.

In a high-stakes conventional war involving an adversary's threatened use of any weapons of mass destruction, the only rational option might be for China to raise the prospect of its own first use of nuclear weapons, a prospect that has now been made explicit in Chinese publications. The issue concerns the possible escalation of a future conflict in the Taiwan Strait and the intervention of the United States, as we shall see in the final chapter. Newly published scenarios assume that the very possibility of a conflict turning nuclear could help deter Washington from intervening in the first place or ever using nuclear weapons, thus rendering its "New Triad" doctrine impotent.[60] It is this reason that so far causes the PLA to minimize the chances of a limited nuclear strike against China. Although an all-out nuclear strike cannot be ruled out, it is the more limited use of nuclear weapons that most haunts the Chinese debates about the likelihood of possible local wars leading to a U.S.-China nuclear confrontation.[61] We will end this study with an examination of the most recent (as of January 2005) Chinese writings that suggest that a rethinking on the role of nuclear weapons may have begun.

Air Strikes Pose the Main Conventional Threat

With each new generation of technological advances, Beijing's leaders have had to rethink the greatest threats in a future high-tech war. They have repeatedly had to delineate the operational meaning of "high tech," which only entered the army's vocabulary in the 1990s. Some history may help clarify how the steady amendments to that vocabulary were masked by replacing the content of established terminology.

When armed conflicts erupted and escalated along the Sino-Soviet border in 1969, the CMC called for strengthening anti-tank capabilities as the most effective way to defeat the first wave of Soviet armored forces supported by strike aircraft and helicopter-borne troops. Massive tank attacks comprised the overriding military problem, though nuclear strikes against strategic targets were also considered. For more than a decade thereafter, the PLA trained and procured weapons for "fighting tank, aircraft, and airborne forces" (*san da*) and "defending against atomic, chemical, and biological weapons" (*san fang*).[62]

With the end of the Cold War in the early 1990s, the military danger from the north largely disappeared while the United States once again seemed to be ever more hostile or indifferent to the hallowed one-China principle. After the spectacular demonstration of U.S. air power in the 1991 Gulf War, the menace of land-based armored divisions was replaced by that of modern precision-guided munitions deployed on bombers, strike aircraft, and cruise missiles. From that moment, air defense loomed as the nation's fatal weakness. In time, U.S. defense plans, including antiterrorist actions, called for rapid deployment of aircraft and their support facilities to airfields from Korea and Japan to Afghanistan and Uzbekistan and on powerful carrier battle groups, and the CMC seemed justified in concluding that these were "deployed right before our front door." Moreover, planes from these nearby launch positions could fly multiple sorties and attack China from unpredictable points on the compass. That the Chinese felt squeezed or encircled became a common theme in the PLA's seminars and debates.[63]

In time, the PLA concluded that air strikes would most likely constitute the opening phase of a high-tech local war, and air domination would eventually decide its outcome.[64] As chairman of the Central Military Commission, Jiang Zemin in the early 2000s advanced the urgent case for building a national air defense system capable of downing jet aircraft and cruise missiles and defeating precision guided munitions: "The threat from the air is the most direct, realistic, and serious threat to our country's security at present and for some time into the future. . . . Air defense constitutes the core of our country's defenses." He ordered his General Armament Department and the nation's defense industry connected to it to strengthen that core.[65]

At this time, vigorous air defenses became the essence of a successful high-tech local war. Procurements and training would now concentrate on "fighting stealth aircraft, cruise missiles, and armed helicopters" (san da) and "defense against electronic jamming, precision attacks, and reconnaissance and surveillance" (san fang).[66] The anti-Soviet san da san fang doctrine glided nicely into air defense doctrine with the same characters. When reading Chinese military treatises, it is necessary to track the content of key terms in order to comprehend changes hidden by familiar shorthand vocabulary.

Moreover, the doctrinal migration continued in 2000 as information warfare supplemented air defense as the dominant concern, and the CMC once more altered the meaning of san da san fang. The term "san da" now referred to "fighting aircraft, missiles, and command-control-communications-computer-intelligence-surveillance-reconnaissance [C⁴ISR] systems," and "san fang" highlighted the need to defend against "precision munitions, cyber warfare, and reconnaissance and infiltration [by special forces]."[67] The new san da san fang reflected the military's assessment that this type of "high-tech" assault could cripple the nation's capacity to conduct a sustained and coherent defense. The PLA had studied the U.S. air and C⁴ISR-directed campaigns from the first Gulf War onward, and the subsequent conflicts in Afghanistan and Iraq only confirmed the validity of the new doctrine. The requirements to meet the objectives of this complex doctrine, however, confounded China as never before and helped underscore the wisdom of Deng Xiaoping's guiding principle of maintaining a low posture, solving external disputes, and refusing to be drawn into war for decades to come.[68]

The Influence of New Threats on the "Active Defense" Doctrine

The essence of the People's War doctrine is the concept of "active defense," which we will treat more fully in our final chapter. The doctrine has served as the basic underpinning of Chinese strategic thought since Mao took command of the Chinese revolution in the 1930s. The enduring adherence to that military strategy can be traced to both realism and philosophy, but here again the doctrine's content has been adjusted to meet a range of new circumstances. The permanent reality that justifies the term is the military's recurrent confrontation with more powerful adversaries.

Though dictated by necessity, "active defense" from the philosophical perspective draws on the stratagems of the ancients as translated by Mao and his revolutionary lieutenants. Once more we encounter the ideas of conflict avoidance, strategic guile, and as a last resort carefully picking the battlefield and the battle. In contemporary China, the doctrine gains strength from growing nationalism or, as a Chinese proverb puts it, "an army burning with indignation is bound to win" (ai bing bi sheng). The best defensive posture builds on national spirit and cohesion and on linkages to international support for China as victim. Mao once stressed that strategic defense "is vital to the very existence" of the Chinese military, a dictum that is repeated today in the PLA's classrooms.[69]

In April 1955, Mao once more elaborated on "active defense" and termed it "China's strategic guiding principle." Then as so many times before, he gave the strategy a new twist, saying, "China will never make a preemptive attack [against other countries]" and yet, he elaborated, "Active defense is defense in offensive posture."[70] It was this somewhat paradoxical statement that Deng Xiaoping sought to interpret a quarter century later. In 1980, with the Vietnam border war still fresh in his mind, Deng told his colleagues to apply active defense equally to conflicts outside and inside the country.[71] He was implying, however, that the relationship between defense and offense would differ in the two cases. Two years later he said, "I am in favor of 'active defense.' . . . Active defense itself does not only comprise defense, [but] defense [also] contains offense."

In this more recent interpretation, "active defense" in practice is made to fit the contradictory requirements that arise before and after the outbreak of war. Sun Tzu would have lauded this distinction. The "defense" component of the strategy is most prominent in the pre-conflict environment and rationalizes the politics of caution and the avoidance of provocative actions that could trigger an attack. With the outbreak of war, however, the "active" element in the strategy takes over and would have much in common with the saying, "Offense is the best defense." This side of the strategy would mandate an offensive posture to attain defensive objectives and more aggressive "activeness."[72] PLA strategists like to explain the new posture as strategically defensive and tactically offensive. Part of this, of course, sounds Orwellian and serves propaganda: By definition, we are the defender; the enemy is the aggressor. But, part of the explanation is meant to instill the mental agility to exploit the evolving situation, a metaphor for Sun Tzu's "terrain," and to go on the attack.

In peace and war, the "consistent" doctrine is "active defense," a doctrine that unabashedly dictates "winning victory mainly through active offensive actions."[73] As some candid PLA theorists admit, in the name of "active defense," China's armies have shifted to the offensive in all local conventional conflicts since 1949.[74] As a case in point, in the Sino-Soviet border clashes of 1969, the PLA deliberately escalated the crisis by ambushing a Soviet company on the disputed Zhenbao Island and legitimated the unprovoked attacks as "active defense."

Seen in this light, "active defense" can justify preemption even before the enemy has struck because the enemy *intended* to strike first, the thought being equal to the deed. One theme that emerges in this study is that preemption or first-strike actions have become more attractive, almost necessary options in China's conventional and nuclear doctrines. Thus the convoluted evolution of "active defense" more often translates into "active offense," because advanced conventional and nuclear weapons blur the zone demarcating peace and war and raise the price of delay and inaction.

Take, for example, Mao's "16-character rhymed formula": "If others let me alone, I'll let them alone; if we are attacked, we will certainly counterattack" (*ren bu fan wo, wo bu fan ren; ren ruo fan wo, wo bi fan ren*). Mao interpreted the formula quite flexibly, especially once the battle had begun. The injunction not to take preemptive, surprise actions vanished as a conflict unfolded and could be easily set aside as the red line between not being "left alone" and being attacked so easily blurred. When Mao warned, "You can fight inside China, [but] we, of course, can fight outside China,"[75] he transformed a warning into a threat to act preemptively, though masked in defensive language.

In 1965, Mao noted the aggressive aspects of active defense strategy in a discussion with his subordinates of the possibility of an invasion by China's adversaries. He formally stressed the "activeness" of the strategy. He said, an invasion "was not so terrible. It is no more than a movement of mankind on the globe. You come to my place, and we go to your place."[76]

The Chinese leader's warning to Moscow after the Soviet Army's invasion of Czechoslovakia in 1968 typifies the gray area in active defense and its potential aggressiveness. At about that time and upon receipt of an urgent message from Albania of Moscow's increasing threat against Tirana, Mao summoned the Soviet ambassador and delivered his message: "You intend to send troops to Albania, don't you? Europe is far from us. We won't go there. . . . However, we have such a long boundary with you. We can go wherever we like. There will be no boundary [between us] if a war really breaks out!"[77] The ambassador, we are told, could not be sure whether Mao's "active defense" of Albania was a bluff or a genuine warning of a retaliatory attack on his country.

More recently, the traditional "cautiousness toward the first battle" noted earlier has been modified as the Chinese appear to have accepted part of the U.S. military's idea that by seizing the initiative it can define the battlefield and often determine the final outcome. The PLA continues to appreciate the implications of making early risky mistakes, but some of its leaders now see how essential it is to seize and maintain the initiative through offensive action or at least not to relinquish the initiative to the enemy. The loss of initiative by the weaker side in the opening phases of a war may not be reversible, a price far higher than the unknown cost of making early mistakes.

This calculation may have a special strategic significance when weighing all the factors in a high-tech local war, because yielding the initiative to a foe equipped with precision-guided munitions may irreparably damage the nation's C⁴ISR systems, a key element in the current version of the san da san fang strategy.[78] In March 2003, a PLA theorist noted that in the Iraq War then underway U.S.-led forces had seized the initiative through high-intensity air strikes combined with a fast-moving high-tech land assault. The Iraqi army was never allowed to take the initiative.[79]

Yet, it is one thing to grasp the problem and change theoretical direction but it is quite another matter to develop, pay for, and deploy the capabilities needed to fight and win a high-tech local war. The cognitive changes have been remarkable, and now the entire defense establishment must be mobilized to respond even as other developmental priorities still take precedence. At the intellectual level, all possibilities for achieving "activeness" are on the table, and some long-dismissed alternatives, even a preemptive or preventive war, cannot be excluded.[80] The chapters that follow will test the degree to which the Central Military Commission has prepared for those alternatives in the event of actual conflict.

The conditions that would warrant resorting to such alternatives are part of the PLA's extraordinary evolution over the past several decades, and they help provide the context that began to develop following the missile crisis of October 1969, the subject of the next chapter. The current answer seems relatively clear: If an enemy irreparably violates China's sovereignty, it is deemed to have struck first and any "no first strike" restraints disappear. At that moment, the PLA is empowered to respond even though the offending act may have been political. Operationally, the Chinese might counterattack locally or launch strikes against the enemy's overseas bases or other high-value assets and, depending on the weight given to possible retaliation, take the war directly to the enemy's homeland, the so-called source of the war.[81] Sun Tzu had cautioned against attacking the enemy's army on the battlefield and especially against striking its fortified cities, but he could not have foreseen the age of ballistic and cruise missiles and the B-2 bomber.

Inexorably and step by step, the realities of modern technology are eclipsing centuries of tradition. The course of this evolution will define the direction of our inquiry and the findings with which we will end.

THREE

Strategic Challenges and the Struggle for Power, 1964–1969

In the early 1960s, China's traditional and revolutionary strategic culture collided with Chairman Mao Zedong's enduring social vision. At the level of grand strategy in 1964, the People's Liberation Army had launched an all-out effort to build a viable nuclear deterrent. Its R&D organizations were racing to complete China's first atomic bomb that October, to build and deploy its first-generation ballistic missiles, and to restart a long-delayed nuclear-powered, ballistic-missile submarine program.[1] Having only recently waged a border war against India and facing mounting crises with an ever-more-hostile Soviet Union and American power moving into Indochina, the Chinese had to make strategic choices.

Mao had long proclaimed that all doctrines must be validated in practice, but practical lessons were pouring in from many sources that confounded his final fantasy of perpetual revolution. Most important, decisions on the nation's social and political direction split the high command and presaged an astonishing decade of deliberate chaos. Emerging from the devastation following the collapse of his grand social experiment, the Great Leap Forward and the rural people's communes launched in 1958, the Chinese leader had, in his own words, been placed on a shelf and a more bureaucratic and in his mind "revisionist" elite had seized power. In the years from 1964 through 1969, Mao was forced to choose between his dream of revolutionization and his commitment to modernization as the foundation for lasting national security.

Even as the Sino-Soviet conflict and the fight for Vietnam were escalating, a grand struggle for power within China was heading for yet another decisive moment in what was to become the tumultuous Cultural Revolution of 1966–76, and the multiple crises combined and fed on one other in the years 1964–69. The questions of war and peace provided the framework for political maneuvering, and for some months in 1969, the Chinese military went on full alert. For the first time, Chinese nuclear forces joined the alert as part of a hidden plot to propel Mao Zedong's heir-apparent, Lin Biao, to a position of supreme power.

To Mao, the coming together of external and domestic challenges was not accidental, and in dealing with them, he presumed that his "Khrushchevite" foes in both Moscow and Beijing were linked in spirit if not conspiracy. By making that linkage, he could play the cards of patriotism and nationalism against alleged corrupters of his revolutionary message, and he thereby set in motion a five-year period of intrigue and treachery that would end in the nuclear alert of October 1969. We briefly review that oft-studied period to explain the security-related outcomes of the October crisis: shake-ups in the factional alignments in Beijing, reorganization of the national command-and-control system, changes in policies toward the Soviet Union and the United States, and broad implications for nuclear deterrence and global stability.

ONE FRONT OR TWO?

The year 1964 began with vocal and unambiguous expressions of Mao's hostility toward Moscow. On March 31, for example, the eighth in a series of Chinese commentaries on an "open letter" from the Soviet Communist Party railed against "Khrushchev's revisionism" only to be followed by similar diatribes against "Khrushchev's phoney communism and its historical lessons for the world" (July 14) and against the Russian leader soon after his ouster that October.[2]

The diametrically opposed ideological points of view and frequent border clashes that year had become ever more intense, and Mao was predicting the likelihood of war.[3] He connected the threat from the north to the threat from within and became increasingly paranoid about a grand conspiracy.[4] The stage was being set for his violent comeback in the Cultural Revolution that began in the spring and summer of 1966.

Mao's rage toward Moscow transcended politics and was fueled by his personal contempt for Nikita Khrushchev. The stories of that hatred are legendary: His bodyguard, for example, once made the mistake of shaving his head, which Mao immediately connected to the bald Khrushchev and berated the soldier. From then on, shaved heads became a taboo in Mao's personal entourage.[5] By 1966, his hatred for the purged former leader had festered for a decade, from the time of Khrushchev's de-Stalinization speech at the 1956 Soviet Party Congress.[6] That hatred blurred his strategic priorities and blinded him to the menacing rise of Marshal Lin Biao.

In November 1964, Mao approved a report to relocate key industrial and research facilities to China's interior.[7] The report divided China into three regions: the coastal provinces and the northeast were the "first line," Yunnan, Guizhou, Sichuan, and other interior provinces the "third line," and all in between the "second line."[8] The massive relocation that followed moved much of industry and defense facilities from the first and second to the third line.[9] Mao quite consciously had chosen to relocate China's industrial bases far from Soviet bombers but, ironically, closer to American air bases.[10] To plan for the third-line construction, Mao first gave top priority to the two iron and steel complexes in Jiuquan, Gansu Province, and Panzhihua, Sichuan Province. Later, he decided that the complex in Panzhihua should claim precedence over that in Jiuquan because the latter was too close to the Soviet Union.[11] Mao no longer equivocated: Moscow was his principal foe.

The clarity of the third-line policy, however, was almost immediately complicated by the events in Vietnam in late 1964 and early 1965. The Americans were waging and escalating the war to China's south and could not be ignored. As an attempt to deal with the menacing Indochina crisis in April 1965, the Central Committee called for war preparedness on two fronts,[12] and Premier Zhou Enlai a month later told his generals to prepare for "an early war, an all-out war, and a nuclear war on the two fronts."[13] While Mao apparently continued to believe that the Soviet Union posed the immediate danger, few in Beijing appear to have shared his view.

Mao's primary concern, it now seems clear, was more domestic than external, and he was even then plotting against his perceived internal rivals and reformulating his strategy toward Vietnam. According to the recollections of Le Duan, then the first secretary of the Vietnamese Communist Party, Hanoi had begun pressing Beijing and Moscow to form a united front against the United States. He later recalled a meeting with Zhou Enlai, among others, and stated that they accepted the idea of building a front and passed the proposal to the Politburo Standing Committee. When Mao received the proposal, he promptly rejected it.[14] Mao, we believe, based his rejection on his fear that any alliance or relaxation of tensions between Beijing and Moscow would impede his purge of "revisionists" at home.

Yet despite Mao's own anti-revisionist obsession at home and abroad, his language in 1965 did reflect his nominal acceptance for a while of a two-front threat. In a major speech at the time, he said: "pay attention not only to imperialism but also to revisionism. . . . We must keep an eye not only on the east but also on the north. . . . We must prepare for fighting wars on two fronts."[15] The possibility of fighting "on two fronts" appears to have reflected Mao's preoccupation with the worst case, but Mao in unguarded moments often revealed his true fears. He more than once asked visitors with access to the Kremlin whether it was "possible for the Soviet Union to send troops to occupy Xinjiang, Heilongjiang, and even Inner Mongolia."[16] Throughout 1965 and 1966, as the war in Vietnam escalated, the Chinese leader remained fixated on the feared offensive from the north.

On one occasion in this period, he told his generals to repudiate Chiang Kai-shek's surrender of large territories to the Japanese and thereby modified his own doctrine on "luring in deep" in a protracted war. In a future war against a Soviet invader, he said, the PLA must resist the initial assault,[17] and he ordered the Central Military Commission (CMC) to switch the nation's defenses from the south to the three northern regions (*san bei diqu*); namely, northeast, north, and northwest China.[18] The CMC rapidly transferred two-thirds of its engineering regiments to san bei to build fortifications and directed six of the nine living PLA marshals to consider ways to "fight a war in the northeast."[19] On November 11, 1965, the main Party organs published an editorial against Moscow's "new leaders" and the policy of "united action" against the United States with the chilling rebuke: "On all the fundamental issues of the present epoch, the relation [between our two countries] is one of sharp opposition; there are things that divide us and nothing that unites us."[20]

By the spring of 1966, Mao had retreated to his southern compound in Hangzhou, where he would finalize the opening moves of the Cultural Revolution. In March, Liu Shaoqi, Zhou Enlai, and Deng Xiaoping, apparently largely unaware of the political storm that awaited them, convened an enlarged meeting of the Politburo Standing Committee to debate the pros and cons of sending a Party delegation to Moscow to participate in the Twenty-third Congress of the Communist Party of the Soviet Union. As an example of how out of step they were with their chairman, they decided at the meeting to send a delegation with Liu Shaoqi as its probable head. Amazingly, the meeting participants did not seem to grasp that Mao had left Beijing in order to plot his actions for their impending purge even though the power struggle had already begun in the PLA.[21]

Predictably, Mao flew into a rage when he received the meeting report and flatly rejected it.[22] He labeled his strategy "provocative" but no more so than allowing "the enemy army to reach the city gate" and of "bolting the door to beat the dog" (*guanmen da gou*), as Zhou Enlai's biographer later put it.[23] Reconciling with Moscow for whatever reason would weaken Mao's ability to eliminate the "revisionists" within the walls of Zhongnanhai, the compound adjoining the Forbidden City and the seat of the Party and government.

SINO-SOVIET BORDER CONFLICTS

By 1966, Moscow was providing Mao the evidence he needed to proclaim that the main danger would come on one front, not two. The Soviet Army was rapidly beefing up its frontline divisions and rocket forces in Mongolia, and in February that year, the Soviet Union and Mongolia signed a new military treaty.[24] In a discussion with several of his PLA marshals, Mao predicted that Moscow would attack within two years.[25] As Soviet bases in Mongolia were clearly becoming stronger and more permanent, the Chinese responded in kind.[26] In 1967, the CMC assigned the motorized Thirty-eighth Corps in the north as an elite quick-reaction unit and put the entire Inner Mongolia Military District under the jurisdiction of the Beijing Region Command.[27]

As Mao had predicted, Moscow did launch a large-scale military action, which came in August 1968, but the target was Czechoslovakia, not China.

Almost immediately, the Chinese upgraded the probability of a Soviet invasion against them.[28] In preparation, the Politburo decided to react more aggressively toward all future border incidents as a deterrent and to galvanize popular patriotism by then largely eroded in the mass upheaval during the preceding two years of the Cultural Revolution. Cries to defend the nation echoed alongside the campaign against hidden traitors, plotters, and revisionists.[29]

In the winter of 1968–69, Mao via the CMC instructed the Shenyang Region Command to plan an ambush of Soviet troops on the disputed Zhenbao Island in the Ussuri River.[30] The command selected three reinforced companies from three corps and speeded up their special training. The General Staff and Foreign Ministry accepted the command's operations plan on February 19, 1969, and passed it and the relevant operational directives to the CMC. In its approval order, the CMC assumed direct control of the ambush. The region commander and a vice foreign minister each headed a team at the Beijing command post, the first to oversee the battlefield and the second to monitor incoming foreign intelligence.[31] Together with the CMC's "operations system" (*zuozhan xitong*)—consisting of the chief and a deputy chief of the General Staff and senior officers from the General Staff's Operations, Intelligence, Technical, and Communications departments and Confidential Bureau—they reported to Zhou Enlai, whom Mao had authorized to make the final decision.[32]

Zhou, it should be noted, often managed the urgent operations of the CMC even though he was not then one of its formal members.[33] Because so much emphasis has been given to Mao's role in the revolution and early Communist state and to his legendary distrust of subordinates, the importance of those subordinates is often missed or underestimated.[34] Capricious though he may have been, Mao had to rely on others, though his trust in them was always limited and short-lived. During this pivotal period in the Cultural Revolution, Mao turned to Zhou to manage emerging external crises (as well as the strategic weapons program[35]), and he gave him much greater authority within the CMC, in part to monitor and curtail the actions of its other members.

On March 2, 1969, the Chinese brutally ambushed and killed the Soviet post commander and a number of his men, and for two weeks the two sides prepared for a regimental-sized engagement that came with full fury on

March 15. On the night of the sixteenth, Mao and Lin Biao, by then Mao's heir-apparent, called in senior officials to discuss countermeasures against the escalating border clashes and told them to make ready for war. Mao ordered the nuclear industrial installations to guard against Soviet bombers, but added: "That's all. Don't fight," though hand-to-hand fighting already had occurred on Zhenbao Island. As intelligence specialist Arthur Cohen has noted, despite the bloodshed at Zhenbao, both sides had clearly "cooperated in escalation control" and kept the firefights conventional, relatively small, and short.[36]

In the days leading up to and following these events, each side issued stern warnings, and eventually the Soviets stopped coming to the island. After the showdown on the fifteenth, the Kremlin repeatedly tried to contact Zhongnanhai, and at one point, Soviet leader Leonid Brezhnev put in a call to Mao via the hot line with terminals at the Kremlin and Zhongnanhai, but the Chinese operator refused to put him through. On the night of March 21, Premier Alexei Kosygin used the separate Foreign Ministry hot line and told a Chinese official that he wished to talk to Zhou Enlai. At midnight, the chargé d'affaires in Beijing visited the Foreign Ministry to deliver the same message from the Soviet premier.[37]

Zhou quickly passed these reports to Mao and recommended that China "prepare immediately for negotiations." Before daybreak the next day, Mao made his response. By then, the Chinese had intelligence that persuaded them that the Russians would welcome diplomatic talks.[38] So, although we are told that Mao did not consider it proper to speak directly to Soviet leaders on the phone, he authorized the Foreign Ministry to tell the chargé d'affaires that the Kremlin should make a formal proposal via diplomatic channels. He ordered Zhou Enlai to begin working toward negotiations.[39]

At this moment in the Cultural Revolution, Mao's distrust of his official advisors had grown, and he often confided in personal aides, including his chief nurse. Strikingly, she was one of the first to learn of a change in Mao's strategic thinking, when he told her, "China and the Soviet Union are now at war. . . . Hasn't the American global strategy given [us] a signal? The U.S. expects to fight 'two and a half wars.' Just think how they would act if they only needed to fight one and a half wars."[40] Beijing would move closer to Washington, and the battle lines in the global struggle would be redrawn.

WAR PREPARATIONS AND
THE RISE OF LIN BIAO

The timing of the battles on March 2 and 15 coincided with bold actions by Lin Biao to seize control of the military and eventually the nation. Planning by early March was well underway for convening the Ninth Party Congress (held April 1–24), where Lin as Mao Zedong's "close comrade-in-arms" would present an unprecedented political report and would push through a revolutionary-style Party constitution.[41] Lin's report proclaimed that the "storm of the great revolution has destroyed the 'palaces of hell-rulers,' big and small, and has made it possible for Mao Zedong Thought to reach the broad revolutionary masses directly."[42] A few days later, the Party Congress adopted the constitution that named Lin Mao's chosen successor.[43]

As Lin was making his move, the Kremlin was acting in ways that apparently convinced the Chinese side that it was pursuing scare tactics and psychological warfare. On April 3, Zhou wrote Mao and Lin Biao that the recent Soviet shelling of Zhenbao Island was to "purposely make an empty show of strength and act in a play for viewers" or "saber rattling as an exercise in psychological terror."[44] On April 28 at the first plenary session of the Ninth Central Committee, Mao made decisive shifts in emphasis in his call for getting ready to fight: War was no longer considered imminent or essentially a matter of weaponry. The nation would have to be prepared "year after year" and "war preparedness mainly means to be prepared psychologically," he said. "To be psychologically prepared means that we should be spiritually prepared to fight."[45]

For Lin, spiritual preparation required squashing the enemies he thus far had created in the Cultural Revolution, and though he clearly was on the rise, his power base remained incomplete. While the Central Cultural Revolution Group (CCRG) had effectively replaced the Politburo and Central Secretariat as the main power center, Premier Zhou Enlai controlled many (but not all) of the ministries under the State Council, and Mao held sway over the military and the masses on the streets.[46] Lin could only recommend appointments to key positions even though he was in charge of the CMC's daily affairs. After the outbreak of the Cultural Revolution, Lin was heard to complain that Mao had "attained his goal, but I haven't attained mine."[47] The CMC Administrative Group, the body responsible to Lin for the

CMC's daily affairs, could only move units below the regimental level, while movements of regiments and above had to be approved by Mao.[48] Even the movement of a company under the Beijing Garrison Command needed Mao's okay.[49] Moreover, Jiang Qing, Mao's wife and a deputy head of the CCRG, was a force to be reckoned with and had begun to resist Lin. From Lin's vantage point, the border clashes had highlighted the indispensable role of the military, and for a time, he had neutralized Jiang's opposition.[50] He calculated that he could do so again as he began to set a course away from Mao's spiritual preparations.

In April, Lin told Long Shujin, commander of the Xinjiang Military Region, that the Sino-Soviet frictions came from their contention for the leadership of the international Communist movement and, therefore, existing border conflicts would unlikely end in a full-scale collision between the two countries. "It is good [for us] to have some border clashes that might raise the prestige of the military and give added weight to several commanders in the mind of the central leadership," Lin stressed. In his capacity as a field commander, Long originally worried about the escalating border actions, but felt relieved as he returned to Xinjiang.

Over the coming weeks and months, however, the war of words between Moscow and Beijing intensified, and as armed preparations quickened on both sides, four generals then in charge of the Administrative Group endorsed Lin's new conclusion that a large-scale Soviet invasion could be imminent.[51] Moreover, Chen Boda, head of the CCRG, shared that opinion and further deepened the crisis mood so important to achieving Lin's ambitious aims.[52] During a military crisis, the judgments of Lin and his supporters would carry far greater weight, especially because they could readily cite fresh and alarming evidence for those judgments from recent Soviet "provocations."[53]

In the months after April, Moscow had speeded up its buildup along the Soviet and Mongolian borders with China and had officially defined the Great Wall, less than 100 kilometers north of Beijing, as the true historical boundary. It was at this moment, according to Chinese sources, that the Soviet military threatened China with "a crushing nuclear retaliation" with "nuclear-armed missiles with unlimited destruction," and Russian authors confirm that Moscow reached a decision to "threaten nuclear retaliation in the middle of August."[54] These and other Soviet actions were deemed harbingers of a Soviet preemptive nuclear assault against China.[55] The moment for Lin to act seemed to be at hand.

Starting from June 20, the CMC Administrative Group convened a two-week planning meeting for a possible conflict in the three northern (san bei) regions.[56] The conference approved the PLA demand to increase the defense budget by 34 percent over the previous year.[57] When Lin attended the meeting on July 2, he added to the war hysteria by directing that "the nuclear fuel plants in Jiuquan and Baotou must be moved to the third-line region by 1970." On August 12, Zhou Enlai stopped the removal but only after the entire nuclear program had been thrown into a panic.[58]

Also in June, Mao had ordered the CMC Administrative Group to hold a forum on preparing for war.[59] He told his generals not to worry if the Soviet Union dropped several atomic bombs on China, a vast land with a huge population. "Besides, we, too, have atomic bombs," Mao added.[60] In mid-June, Mao approved the group's proposals to bolster the administrative structures of the General Staff and General Logistics departments as a measure to prepare for fighting the Soviet Army.[61] Shortly thereafter, the General Staff held a two-week meeting of communications specialists and then ordered its communications units to build an emergency underground cable network for those structures.[62]

Mao's attempt to involve Washington in the explosive Sino-Soviet confrontation followed the ancient dogma of "playing one barbarian off against the other" (yi yi zhi yi).[63] Facing a likely Soviet attack, Mao told Zhou Enlai not to highlight U.S. Taiwan policy.[64] Silence would greet the anniversary of Truman's decision in June 1950 to deploy the Seventh Fleet in the Taiwan Strait.

From June through July, orders flowed from the high command. Mao, for example, approved a decision of the Politburo to further simplify the departments of the Central Committee and the ministries of the State Council and to introduce deep personnel cuts. Around 210,000 officials soon headed for labor in the nation's interior, and more of the ministries fell under Lin's rule. Most important, the Party's Central Investigation Department (intelligence) merged into the General Staff Intelligence Department.[65] All these actions favored Lin, and by July, he seemed unstoppable.

On June 30, as the Administrative Group's forum was still in session, senior generals in attendance demanded a dramatic increase in funding for the ordnance industry. Qiu Huizuo, then deputy chief of the General Staff and a Politburo member, agreed and advocated abandoning the long-standing guideline on developing the economy in a planned and proportional way.

War fighting, he proclaimed, was the immediate priority, and rote adherence to the "planned, proportional way" was obsolete and dangerous.[66] At that moment, the ever-agile Zhou Enlai was forced to take sides after some in the room urged him not to violate the very guideline that was associated with his name. Zhou's response was feigned anger. "What do you mean by saying 'planned and proportional'? The needs [of war] are the plan, and war determines the proportion."[67]

In addressing those needs, war preparedness rapidly spread from the center to province-level authorities by mid-1969. In June, Beijing ordered every province to build ordnance factories in its own strategic rear, called "minor third-line areas," and set up a War Preparedness Leading Group to oversee local mobilization and civil air defense.[68] An emergency atmosphere quickly engulfed the whole nation, and, according to a later top-secret document condemning him, Lin apparently made a brief "inspection tour" on July 23, which allegedly "used preparations for war as a pretext for seizing power."[69]

With the onset of summer, the verbal exchanges between the two Communist states grew more feverish, and war preparations reinforced the unrestrained hyperbole. Mao's doctor recalls the entire land being energized for war: "Tens of millions of people were evacuated from the cities and shipped to rural areas in a variety of guises. . . . As the war scare grew, others were evacuated away from the borders. In August 1969, the remaining city residents were mobilized to 'dig tunnels deep' in preparation for aerial, possibly nuclear, attack."[70]

In some provinces, factional armed conflicts between bitterly opposed mass organizations frustrated the local war preparedness campaigns, and the center's watchdogs had to intervene. On July 23, for example, the Party central leadership issued a decree demanding Shanxi Province restore public order by forcing local mass organizations to surrender their weapons and soon afterward extended the proclamation to all provinces. The PLA sent armed detachments to help collect the seized weapons, and shortly thereafter, factional battles subsided, allowing the local rulers to reimpose their control and resume the mandated military preparations.[71]

By the end of the summer, the military buildup along the northern border had accelerated, and the danger from America had almost vanished from public discourse. A report by four PLA marshals on July 11 restated the obvious conclusion that the "Soviet revisionists have made China their main enemy, imposing a more serious threat to our security than the U.S. imperialists."

The four added: "We have made full preparations, and we are ready to defeat any enemy who dares to invade our territory."[72] Despite some unresolved questions at the highest level, the CMC made the strategic mandate crystal clear: "Currently, Soviet revisionism is our biggest threat. We must prepare first against Soviet revisionism and switch our key target to Soviet revisionism [from U.S. imperialism]."[73] Mao's strategy now targeted the single front to the north.

THE CRISIS MOUNTS

From March to July, in visits to France and Asia and in other public settings, President Richard Nixon and his leading foreign policy advisors began floating ideas about developing "parallel relations" with China and the Soviet Union. Secretary of State William Rogers, for example, told a meeting in April that the United States would "take the initiative to reestablish more normal relations with Communist China." During the next months, the United States modified trade controls and began the slow process of reciprocal relaxations of the U.S.-China tensions. On July 25, the president told reporters that he accepted the principle "Asia for Asians," and a few days later asked the Pakistani president to convey his sentiment to Beijing that "the US should not be party to any arrangements designed to isolate China."[74]

Zhou Enlai immediately picked up on these signals. While he and other Beijing leaders reportedly were closely monitoring the declared changes in U.S. policy, they did not overestimate their significance. They deemed these changes far from fundamental, though they did appear to fit Mao's conclusion that the threat to China came less from the United States than from the Soviet Union.[75] The more compelling signs of change would come that fall.

An action-reaction chain between Beijing and Moscow, moreover, was pushing the crisis to a climax. Moscow, stunned by Mao's fierce anti-Russian xenophobia, for months had accused the Beijing leaders of plotting to launch nuclear weapons against the Soviet Union. Because these leaders knew full well that they had no ability or intention to initiate that strike, the best-informed Chinese could only conclude that Moscow was readying its public for a preemptive Soviet attack. Mao, however, reportedly paid little heed to the Kremlin's motives, one way or the other, and pressed ahead in the certainty that the day of reckoning was looming ever closer.[76]

August witnessed a further deterioration of the bilateral relationship as skirmishes erupted all along their common border in Xinjiang. On the thirteenth, Soviet troops killed thirty-eight PLA soldiers in an ambush, and several reporters working in Xinjiang died in a follow-on firefight.[77] In response a few days later, the CMC with Mao's approval issued a directive calling for the PLA to heighten its discipline and alertness in the region and warning all senior officers that any violators of the order would be severely reprimanded.[78]

In the same month, Beijing's high command was made acutely aware of the Kremlin's "nuclear blackmail," though knowledgeable Russian specialists deny that an explicit ultimatum was ever issued. Still, authoritative Chinese sources state that General Andrei Grechko, the Soviet defense minister who had planned the 1968 invasion of Czechoslovakia under the pretext of Warsaw Pact exercises, had threatened to "punish" China with a nuclear assault, and that Soviet specialists had made the rounds to American think tanks to ascertain Washington's likely response to a bombing of China's nuclear facilities.[79] About this time, CIA director Richard Helms released a secret report saying the Soviet Union had probably discussed the possible nuclear attack with its East European allies, and on September 16, a known KGB agent, Victor Louis, warned in the *London Evening News* of a probable Soviet nuclear attack on those facilities.

By then, Zhongnanhai had sufficient evidence to regard these warnings as more than a bluff, and few in the leadership could give much credence to the voices of Kremlin "moderates."[80] On August 28, Mao ordered the establishment of the National Civil Air Defense Leading Group and made Zhou Enlai its head. This group took charge of the nation's air defenses and mass evacuations and set up an administrative organ within the General Staff Operations Department.[81] Mao simultaneously issued an urgent instruction to protect many more key installations from a sudden nuclear strike.

On the same day, Mao approved yet another urgent directive, this time in the name of the Central Committee, to "prepare to smash the armed provocations by the U.S. imperialists and the Soviet revisionists at any time and to prevent them from launching surprise attacks."[82] The nine articles of this "Order for General Mobilization in Border Provinces and Regions (August 28)" detailed plans for the conduct of an expected conflict.[83] That day, too, the CMC ordered all its troops in the three northern regions to undertake emergency training.[84] The implementation of this order, simplified as the "August 28 Order," was deemed the precursor of general mobilization. It marked the high tide of the country's war passions and even Mao was swept up by it.[85]

Mao's generals still remained skeptical, though divided, even as the four marshals had been on July 11. Zhu De, the most senior marshal, shared their skepticism.[86] The chairman had told the General Staff to reexamine the evidence for a possible Soviet attack, and, echoing the marshals, it reported to him that an attack "was not very likely."[87] Other high-ranking aides, on the other hand, told him that the Soviet Army had a history of preemptive strikes; witness its invasion of Czechoslovakia the year before. The always-suspicious Mao was torn, but fell back on his penchant for assuming the worst. He reportedly said, "It is not good for all central officials to assemble in Beijing. Even one atomic bomb will kill many of us." Shortly thereafter, the evacuation of China's top leaders from the capital began.[88]

At this moment of high drama in Beijing, Vietnam's aged president Ho Chi Minh, a long-time revolutionary comrade of the Chinese Communists, died on September 3. Zhou Enlai and Marshal Ye Jianying immediately flew to Hanoi to pay their respects but did not even stay overnight because of the crisis at home.[89] Zhou reportedly had bought into the idea that "a nuclear surgical assault" could come soon using negotiations as a "smoke screen," and by then he also was becoming increasingly concerned about a possible hostile reaction by Washington, which regarded Ho Chi Minh as its enemy.[90]

The whirlwind of war preparations in China had become the all-consuming obsession in the Kremlin. Once again the Soviet leadership called on Premier Kosygin, whom the Chinese knew to have been an advocate of diplomacy in the aftermath of the March crisis, and soon thereafter communicated its interest in negotiations to Beijing. Kosygin, too, was in Hanoi for Ho's memorial services. Mao immediately recognized an opportunity: Would not the Soviet request for negotiations, if leaked, stimulate the Americans to improve their relations with Beijing?[91]

For several days Kosygin had been cooling his heels in Hanoi waiting for a Chinese response, and finally had given up and was en route home when a radio message came from Beijing. His plane changed course and landed at the Beijing airport on September 11, where he was met by Zhou Enlai. In their long hours of discussion at the airport, Kosygin and Zhou covered border issues, conflict avoidance measures, dispute resolution, exchanging ambassadors, and, most especially, the near-term convening of border negotiations.[92]

Nothing was resolved, to be sure, and the hostile propaganda exchanges continued to poison the atmosphere.

Behind the scenes, moreover, the Chinese were taking nothing for granted. Many in the high command had suspected that the incoming Kosygin plane might really be carrying special forces as had occurred during the Soviet invasion of Czechoslovakia. With the Soviet resort to "Trojan horse" tactics during the August 1968 attack on Prague still fresh in their minds, the paranoid Chinese feared a repeat sneak assault on the Beijing airport. While Kosygin was still in the air, Mao ordered Zhou to place military units on alert and move several specially trained battalions to safeguard the airport.[93]

In the days that followed, Beijing was rife with rumor and debate. For its part, the Politburo met on September 16, 18, and 22 to make its assessment of the talks and next steps, and one topic on the agenda was the effect of the airport meeting on the Americans. These Chinese were devouring incoming intelligence and news reports, none of which encouraged a relaxation of the nation's vigil. The senior leadership worried that Kosygin had avoided answering Zhou Enlai's allegations about a possible Soviet nuclear strike even though the Chinese premier had raised the possibility at the airport.[94]

Why, the Chinese asked, had senior Soviet officials not met Kosygin's plane when it landed in Moscow? Why had Moscow not fully acknowledged the understandings reached at the airport and that had been "clearly defined" in Zhou's letter to Kosygin of September 18?[95] Why did the Soviet UN representative tell his American counterpart that a military trial with China was inevitable if Beijing continued its hostility toward the Soviet Union? Moreover, Soviet generals had only recently threatened to launch missiles against China, and then there was the above-mentioned inflammatory article published by Victor Louis on September 16.[96] Viewed from Zhongnanhai, Moscow was up to no good. Was it not probable, they argued, that the Soviets would launch a surprise attack while Beijing awaited negotiations, and what better time to attack than October 1, China's National Day, or upon the arrival of the Soviet negotiators in Beijing shortly thereafter?[97]

Once more the four marshals weighed in on the debate. They opened their newest assessment, "Views about the Current Situation" (September 17), with the declaration: "Just at the time when the Soviet revisionists have daggers drawn, the U.S. imperialists are fanning the flames, and China is making war preparations, Kosygin suddenly made a detour to Beijing. . . . What is his purpose?" They then asserted that the Kremlin still harbored the intention to initiate a war against China but quickly added that they could not "reach a final decision" on that intention because of political considerations, one of which was "possible Sino-American unity." In the end, being "firm on principles and flexible on tactics," they endorsed the negotiations with the Russians and the eventual resumption of Sino-American ambassadorial talks.[98] Mao agreed with their judgments but stressed the need for self-reliance in the face of a Sino-Soviet war. He noted that the United States had not participated in the two world wars until "other countries had fought for two years."[99]

The Politburo dutifully ordered the preparations for war to continue. Starting from mid-September and continuing into the next month, Mao ordered the CMC to transfer several crack units from the south to the three northern regions.[100] The Twenty-seventh Corps moved from Wuxi, Jiangsu Province, to Yanqing County near Zhangjiakou as reinforcements to the Sixth-fifth Corps there because Zhangjiakou provided the sole natural defense for Beijing itself. Soon thereafter, the air force began redeploying several surface-to-air missile battalions to Zhangjiakou, and the CMC added manpower to most of its divisions and formed eighteen new infantry divisions.[101] The total number of infantry officers and men increased 20.9 percent. The CMC then disbanded most of the tank regiments attached to infantry divisions and reorganized them into more powerful tank divisions or independent tank regiments as a way to better engage Soviet armor. The Engineering Corps grew from four to ten divisions and from sixteen to thirty-four regiments, and many of these as well as expanded construction battalions launched a crash program to build hardened air-raid shelters and other defensive positions.[102] Simultaneously, civilian authorities pushed the construction of shelters throughout the nation.[103]

For Mao, all these preparations could not come soon enough. To make the point, Mao added one more slogan to the twenty-eight that Zhou Enlai had routinely prepared for the National Day. He wrote that the people of the world must "specially oppose any war of aggression, especially one in which atom bombs are used as weapons."[104]

THE ALERT

Driving much of the defense analysis throughout September and early October were intelligence reports that reinforced the Chinese military's conviction that Soviet forces were preparing surgical strikes against China's big cities and key military targets. Mao, Lin, and others reportedly gave great credence to these reports, and on September 20, Mao told the CMC to hold a special meeting to survey once more ways to ready the nation for war. On the twenty-second, Zhou Enlai spoke to the senior generals on the commission and referred to "a new strategic plan," and three days later, generals from all region commands and service arms met at Mao's order to decide how to increase readiness in the three northern regions.[105] The term most often heard in the meeting hall was "the coming Soviet surprise attack."

On September 26, Zhou Enlai received a letter from Kosygin, which recommended that the two delegations begin border negotiations in Beijing on October 10. However, the letter failed to mention the cooperative tension-reduction measures mutually accepted at the Kosygin-Zhou airport talks and noted in Zhou's letter to Kosygin on the eighteenth.[106] The Chinese interpreted this as Russian backtracking and became even more convinced that the Kremlin was not sincere and might even be plotting an attack under cover of the upcoming negotiations. "The military must not slacken off," Mao said, and on the twenty-seventh, Mao and Lin Biao received senior PLA officers then attending the meeting to evaluate the nation's war preparedness and plan for the coming conflict. "We urge you not to stay in Beijing until National Day," Mao said. "All of you must pay close attention to war preparedness after you return [to your headquarters]."[107]

To gain the attention of audiences at home and from Moscow to Washington, Mao turned to his nuclear arsenal as his messenger. He ordered a thermonuclear test to be conducted prior to the National Day to dramatize the nation's unity to "win still greater victories" and "as another great blow at the nuclear monopoly of U.S. imperialism and [Soviet] social-imperialism."[108] On the twenty-third, the Lop Nor test site had conducted its first underground explosion, and six days later set off a 3-megaton thermonuclear weapon. Moreover, during the coming months, Chinese missiles targeted on the Soviet Union increased to fifty.[109] Few in Moscow missed the unmistakable messages.

Meanwhile, massive military movements were still underway, and Mao needed more time to complete them before commencing the border negotiations. On September 29, the Foreign Ministry handed a "verbal notice" to the Soviet chargé d'affaires to postpone negotiations from October 10 to 20. Still anticipating a Russian sneak attack on National Day, Lin Biao the next day ordered the CMC Administrative Group to monitor the dispersal of most military aircraft from key airports near Beijing and the implementation of measures against a Soviet preemptive strike against the airports. Because Lin believed the three huge reservoirs outside Beijing could flood the city and its outskirts if their dams were destroyed, he told the local authorities to release their water, but Zhou Enlai considered Lin's proposed solution as bad as an actual attack and reversed the directive.[110]

Lin, with Mao's approval, gave the group an additional order to place all PLA units on a first-grade or highest-state alert. Although he sometimes appeared to downplay the likelihood of a Soviet attack when speaking to his generals, he invariably demanded they intensify war preparations if only as a deterrent.

Yet, those very preparations for a possible attack on October 1 magnified the fears for their personal safety among the top elite, and stories concerning their precautions taken in secret rapidly circulated. Helicopters were stationed behind the Tiananmen, PLA intelligence and operations teams with full communications gear were placed on the viewing rostrum before National Day,[111] and an underground shelter was built for evacuation of the leaders to the western suburbs. Lin Biao practiced horseback riding in his backyard for his own personal escape or some say for his heroic return to the battlefield,[112] while Mao's wife, Jiang Qing, had a shelter constructed in her yard and learned to drive for her getaway.[113]

Despite all these actions and angst, National Day came and went without incident, and as students of failed prophecy would have predicted, the rumors of war thereupon multiplied.[114] The date may have been wrong, but, the CMC appeared to believe, the Russians were still coming. On the fifth, Lin Biao flew to Zhangjiakou for an urgent inspection of its defense fortifications.[115] And, when Zhou Enlai received Kosygin's letter of the fourteenth, which said the Soviet negotiators would arrive by October 20, the Chinese had their new crisis date even though they were the ones who had first proposed the alternative meeting time.[116]

By the second week of October, Mao had begun to panic and seized on each scrap of intelligence warning of possible Soviet military movements as proof of Moscow's evil intentions. The most alarming piece of intelligence in Mao's eyes claimed that Soviet troops would launch a large-scale assault on the twentieth under the umbrella of the border talks. This was quickly followed by a secret report allegedly originating in Moscow itself that Russian technicians had begun retrofitting the plane carrying the Soviet delegation to Beijing with nuclear-tipped air-to-surface missiles.[117] When a "reliable" East European source confirmed the D-day, Mao needed no more convincing.[118] He could see himself vanishing in a mushroom cloud within days.

With the latest intelligence messages in hand, Mao again called the Politburo into action.[119] He told his colleagues, "The international situation can deteriorate suddenly," and directed most of the central leaders to depart Beijing before the twentieth.[120] The ever-worried Mao entrained for Wuhan on the fourteenth, and Lin Biao flew to the city of Suzhou near Shanghai three days later. But, some had to stay and, should they survive, to put on a good face for the arriving Russians. Zhou Enlai, General Huang Yongsheng, and Jiang Qing would bravely remain in Beijing.[121] Zhou would serve as the central crisis manager; Huang, who headed the CMC Administrative Group as chief of the General Staff, would oversee the CMC's daily affairs as the representative of Mao and Lin Biao; and Jiang Qing volunteered to be the chairman's eyes and ears in the capital.[122] Before he departed for Wuhan, Mao met with selected officers from PLA headquarters, praising their loyalty and courage, and he said to Zhou, "I go first. Please tell Comrade Lin Biao to leave Beijing as soon as possible. Enlai, you should also depart Zhongnanhai for the [underground command center in the Western] Hills. I will give you a phone call after I arrive in [Wuhan]."

On the sixteenth, General Huang Yongsheng met the senior officer in charge of the General Staff Operations Department, Deputy Chief of the General Staff Yan Zhongchuan, and directed him to set up an advance command post to serve as the CMC's operational center in the opening phases of the anticipated conflict.[123] As stipulated in standing orders, officers for the post would come from the Operations Department with staff support from the General Staff's other key departments. The same day, Huang ordered the mobilization of the strategic reserve consisting of several ground corps, an airborne corps (Fifteenth Corps), and several tank, artillery, and air defense divisions to face the expected Soviet onslaught.[124] For his part, Zhou Enlai approved the removal of key documents from Foreign Ministry archives for safe storage in the interior.[125]

On the seventeenth, General Yan and his staff retreated to the blast-hardened wartime command center under the Hundred Hope Mountain (Bai Wang Shan) in Beijing's Western Hills, and General Huang led a contingent of the CMC Administrative Group to the advance command post.[126] General Yan had kept the move completely secret until the last minute and isolated his staff from all outside contact. For months, the families of these staff members had no idea of their whereabouts, never a good sign during the chaotic period of the Cultural Revolution that year. At the same time, the State Council and the Party's Central General Office fled to their own emergency administrative centers in hardened silos in Elephant Nose Valley (Xiangbizi Gou) near the CMC's advance command post.[127] And not to be outdone, the Ministry of Public Security executed some of the most dangerous prisoners and moved the rest of the prisoners to remote county-level jails.[128]

Perhaps, the heaviest demands fell on the General Staff Intelligence Department and the air force Intelligence Department and other intelligence agencies as the advance command post required hour-by-hour updates.[129] These agencies apparently learned that the force protection of three Russian missile divisions on the border with China had been increased and might have mistaken it for an increase in alert. Within the everyday state of force readiness (*postoyannaya*), there is a condition of "concern" (*nastorozhennost'*), which was often regarded by foreign intelligence as an increase in the alert status. In this condition, the commander and his staff on the strategic missile bases would move to the bases from their off-base residences, but there would be no movement or increased readiness of the weapons.[130] However, these subtleties were lost on Chinese and other foreign intelligence, and the possibility that Soviet strategic forces had gone on alert was met with alarm in the advance command center. Later, Lin's son, a senior air officer, explained why the Soviet and Chinese militaries almost simultaneously had placed their strategic forces on alert: "Neither of the two sides could determine the other's real intentions. Each worried about possible preemptive action by the other."[131] Prudence dictated that the Chinese respond.

NO. 1 ORDER

By this time, Lin Biao, still in overall charge of the CMC's daily affairs but now working in Suzhou, had become obsessed with the possibility that the Soviet airplane carrying the negotiation team would launch its smuggled nuclear missiles upon entering Chinese air space on October 19. At 1700 on the eighteenth, therefore, he dictated a priority message to General Huang

Yongsheng.[132] Entitled "Urgent Directive Regarding Strengthening Combat Readiness to Prevent an Enemy's Surprise Attack," the message made six main points, all ordering preparations for a surprise attack.[133] The strategic missile forces, the Second Artillery, were to be placed on full alert, and all PLA units were ordered to reach a state of total readiness, with their personnel confined to their posts. Lin stressed that any missile launch would have to be approved by Mao himself.[134] To avoid any possible misinterpretation or mistakes, Lin told an aide to deliver the six-point message about two hours later by encrypted phone to Huang as the chief of the General Staff. Lin's wife, Ye Qun, told the aide that she would personally report the urgent directive to Mao in Wuhan.

According to Lin's aide, Ye Qun did report the content of Lin's six points in a call to Wang Dongxing, Mao's chief bodyguard, on the eighteenth and somewhat earlier than Lin's message had gone to Huang Yongsheng.[135] Later, Ye said that Mao expressed no opinion on the content of the Lin directive.[136] Nonetheless, Lin and Ye did not inform Mao about the directive's actual issuance by the advance command post until a few hours later, and the timing forever after has been a matter of controversy. In the 1980s, a team of military prosecutors searching Mao's archives in Zhongnanhai found a written document that recorded an oral message from Lin and Ye to Mao on the directive, but there was no evidence that Lin had requested Mao's approval before sending his six-point message to the chief of the General Staff for implementation.[137] Whatever the reality, there is no doubt, however, that Lin had made a monumental mistake in the eyes of the angry chairman.

At 2000, after he had received Lin's directive, General Huang put in a call to General Yan Zhongchuan, his operations chief at the advance command post, and told him to phone the directive to all military headquarters. After returning to the duty room, Yan made another fateful decision. He decided to rewrite Lin's six points into four separate orders and dictated each of the four to a staff officer. Yan recognized that these four documents would be the advance command post's first directives and, to the bafflement of all later historians, decided that he should number them individually one through four and collectively term them the No. 1 Order, though the first of the orders alone would also be called the No. 1 Order (but to avoid confusion here, we will simply call the four orders "directives"). Each of the four directives honored the spirit of Lin's original six-point directive, but General Yan had made remarkable and potentially perilous changes to Lin's original language.[138]

Once the four-part No. 1 Order had been drafted, Yan told an officer to submit the documents to Huang for final approval, but by then the general had taken sleeping pills and fallen asleep. The time was 2130. Pressed for time because the Soviet airplane was already in the air and would enter China's air space within about ten hours, Yan felt he must act. Within minutes, "Vice-Chairman Lin's No. 1 Order" had been sent.

The order has a special place in the history of the Chinese military as the first and only time the command was given to place its strategic forces on full alert. Coming at a critical juncture in Cultural Revolution politics, Sino-Soviet tensions, and the initial deployments of China's strategic weapons, this unprecedented document and its ultimate consequences were to shape the high command's judgments on the control of the nation's weapons and the efficacy of their threatened use. The full text of Directive No. 1 of the No. 1 Order follows (and for historical accuracy is translated as the No. 1 Order).

No. 1 Order

Vice-Chairman Lin issues these directives at 2130, October 18, 1969:

U.S. imperialism and Soviet revisionism have taken abnormal actions in the past two days. The so-called Soviet delegation is scheduled to come to Beijing tomorrow (the nineteenth) for negotiations. We must prevent Soviet revisionism from deceiving us by keeping full vigilance. We should especially pay close attention to [the events on] the nineteenth and twentieth.

Various region commands, especially the region commands in the three northern regions [san bei], must immediately disperse and protect their heavy weapons, such as tanks, aircraft, and artillery.[139]

The region commands in the coastal areas also should be on the alert to prevent U.S. imperialism and Soviet revisionism from launching surprise attacks. Do not be caught off guard.

Rapidly accelerate the production of anti-tank weapons such as 40 [mm] bazookas and anti-tank guns (including recoilless guns and 85 [mm] anti-tank artillery).

Immediately organize chosen command teams to proceed to wartime [advance] command posts.

Senior officers at various levels must be on duty to keep abreast of new developments on a real-time basis. Quickly report the implementation of this order.

With regard to Directive No. 2 of the No. 1 Order, Lin's decision putting the Second Artillery on high alert, General Yan deemed it wise to exclude its terms from the first directive of the No. 1 Order in view of the possibility that the implementation of this directive, if leaked, would frighten the Chinese people and foreigners. He need not have worried because its text has not been divulged to this day. We do know that Directive No. 2 called on the Second Artillery headquarters to ready its nuclear-armed missiles for immediate launch. In accordance with standing orders and for security reasons, the advance command post did not even copy Directive No. 2 to other units because of its highly sensitive nature. The advance command post told the Second Artillery to report on the directive's implementation and then to submit its responses to the advance command post for transmittal to the CMC.

Directives No. 3 and 4 were far less confidential, but their contents, too, have not been made public. To further interpret Lin's six-point directive, Yan Zhongchuan drafted Directive No. 3 to the General Staff's Intelligence and Technical departments to maintain round-the-clock surveillance and signals reconnaissance, while Directive No. 4 was sent to the PLA's General Staff, General Logistics, and General Political headquarters, the other arms units (such as the navy and air force), the National Defense Industry Office, and the Defense Science and Technology Commission. Both the third and fourth directives detailed specific requirements to complete their readiness for war.

At 2144, less than fifteen minutes after the four directives had been dispatched, General Yan received word from Lin's office in Beijing that the texts had been received. He then turned to one of his Operations Department deputies and told him to transmit Directive No. 1 to the san bei region commands (Beijing, Shenyang, Lanzhou, and Xinjiang) and then to the other region commands (Ji'nan, Nanjing, Fuzhou, Guangzhou, Kunming, Wuhan, Xizang, and Chengdu). Directives No. 1 and 4 were then phoned to the navy, air force, and Beijing Garrison Command. Presumably, Directives No. 2 and 3 had already gone through highly classified channels to the Second Artillery (No. 2) and the two General Staff departments (No. 3).

Almost immediately, we are told, Yan realized the magnitude of what he had just done. The entire transmittal process had taken about two and a half hours, a brief moment that would shake the nation. Moreover, how could Yan be sure he had gotten the messages right? His chief, General Huang Yongsheng, had only given Yan oral dictation and should have carefully reviewed and approved the final texts. But, Yan apparently feared the wrath of his boss roused from a deep sleep posed a bigger risk at the moment of decision than the future anger of Chairman Mao, let alone the potential danger to the nation. In the end, Huang, Yan, and most senior staff present that night in the advance command post paid a high price for their alleged reck-lessness, though their purge did not come for almost two years.[140]

On the other hand, the command-and-control system appeared to work with military precision. The initial response from the region and service commands to Directives No. 1 and 4 had been efficient and disciplined, with the performance of the four san bei military regions later deemed exemplary. Upon receipt of the No. 1 Order directives at 2315, moreover, the Guangzhou Region commander, Ding Sheng, immediately rallied his top officers at his Operations Department, and when their meeting ended, he accompanied his command team to the underground command center outside Guangzhou. Ding quickly sent a message to his region's field armies, air force units, and South China Sea Fleet headquarters to execute their respective No. 1 Order directives. He then phoned his progress report to the General Staff's advance command post in Beijing at 0140 on the nineteenth, some two and a half hours after receipt of the order.

Meanwhile, parts of the process had been sloppy or highly questionable. Where was Zhou Enlai, whom Mao only days before had put in charge of the center's overall operations? Neither the CMC nor the advance command post had bothered to notify him, and for hours, he had no inkling of the No. 1 Order. To date, those closest to the situation and who have told the story have guessed that perhaps the CMC Administrative Group had by-passed Zhou because only military units would be involved.

At the same time, most of the region commanders who held concurrent high offices in their nearby provincial organs had been caught up in the up-heaval of the Cultural Revolution, and some of them transmitted the top se-cret order to unauthorized local officials and even mass organizations. More-over, the sudden movement of military units could not escape the roaming Red Guards, Mao's young rebels with prying eyes. In Yunnan Province, in one case, these mass organizations brazenly copied the secret order onto "big-character posters" and pasted them on street walls overnight. Next of course came the inevitable rumors of a coming war against the Soviet "enemy." The beleaguered local authorities immediately used their own channels to alert the Party center and State Council about the mysterious No. 1 Order and street gossip surrounding it.

Now Zhou Enlai knew, and he quickly learned the danger after contact-ing Mao's chief bodyguard, Wang Dongxing. Even the chairman had been out of the loop, and a political crisis could probably not be avoided. While

Mao knew the contents of the six directives, he did not know these directives would be issued under the title of "Vice-Chairman Lin's No. 1 Order." Even Lin and General Huang did not know this.[141] On the evening of the nineteenth, Zhou summoned General Huang and four members of the CMC Administrative Group and demanded to know the background of the order and its current status. Who, he asked, had named the directives "Vice-Chairman Lin's No. 1 Order," and why had they permitted secret military orders to reach the street? Whose name would be put on a possible No. 2 Order since Lin's name had been given to the first one?

Nevertheless, the moment was not right to dig too deeply, and Mao and Zhou understood that the most dangerous enemy was in the Soviet Union, not China. The hard questions about the contents and issuance of the order would not be raised until Lin's death in an air crash two years later.[142] Still, Lin Biao, only recently chosen the heir apparent, would never again have Mao's full trust, and soon after Lin died in 1971, the episode of the No. 1 Order was labeled "a rehearsal of Lin Biao's counterrevolutionary coup d'état." Indeed, a "relatively objective comment" would not appear in an official publication until 1986, when the Party admitted that Lin's directives followed "Mao's assessment" and others, not Lin, had labeled them "Vice-Chairman Lin's No. 1 Order."[143]

IMPLEMENTING THE NO. 1 ORDER

The real crisis, of course, came in the wake of the order. Mao could not repudiate it or his chosen heir without looking weak at a moment of intense infighting in the Cultural Revolution, then in its fourth year. The entire military had gone on alert, and the people were rallying to thwart the expected Soviet attack that Mao on National Day had said would come soon.

Amazingly, Lin Biao missed the signals of Mao's true feelings or he realized that this was no time for the timid. He clearly believed his own propaganda and worried most about being caught off guard by a surprise attack. He became impatient with the cumbersome reporting process, one that he did not fully control, and told the air force Intelligence Department, where he had more reliable allies, to send him all relevant intelligence without passing it through channels. His dependence on airborne reconnaissance information and his personal ties in the air force were reinforced when they gave him what he wanted to hear. At the same time, Lin continued to receive intelligence reports from the General Staff's Intelligence and Technical departments via its Operations Department, now lodged in the advance command post hideaway. As the alert continued, Operations officers passed follow-on orders from the CMC to the Second Artillery battalions and the other services.[144]

When Directive No. 2 caused the nation's strategic missiles to prepare for "immediate launch," it should be noted, Lin had included the DF-3 intermediate-range (2,650 km) ballistic missile. Apparently, he and the drafters of No. 2 had assumed from his reading of defense-industry reports that the Second Artillery had already acquired these missiles, though they were still in the test phase and more than eighteen months away from initial deployment. Only the 1,250 km DF-2A had been deployed against Soviet targets in Siberia and the Russian Far East since the fall of 1966. Realizing the error but fearful of the repercussions of embarrassing the volatile Lin, the Second Artillery nevertheless immediately reported to the CMC that no base had yet been equipped with DF-3s.[145] How Lin reacted is unknown, but his order is instructive for it reflected the state of mind of Beijing's leaders as they grasped for any means whatsoever to respond to a nuclear attack. It also provides a glimpse into what may be a continuing problem in China as in other nuclear nations; that is, the highest political leadership may have only a limited understanding of the most lethal weaponry at its command.

On October 19, Lin remained fixated on the "nuclear-armed" Soviet aircraft that was carrying the Soviet delegation toward Beijing, an obsession carried over from the earlier Kosygin visit the month before. He told the air force to report to him every few minutes on incoming intelligence. He even delayed his usual afternoon nap—a must for most Chinese bureaucrats at the time—until the delegation members had arrived at and departed from the Beijing airport.[146]

Within a few hours, however, Zhou Enlai on the twentieth began to assert his authority. He drove to the advance command post under the Hundred Hope Mountain and with the CMC Administrative Group took charge of crisis operations.[147] Zhou ordered the General Staff Intelligence Department to brief him every morning at 0800 on reports over the preceding twenty-four hours, and this routine was to last for the next several months.[148] Zhou was taking command on Mao's behalf, and none dared question his decisions.

As Zhou's power increased, Lin's was being circumscribed, though ever so slowly. On October 22, the Central Committee and CMC jointly issued a document in Mao's name entitled "Rules on the Authority to Move and Employ Troops." It stipulated that all military actions on the Sino-Soviet or Sino-Indian border must be reported in advance to the CMC and approved by Mao personally.[149] The chairman was looking to prevent any unwanted outbreak or escalation of border conflicts by taking all troop movements out of Lin's hands, and Lin could do nothing but obey.

One week after the border negotiations had begun on October 20, Lin Biao began to step back from the crisis he had created. He no longer expressed an interest in military intelligence. By late November, the divisions that had bivouacked in the bitter cold along the border for some weeks began complaining to their commanders, and with no obvious serious threats coming from the other side, they began questioning the CMC and requesting to return to their bases. Lin was understood to agree, saying, "The troops can now return to their barracks." His wife Ye Qun, on the other hand, disagreed: "If the troops now return to their barracks, who will bear the responsibility if war breaks out?" Although we must always be wary of sources that place blame for failures and errors on Lin, his wife, and allies, it seems clear that Ye did prevail as her husband weakened, and one million troops spent the next months in the frozen open.[150]

By this point, Mao and Zhou Enlai had expected Washington would react negatively to the highly visible Kosygin-Zhou talks, and they apparently thought that the reaction would favor China. But for weeks nothing visible happened, though behind the scenes in Washington President Richard Nixon and his national security advisor, Henry Kissinger, were debating a strategy to put pressure on Moscow to convince the Kremlin to end the Vietnam War. Furthermore, months before, Kissinger had told the National Security Council's Senior Review Group that aligning with China would be a sound strategy, noting "it is better to align yourself with the weaker, not the stronger of two antagonistic partners."[151]

Unknown to the Chinese, the White House was preparing in secret to place the Strategic Air Command on nuclear alert, and on October 25, almost two-thirds of America's main strategic bomber force was loaded with nuclear weapons and scrambled on the SAC runways.[152] The remarkable history of what followed is told by Scott Sagan and Jeremi Suri: "On October 27 and 29, eighteen nuclear-armed B-52s flew eighteen-hour missions over the northern

polar cap. The bombers flew north, along the Canadian coast, toward the Soviet Union . . . and flew oval patterns toward the Soviet Union and back." [153]

Chinese histories state that Beijing became aware almost immediately that
Washington had placed U.S. forces in the Asian-Pacific region on "full-scale
alert" (*quanmian jiebei*), and that U.S. nuclear bombers were in the air. [154] By
contrast, as the Chinese alert lasted into November, the United States was either unaware or was ignoring it. U.S. pressure was clearly one-sided in favor
of Beijing, a fact that became even more pronounced that month when Washington told the Chinese Foreign Ministry that the destroyers of the U.S. Seventh Fleet would cease patrolling through the Taiwan Strait. [155] The decades-
long "Formosa Patrol" had ended. Zhou was ecstatic and told Mao: "We have
found a way to do it. Now, we can knock on [America's] door." Mao believed
he had found a potential partner to neutralize the Soviet Union.

To get things started, Zhou, who was rotating between the advance command post and Zhongnanhai, ordered the release of two American yachtsmen
detained for violating China's territorial waters. [156] On December 4, Zhou
told Mao that he considered it necessary to resume the ambassador-level talks
with the Americans in order to "bring pressure to bear on Moscow in the border negotiations." These talks, Zhou said, would "increase the doubt of Soviet
revisionists and the growth of U.S.-Soviet contradictions." Mao agreed. [157]

With U.S.-China relations on the upswing, Beijing's leaders could concentrate exclusively on the crisis with the Soviet Union, and the alert of the
nation's military forces, including its strategic missiles, remained in effect.
On December 20, Zhou Enlai in a speech to a military conference called to
discuss war preparedness began to sound upbeat for the first time: "Currently, the international situation is moving toward a direction beneficial for
the people." Two months later, on February 13, 1970, Zhou said, "The U.S.
government's military budget is mainly to cope with the Soviet Union," not
China, implying that the United States would act ever more favorably toward Beijing. [158] Only Lin Biao stood firm, and most officers of the advance
command post stayed confined in their hardened silos. Mao seemed to float
above it all in his Wuhan retreat, while he became more and more agitated
about his chosen successor and close comrade-in-arms.

By mid-February, Zhou had enough bunker time and permanently left its
dubious safety for his residence in Zhongnanhai. [159] Soon afterward, the
officers in the advance command post followed suit and returned to the General Staff headquarters. Yet, the CMC did not allow most of the one million

soldiers freezing on the border to move back to their bases, and it was not until April 24, 1970, that the CMC issued a "Directive Concerning the Dispersal of Troops," which allowed those soldiers and their heavy weapons to move back to their bases.[160] Presumably, it was about this time that the nuclear missiles were allowed to stand down.

In the years that followed, however, Directive No. 2 to the Second Artillery would continue to trouble a number of senior PLA officers. They would voice the gravest misgivings about the reasons the missile battalions had been placed on highest alert in the first place and then left there indefinitely. To be sure, these battalions had responded well, but their commanders had learned of the flawed knowledge in the top leadership about the status of the nation's nuclear weapons. Moreover, they would come to know the awesome capability of the Soviet Strategic Rocket Forces as information on them began leaking almost as soon as the U.S.-Soviet Strategic Arms Limitation Talks (SALT I) began on November 17, 1969, in Helsinki. As they were becoming more fully aware of the global balance of strategic forces, their confidence in their own deterrent waned.

In time, these officers began to question whether the Second Artillery could have survived and performed effectively if the crisis had escalated to nuclear war and required a retaliatory response. They concluded, for example, that the military could not have long concealed the locations of its command centers, because their construction activities and their equipment and communications emissions made them easy prey. Once located, they could be targeted and destroyed. For the next decades, the uncertainties concerning the survivability of the command-and-control complex still plagued PLA commanders, though 1969 for most of them was to become ancient history.[161]

DEFINING THE FUTURE

Many of those closest to the 1969 alert did not long survive, and we should briefly note, though not dwell on, the events that served as the context for reaching the lessons of that fateful year. The Cultural Revolution was not yet half over, and its fury had hardly run its course. The factionalism and paranoia wrought by Mao's policies and personality continued apace and impeded decisions on urgently needed political and military changes. Lin Biao and some of his allies only died in September 1971, while fleeing the summer resort of Beidaihe after his alleged plot to assassinate Mao had failed. Within those same two years, in July 1971 U.S. national security advisor Henry Kissinger had made his secret trip to China, and a new era in global politics had begun. The Vietnam War would not end for years, but despite Soviet and Chinese military support for the North Vietnamese and a number of hostile encounters between the Americans and Chinese before the Kissinger trip, the White House doggedly pursued Nixon's policy of "parallel relations" with the two Communist giants.

On May 26, 1972, four months after Nixon's journey to meet Mao and Zhou and hammer out a rapprochement, the U.S. president and General Secretary Leonid Brezhnev signed the ABM and SALT I agreements. The part played by the Chinese and American strategic alerts became sealed in secret archives and was almost lost to history.

Those Chinese who lived that history, however, knew that the future would never be the same. For them, six major lessons stood out:

1.   China would benefit from the evolving triangular relationship. When threatened by one of the superpowers, China would be protected by the other so long as the two superpowers were contending for dominance. The key lesson throughout the next years of the Cold War was that the nation would be saved by the less aggressive superpower.[162]

2.   Nuclear weapons would never again be called "paper tigers," Mao's favorite characterization after the explosion of the first American bomb. Faced with the reality of nuclear war, China would begin to act as if nuclear deterrence existed, though none could utter the term until after the chairman's death in 1976. But, from 1969 through 1976, Mao began to enunciate the main principles on the limited development and use of nuclear weapons that remain in force to this day.[163]

3.   The integrity and wisdom of the national command authority could never again be taken for granted, and the awesome implications of politicizing China's vital interests and security would be a lasting memory. Domestic power struggles could weaken national security and distort decisionmaking at the highest levels. They could alter intelligence and pit the Party and state against elements of the military high command. They could destroy trust in the system. The military culture built up in tradition, revolution, and the Korean War was in shambles.

4.   Although command and control (C^2) had worked well, major flaws and the backwardness of the PLA's C^2 had been exposed. Lin had

easily bypassed the chain of command, and Mao's chosen crisis manager, Zhou Enlai, had been kept in the dark. The validation of orders
had failed, the state of affairs in remote commands had often not
reached the center, and in the melee of the Cultural Revolution, military secrets had been divulged on "big character posters." Command
and control needed a dramatic overhaul, but no mechanisms were in
place to do the necessary post mortem.

5. The Second Artillery had supposedly performed well, but its first-
generation missiles, the Chinese now knew, could be spotted by satellites, targeted, and destroyed. The SALT process had revealed the
capability of Soviet national technical means and the accuracy and
power of its missiles, and the Second Artillery would be no match for
decades. Political compromise would have to replace revolutionary
zeal in protecting the nation, even as the production and deployment
of the next-generation missiles would have to be accelerated.

6. Lost sight of for a time was the weakness of the Chinese air force.
One incoming plane bringing Soviet negotiators had spawned a panic
and a national alert, and it soon became clear that the weak links
were air power and air defense. The problems with the air force had
long plagued the PLA and had been magnified in the Cultural Revolution, and for the first time the nation's generals recognized the relationship between missile retaliation and air defense.

These six lessons, though vaguely understood when the military alert
ended in April 1970, shook the conventional wisdom that had governed the
Chinese security establishment and gradually caused the high command to
reach out for new solutions. The alert of 1969 served as an alarm call for
the new commanders who would replace Lin Biao, Huang Yongsheng, and
the others allegedly responsible for the debacle. That call coincided with the
opening to the West and the beginning contacts with security and military
specialists in the United States, and gradually the two conceptual worlds, increasingly shaped by new technologies and new wars, began to converge.

The last four of those lessons related to national command authority, command and control, the Second Artillery, and air power in time came to dominate the search for a modern national security and military system. That quest
did not begin in late 1969 and early 1970, but it took on new urgency and a
new direction at that time, and the crisis of those months helped define the
future. We deal with the most significant changes in the following chapters.

PART TWO

Lessons Applied: Security Policymaking and Military Operations

FOUR

National Command Authority and the Decisionmaking Process

Over the past half century, Chinese Communist Party (CCP) leaders have labored to mold a highly centralized and unified national command authority. When reacting to external threats to the nation or its sovereignty, they have exhibited a trademark caution mixed with periodic and unexpected audacity, an apparent contradiction created by the paradox of constant insecurity and growing global influence. For them, this is principally a political challenge, and they repeatedly question how China's central political authority should be configured and how it should function and prevail during emergencies.

From its years of fearsome struggles in the revolution and the political-military trials thereafter, the central leadership came to understand the vital need to use interrelated but functionally distinct Party and army institutions for deciding on and handling dangerous matters of security and survival. That understanding long ago became an essential component of the enduring political culture. Having its own well-defined bureaucratic "systems" and channels of communication, each of these institutions gained a high degree of operational autonomy within its own well-defined domain.

Yet, the authority of each domain would change when the divide had been crossed between peace and war. The Party leader, always the sovereign and ultimate commander of the gun, had the last word in matters of peace and going to war. Until the fateful decision for hostilities had been reached, he and his most powerful chosen colleagues alone served as the national command authority throughout the rule of Mao Zedong and thereafter. True to the spirit of Sun Tzu's principle against the sovereign interfering with his generals, however, the Party high command would constitute that authority only until the decision for war had come, and with the call to battle, the Party's military body, the Central Military Commission (CMC), would take over.

To achieve and regularize the Party-military balance in times of enduring crisis, the senior policy and command institutions have undergone extensive restructuring in recent years, and many of the newest arrangements have still not been proven or finally approved. Moreover, those institutions are now experiencing a generational turnover, and none of the likely future successors has ever exercised command in wartime. When Jiang Zemin, like Mao Zedong before him, decreed that man still matters more than technology or weapons, he was stressing the urgent requirement to train qualified command personnel and empower them to manage the transformation of the nation's security system.[1]

While describing and evaluating the central command authority— frequently referred to loosely as "the center" (*zhongyang*) without specifying its actual composition—this chapter discusses how it is organized in depth and how that authority in its entirety reaches and oversees decisions and manages crises. Chinese sources have exposed the salient characteristics of their decisionmaking processes as well as the functions of the principal leadership organs in the execution of national command. As we shall see, since the 1950s, those bodies have undergone important modifications intended to reinforce the center's capacity to act during crises and avoid a repeat of the near-fiasco of the 1969 military alert.

THE CENTRAL SECURITY DECISIONMAKING APPARATUS

The Communist Party, not the National People's Congress (NPC), has governed the People's Republic of China (PRC) since its founding on October 1, 1949. For eight and a half years from July 7, 1966, to January 13, 1975, neither the congress nor its Standing Committee met even once. During the Cultural Revolution in those years, Mao stationed a military control team in the NPC and its Standing Committee and then shut them down.[2] After the Cultural Revolution, the power of these legislative institutions was restored or increased, though principally in areas other than national security.

The NPC, which convenes annually as China's supreme legislative organ in name, does not play any significant role during crises and acts mainly as a rubber stamp on most matters of high policy. Under Article 62 of the state constitution, it has the "functions and powers" to "decide on questions of war and peace," and according to Article 67, its Standing Committee has the "functions and powers" to "decide, when the National People's Congress is not in session, on the proclamation of the state of war in the event of an armed attack on the country or in fulfillment of international treaty obligations concerning common defense against aggression; [and] to decide on general mobilization or partial mobilization." Because China has never declared war, though the PLA has fought on many fronts, these "functions and powers" have never been put to the test, and few NPC members or any present-day Chinese could imagine their involvement in such a test. The power to set the national security agenda belongs exclusively to the Party.

The Politburo and Its Standing Committee and Secretariat

The Party exercises its core leadership through four central organizations: the Political Bureau or Politburo and its Standing Committee, the Central Secretariat (or Secretariat), and the Central Military Commission. Under Party rules, a relatively clear division exists among these four organs and their primary responsibilities. Nonetheless, Party practice and tested experience over the course of the past five decades have altered the relationships among them and strengthened some lesser bodies that now exercise considerable authority, even in times of great uncertainty or national emergency.

The Standing Committee and full Politburo—most often the referent for "the center"—sit atop China's entire power pyramid, and before examining their evolution and present-day positions and roles, we should briefly note their membership. As of early 2005, the Standing Committee was composed of nine members who had been formally endorsed by the Party Central Committee. Listed in order of their ranking, the Standing Committee members chosen by the Sixteenth Central Committee on November 15, 2002 were Hu Jintao (General Secretary), Wu Bangguo, Wen Jiabao, Jia Qinglin, Zeng Qinghong, Huang Ju, Wu Guanzheng, Li Changchun, and Luo Gan. Trained as engineers, all nine began as technicians and then moved up in the Party-state hierarchy; none had military experience. Also in November 2002, twenty-three men and one woman (Wu Yi) were approved as Politburo members, and one was chosen as an alternate member.

Chosen in theory by the Party Central Committee, the Politburo and Standing Committee are in overall charge of the work of the entire political-military system and have the right under the Party constitution to make decisions on all central policies during the period between plenary sessions of the Central Committee. The reality is that the Standing Committee acts as the ultimate political authority unless the top leader serves without a position inside the Politburo, as was true of Deng Xiaoping from 1987 to 1997, in which case the Standing Committee acts under his direction. As in any political bureaucracy, personal power in China can overshadow formal authority. Who has the final say is seldom in doubt, though it can appear convoluted to outside observers.

During the revolution and the early years of the PRC, the Central Secretariat exercised real power, at first because their distant and widely dispersed locations prevented the Politburo members from convening "once every half a month" in one locale, and then because necessity had become the custom. As a makeshift measure, the ranking leaders usually reached decisions on significant issues at the Secretariat meetings, and this practice continued into the People's Republic.[3] As an example, China's decision to build the atomic bomb was made at an enlarged meeting of the Secretariat chaired by Chairman Mao Zedong on January 15, 1955.[4]

At the Eighth Party Central Committee meeting in 1956, however, Mao altered the power balance in the high command. He downgraded the Central Secretariat and gave most of its responsibilities to the revived Politburo Standing Committee, making it the nation's highest policymaking organ and a mirror image of the eclipsed Secretariat. This committee, it should be noted, had existed in the revolutionary years, but had been deactivated and its power eventually replaced by the three-person Secretariat in March 1943, when Mao became chairman of the Secretariat and Politburo.[5] Then composed of the Central Committee chairman and vice-chairmen and the general secretary of the Secretariat, the Standing Committee was empowered to make all significant decisions between the plenary sessions of the Politburo.

From 1956 on, the Secretariat became the "working body" of the Politburo and its Standing Committee.[6] In making this change, Mao intended to shore up his own position while reducing that of the Central Committee departments and state bureaucracy. At the same time, he elevated Deng Xiaoping to general secretary and the leadership's inner circle for the first time and granted him a power-sharing role with Liu Shaoqi, the nation's president and then Mao's heir apparent.[7] Whether intended or not, the creation of the Standing Committee lessened the power of the full Politburo and produced an alliance between the new committee and the slightly enlarged Secretariat.

Moreover, even before this calculated downgrading of the Politburo in 1956, Mao reportedly did not regard the Politburo as "a leading body" (*lingdao jigou*). When he formalized this view, therefore, he forged an unequal triad of Standing Committee, Secretariat, and Politburo, and from then on he made most decisions at the enlarged meetings of the Standing Committee. Following the 1956 reorganization, only those Politburo members on the Standing Committee regularly participated in the center's daily functions and major decision meetings.[8]

Its work shrouded in secrecy, the Secretariat reports to and operates under the Standing Committee and manages the Party's daily operations in accord with the guidelines of the Politburo and its Standing Committee. Its duties encompass implementing their policies, administering the distribution of central-level tasks, and serving as the switchboard for communicating instructions from and receiving reports destined for the Standing Committee and the larger Politburo membership. In name, the Secretariat is an "administrative organ" (*banshi jigou*) of the Politburo and its Standing Committee, but in fact, it acts as a partner of the Standing Committee, because since 1987 the committee nominates and works intimately with the Secretariat's members.[9]

This small body, which was composed of seven members in 2005, stayed relatively powerful even after its demotion almost fifty years ago. In April 1959,

Mao, the Party chairman, told General Secretary Deng to take charge of the implementation of all central directives, saying, "You have now assumed authority. You should exercise authority once you have power at hand. Do you dare to do it?"[10] A few days later, he added, "I take command with Deng Xiaoping as deputy," and about this time, Liu Shaoqi ordered the Central Secretariat to assume additional responsibilities and warned Party officials not to regard it as "a mere secretarial department."[11]

The Central Military Commission

During the tumultuous years of the Chinese civil war (1927–49), factionalism scarred Party life. It drastically undercut Mao's authority until he began to have a firmer hold on the leadership during the Zunyi Party conference (January 1935) in the course of the historic Long March (1934–35), only to reappear many times thereafter. In November 1935, after the survivors of the Long March finally reached northern Shaanxi Province, Mao became chairman of the Central Military Commission and further solidified his position against factional rivals.[12] Reflecting on the Party's history in 1938, Mao made his famous statement that "Political power grows out of the barrel of a gun" and added: "Our principle is that the Party commands the gun, and the gun must never be allowed to command the Party. Yet, having guns, we can create Party organizations. . . . We can also create cadres, create schools, create culture, create mass movement."[13] Mao was one of those cadres created by the gun.

The modern-day Central Military Commission with its constitutional standing in both the Party and state also had its origins in two organs, one in the Party and one in the government. The Party's CMC was established in 1926 and had a complicated evolution thereafter.[14] As noted by John Gittings long ago, the government's Military Commission has "existed since the end of 1931 under one name or another, when its formation was called for by the first All-China Soviet Congress."[15] Ever since, the commission has run the nation's military affairs under central Party leadership. Often referred to as the "supreme command," the CMC "directs and assumes unified command of the nation's armed forces [and] exercises operational command over the whole PLA and leadership for the development of the PLA." In March 2000, the National People's Congress enacted the Legislation Law of the PRC, which for the first time expressly defined the legislative power of the state's CMC and all subordinate military organizations, and thereby granted this CMC the power "to formulate military statutes in accordance with the Constitution and laws."[16]

Despite the official standing of the state's CMC, it is the one wearing the Party hat that controls, though the membership of the two is identical. Two years before the reestablishment of the Politburo Standing Committee, on September 28, 1954, the Politburo made a decision to keep the CMC under the supervision of the Politburo and the Central Secretariat.[17] The Secretariat's responsibilities in this regard passed to the Standing Committee in 1956. In practice and keeping the foregoing in mind, the CMC assumes national command once the decision to take military action is made by the most senior Party leaders.

Prior to the Thirteenth Party Congress in November 1987, the CMC chairman had to be a member of the Politburo Standing Committee, but Article 21 of the new Party constitution that year said: "The members of the Military Commission of the Central Committee are decided on by the Central Committee," in practice meaning the Standing Committee.[18] This provision paved the way for Deng Xiaoping and later Jiang Zemin to head the CMC, while not serving formally as Standing Committee members. We will return to the CMC in our discussion of PLA command and control in the next chapter.

MAN ABOVE INSTITUTIONS: MAO AND HIS SUCCESSORS

At first glance, the present-day organizational arrangements in the high command remind one of the overlapping hierarchies of the Mao-era People's Republic. In those years (1949–76), the Party leadership set the strategic direction or "political line" and made national security decisions at both regular and special enlarged meetings of the Politburo and its most senior leaders. Two developments shaped the reality of power under Mao's rule: First, starting from 1959, Mao elevated himself above the Politburo and even its Standing Committee; and second, in 1961, the Party center appropriated most political and economic planning powers from provincial-level Party committees by forming six CCP central bureaus in different regions to supervise those local authorities.[19] These and related moves toward absolute power under Mao proved to be momentous steps in pushing the nation toward the Cultural Revolution in 1966.

As we have seen in Chapter 3, those moves at the time did not contradict the prevailing modalities in reaching national security decisions. Chairman Mao had already arrogated supreme power to himself, and all civilian and military leaders followed the chairman or paid dearly. In the 1950s and 1960s, for example, Mao chose Marshal Nie Rongzhen as a nonvoting delegate to attend the Central Secretariat and later the Standing Committee meetings. Nie could express his views on major agenda items relevant to the PLA and then relay relevant center directives to the CMC. On many occasions, however, in order to show his irritation with Nie or the military, Mao would not invite Nie to some key security-related meetings and would designate no replacement.[20]

Throughout his rule, Mao had the final word on national security issues, usually after seeking the counsel of senior military officers and Party associates. His control of the military was rarely tested, though the events of 1969 demonstrate that it could be subverted. For the PRC's first quarter century, the record shows that in most but certainly not all critical national security decisions and operations, he drew on the recommendations and expertise of a wide variety of military and security specialists as well as his closest political associates. Nevertheless, Mao could go it alone, and when he did, he was prone to making huge mistakes.

Moreover, the chairman often wrestled against the findings of objective intelligence and the requirements of technical expertise and even his own protection, and he increasingly flaunted those requirements from the 1950s to his death in 1976. For instance, in the spring of 1956, Mao decided to make his first swim in the Yangtze River, later memorialized in one of his poems. Luo Ruiqing, the minister of public security, balked, saying he could not dispatch the security forces to escort Mao without "approval from the central leadership." Mao replied in anger, "To whom do you want to report? I am the chairman of the Central Committee!" Caught in the middle, the local security officers remained steadfast and refused to join Mao's bodyguards without Luo's order, and Mao was stymied and could not swim in the Yangtze until many weeks later. Within a decade, Luo's repeated reliance on Party rules to defy the chairman would result in his purge. Mao could not shake the imperial belief in his own infallibility.

As another example of this enduring belief, in the first half of the 1960s Mao and Liu Shaoqi sharply disagreed on ways to resolve economic crises and handle internal "class struggle." In July 1962, Liu persuaded Mao to quell the social instability resulting from the nationwide famine following Mao's Great Leap Forward and rural communization, but then Mao berated Liu for overestimating the scope of the domestic crisis. In the winter of 1964–65, the two leaders again crossed swords over measures to check the momentum of liberalization in China, with Liu directly opposing Mao's extreme measures against dissenters. Mao reportedly railed at Liu: "Don't think you are terrific. I am able to knock you down even if I only move my little finger." Despite the outburst, Liu defiantly stood fast, and Mao failed to gain the assent of the Standing Committee. But, by defying the chairman, Liu had sealed his fate, and the unforgiving Mao would take his revenge against his erstwhile heir apparent eighteen months later in the opening days of the Cultural Revolution.[21]

Whatever collegiality had existed in the high command collapsed in mid-1966, when the Politburo Standing Committee suspended the work of the Central Secretariat.[22] The following February, Mao ordered the Central Cultural Revolution Group (CCRG) to assume all the powers of the Politburo and Secretariat,[23] and then suspended their operations until the Ninth Party Congress (April 1969) elected the new Politburo.[24] From then on, Mao orchestrated policymaking at special enlarged meetings of the Standing Committee or in the CCRG.[25] Until his death in September 1976, the central command apparatus assumed a Byzantine character, and this anomalous and erratic system put personal politics in command and caused widespread havoc.[26]

The story of the decade of the Cultural Revolution has been told many times in rich detail, but for our purposes the important fact is that the national command authority passed among power holders with shifting ties to Chairman Mao and his comrades of the moment. Only his death in September 1976 ended the long nightmare and within a year provided the opening for Deng Xiaoping to become the supreme leader.

The Ruling Triad Since 1980

After Mao's passing and the overthrow of the radicals allied with him, the status quo ante was mostly restored. Following the reestablishment of the Central Secretariat in 1980, the Politburo, its Standing Committee, and the Secretariat again became a fairly stable triad for managing the nation's internal business and dealing with international problems. To be sure, bitter disputes have sometimes erupted and forced the leadership to settle its "inner-Party contradictions" within larger groups, even ones that involved retired Party elders, but these are the exceptions that prove the rule. As examples of these struggles, Hu Yaobang and Zhao Ziyang, general secretaries of the Central Committee in the 1980s, were dismissed at "inner-Party political life meetings" after they had lost the confidence of the real power holder, Deng Xiaoping.[27]

As has been the case with other Party leaders with authoritarian impulses, Deng winked at Party rules and mobilized powerful supporters outside the Politburo if the normal processes for settling such "contradictions" did not suit his personal purposes: The claim could always be made, sometimes with justification, that irregular measures were needed to defeat opponents who could endanger the rule of the supreme leader and the Party. The possibility of that claim reemerging will always linger in the background so long as final authority is based on a culture of man over institutions and a single institution, the Party, monopolizes all power.

As of this writing (January 2005), the assignments and responsibilities within the center's policymaking apparatus exhibit many superficial similarities with the Party structures found in the early years of the People's Republic, though, of course, without the domineering presence of Mao and with the lessened role of the uniformed military and the greater value given to expertise. Information is now disseminated much more widely, and the policy process has achieved a modicum of transparency so absent at the beginning. Reminiscent of that earlier period, job specialization has reappeared among the "generalists" within the high command and the leadership triad.

What this means is that the Standing Committee acts on all critical matters, especially those involving national security and the fate of the Party, between plenary sessions of the Politburo, and even in full Politburo meetings its members have the governing voice. Nevertheless, the most important of these decisions are usually reached in special enlarged meetings because of the need for consensus building, Party unity, and well-informed counsel.

The Politburo will not depart from this routine except in genuine emergencies. One of the most important "emergencies" occurs when the Standing Committee, acting as the central decisionmaker, cannot hammer out a consensus on vital issues and stays deeply divided. Most such issues fall in the category of domestic security or ideological direction, because for more than three decades the political line and main policies on international security have been mostly noncontroversial. Long-term stability, greater openness and multilateral cooperation, and avoidance of war are the hallmarks of that policy. Even when that policy is overshadowed by the specter of Taiwan's independence, the center stands together. Thus, it is principally over domestic and ideological direction that the Standing Committee requires and seeks general endorsement from the full Politburo. That endorsement must also be sought when entering a war or dealing with life-and-death crises.

The Central Secretariat, as we have seen, became responsible in 1956 for handling the Party's daily affairs in line with the guidelines and directives of the Politburo and Standing Committee. It lost that responsibility for a time in the Cultural Revolution, but in the more than quarter century since then it has served as the leadership's administrative organ. It implements and tracks the decisions of its bosses and is the Party's central memory bank.[28]

Although the triad works reasonably well, it is neither efficient nor effective when decisions must be reached quickly and decisively. The result all too often has been lost opportunities or miscues over Taiwan, failure to take advantage of openings with the United States and other states, and a risk-aversion culture that is quite unsuited for fast-moving events. Although the Standing Committee acts as Beijing's top-tier decisionmaking organ, the comparative political clout of its individual members is unequal in practice, and some members can even be excluded from especially sensitive decisions. This occurred most often under Mao, who after 1959 frequently did not allow Zhu De and Chen Yun, both official members, to attend the committee meetings.[29]

Moreover, the Central Secretariat could use its bureaucratic know-how and powers to delay or reshape the Standing Committee's instructions. By the mid-1960s, Mao had come to believe that his decision to enlarge the role of the Secretariat had resulted in his "loss of power," and, as noted, he shelved it for ten years during the Cultural Revolution.[30] The allocation of tasks within the leadership triad had in fact left the power of the Secretariat largely unchecked and sometimes unresponsive, and Mao abhorred its impingement on his authority. Adherence to collective leadership remained the Party doctrine, but Mao believed that his vote should outweigh all others combined.

Following his death and the return of Deng Xiaoping, moreover, the powers of the dominant leader continued unabated but the Secretariat reacquired its earlier administrative jobs. When Deng died in early 1997, the triumvirate of the Standing Committee, Politburo, and Secretariat regained most but not all of its former vitality and cohesion, though the perpetuation of Jiang Zemin's chairmanship of the CMC delayed the complete restoration of the triad's original status until after his retirement in 2004.

Leading Groups

When Deng consolidated his power in the early 1980s, he faced a shattered triad and state bureaucracy. Even as he was rehabilitating his deposed supporters and returning them to high positions, he needed to find ways to reorganize and invigorate the nation's policymaking system. His solution was to resurrect a mechanism, the "leading group" (*lingdao xiaozu*), which Mao had assembled in 1958 and which had even resurfaced on an ad hoc basis in the Cultural Revolution. These interagency groups and their offices play a central role in today's China, a role that encompasses jurisdiction over national security matters.

Over the years, the Chinese have adopted many terms—some colloquial, some formal—to label interrelated Party, state, and military establishments. For example, they use *kou* (gateway), *xitong* (system), and *bumen* (department) interchangeably to describe the network of units under a single ministry-level organization. These terms relate mostly indirectly to the decisionmaking mechanisms, including the leading groups, under the national command authority. The major function of a leading group is to facilitate the coordination of operations conducted by a number of systems or departments. The Party and state have authorized these groups to implement the highest-level decisions and to strengthen trans-departmental work.

As the established councils for detailed policymaking and bureaucratic oversight under the Standing Committee's direction, the leading groups are Party-military bodies whose composition reflects the overlapping of senior Party and military officials within the Politburo as a whole. For example, from the Sixteenth Party Congress until September 2004, former Party general secretary Jiang Zemin and his successor Hu Jintao were chairman and first vice-chairman respectively of the CMC, the two CMC vice-chairmen, Generals Guo Boxiong and Cao Gangchuan, served on the Politburo, and a member of the CMC, General Xu Caihou, sat on the Central Secretariat.[31]

Headed by a member of the Standing Committee and manned by senior Party and state officials and several top generals, the five leading groups of greatest interest here are those for National Security, Foreign Affairs, Taiwan Affairs, Counter-Terrorism, and "Three Anti" (*sanfan*). The first four directly deal with external crises and conflict resolution, and all draw on parallel state ministries and PLA command and technical systems for information and support.[32] Set up in 2004 by the Politburo and CMC, the Three-Anti Leading Group was tasked to ferret out "spies, special agents, and hidden traitors" after the exposure of alleged Taiwanese spy networks from 1999 to 2004 and as mainland-Taiwan relations sharply deteriorated.[33] The next section will illustrate how these leading groups function at the Party's direction.

NATIONAL COMMAND AUTHORITY IN CRISIS AND WAR

In the paragraphs that follow we shall review typical approaches in Beijing's decisionmaking, including the management of crises, the activation and coordination of departments and agencies, and the mobilization of military units. Through this review, we can understand the different functions of China's central policymaking apparatus and the special roles played by relevant departments and agencies in the course of security crises.

In the initial stages of a pressing security problem requiring its decision, the Standing Committee takes the lead. It receives intelligence briefings, reviews the relevant documents screened by the Central Committee General Office, and debates alternative courses of action. Members of the Standing Committee, which has never included women, make presentations based on their career "specializations"; that is, their personal diplomatic, military, economic, or domestic political perspectives. Over time, these individuals become the expected and respected spokesmen on those perspectives derived from their earlier careers.[34] The committee normally acts with great deliberation and solicits advice from the ministers of defense (concurrently the CMC vice-chairman) and foreign affairs, the intelligence agencies, and other departments.[35] Occasionally, trusted scholars or recognized experts will be invited to these meetings in order to provide important knowledge and opinion on a wide range of topics relevant to handling the problem.

If the Standing Committee cannot reach a consensus on its overall approach to the crisis, some members may propose that the central leadership call a plenary session of the Politburo for its approval of highly significant or controversial proposals. Once the committee has reached a consensus on a practicable approach, it normally will pick one of its members to convene meetings to debate and draft the contingency plans and policy directives. In practice, this member becomes the crisis manager.

In an emerging crisis, the crisis manager will summon the ministers of defense and foreign affairs, the head of the Ministry of State Security (or earlier, its intelligence predecessors), the chief of the General Staff, and head and deputy head of the General Staff Operations Department. He might send for the heads of other departments, as needed, and together these officials constitute what might be called the crisis action team. (In recent years, one of the "other departments" is quite often the Central Committee United Front Department because so many foreign security issues affect minority and religious groups.) The team members must come to the crisis manager's office throughout the emergency, and at their meetings, the participants are expected to engage actively in the dialogue, offering their professional expertise and personal judgments. After summing up each session, the manager will inform the Politburo Standing Committee by phone or in writing and, when he is comfortable with the team's agreed plan of action, submit written proposals to the Standing Committee for a decision. Throughout this process, the committee members and crisis manager typically consult by phone or in small group sessions with their own advisors.

This process is best suited for slowly evolving but somewhat predictable crises, such as the downing of the U.S. EP-3 spy plane on April 1, 2001.[36] Following the collision of the U.S. plane with a Chinese J-8 fighter, both sides initially engaged in mutual recriminations and uncompromising demands. Within a few days, however, the issue became the return of the American crew and the aircraft, and negotiations got underway. At that point, tensions, though high, became manageable, and it quickly became obvious that a deal would be struck. Moreover, even as the reconnaissance flights resumed, Beijing and Washington embarked on more general discussions on how to avoid such incidents in the future. While the crisis had moments of high drama, the system for handling it worked pretty much as it was designed to do.

Following the committee's endorsement, the manager, always a member of the Standing Committee, will pass its decision to the Secretariat and the relevant leading group or groups with instructions for implementation. In the key security areas, one or more of the four earlier-mentioned leading groups (National Security, Foreign Policy, Taiwan, and Counter-Terrorism) would be notified and activated, and some interview evidence suggests that intense jockeying occurs before the group selections are made. Such jockeying appears to reflect each Standing Committee member's political instinct for sharing the responsibility and thus the blame in case of failure.

In late 2000, the Politburo established the National Security Leading Group (Guojia Anquan Lingdao Xiaozu) in order to coordinate all security ministries and organizations and departments under the CMC. In a leadership preoccupied with domestic problems and lacking a foreign policy figure of the stature of a Zhou Enlai, the group was formed to expedite the center's decisions at the highest level.[37] Jiang Zemin headed this group until sometime in 2003, when he was replaced by Hu Jintao, and former senior foreign affairs official Liu Huaqiu became the group's secretary-general. Liu was picked over other candidates such as Deputy Chief of the General Staff Xiong Guangkai, the secretary-general of the Taiwan Affairs Leading Group.

As of early 2005, the relationship between the National Security and Foreign Affairs leading groups was not fully resolved, even as their mission was becoming identical, and Chinese were referring to them as "one organ with two signboards."[38] Loosely organized and thinly staffed in its first year or so, the National Security Leading Group now functions more smoothly and responsively, as was seen in the rapid-fire decisions taken toward Washington on and after the terrorist attack on the United States on September 11, 2001, and in response to the Iraq and North Korea crises in 2003.

As is the norm with each of the leading groups, functional power gravitates to the office-in-charge under those groups, and in this case, one powerful office serves two masters. How this happened was a classic ploy in a bureaucratic power struggle. The head of the long-standing office of the Foreign Affairs Leading Group, Liu Huaqiu, also served as the head of the Foreign Affairs Office of the State Council. In reality, there was only one office, operating under two different names. When the Foreign Affairs Office of the State Council was disbanded (in actuality, when the name was simply dropped), Liu, as the National Security Leading Group's incoming secretary-general, outmaneuvered his rivals to become head of the "new" influential group's office. Again, this simply involved a shuffling of signboards (*paizi*) on the front gate. Liu's office retained the name "office of the Foreign Affairs Leading Group" and added the paizi of the "office of the National Security Leading Group."

This explains why this well-seasoned and well-connected body could easily make the transition to take on its expanded mission. The office now provides integrated support for the two leading groups, and Chinese sources affirm that by these maneuvers, Liu, a veteran diplomat and former vice foreign minister, had reinforced the hold of Foreign Ministry officials on the national security process, a hold whose origins can be traced back to the powerful position of Zhou Enlai as Mao's chief foreign policy lieutenant.[39]

This emerging synergy among the leading groups is repeated in other sectors. The Taiwan Affairs and National Security leading groups, for example, have the authority to coordinate across ministries and military departments, thus blurring the distinction between Taiwan as a domestic concern and as one lodged in the foreign affairs arena.

The leading groups and their offices have the power to defuse bureaucratic conflicts and factionalism that plague most vertically organized hierarchies and that can become especially acute in the Chinese bureaucracy. A senior Party leader heads each of the leading groups, whose subordinate secretaries-general in the case of Taiwan Affairs and National Security have a history of personal rivalry. The leading group office directors reportedly have toughened the quality and efficiency of these groups and given them the stature, though not yet the fully qualified staff or national visibility that is comparable to the American National Security Council.

With approvals from the Politburo Standing Committee and staffing support from their offices, National Security and Foreign Affairs, like other leading groups, have the clout to override bureaucratic resistance and passivity in achieving successful trans-departmental operations. In the course of crisis management, they are responsible for the timely assessment of the situation, coordination among Party and government departments and agencies, and engagement of diplomatic and military actors. Throughout that process, they become the action centers through which the Foreign Ministry, the PLA General Staff, the ministries of State Security and Public Security, government agencies for international trade, and the Central Committee departments of International Liaison and United Front will participate in the intensive debates and decisionmaking from the beginning to the end of a crisis.

Earlier we noted that the CMC is the national command authority once the decision to begin a conflict has been taken, but here we enter the realm of the theoretical or ideal system because the "last war" was fought for a mere twenty-nine days more than a quarter century ago against Vietnam. What we have been discussing is how those senior Party organs deal with emerging and ongoing crises prior to the outbreak of a conflict or direct military action. When that outbreak occurs, the CMC takes charge of military operations, though the top-level CMC military officers on the Politburo must keep the Standing Committee informed, recommend new related national policies to it, and pass those policies to the CMC for action by the General Staff Operations Department. The deeply ingrained synergy between military and civilian Party officials does not end with the transfer of authority in wartime.

We shall discuss how military command and control work in the next chapter, though once again the reader should keep in mind that none of the command or control systems being readied for actual conflict has ever been tested in wartime. Moreover, the picture we paint of high-level responses to emergencies is flawed by the inadequacy of the sources currently available to us. The ways the response mechanisms do or would work in the real world remain unclear or untested, though some data strongly suggest that even in routine times communication breakdowns, personal rivalries, and incompetent or indifferent leaders all too frequently tarnish the somewhat ideal models we are describing.

As the crisis evolves prior to the decision to commit military forces to combat, pre-positioned ministry-level units become activated during each crisis, and for them the Standing Committee and its relevant leading groups constitute the final authority. As always, that committee has the last word or veto, though the exigencies of war and dominant personalities can blur its decisiveness and powerful image.

Each ministry has established a contingency apparatus, and we know the most about the one under the Foreign Ministry and the comparable military system. The Foreign Ministry has assigned a vice-minister to lead its contingency teams (*yingji xiaozu*) for handling emergencies, and each team is composed of officials from the geographical area and functional departments and ministry Party committee. For dealing with the North Korean nuclear issue in 2003 and 2004, for example, the vice foreign minister chaired the team meetings that were attended by the team leader (a special envoy for North Korea), by his senior staff officer, by officials from the departments of Asia, America, and International Affairs, and by invited specialists from the General Staff, the Ministry of Science and Technology, the China Atomic Energy Authority, and the National Nuclear Corporation. After reaching a conclusion on the nature and peril of the North Korean program and how to deal with it, the Foreign Ministry submitted a summary for reference to the National Security and Foreign Affairs leading groups via their offices. At the same time, other departments activated their contingency teams and submitted their summaries to the two leading groups.

In a crisis, long-tested think tanks under the Party, the military, and the principal security-related ministries are encouraged to draft suggestions and ideas that will be presented to the Foreign Affairs and National Security leading groups. The Party has issued three somewhat vague "guidelines" that govern the formulation of the contingency plans or countermeasures: They must "conform to the national interest," "adhere to the principle of upholding justice," and "be accepted by the ordinary people."

Other research bodies such as the institutes affiliated with the Ministry of State Security, selected military establishments including the Academy of Military Science and National Defense University, and research facilities under the New China News Agency and China Academy of Social Sciences can present their suggestions and opinions during the early stages of some crises. However, policymakers regard these and similar organizations as academic institutions and permit them to make their presentations only when the situation is not pressing (*changxian xiangmu*), while policy think tanks noted in the paragraph above are responsible for projects at the more urgent stage of "pressing demand" (*duanxian xiangmu*).

In addition to the National Security, Taiwan Affairs, and Foreign Affairs leading groups, the Politburo has commissioned several other leading groups to handle problems with both domestic and international implications.[40] One of these is the Counter-Terrorism Coordination Leading Group, which presumably was set up to combat antigovernment groups in Xinjiang and to join forces with the Tashkent-based counter-terrorism "agency" under the six-nation Shanghai Cooperation Organization; that agency became operational in 2002.[41] This leading group has the same civil-military structure as its sister groups, and in addition it draws on officials from the Armed Police, the General Staff Intelligence Department, local counter-terrorism offices, and airline, railroad, customs, and medical organizations.

Moreover, Beijing continues to experiment with the leading-group format as a more general problem-solving mechanism. In September 2002, the Politburo Standing Committee elevated the State Informationization Work Leading Group and renamed it the State Informationization Leading Group. Former premier Zhu Rongji was appointed the group's chief (replaced in

March 2003, by newly appointed Premier Wen Jiabao), making this civil-military group technically responsible to the State Council rather than the Politburo.[42] A more dramatic example of the leading group as the crisis mechanism of choice came in the third week of April 2003, when the Politburo formed the Leading Group for Prevention and Treatment of SARS, headed by Party General Secretary Hu Jintao with deputy heads Premier Wen Jiabao, Chief of the General Staff Liang Guanglie, Executive Vice-Minister of Health Gao Qiang, and Wu Yi, the new health minister and head of the National SARS Prevention and Control Headquarters.[43] That this emergency leading group was created with a military style headquarters rather than a typical "office" suggests how flexible the leading group mechanism has become.

With respect to national security issues, moreover, this mechanism may be undergoing ongoing restructuring and experimentation to improve both its relevance and efficiency. In general, all of these changes are intended to augment the leadership's prediction and prevention abilities. They respond to the recurrent criticism that the leadership's repertoire of measures to anticipate and stop crises pales in comparison to its post-disaster capabilities.[44] If the Standing Committee's agreement on the seriousness of the problem can be assumed, the most significant changes will probably go in these directions in the coming years:

Possible merger of security-related leading groups.

The National Security, Foreign Affairs, Taiwan Affairs, Counter-Terrorism, and Three-Anti leading groups, which already overlap to a degree, may merge into a smaller number of super-groups. The first two already have a single office, and the ongoing debate concerning the need for a National Security Council on what Chinese analysts believe to be the U.S. model highlights the importance attached to establishing a strong, high-visibility policy body that can unify decisions while coordinating and checking the lower-level ministries and commissions.

Greater integration of leading groups with the Central General Office.

The merged super–leading groups, if the decision to approve them survives bureaucratic opposition, will have to draw even more heavily on the Central Committee General Office. Serving as the Party's central administrative organ, this office transmits policy directives from the Standing Committee via the Central Secretariat to the entire Party, state, and military. Discussed more fully in the next section, this Party "nerve center" already provides the Foreign Affairs/National Security leading groups with the bureaucratic muscle to control the most difficult trans-departmental operations and activities. In reality, though not in formal structure, this combination has begun to rival the U.S. National Security Council when it has functioned at its best.[45] Nonetheless, the system still lacks the institutional integrity to operate seamlessly in times of stress and uncertainty.

The possibility and the likely timing of these or any other changes that have been mentioned will continue to be debated in China and abroad until the Party finally reaches and announces its decisions on the fate of the senior bureaucracy. How the evolving interagency leading groups will function within the well-established Party and state organs thus remains a pressing question. Even as he gained further power with Jiang's retirement from the CMC, Hu Jintao faced the tasks of simplifying the relationship between these interagency leading groups and further streamlining China's policymaking mechanism.[46] Institutional readjustments are already underway, and many others are being discussed. Mao's call for the Party to "get organized!" still echoes throughout the halls and offices of China's high command.[47] Impeded by archaic ideology, obsolete technology, and complicated developments in the international environment, a stable, institutionalized national command authority remains an unfulfilled goal.

Yet, despite all this tinkering with the power and functions of the leading groups, there is, of course, a ready-made national security organization in place and operational. Simply put, the Politburo Standing Committee, the Central Secretariat, and General Office currently play that role on a daily basis. Once that committee makes a decision, its working bodies can command the specific leading group or groups to carry out the necessary trans-departmental operations, and another super-leading group could be redundant or become a dangerous rival. The current leading groups, on the other hand, help extricate the committee from daily routines and allow it to concentrate on strategic policymaking. Thus, the committee simultaneously functions as the Party's supreme policymaking apparatus and the government's national security council. The "one organ with two signboards" style also applies to the Central Military Commission, which we discuss in the next chapter.

STRUCTURE AND OPERATIONS
OF THE CENTRAL GENERAL OFFICE

The one component that seems to be reasonably fixed within the national hierarchy is the Party's Central General Office. Within the senior bureaucracy, the office acts as a cabinet secretariat and gatekeeper in the acquisition and processing of information on all major security and foreign policy issues. The Standing Committee and Secretariat rely on the office to communicate, coordinate, and oversee the implementation of critical Party-state decisions, including some down to the provincial level. The office director has cognizance over all intelligence agencies and plays an important role in the political chain of command.[48] Serving much like a cabinet office in Western governments, the office manages the overall information flow and supports and insulates the general secretary by selecting what he and his colleagues read, adding its own background research and comments. Located in the southwestern part of the Forbidden City's Zhongnanhai, the General Office is the administrative organ jointly serving the Standing Committee, Politburo, Secretariat, Central Committee, and leading groups.[49] Chart 1 provides a simplified overview of the administrative chain of the central leadership.

The daily caseload and information throughput is staggering. All major Party, state, and military institutions and each of the hundreds of research and policy organs throughout the nation have the right to transmit their reports to the General Office through predesignated channels, but the screening powers of the office are absolute and without appeal. Prior to high-level meetings, not to speak of emergencies, the communication channels can become overloaded and vulnerable to false or misleading signals.

In 2002, the State Council created the State Informationization Office (SIO) under the above-mentioned State Informationization Leading Group and directed it to oversee the modernization and integration of the entire Party-state information structure, with the General Office and its administrative network given the highest priority. In that year, large sectors of the nation's communications system, including the nation's broadcast satellites, had been compromised several times, and, according to one official, the last straw came when the outlawed religious-political movement Falun Gong tapped into the computerized phone switchboards and sent recorded messages to

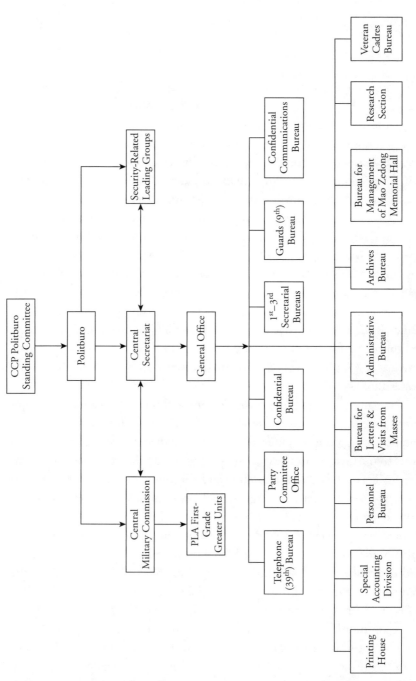

Chart 1. Central Administrative System of the Chinese Communist Party

almost every leader in China. He said: "The phone rang in my office, and when I hung up, it started ringing again. You couldn't really end the call until the message had played fully several times."[50] Supposedly protected computer and satellite broadcast networks, it turned out, could all too easily be compromised and were already deemed to be antiquated and unreliable. The answer was to initiate the largest and most secure civil-military information system in the world, China's version of e-government.

This system is being designed to connect all levels of the Party and government, the military, and state-owned corporations, and as a result the PLA would expect to receive support from the information security department of the SIO and several affiliated entities to validate the confidential communication networks linking its command components to the state and Party. The present-day organization of the General Office, the Chinese point out, aggravates slow and often untrustworthy information transmission, a problem that has been given to the SIO and its partners to solve. The current arrangement attaches greater importance to telecommunications security and information secrecy than to well-grounded and efficient decisionmaking, but the official e-government plans place security and efficiency on a roughly equal, but very demanding, plane.

The General Office consists of at least the seventeen sub-units listed in Chart 1, including the First through Third Secretarial bureaus, Confidential Bureau, Confidential Communications Bureau, Telephone Bureau (Thirty-ninth Bureau), Guards Bureau (Ninth Bureau), and other organs.[51] The seven just-named bureaus are the most relevant ones in our effort to understand the national command decisionmaking process.

The staff members in some of the bureaus have near total access to the state's most closely guarded plans and other classified documents. They can receive secure phone calls from the outside, but they can initiate calls to the outside only through a tightly controlled telephone switchboard. Encryption technologies help ensure the confidentiality of internal communications,[52] and confidential "red phones" are the hallmark of every senior leader's desktop.[53] The Telephone Bureau provides the leaders and their chief assistants with specially designed telephones to ensure their ability to reach any domestic destination quickly and to protect their lines from electronic tapping, eavesdropping, or even monitoring by the bureau's own switchboard operators.[54]

Many leaders reportedly worry that even encoded documents and encrypted phone calls might be illegally deciphered, and when discussing highly classified issues they often employ predesignated codes substituting key words and phrases in order to confine the message to those who need to know.[55] For maintaining secrecy, the General Office runs a shop for printing top-secret documents for a highly limited circulation.[56]

Several bureaus of the General Office function as its administrative wing. The most important function of these bureaus is information control, and it is this function, if operated as planned, that would be revolutionized as part of the overall e-government technology program in the coming five to ten years. The existing safeguards limit whether and how individual leaders acquire the intelligence and screened advice necessary for informed judgments, and it is the Confidential Bureau that controls the codes and related technologies for enciphering messages and ensuring cryptographic protection.[57] Many of this bureau's staff have graduated from a highly secret school in Changchun, Jilin Province,[58] and their main job is to submit reports to central leaders based on incoming encrypted cables and phone messages.[59] The Confidential Bureau maintains contact with comparable departments in the State Security and Public Security ministries, especially when developing new codes and improving or innovating encryption technologies.

The CMC and PLA General Staff have fashioned separate measures for preparing military codes, enhancing the requisite encryption technologies, and managing the delivery of military documents. The current lack of interoperability of the secure military and civilian networks has proved to be a major difficulty in some key sectors, such as air traffic control emergencies when civilian aircraft stray out of the rigidly defined air corridors and are challenged by air force fighters operating on incompatible frequencies.[60] A primary task of e-government will be to reconcile the many diverse encryption schemes and telecom frequencies and to begin to overcome the extreme compartmentalization of China's highly security-conscious and bureaucratized military-political operations.

The delivery of classified documents between the General Office and all the senior Party and state organs at the provincial or ministry level and above is the responsibility of the Confidential Communications Bureau. It dictates how all recipients of classified materials handle them and for how long; most such materials must be routinely returned within two months for archiving and preparing the historical record.[61] Although other agencies have reportedly had their secret documents lost or stolen, as was the case of nuclear weapons papers that reached the United States and became part of the Cox Report in 1999,[62] the bureau reportedly enjoys the reputation of having had very few documents in its care to have ever gone missing.

The three secretarial bureaus taken together function as the General Office's most active transmission channel. Reports destined for the central triad are funneled through one of these three. This powerful bureau evaluates and selects reports and research papers routinely submitted by Party, state, military, and academic institutions and decides whether to submit them and if so to whom. For the most sensitive reports, the supreme leader can contravene the ordinary distribution rules and deny particular officials access to them on a need-to-know basis. This bureau dispatches Standing Committee directives to the authorized distribution list and edits the *Daily Report* (*Meiri Huibao*), the leaders' morning briefing paper on major issues and intelligence.[63]

Another secretarial bureau drafts the language of most routine central documents and the speeches of the principal leaders. And, the last of the three secretarial bureaus arranges the leaders' daily schedules. This bureau also prepares a daily memorandum on the recent and forthcoming activities of the top leaders for use in editing the *Daily Report*.

The PRC Law on the Protection of State Secrets (September 5, 1988) with its Implementation Measures (May 25, 1990) governs the handling of all confidential materials, and the Party-State Central Secrets Protection Commission and the All-Army Secrets Protection Commission enforce it. Those serving in the three secretarial bureaus face additional and more stringent security regulations, all intended to "limit the number and type of officials having access to classified materials" (*jinliang jianshao zhimi mian*). Top secret intelligence, for example, can be transmitted only at the last minute to the cleared secretary in charge.[64] The motto emblazoned on all secretarial training manuals is: "Do not talk about what you know! Do not ask about what you do not know!" Party histories proclaim that the confidentiality rules have been strictly observed in the past several decades but express the worry that the money-driven psychology of today's China is corroding that discipline.[65] A veteran revolutionary was heard to complain, "Now people doubt many state secrets can still be closely held!" His solution was heavier punishments for violators.[66]

Keeping secrets is only one concern when picking secretaries. The secretary's position historically has sometimes brought special influence to its holder, as has sometimes been the case with other positions such as that of translator. Party documents speak of the "dictatorship exercised by secretaries" and warn of deficient administration and corruption that can result.[67] Nevertheless, personal bonds and trust so critical in any political body grow with time and success, and leader and secretary in China come to share a common fate. Some high officials accord their secretaries additional powers and before their own retirement recommend them for promotion.[68] One of the secretaries' unspoken tasks is fortifying their bosses' "relational networks" (*guanxi wang*) and building their own networks with other well-placed counterparts.[69] This hidden power corrupts and adds to the complexity of the national command authority in moments of crisis and confusion but routinely moves and motivates the policy process.

The General Office Research Section (Bangongting Yanjiushi) runs selected research projects needed by the Party's central departments. This small section routinely coordinates with the Party Central Policy Research Section (Zhonggong Zhongyang Zhengce Yanjiushi), a higher-level organization equivalent in rank to the General Office and tasked to work principally on domestic issues for the Party general secretary.[70] This second research body and its many bureaus have evolved in ways that have expanded its reach and importance.[71] It checks all draft documents and verifies their congruence with the accepted political line, and its output on national and international security problems reportedly complements well that of the office's Research Section.

Taken together, the General Office bureaus have billets for about 3,800 staff members.[72] All these bureaucrats support the daily routines of the leadership, but their primary purpose is to guarantee the bureaucracy's focused and uninterrupted performance in times of crisis and the conduct of high-profile national tasks, such as summit meetings and other senior-level Party and state gatherings.

At the level of the Party high command, the General Office makes the administration function, and within it strong links have been forged to the military's command-and-control structure discussed in the next chapter. The flow of decisions between the Party and the military exemplifies political command in action.

PROTECTION OF THE CENTRAL ELITE

We now turn to that part of the General Office that directly interacts with the entire central leadership and ensures its ability to function in all environments. Complementing the communications and operations sector of the General Office is its highly feared Guards Bureau (normally referred to as the Ninth Bureau), which operates like the U.S. Secret Service and provides personal protection to the top leaders and their families. In addition to placing a protective envelope around the central leadership, the bureau director must block any threatening or unwanted contacts or messages.[73]

His organization consists of separate divisions to protect Chinese leaders and senior foreign guests as well as several other organs for security and logistics and administers the Central Guards Regiment, which safeguards Zhongnanhai, Tiananmen Square, the Great Hall of the People, and important meeting locations and travel routes.[74] The bureau assigns guard "secretaries" to assure the safety of most Party leaders and senior officials in their offices and residences and during travel. Although in the past the CMC Guards Bureau provided comparable protection for senior military officers, the central leadership has begun integrating the military-political leadership protection bureaus, and the result may now be a single Party-state-military Guards Bureau providing three-way security.[75]

The Central Guards Regiment, once code-named Unit 8341, has more troops and firepower than most regular regiments. (The unit's designation, 8341, was the code name of a military warehouse, until the General Staff gave it to the Guards Regiment. Over time, the legend spread that the code name referred to Mao's eighty-three-year lifespan and the forty-one years of his reign since the 1935 Zunyi Conference until his death in 1976.[76]) In emergencies, the Guards Bureau director can augment the regiment by calling on the Beijing Garrison Command, the Armed Police, the Beijing Bureau of Public Security, and the ministries of public security and state security for troops. Because the Guards Bureau concurrently is the Ninth Bureau of the Ministry of Public Security, the director also commands highly trained and well-equipped public security units and has access to their intelligence sources.[77]

The Guards Regiment receives its orders from the General Office and Guards Bureau and receives help from the PLA General Staff regarding the regiment's staffing, training, and logistics.[78] The chief of the General Staff also can determine the concrete requirements for the regiment's readiness preparations to the extent that he has the ear of the supreme leader.[79]

The Beijing Garrison Command's Cadres Detachment selects the roughly two hundred bodyguards who protect the Politburo leaders and such luminaries as Deng Xiaoping and the retired Jiang Zemin.[80] These handpicked soldiers are platoon or even company commanders recommended by the elite combat divisions of the ground forces.[81] From the days of revolution, wartime guerrilla fighting, and the civil war to modern-day terrorism, those leaders have felt the most vulnerable while traveling, and the Guards (Ninth) Bureau goes into high gear whenever they leave their compounds. The specially selected escort teams, ranging in numbers from tens to more than one hundred, maintain "interior security" (*nei wei*) while local security forces and military units en route ensure "exterior security" (*wai wei*).[82]

In 1976, the CMC expanded the Guards Regiment into a Guards Division (Jingwei Shi) with more than ten thousand officers and men, but in December 1978, the Third Plenum of the Eleventh Central Committee reduced it to a regimental-sized organization. Apparently, Deng Xiaoping had in mind lowering the stature of Maoist holdovers Hua Guofeng and Wang Dongxing by decreasing the number of their guards and also was seeking to restore inner-Party political life to pre–Cultural Revolution norms.[83] The regiment now has something over seven thousand officers and men, including those units affiliated with the Guards Bureau.[84]

Over the last quarter century, the Standing Committee and the CMC have worked out the job division between the Guards Bureau and Guards Regiment. As a way of integrating these two units and reducing bureaucratic friction, ranking officers from each of them are assigned to concurrent and comparable jobs in the other unit.[85]

With support from the Beijing Garrison Command, the Guards Bureau protects the several underground bunkers built for evacuation of designated officials to sites either near their offices or at the hardened emergency center in Elephant Nose Valley near the CMC's advance command post in Beijing's Western Hills.[86] The bureau also has posted full-time guards to all airplanes flown by the leaders. These guards travel aboard the planes and stand guard over them at both domestic and foreign airports.[87]

Less well known is the bureau's mission to conduct surveillance over any suspected political opponents of the senior leadership. In name, the General

Office director is responsible to the entire central leadership, but in reality, he must give unflinching loyalty to the top man, a task that can become particularly dicey when the power of a Deng Xiaoping or Jiang Zemin exceeds that of the general secretary. The political terrain becomes especially treacherous, moreover, when the supreme leader orders the bureau to place a Party colleague under surveillance in addition to monitoring his or her communications. In such cases, the supreme leader receives daily reports from the office director, whose job comprises weaving these reports into a profile of the top leader's proven or potential adversaries.[88]

EVALUATING AND TRANSFORMING THE SYSTEM

The complexity and domestic orientation of the General Office and protection organizations we have described produce delay and minimal international risk-taking, and the process is highly susceptible to personal power and influence. To understand why this is so, we need to move somewhat abruptly from the detailed inquiry into Party operations to the most general level of political culture as it affects strategic decisionmaking. Much depends on the working styles of the Standing Committee and the CMC, and the needed innovations must overcome the strong bureaucratic impulses of the General Office. We have written elsewhere, "No external issue except the future of Taiwan could compare to the dangers or the opportunities within the nation. . . . The logic behind Beijing's strategic calculus mostly remains in place: the perpetuation of Party rule needs domestic political stability, prolonged political stability requires sustained economic development, and that development depends on a peaceful international environment."[89]

The operational character of the General Office and its counterparts in the military buttress that domestic priority and the dominant strategic calculus. In this sense, the national command authority may not be ready for the brutal test of war. Achieving such a state of readiness would now seem to depend more on China's own revolution in military affairs—a change in what we call political-military culture—as much as any tinkering with operational mechanisms.

During his thirteen-year tenure as Party general secretary, Jiang Zemin attempted to define and press for the needed changes, though all too often his case for a radical transformation in thinking was couched in politically correct euphemisms and sloganistic pablum. His speech to the Party's senior leadership on May 31, 2002, is a case in point. Jiang Zemin reaffirmed that China must adopt or accept a wide range of bureaucratic changes at an accelerated pace or face falling behind in the race to build a modern, powerful state.[90] On the eve of his formal retirement, Jiang had his eye on changing the established processes of staffing and decisionmaking of the national leadership in accordance with the constitutional requirement of taking the "three represents" as one of its major guides to action. He thereby laid out a program of active "multilateral diplomatic activities" and cooperation that would ward off conflicts.[91] "The road is tortuous, but the future is bright," he predicted.[92]

In taking that road, the Party would have to move forward on a broad and largely unfamiliar front, and here Jiang's remedies became somewhat less opaque and would become the Party's action guidelines for the remainder of his own rule and much that followed his Party and state retirement. Seven bureaucratic changes that could help transform the national command authority are underway:

Accelerated openness to foreign political and ideological concepts.

In the Maoist era and even under Deng Xiaoping, the Party rigidly excluded Western concepts as revisionist and dangerous. Mao pursued the Soviet model with "Chinese characteristics" to govern the national command system, but that pursuit ended with Jiang Zemin and Hu Jintao. As Jiang, in all-too-familiar slogans, put it to the Sixteenth Party Congress, "Innovation requires emancipating our minds, seeking truth through facts, and keeping up with the times."[93]

In a significant way, Jiang was turning away from his Chinese and Marxist heritage that had been the hallmark of his predecessors' pursuit of reform. Dealing creatively with external threats would require emulating some of the more effective foreign institutions and absorbing their procedures as well as their ideas and technologies, and this has caused the leadership to send researchers abroad to study European democratic parties, the American National Security Council, the U.S.-inspired revolution in military affairs, and much more.[94] Some of their findings are being incorporated into China's own policymaking, though the process is still proceeding with great deliberateness.

A case in point is the establishment of the National Security Leading Group, and another is the increased incorporation of Western-trained strategists and scholars into the General Office and other central decision bodies. At first relegated to the margins, these returnees are now playing a more important role and gradually are introducing Western concepts and practices. Their emergence in the national polity sheds light on a growing tension between the grand China-centric tradition and the onslaught of modernity and globalism.

Increased practice of collective decisionmaking.

During his dictatorial rule, Mao all too frequently insulated himself from his comrades and the information support structure, and the results often led to disaster. Deng Xiaoping, too, adopted Mao's approach in his later years, and we should keep in mind that the God-complex is not unknown even in Western democracies. Starting with Jiang and continuing under Hu, the high command, especially those on the Standing Committee and the CMC, adopted a collective working style especially in the initial years after assuming power.

Although traces of a strongman mentality can still be found in today's Beijing, collective leadership has steadily become the norm even after the supreme leader has consolidated his position. This new norm has tended to make the policymaking apparatus less ideological, more flexible, and more transparent. This is apparently what Deng Xiaoping had in mind roughly eight years before his death, when in the aftermath of the Tiananmen crisis of 1989, he delivered a number of talks on the leadership that would come after him.[95] "If your leading body is going to succeed, it is essential for you to form a collective leadership," he said. "You must be a collective in which each member cooperates closely with the others, and a collective that thinks independently. You should . . . complement each other's thinking and help correct each other's mistakes and shortcomings." Within that collective, he designated Jiang Zemin the "core."[96]

Greater concern with public opinion.

Beginning in the 1990s, the Party line committed the nation to "reform and opening up" as the "only way to make our country strong" through steady economic development, the nation's "top priority."[97] That priority was said to require long-term regional peace and internal order, the exact opposite of Mao embracing continuous revolution and "great disorder under heaven" (*tianxia daluan*). In his time, Mao cared little for popular support for his policies, though he craved mass adulation, and Deng Xiaoping made the disastrous decision to unleash troops against peacefully demonstrating citizens in the dark days of the Tiananmen debacle. Over time, especially as the nation cautiously adapted and then succumbed in an astonishing era of growth to the information and telecommunications revolution, the need for stability subtly became transformed into the perceived need for media visibility and broad acceptance.

The largely unforeseen eruption of divergent, vocal, and often well-informed public discourse and opinion must have struck advocates of the "mass line" in the People's Republic as supremely ironic and hardly welcome in light of the priorities for stability and resurrecting the Party's waning prestige. It began first within the large cities in China's coastal provinces and became magnified as outspokenness and Internet access spread among the educated youth. With the populace less and less tuned to the center's edicts and pronouncements, the Party came to realize it needed the support of the Chinese people more than the people needed it.

Currently, before adopting novel foreign policies, the leadership must try to gauge their acceptability in the general population, and, to the old revolutionaries' chagrin, the Party has come to heed the major opinion polls when determining how far those policies can go and in what direction. This became especially true of any policy that might affect the future of Taiwan. It has become more routine for some senior officials, such as the foreign minister, to answer questions concerning the nation's foreign and security policy raised by thousands of Internet users, and monthly Politburo "study sessions" have become well-publicized events.[98] Chinese sources now list popular "acceptability" as one of the three basic requirements for fashioning any external policy; the others, as discussed earlier, are conforming to China's national interest and "justice."[99] Decisions on war and peace can no longer take for granted those long lumped together as the "masses."

Greater use of enforcement agencies to ensure compliance.

Mao's attitude toward opposition and social deviance echoed the traditional disdain for the law, and he seldom relied on law enforcement agencies to enforce his policies. Rather, he put his faith in propaganda, social pressure, and "reform through labor" to compel obedience. Early visitors to China after the Cultural Revolution routinely reported the dearth of laws, lawyers, and violent, even petty crimes.

All that has now passed into history. Over the past decade the Party has faced a steady loss of public backing and ever-greater indifference, and step by step, it has come to depend on the state's legal agencies to guarantee compliance. Even during external crises, it has enlisted these agencies to tighten its control and ensure domestic tranquility. Whereas Mao energized mass movements and berated bureaucratism, his successors have taken the opposite road, especially after the Tiananmen turmoil in the spring of 1989.[100] As a result, the Armed Police and ministries of public and state security have a louder voice in decisionmaking and a bigger stick in combating disobedience. As early as 1983, Deng in a speech entitled "Crack Down on Crime" told leaders in the Ministry of Public Security to conduct investigations with the advice of "veteran policemen" and added "[We] have to strike hard, fast, and according to law" to combat crime.[101] "Crime" in today's China can often have a perverse meaning, including endangering state security, and legalization of the bureaucracy has taken the place of trust and loyalty to an ever-greater degree.

An ever-younger leadership.

The Confucian ideals, though often vilified by Mao and Cultural Revolution radicals, penetrated even the Communist hierarchy and perpetuated the esteem accorded the Party elders. Age and seniority mattered. The deeply rooted relational networks depended on keeping the most senior person in power, no matter how infirm or even senile he might be.

Contemporary knowledge, often acquired in foreign universities, and the demands of the expanding market economy and advanced technology have gradually replaced the ancient principles and lessened reverence for the old. Now the vigor of youth and the age of the computer set the tone of China's rapid transformation. In the summer of 1989, Deng called for the formalization of mandatory retirement within the Party, state, and military elites: "We must have some young people as leaders, or it will be difficult to carry on. . . . Under a retirement system, it will be fairly easy to replace leaders with new ones. . . . Let's consider this settled."[102] Despite some glaring exceptions, retirement ages are taken seriously throughout the leadership, and the Party elders, once so important to warding off genuine political modernization, now grumble in retirement at home.

That is not to say that the rich and powerful cannot influence their succession. The succession of Party heads from Mao to Jiang Zemin sometimes had disastrous results for the heir apparent, and only Jiang stepped down according to the rules, though even he did not fully retire for almost two years until resigning the CMC chairmanship. Moreover, he handpicked key Party and state replacements and most members of the Standing Committee, but it needs to be said that General Secretary Hu, though personally chosen by Deng Xiaoping as Jiang's successor, undoubtedly needed the prestige and endorsement of Jiang as he wove 'together his own networks and reinforced his base. The dominance of the old ways was clearly slipping, but Machiavellian methods and personalistic politics remained firmly in place.

All political systems have mixed values and behaviors, and deference to age or youth is only one of them. Yet, a vivid experience of one of the authors who visited the same military-security organization in Beijing over many years has been watching the generational succession in practice, and slowly the younger generation's expertise and even its opinions are coming to be valued. In the most command-sensitive environment, highly trained specialists in their twenties and thirties now speak with increased authority and are listened to tolerantly or with genuine respect. Seniority is still highly valued, but the excitement, the jargon, the technical competence, and the boldness of the young are coming to have a more dramatic influence on the old than the other way round. History may well record this as one of China's most fundamental revolutions, assuming it is allowed to continue.

More tolerance toward inner-Party dissent.

On July 2, 1941, the Party's quintessential organization man, Liu Shaoqi, delivered a lecture to the Party school in Yan'an "On Inner-Party Struggle."[103] His message was that permissible "struggle" must not "weaken the Party's organization, solidarity, discipline, and prestige or hinder its work"—all prescriptions that became weapons to stifle dissent in practice. Disputes had to be "principled," and Liu added: "Everything must be based on reason and be rationally explained, and everything must be done with good sense. Nothing else will do." The catch was only the top leader could be the ultimate judge of what was reasonable, rational, and done with good sense, and under Mao, incautious dissent could prove suicidal. We have already seen where dissenters won the day and survived at least temporarily, but Mao and to a certain extent Deng and their successors have insisted on unanimity and suspected the most well-intentioned dissenters of latent disloyalty.

Modernization, tolerance of foreign or novel concepts, the erosion of ideology, and the rise of the young are both causing and legitimizing honest debate in the People's Republic. This greater tolerance of such "constructive dissent" has begun to permeate all echelons of the national command authority as well as the nation at large. The intolerance of the hardliners is waning, and that authority increasingly reflects dedicated consultation and compromise. The ever-greater recognition of international diversity and the commitment to cooperation, multilateralism, and the peaceful resolution of conflicts suggest the positive influence of fact-based, constructive disagreement on national security policy.

Counter-trends: Greed, corruption, and the decline of selfless service.

Common to the six changes we have described is their endorsement by the Party and their presumed positive influence on central command functions. There are, however, countervailing trends that vie with the ongoing desired transformation and complicate any assessment of its likely outcome. China has paid a high price for its rapid economic progress and opening up to the capitalist world, and perhaps the money-oriented culture has exacted the highest toll on the spirit of egalitarianism and service to community and nation. Corruption has penetrated all aspects of life from the Party to the military, and more than once visitors have been startled to see giant billboards in Chinese cities pressing the campaign against corrupt practices. Some legal actions against those practices have been draconian, but the more subtle infusions of greed, plagiarism, theft of intellectual property, and fraud remain largely unchecked.

Whether the Maoist ideal working style of "serving the people" is gone forever remains uncertain, though its decline in business and the academic community does not augur well for the future.[104] A casualty of this loss of integrity has arisen within the scholarly community that once was the backbone of centers of strategic studies. These centers are now providing only marginal assistance to the nation's security policy, though most think tanks and the intelligence services within the Party's inner sanctum appear to be resisting the temptations of the money economy.

. . .

This review of the workings of the national command authority may well seem familiar to students of politics in the West. Personality and relational networks in both East and West transform and complicate hierarchical structures and command operations. The Party center in China speaks with a more moderate, collective, youthful, and informed voice, but in close association with the Central Military Commission when dealing with matters of security and sovereignty, its voice can engender a disciplined response.

Working through powerful interagency leading groups and the Central General Office, the Standing Committee, as anchored to the full Politburo and Central Secretariat, makes the final decisions. In reaching those decisions, the triad serves the Party general secretary, the nation's commander-in-chief, and in the final analysis the Party does rule the gun. Yet, once the decisions for war and military action are made, the People's Liberation Army takes charge, and should it ever come to nuclear war, it is the CMC chairman who has his finger on the button. How those decisions are implemented and how the strategic forces are organized are the subjects of the next two chapters.

FIVE

Military Command, Control, and Force Operations

As their arsenals grow and technologies advance, the commanders of the People's Liberation Army (PLA) are conducting trials of steadily improved military units and devising survivable and effective command systems and strategies. Until the national command authority's decision to go to war, they will be testing and evaluating battlefield concepts and command procedures. The details on these concepts and procedures presumably will continue to evolve, but the sources available to us strongly suggest that their main characteristics have been determined. Based on these sources, this chapter builds on our knowledge of the national command authority and reviews China's efforts to put in place a modern command-and-control organization.

As used in the U.S. military, "command" refers to administration and personnel placement, promotion, training, and mission assignments, whereas "control" refers to the operational deployment and employment of the armed forces.[1] We deal with the organization of the PLA and how it has evolved in recent years and attempt to discern how the Chinese employ the concepts of command and control. What "lessons" have forced the leadership to restructure that organization, and have the changes proved workable? Can command and control operate effectively in a high-tech local war for which the PLA is now preparing?

After addressing these questions, we turn to a detailed case study of the command-and-control process leading to the Sino-Vietnamese border war in 1979. This study presents concrete though somewhat dated insights into how the high command acted in past crises and what it learned from them. That background provides the context for later Chinese writings on ways to revamp command and control at all levels. We discuss how Beijing has responded to the lessons derived from this case and from U.S.-led military actions from the Gulf War in 1991 to the Iraq War twelve years later.

This chapter analyzes these responses as they apply to organizational experiments, planning priorities, and military exercises. It concludes that adjustments to command and control have become more technical and sophisticated and that some long-standing wartime operations under the Central Military Commission (CMC) and its departments are being transformed.[2] Coupled with administrative actions generated by internal political reforms, the current tendency is toward a weakening of the Party's influence in the overall military domain.

THE MILITARY DECISIONMAKING APPARATUS

Throughout the years of revolution and state building, we must stress again, the roles and powers of the Party and army have been strictly demarcated in theory though often blurred under power's corrupting influence.[3] We have seen that an institutional change occurs at the moment the Chinese nation crosses the boundary between peace and war, and the two power centers exchange roles. Up to the decision to fight, the Standing Committee of the Politburo has the sole power to determine the specific direction of state and security-military actions, though it routinely attaches the greatest importance to the voices of senior military officials when dealing with issues of national defense. In times of peace, not excluding the most intense crises involving armed threats and military deployments, the Standing Committee alone acts as the supreme national command authority. Once war occurs, however, the burden of command authority passes to the Party's Central

Military Commission, which, while led by Party civilians, would be dominated by senior PLA officers. True to tradition, the political sovereign would stand aside, though consultation would be expected, even mandatory.

We now turn to the CMC, its internal organization and operational system, and how its structure and functions have evolved to get ready for and to carry out wartime operations. The CMC is the national command authority in waiting, and its ongoing organizational evolution reflects missions that the People's Liberation Army is expected to perform in defense of the nation.

Determining the membership of the CMC falls to the Standing Committee, though constitutionally its selection requires the endorsement of the Central Committee. In addition to Chairman Hu Jintao, the membership of the CMC (as of January 2005) comprises three vice chairmen, the heads of the four general departments (Staff, Political, Logistics, and Armament), and the commanders of the air force, navy, and Second Artillery.[4] All of the PLA's "first-grade greater units" (*yiji da danwei*)—equivalent in status to a "greater military region" (*da junqu*)—come under the CMC's direct control.[5]

The CMC General Office administers the commission's daily affairs and staff. Currently, the office consists of the Guards Bureau, Confidential Bureau, Confidential Communications Bureau, Joint Operations Bureau, Research Bureau, Policy Planning Department, Secretarial Bureau, Foreign Affairs Bureau, Administrative Bureau, and other units. The Guards Bureau, working in parallel with the Guards Bureau under the Party General Office, ensures the personal safety of the CMC leaders and other high-ranking officers. The Research Bureau studies foreign military developments, while the Policy Planning Department focuses on problems within China's armed forces and in civil-military relations. The recently established Joint Operations Bureau attempts to balance the demands of the individual services and promote integration among them as the emphasis shifts to joint operations.[6] Moreover, the assignments of some CMC General Office bureaus mirror those of the General Staff's General Office and departments. Checks and balances as well as cooperation are in play between these CMC and General Staff organs, though in some cases these organs are the same.

Faced with ever more complex and threatening battlefield scenarios and the increased need for communications integrity, PLA planners have sought to enhance the survivability and effectiveness of the communications networks of the army, air force, navy, and Second Artillery—collectively referred to throughout our study as the "services." For these purposes, the CMC has long assigned its Confidential Bureau to establish classification standards and encryption policies and has made the General Staff's Confidential Bureau, Communications Department, and Technical Department responsible for encoding, transmitting and receiving, and deciphering messages. The two confidential bureaus oversee and coordinate the modernization of their respective communications networks.[7] The General Staff assigns the army's best mathematicians to Institute 51 for encryption and network security research in collaboration with the State Informationization Leading Group, its associated state organs, and selected electronic industry institutes.[8]

The CMC and its General Office were previously located in a compound in Sanzuomen (Three Gates) next to Zhongnanhai in Beijing, though in the late 1990s most of the bureaus and departments under the office moved to the recently built CMC headquarters on Fuxingmenwai Street west of Tiananmen and adjacent to the Military Museum. The CMC chairman's personal office director regularly visits the new headquarters and briefs the staff, with special attention given to senior personnel changes.[9]

All CMC members and their staffs have offices in the Fuxingmenwai complex, though many of them spend most of their time at their other offices. The main purpose of the headquarters facility is central administration or "command," while "control" is routinely handled elsewhere, though the lines between their command and control duties are seldom sharply drawn and often deliberately blurred. The CMC's vice-chairman in charge of daily affairs usually handles all routine and non-crisis business at his Fuxingmenwai office, and the deputy chiefs of the PLA General Staff in charge of operations and intelligence typically work there as well. This compound houses the "operations system" (*zuozhan xitong*) composed of task teams from the General Staff's Operations (First), Intelligence (Second), Technical (Third), Radar and Electronic Countermeasures (Fourth), and Communications departments and Confidential Bureau. This system is on permanent alert status, and its teams must be prepared at all times to brief their superiors on essential defense-related matters and contingency plans.

For crisis operations that could include actual conflict, the CMC has built a command center (*zhihui zhongxin*) in hardened silos in the Western Hills in the northwestern suburb of Beijing. Built to house 3,000 personnel and stocked with all necessary supplies to last for six months, the center was eventually strengthened to survive a direct nuclear hit. Located in a restricted area, this center is heavily guarded by elite units under the Beijing Garrison Command. The General Staff long stationed two battalions to guard the center but later added a third.[10]

Despite the move to Fuxingmenwai and the effort to consolidate all the senior staff personnel, the CMC still leaves task teams in Sanzuomen and the Western Hills.[11] In a perilous crisis or conflict, these teams are organized and trained to work together as the CMC's command posts, and may be further dispersed if one of the teams is put out of action. Similarly, other CMC command centers have been created to serve as "alternate" or "advance" command posts.[12]

In Chinese military parlance, several types of command posts exist. The PLA creates its "main command posts" (*jiben zhihuisuo*) for regiments and above; prior to an impending conflict, it adds "alternate" (*yubei*), "rear" (*houfang*), and "advance" (*qianjin*) command posts. Alternate posts replace damaged or destroyed main command posts; rear posts provide logistical and technical backup and stand-by or replacement personnel; and advance posts serve frontline units and provide the "primary direction" for the battle.[13] The prescribed redundancy and related contingency plans for further dispersion as needed reflect a strong concern for survivability of command and control in wartime.

Directly under the CMC are the previously noted four general departments, each of which is represented on the CMC. The most important of these is the General Staff, through which the CMC ensures overall command and operational control of its forces. In peacetime, most of the General Staff's work involves administration and other routine command jobs. It administers the buildup and oversees the quality of the services even as it researches and recommends strategic options for these forces. In times of mounting crisis or actual conflict, it supervises all theater operations and controls the nation's combat forces at and above the corps (*jun*) level and air and naval units at the division (*shi*) level. Charged with insuring the readiness and fighting capacity of those forces, the General Staff is the PLA's operational headquarters.[14]

During emergencies that could end in armed confrontations or war, the CMC has standing orders for the General Staff to convene meetings with predesignated senior officers at the Operations Department's command center. The General Staff is authorized to summon representatives from the key military departments, services, and relevant greater military regions.[15] It can assign them to assist in formulating battle plans, establishing command posts, coordinating interservice operations, designing theater operations, securing logistical support, ensuring communications, and finalizing the operation's budget. During the actual fighting, these representatives regularly assemble at the command center for battle assessments, follow-up planning, and the formulation and transmittal of tactical orders to the combat units.[16]

In the late 1990s, however, this preset and somewhat time-consuming, even ritualistic process came under repeated criticism and review when the military was directed to prepare for a high-tech local war. From its appraisal of the Gulf War and later American-led military operations, the CMC recognized that modern warfare is unpredictable, fast moving, and highly threatening to command and communications centers.[17]

Forced to rethink and reorganize its time-honored approaches to joint command, the PLA leaders examined a variety of standing orders and existing C³I technologies and experimented with several promising alternatives. The CMC then issued a revised version of the "Regulations on Headquarters," which detailed the General Staff's responsibilities for coordinating all military departments and services and solving any differences among them. These standing directives increased the General Staff's authority and the power of "chiefs of staff" down to the regimental headquarters.

It should be noted that the term "staff department" (*canmou bu*) is used only for the General Staff, which is called Zong Canmou Bu. All military commands are called *silingbu* or "headquarters." Chiefs of the staff serve as the executive officers in these headquarters, but the commander and the political commissar in each command are in overall charge of the headquarters and its political, logistics, and armament departments.

When preparing for battle, the PLA high command searches for a specific winning strategy to defeat its better-armed foes and routinely mobilizes the country's best minds for this task. For its part, the CMC has created an array of policy planning and intelligence bodies to conduct research on the strategic, tactical, and technical elements of modern military operations and their connection to broad national security policies and directives. At the pinnacle of these organizations, the General Staff is responsible for mandating and evaluating the highest-level security research; finalizing reports on strategies, weapons requirements, and proposed deployments; and submitting reports on behalf of the CMC to the Politburo and, as needed, the central government for approval.[18]

The PLA has two highly secretive research units that conduct time-urgent studies on global strategy and potential crises. What we know about them is limited, though we have been told that both are key organs with significant budgets and well-trained staffs. The first is the Strategic Committee under the CMC, about which virtually nothing is known.[19] The second, the International Situation Research Team, comes directly under the General Staff and works closely with its Operations, Intelligence, and Technical departments. Its members come largely from these departments and the Academy of Military Science Department for Foreign Military Studies. It submits monthly reports to the CMC for crisis assessment and carries out special projects assigned by the CMC. Directly under the Operations Department ("Operations"), two division-level offices serve as the research staff for this team and the Strategic Committee, respectively.[20] In comparison to the Intelligence Department, this team is smaller but similar in rank. The chief and deputy chief of Operations concurrently serve as leader and deputy leader respectively of this team as well as office director and deputy office director of the Strategic Committee. In reaching its decisions, the CMC relies more on the two units than any other research groups. The other less important but far better known research organs linked to the General Staff include the General Staff Intelligence and Technical departments, the Academy of Military Science, and the National Defense University, all of which have access to the most sensitive policy decisions and intelligence.

Within the General Staff, the Operations, Intelligence, Technical, Radar and Electronic Countermeasures, and Communications departments and Confidential Bureau directly participate in command and control. The most important is the Operations Department, which serves as the nerve center in the communications chain from the CMC to battalion-level combat forces. This department performs like a telecommunications switching center for the transmittal and retransmittal of all central orders and reports. Even deputy chiefs of the General Staff, if they are not in charge of operations, must frequently check with Operations for reliable and timely information, especially during emergencies.[21]

Prior to October 1949, Operations reported directly to the CMC, but the following year, Mao placed it under the General Staff.[22] Its detailed situation reports for the CMC would now carry the General Staff's chop. It drafts most operations plans, transmits and monitors all decisions on military deployments and employment, briefs the General Staff leaders as well as the CMC on the results of implementing central orders, and in wartime, updates plans in real time, and recommends tactical actions and countermeasures. Few foreigners have ever penetrated this department, and few of its decisions have ever been leaked.[23]

Until the mid-1990s, the department was composed principally of officers from the PLA ground forces. In an attempt to ready the military for a high-tech local war, however, many air, naval, and Second Artillery officers thereafter were assigned to Operations' functional bureaus.

In addition to the offices of the Strategic Committee and the International Situation Research Team and an Administrative Section to handle routine assignments, Operations' nine principal bureaus are Frontier Defense and Garrison, Regional, Comprehensive Planning, Operations, Joint Operations, Naval, Air Force, Strategic Forces, and Air Defense.[24] Chart 2 shows these Operations Department bureaus and more generally outlines the command-and-control organization under the CMC during wartime theater operations, which will be discussed below.

The Operations Bureau coordinates the other bureaus and service-specific plans and contains the round-the-clock command duty office (*zuozhan zhiban shi*) at the heart of the General Staff's operations system.[25] The nominal assignments of most of the other bureaus are quite clear and need little explanation. The service-specific bureaus make requests for equipment, personnel, and funding through the Operations Department to the General Staff, which is assigned to forge a comprehensive understanding of ongoing buildups and readiness.

The Strategic Forces Bureau oversees the operations of the nuclear forces of the Second Artillery, the special nuclear-armed air force squadrons, and the navy's nuclear-powered ballistic-missile submarine force. The bureau helps the CMC keep a tight rein on all nuclear units and how they fit into the overall national strategy. Only the CMC chairman—not China's president—has the authority to launch any nuclear weapons after getting the concurrence of the Politburo Standing Committee and CMC.

Specifically, the defense White Paper for 2000 states: "China's nuclear force is under the direct command of the Central Military Commission," and the one for 2002 says: "The strategic nuclear missile force, under the direct command of the CMC, constitutes the main part of China's limited nuclear counterattack capability." The strategic nuclear missile force is, of course, the Second Artillery, the subject of Chapter 6. The 2002 version adds, "Its primary missions are to deter the enemy from using nuclear weapons against China, and, in the case of a nuclear attack by the enemy, to launch an effective counterattack in self-defense independently or jointly with the strategic nuclear forces of other services, at the order of the supreme command." [26] Presumably, the other nuclear forces are those deployed on China's ballistic missile submarine and bombers and fighter-bombers.

Two of the Operations Department's bureaus require special comment. The Comprehensive Planning Bureau, as part of its duties, provides general guidance to the various military departments, formulates the General Staff's comprehensive buildup plans, and approves the budget for any buildup. The Regional Bureau, assisted by the previously mentioned bureau, conducts contingency war planning for the relevant military theaters and oversees the implementation of that planning. The assignments of the two bureaus supplement and even overlap those of Operations' other bureaus.

In order to balance the demands of the services and promote their integration, the mission of the Joint Operations Bureau is to study theories on joint operations and "sum up" its conclusions from large or joint exercises. The General Staff has transferred many experienced officers from the operations departments of the air force, navy, and Second Artillery to create a "joint" dimension to this bureau. In peacetime, the bureau sends groups of officers to supervise joint exercises and help the seven greater military region commands form similar units at and above the division level.

In order to convey how this joint dimension is designed to work, we must briefly describe the history of the greater military region (which we simplify in this study as "military region" or "region"). In 1950, following the military takeover a few months earlier, the CMC divided the nation into six multiprovincial regions with the aim of enforcing the Communist-led "democratic dictatorship," as Mao called his initial government. As part of the Sovietization of the PLA, it restructured these into twelve smaller regions in 1955 and added one (Fuzhou Military Region) the next year. The frontier military regions (Xinjiang, Xizang [Tibet], and Inner Mongolia) were disbanded or "reallocated" over time, and in 1985 Deng Xiaoping reorganized the country into the current seven regions. Now, the name of each headquarters city is given to that region (for example, the Nanjing Military Region or Shenyang Military Region), and the constituent provinces or major cities within each

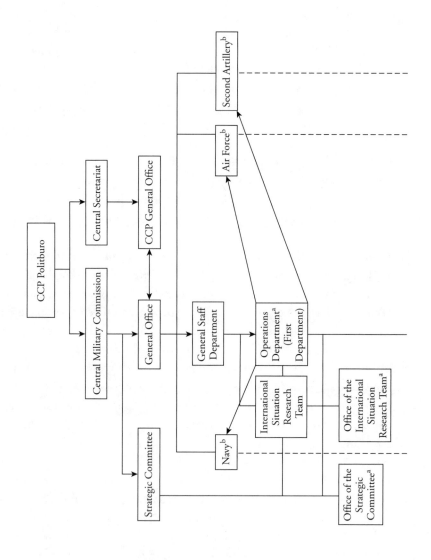

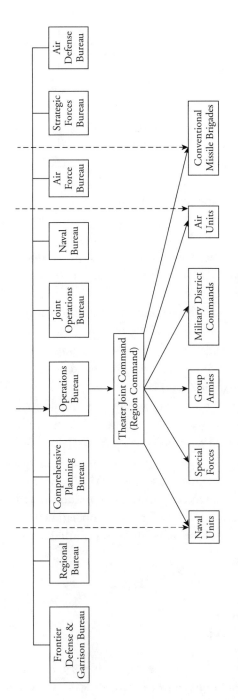

Chart 2. Command-and-Control Organization in Conventional Theater Operations

region are its military districts or garrison commands. We shall encounter the structure and tasks of the military region throughout our study. Our goal is to understand both its central place in PLA command and control and its changing organization and responsibilities when the CMC orders joint or trans-regional operations or conducts large military exercises.

If fighting breaks out, the Joint Operations Bureau will dispatch task teams to coordinate the troops attached to the joint command in the "theater of war" (*zhanqu*). The PLA considers each military region equivalent to a theater of war, and now uses the former term in peacetime but the latter in extreme crises (such as those in the Taiwan Strait) or war.[27]

In theater wars, the CMC will create a theater joint command (*zhanqu lianhe zhanyi zhihuibu*) and advance command posts to manage operations in the different battlefields. The General Staff will direct the head of Operations to coordinate peripheral actions and provide additional air cover and logistics. In trans-theater operations comparable to the 1979 Vietnam border war, the CMC now will set up a trans-theater joint command consisting of senior officers transferred from the four general departments, the different services, and the commands of the relevant theaters for managing the expanded operations. In such circumstances, the advance command posts will come under the control of the trans-theater joint command.[28]

Throughout the fighting, Operations will continue to play the decisive role. It will station a team of some twenty of its senior staff in a specially guarded compound in Zhongnanhai. These officers will provide liaison and advice to Beijing's political leaders. Through this team, the leadership will maintain active contact with the department. As noted, the CMC has ordered the department to construct several centers for ensuring the uninterrupted flow of commands. During nuclear crises, the CMC can issue operational orders to the main center (or its alternate in case of need) for transmittal to the Second Artillery and other services.

CENTRAL COMMAND AND THE LESSONS OF HISTORY

Today's command-and-control policies bear the stamp of history and are heavily weighted by revolutionary traditions and well-studied "lessons," even though much of that history is confined to outmoded infantry operations and short-term demonstrations or skirmishes.[29] Nevertheless, Beijing has enshrined and encoded the historical experience from the Korean War (1950–53), the first and second Quemoy crises (1954–55, 1958–59), the Sino-Indian border conflict (1962), the Sino-Soviet border battles (1969), and the Sino-Vietnamese border war (1979). This "summing up" is used to make each succeeding crisis or actual military action fit and update previous standardized war summaries or "models," and so long as the future appears to fit the pattern, Chinese responses will have a certain order and predictability.

By contrast, revolutionary leaders often fought from a position of extreme weakness and had to confront their enemies' strategies, to use Sun Tzu's expression, and to make constant trial-and-error adjustments as fighting evolved. Those who became trapped in predetermined tactics usually courted defeat. Conventional wisdom based on accepted lessons seldom substituted for solid intelligence and situational creativity.

What happens after a decision has been made, of course, directly affects the final result. Beijing's leaders often hint at what is to come by passing a covert message to selected foreign guests or issuing a public announcement or warning, though it has usually proved impossible to separate genuine hints from bluffs and bluster. Mao's message to Edgar Snow in 1970 about a possible opening to Washington is one of the best-known examples.[30] Foreign leaders, however, seldom distinguish legitimate from deceptive messages, and it does little good to say that they failed to understand because of their ignorance of the Chinese mind. Indeed, Beijing's leaders have belatedly recognized that such messages might be missed or misconstrued, a dangerous outcome in the nuclear age.[31]

When the central leadership faces a regional crisis, the Operations Department will automatically begin devising a theater operations plan, and the step-by-step process leading to the final plan is strictly prescribed as follows:

- Operations formulates an overall operations plan and submits it to the deputy chief of the General Staff in charge of operations for review and possible revision.
- Operations submits the revised plan to the chief of the General Staff for examination and finalizes it in accord with his opinions.
- The relevant service and region commands devise specific operations plans in accordance with the approved overall plan and submit them to Operations.

- After reviewing and revising these specific plans, Operations submits them to the deputy chief of the General Staff in charge of operations and then finalizes them in accord with his opinions.
- Operations formulates various logistical and technical plans and drafts relevant orders and directives.
- The General Staff passes all plans, orders, and directives to the CMC for final approval.

Once the CMC has given its approval, the General Staff will order the Operations Department to commence theater operations, if required.[32]

This formulaic process of decisionmaking in a crisis, however, has sometimes broken down. When domestic politics have become irrational, national security can be sacrificed. The power struggles between Mao and Lin Biao discussed earlier exemplify how foreign security policy can be affected, and the paragraph that follows suggests some of the dimensions of the possible problem of mixing nationalism, domestic factionalism, and security threats—a problem, one might add, that is not unique to China.

In the summer of 1971, Mao's struggles against Lin Biao caused him to mix foreign and domestic politics in an explosive fashion. In September, Mao ordered a massive military buildup in Beijing and its environs as a contingency plan to prevent a coup d'état at home and simultaneously, he thought, to neutralize Soviet military pressure. At the time, most of the top military departments were still under the influence of Lin and his associates. Through Zhou Enlai, who then did not hold any senior position in the CMC, Mao added six divisions to the Beijing Garrison Command and assigned it unprecedented powers.[33] Following Zhou's directives, the command reported only to Mao and Zhou and circumvented the CMC Administrative Group (an organ responsible for the CMC's daily affairs), General Staff, and Operations Department.[34] By this action, Mao, whose power to make such rapid adjustments was unique, had created competing power centers within the PLA and probably averted further civil strife, but the result could have been a serious rupture of command authority.

In early 2004, the CMC approved the reorganization of the Operations Department to meet the rigid requirement for waging a high-tech local war. The readjustment reportedly was based on the Chinese understanding of the operational structure of the U.S. Joint Staff under the Joint Chiefs of Staff. The reorganized department was reported to consist of ten division-level units, including an office, a military command center, and eight bureaus for operations organization, operations planning, joint operations, special operations, war environment, strategic targeting, war preparedness, and exercise management, respectively.[35] To what extent Operations' new structure will overcome a generation of bureaucratism and service rivalry will only be known in a future war.

FIGHTING THE LAST WAR: VIETNAM 1979

The rethinking that has gone into planning for that possible war stretches back to the little-known battles fought in the mountains of North Vietnam more than twenty-five years ago. By way of background to China's "last war," it is necessary to recall that Beijing's relations with Hanoi had been deteriorating since the mid-1970s. Mistreatment of ethnic Chinese in Vietnam had driven many of them to flee, and skirmishes along the Sino-Vietnamese common border had steadily increased. After Vietnam joined the Soviet-dominated Council for Mutual Economic Assistance (Comecon) and signed the Treaty of Friendship and Cooperation with the Soviet Union in November 1978, China branded the new ties a military alliance against it. The following month, the Vietnamese army invaded Kampuchea (Cambodia), ousted the pro-Beijing Pol Pot regime in Phnom Penh, and overran the country.

At the same time, Sino-American relations had been normalized. Deng Xiaoping's assessment appeared to be that China could contain Vietnam's "expansionism" in Indochina, challenge the Soviet commitment to Hanoi with impunity, and "please" his new American friends.[36] For the purposes of this study, however, our interest is how the ensuing twenty-nine-day war would test the PLA's command-and-control system in preparation for a major war.[37]

By focusing on this aspect of the war, we do not do full justice to Deng's role in the invasion or to combat operations. In every sense, the strategic thinking behind the assault was his as was the determination of the war's objectives and scale. He chose his top warriors as the field commanders, mobilized the relevant provinces to support the fighting, approved the details of the operation, and gave the order to launch the attack. This was Deng's war, and here we examine how its command and control functioned.

The record of the large-scale but limited war with Vietnam in February 1979 contains details on the planning and execution of reasonably modern theater operations. For the PLA, this "lesson teaching" offensive more than a quarter century ago is its last war and the only recent case of how it prepared for actual offensive operations. At the end of the short-lived fighting against a tenacious and battle-tested army, the Chinese probably learned more lessons than they taught Hanoi.

Let us digress before proceeding in order to highlight the Chinese sources that we use in this section. The overall view of the operations of PLA command and control in China's Vietnam War was provided by General Zhou Deli, the chief of staff of the Guangzhou Region Command leading up to the conflict.[38] As we noted in Chapter 1, however, memoirs can be self-serving and limited to one individual's recollections. We have supplemented this account with three classified documents that were circulated at the division, regimental, and company levels, respectively, within the PLA. Each of these reprints highly classified documents, including orders, summaries of battlefield lessons, and other war-related records.[39] The division-level documents were promulgated within months of the war, while the other two were circulated a year later. The memoir and these documents are the only direct evidence from PLA sources that we have uncovered, though undoubtedly much more exists.

An astonishing problem surfaced as war preparations began and has only recently been fully addressed. Though Vietnam had for several years been considered a potential adversary, no contingency plan existed in case a conflict occurred, and months would pass after the preliminary decision for war had been made before any operations plans would be formulated. According to General Zhou, the CMC only in September 1978 set out to formulate preliminary plans for a large-scale invasion of Vietnam. Early that month, the General Staff notified the Guangzhou and Kunming region commands that it would send airplanes to pick up teams chosen by them to attend a war planning meeting in the CMC's Sanzuomen headquarters. Zhou chose officers from his Operations and Intelligence departments as his team members.[40]

After the General Staff Intelligence Department had briefed them on the ongoing Sino-Vietnamese border skirmishes and their "Soviet connection," the General Staff Operations Department organized two groups from the Guangzhou and Kunming regions to discuss alternative scenarios. Their superiors in the department would use their conclusions to refine the overall and specific operations plans.

From September to December, the Guangzhou Region Command accelerated war preparations. Under orders from the CMC, it gave precedence to making all the forces battle ready. Because many division and lower-level commanders had not been in combat before, it transferred battle-tested officers from higher- to lower-level headquarters, postponed retirements, and ordered the most-capable junior officers to take command of the deployed companies and platoons. All commanders were ordered to designate and publicize a first and second successor should they fall in battle. The CMC authorized all units in the Guangzhou and Kunming regions to reassign division-level officers and for all levels simplified the procedures for rapid promotions and reassignments on the battlefield. Other directives came in a flurry and far too late to implement and test them fully before the invasion began.[41]

Equally important, most communications and intelligence collection were antiquated, a perennial problem the CMC defined in terms of weaknesses in the command structure. As stopgap measures, it sent a few technical and intelligence units to the battle zone and directed additional officers from corps down to regiments to go to the lower-level commands. The continuity of command, it held, would guarantee the upward flow of frontline intelligence, but once again little attention was given to the time and effort needed to test all of the changes in order to realize that continuity.

On November 23, presumably after the overall and specific operations plans had been approved, the General Staff directed two new teams to attend a second planning meeting. Senior officers from the air force, navy, and General Staff Operations and Intelligence departments attended this weeklong meeting. Simultaneously the CMC had ordered all the commands in the northeast, north, and northwest regions to go on full alert as a strategic move against a possible Soviet military response.[42] It summarily announced that all troops of the army, navy, and air force in the Guangxi Military District would be attached to the Guangzhou Region Command, a change from the standing practice of having only the ground forces under direct military region command.

After briefing them on the approved specific operations plans and the strategic goals for the campaign against Vietnam, the teams were told to work out their tactical operations. Well-informed sources have testified that a major objective of the campaign was to stop Vietnam's full-scale offensive against Kampuchea, and another was to align Sino-American strategic interests by striking Vietnam, Moscow's ally.[43] The two teams requested that the CMC assist the region commands in mobilizing the strike forces, supplying them, and providing them battlefield intelligence. Armed with the promise of assistance, the teams departed for Guangzhou and Kunming on December 2.

A week later, on December 9, the CMC via the Operations Department ordered the Guangzhou Region Command to write the forward deployment plan, and the Guangzhou Operations Department submitted a preliminary version to Zhou Deli within hours. After his review, Zhou penned his comments, and the department completed its draft, whose details remain secret to this day. The draft plan was then given to the region deputy commander in charge of operations, and the latter passed it to his commander for final approval. On the tenth, Zhou, with approvals in hand, ordered the plan's execution and cancelled all leaves. To maintain secrecy, his order did not mention the plan's military objectives or assignments.

On the eleventh, the region commander convened the first meeting to prepare for the coming battle. The deputy head of the General Staff Operations Department attended this meeting. The commander authorized Zhou to brief the participants on approved deployment schedules and on measures to bring all units up to strength, provide battlefield logistics, and improve communications. For combat effectiveness, Zhou permitted only 5 percent of the officers and men to remain in the rear areas. He demanded virtually complete radio silence by his soldiers during the deployment phase and allowed only urgent messages to be sent from the few centers where relatively advanced encrypted terminal equipment had been installed. In order to deceive Vietnamese and other foreign intelligence agencies, he urged the rear-area offices to run their transmitters according to their usual routines.

After the meeting, Zhou had intended to call a briefing for his department heads, but his commander cancelled it in order to prevent leaks. Instead, Zhou had to visit each department separately to convey its detailed assignments and mission objectives.

At his Guangzhou Region's Operations Department, Zhou discussed the positioning of mobile forces, the timing of their departures and arrivals on station, the technicalities of communications, and the locations of the advance command posts. He then met with his Intelligence Department and reviewed the requirements for battlefield intelligence and the schedules for the reconnaissance teams; and thereafter worked his way through the Technical, Communications, Confidential, Military Affairs, Logistics, and Military Training departments. For example, he left orders with the Technical Department officers about the forward deployment of monitoring stations; with Communications to beef up its uninterrupted field communications; and so on, department by department.

Having finished with the staff officers, General Zhou then made a command tour of the Armored Corps and the Artillery Corps. In these corps, he focused on their detailed readiness, understanding of their orders, deployment, protection from air attack, individual plans of attack, and responses to possible setbacks. On the eve of the battle Zhou seemed to be everywhere making sure his forces understood their responsibilities. By midnight on the eleventh, he had visited a dozen key departments an average of less than two hours each. One wonders how much would have been accomplished by this one overworked commander operating without a break and under great pressure. That he missed or failed to address key issues is hardly surprising.

On the twelfth, Zhou advised the command's Administrative Bureau to look after the needs of the advance command post, helped his Operations Department finalize the movement order, and submitted the order to Xu Shiyou, his region commander, for approval. Xu issued the order on the thirteenth, and the forward forces decamped and began to deploy on the fourteenth.

A week later, on the twenty-first, Xu created an advance command post near Nanning and directed the physical hardening of its command center. The post assumed control of the forward units, and selected personnel from the Guangzhou Region Command to man it. In terms of job division, Zhou designated personnel from the region's Operations Department to oversee command and control, air defense, and the post's internal garrisoning. The region's Military Affairs Department would control the post's perimeter garrisoning and communication lines, and the Administrative Bureau would be in charge of the post's living quarters, supplies, and personnel needs.

To identify the units directly under the post, Zhou gave them codenames. He called the Headquarters Group 1, the Political Department Group 2, the Logistics Department Group 3, the Artillery Corps Group 4, the Engineering Corps Group 5, the air force team Group 6, and the navy team Group 7. Zhou does not mention the action contemplated by the neighboring Kunming Region Command or any contact with that command, which would join the attack, and only Operations in Beijing seems to have had cognizance of the total offensive along the border. Fully coordinated trans-region commands would only come later.

The assault led by Guangzhou would come along three main fronts. Zhou divided the post's operations officers into a "directional team" for each front and ordered them to track and report on that front's operations once the fighting broke out.[44] On January 5, 1979, Xu, now in Nanning, held the second war planning meeting. In addition to the heads of the seven numbered groups, commanders of the corps-level forces and their chiefs of operations and training met to review once more the specific operations plans and recommend changes.[45] Xu quickly agreed to the revisions that were proposed.

Just as the advance command post was making its revisions, however, the CMC also changed the operations plan. On the twelfth, it dispatched a team of senior officers to the Sino-Vietnamese border to make a last-minute field investigation. They almost immediately dismissed the preparations as inadequate and called for additional training. The CMC thereupon postponed the offensive for about a month.[46]

On the twenty-third, Zhou, accompanied by a region operations officer, flew to Beijing for the third time to get the CMC's final instructions via the General Staff Operations Department. The next day, they returned to the advance command post with new directives and ordered the final check on all preinvasion plans. On February 12, Zhou met with officers from the Engineering, Armored, and Artillery corps to put last-minute touches on those plans and passed the changes to Xu. With his approval in hand the next day, Zhou's Operations Department dispatched the plans to the CMC and the General Staff for their chop.

At the advance command post, Xu received the final battle plan and ordered his Operations Department to communicate the D-day orders to the invasion troops and military departments unit by unit. Each organization thus could know only its own assignment and have little understanding of the overall operations. As a result, the post worked feverishly to analyze how the actions of one unit would affect those of others. The onslaught on Vietnam began in the early hours of February 17, and the flaws in command, control, and communications that should have been so obvious preceding the attack almost immediately caused problems in its execution. Sun Tzu would not have been surprised.

Although the Chinese invaders basically declared victory and marched home in the second week of March, they had paid dearly for the victory in casualties, destroyed equipment, and loss of morale. The lessons they learned dominated their planning debates for years to come: their command-and-control system had operated poorly especially across theaters and service arms; communications equipment frequently had failed in mountainous terrain; attack planes could not fly under the low clouds covering that terrain and were grounded; army units could not operate together or flexibly; and weapons and ammunition were not interchangeable. From the very beginning, PLA intelligence on the deployments and fighting capabilities of the battle-hardened Vietnamese proved wrong.

RETHINKING COMMAND AND CONTROL IN THE 1990S

These and other examples of command and control in military actions, especially as tensions with Vietnam persisted, were used for making changes over the next decades. And, confounding the pressing need for military reforms, it was in these years that modern warfare shifted from low- to high-tech. Still the lessons of Vietnam in the coming "high-tech" context following the Gulf War provided painful evidence for the high command, and long-suppressed tales of the Vietnam debacle passed from old hands to new recruits and supplemented comparable lessons extracted from selected foreign military operations. The search for solutions thus became contentious and protracted.

Ensuring Command Information

From its analysis of those lessons, Beijing concluded that the PLA was not ready to fight as an integrated force in a high-tech local war, and in 1987, its theorists stepped up research on joint operations (*lianhe zhanyi*). Their studies generally concluded that the military could engage in only primitive joint operations with low-tech weapons and equipment, and could not sustain those operations over long periods. While some officers clung to the view that such operations were only a special form of combined-arms operations (*hetong zhanyi*), the foreign high-tech wars of the 1990s forced the CMC to recognize that joint operations imposed severe requirements on the combatants and constituted a revolutionary change in warfare.[47]

The theorists came to understand that combined-arms operations only integrated the combat capabilities of various units within a single service. In these operations, the ground forces played the decisive role with the backing of the other services. Joint operations, by contrast, would prioritize the services according to perceived dangers and potential opportunities and would combine the forces of the traditional three services and conventionally armed elements of the Second Artillery. The rules of engagement are only now being rewritten and appear to stress fully joint military actions. Ground forces would no longer automatically enjoy the dominant position, but instead all services would have equivalent status in the command-and-control chain.[48]

As now conceived, the requirements for these operations place a special burden on command and control and focus on the use of mobile forces in fluid and complicated environments. Creating a winning system, PLA commanders hold, depends on sophisticated electronic reconnaissance, rapid and coordinated decisionmaking, and, most essential, high-capacity communications.[49] Achieving dominance in "command confrontation" (*zhihui duikang*) is the goal.[50]

The key to command confrontation is said to depend on developing automated command-and-control networks. In 1977, the CMC tasked Institute 28, Institute 63, and the College of Computation and Command Automation—all located in Nanjing—and other research bodies to quickly develop and test such networks.[51] In the early 1980s, it approved the first prototype for its general departments, the services, and region commands. These research organs steadily improved the prototype and eventually built a computer-aided network capable of securely transmitting documents, electronic messaging, graphic processing, and data retrieval.[52] In 1987, the second-generation network utilized advanced technologies for transmitting and authenticating orders, intelligence data sharing, friend-or-foe identification, anti-jamming, and information security management.[53]

Although the CMC had long identified the lack of advanced electronic equipment as the central problem, changes in command and control moved with agonizing slowness.[54] Only after the dramatic lessons of the 1991 Gulf War were driven home did electronic warfare finally receive the commission's highest priority.[55] More than fifteen years had passed since the 1977 network decision.

By 1993, the new automatic network, which contained some foreign technology, had been adopted by most corps-echelon units. By installing automated equipment in all headquarters of the group armies (ground forces), air corps, naval bases, and missile launch bases, the CMC linked those head-quarters and its combat forces.

Nevertheless, problems continued to plague the system. In the summer of 1995, when three U.S. E-6 aircraft flew close to China's airspace, PLA radars and telecommunications in the relevant commands failed or were seriously interrupted. The CMC generalized this failure and concluded that information capabilities could determine victory or defeat in a future war.[56] Once again, the order went out to modernize the electronic command and control system.

After the installation of the follow-on network, the CMC directed all region commands to conduct war games for equipment evaluation and troop training. In November 1999, the first of these exercises took place in the Beijing Region Command.[57] These and subsequent exercises revealed a number of troubling deficiencies: incompatible and unstable communications, unreliable friend-or-foe identification, poorly integrated foreign equipment, low-quality early-warning and command and control, questionable survivability, and poor control of strategic weapons. The weak links critical to all these deficiencies were low-quality and inadequately connected sensors.[58]

In many cases, these deficiencies stayed long hidden because of the failure to hold full-scale exercises that would test readiness and expose problems. Throughout the first half of the 1990s, for example, even the best group armies lacked funds and fuel even for modest exercises. Of these, the Thirty-eighth and Thirty-ninth group armies had not conducted a single combined-arms exercise above battalion level for years.[59]

The high command understood that a technology fix would be slow in coming and, in any case, was only part of a larger problem. For the near term, the PLA would have to stress innovative concepts to modify its command-and-control procedures. It drew the new concepts from foreign ideas and its own memory banks and termed the resulting product "software." In developing this software, military planners concentrated on each imagined enemy's weaknesses (more than its threats) and on ways to cripple its command and control. They intended to attack its command centers and electronic counter-measures aircraft. Comparable stress was placed on protecting their own command centers, and they began exploring the use of fake electronic equipment, camouflaged and mobile units, and radio and electronic deception.[60] The initial "software" studies highlighted a gap between the proposed tactics and the capabilities of the PLA's command organizations. Although the

CMC actively examined ways to improve training, weapons, and exercises, it reshaped those organizations only in piecemeal fashion.[61] Bureaucratic inertia persisted, but, as we shall see in our final chapter, sufficient progress was made over the next years to hold a massive proof-of-concept military exercise in 2001.

In May 2001, the CMC issued another order calling on all commands to speed up the replacement of their command-and-control networks.[62] The Guangzhou Region Command was one of the quickest to respond and built what was considered the best such network connecting to all regiments. Nevertheless, even that network had limited functionality and operated poorly in complex and dynamic environments. PLA commanders complained about its limited value in wartime.[63] Chinese sources cited U.S. publications that state the PLA had still not deployed true C^4I (command, control, communications, computers, and intelligence) systems for joint operations.[64]

Simplifying Organizations and Chain of Command

Gradually, studies and slogans yielded to more meaningful organizational reforms. The CMC decided first to reorganize the most senior headquarters. It formed the General Armament Department in 1998 with the merger of the Commission of Science, Technology, and Industry for National Defense and the General Staff Equipment Department. Its goal was to reduce the contradictions between weapons R&D and procurement priorities. Moreover, many specialists have criticized the current (as of January 2005) setup of the General Staff's high-tech departments and are debating alternatives and possible ways to overcome strong resistance to change. One favored alternative would affect the Radar and Electronic Countermeasures and Communications departments, which have overlapping functions. An information warfare attack would target them both, and their responses would have to be more closely coordinated. Once a single department that later was split, they now may be remerged.

For the next command level down, the CMC faced far more complex problems as it considered how to restructure the seven region commands and corps-level forces. These commands were already responsible for peacetime military buildup and the direction of wartime theater operations, but they were only in charge of the ground forces and provided them communications, intelligence, logistics, and training. Considered independent, the air force, navy, and Second Artillery units in any region's "territory" ran their own manning, training, and supply operations. Only the CMC and General Staff could order the deployment and employment of these units and assign them to a theater joint command, but these units were the channels through which the region commands could control the air squadrons, conventionally armed missile battalions, and naval flotillas in their territory.[65]

The region commands located along the coast could not obtain intelligence from navy and air force units in their areas. The air force and navy would receive intelligence reports through their own channels and could choose whether to transmit the reports to the region commands. This cumbersome process undermined regional air defense even though the air force was responsible for defending all strategic points in the region. The CMC did not specify the authority of the air force in the command chain or designate how the air defense units of the ground forces, navy, Second Artillery, and militia should work together.

In peacetime, the four services could only cooperate through irregular contacts among senior officers or during joint exercises held every few years. In wartime, the CMC would form ad hoc theater joint commands to attain a workable coordination, again as was shown to be defective in the Vietnam case. The existing regulations did not clearly assign command responsibility in advance of crises. Limiting the power of the region commander to control of the ground forces, we believe, reinforced the center's authority and prevented "warlordism." Beijing was limiting the power of the region commanders in order to assure its dominance of the military, but these limits came at a high cost.

In 1998, the CMC addressed this cost and decided to reform the region command structure. It established theater joint commands for joint exercises whereby the General Staff and service headquarters would now dispatch flag officers to those commands. Under the reorganized structure, which concentrated on the peacetime military, these commands also would receive staff officers from the General Staff Operations Department, the local air and naval commands, and the conventionally armed units of the Second Artillery. Joining each command's operations department, these officers would have a significant voice in drafting specific operations plans and monitoring their implementation. The avowed goal of the 1998 decision was to strengthen coordination among the services.[66]

The following year, the CMC issued the "PLA Outline of Joint Operations," which would give a theater joint command operational control over all assigned and attached field units in the region. Its focus was future crises and conflicts. As a contingency plan for a mounting crisis, the command would be required to set up the main, alternate (or mobile), and rear command posts, and in case of need, an advance command post, all of which were introduced earlier. The outline reduced the bureaucratic powers of the region command's four departments (headquarters, political, logistics, and armament) by replacing them in wartime with five functional "centers" and teams. Each main command post would have centers for command, intelligence, communications, electronic countermeasures, and fire-control coordination. The command center would be constituted as the "core" and would run the other four centers. As planned in the outline, staff officers from relevant services would join these centers.[67] In addition to the five centers, several teams would oversee battlefield liaison, command automation, equipment maintenance, weather forecasting, mapping, political work, logistics, international law consulting, and public relations.[68]

Additional regulations also redefined the responsibilities and powers of the commanders of all military units under normal conditions. They gave each unit commander full authority over all departments and assigned forces in his area of jurisdiction. The regulations downgraded the role of the Party committee but upgraded that of the chiefs of staff at all levels. As the power of political departments is decreased, the clout of the professional line officers is intended to grow. Under the commander, the chief of staff administers the daily affairs of the headquarters and resolves conflicts between the headquarters and other departments. The chief of staff along with the commander and political commissar signs off on all reports and cables, but the chief of staff alone determines the procedures for their transmittal.[69]

Although the focus of the grand reorganization has fallen on the central and region commands, the CMC also extended the new measures to group armies or corps and below. It sought to simplify vertical communications and bolster horizontal ties in the command chain. No single command was initially authorized to supervise more than eight combat units, but like other details in the reorganization, experimentation and flexibility were the rule.[70]

For decades, group armies or their predecessors were the backbone of the ground forces with the corps-division-regiment-battalion hierarchy considered fixed, almost sacred. As the implementation of the stipulated changes has gained momentum, the CMC has introduced a new corps-brigade-battalion organization into a few group armies. Earlier, the brigade principally existed only in the strategic rocket forces and such technical arms as the Artillery, Engineering, and Armored corps. By replacing the divisions and regiments with brigades, the PLA has streamlined communications in joint operations and the command of group armies over their assigned forces. The battalions will operate as an independent cadre or building block to train and control their subordinate companies and will replace the regiment in maximizing fire and technical support.[71] The CMC also has moved combat troops from the technical arms to group armies for buttressing the first-line forces.[72] After it completes its multiyear review of this trial reorganization, the CMC reportedly intends to introduce this structure into such elite units as the Thirty-eighth and Thirty-ninth group armies.

Another change is designed to enhance the survivability of the communications networks and command posts. Our review of Beijing's decision to fight Vietnam identified the use of main and advance command posts, which, taken alone, are deemed vulnerable to a decapitation strike and inadequate for waging a high-tech local war. The CMC has ordered region commands and each of the corps-level organs to establish and disperse their main, alternate, rear, and advance command posts. Most main command posts will now contain at least 40 percent of the headquarters officers and will be headed by the commander. Alternate command posts, headed by a deputy commander, will have 20 percent of the officers and will take over responsibility from the main command post should the latter be destroyed or neutralized. The advance command post will have 10–20 percent of the officers and will also be led by a deputy commander; and the rear command post, headed by a third deputy commander, will provide logistical and technical backup.[73]

The CMC permits considerable flexibility in the composition and mission assignments of each command post in order to take into account local conditions and has introduced other modifications to promote survivability and effectiveness. Now battlefield requirements outweigh hallowed past practices in restructuring command and control from top to bottom. For example, among the many other organizational changes that will affect but do not directly relate to command and control is the proposed merger of the Logistics and Armament departments during crises or conflicts.

In 2003, the CMC further improved the communications for joint operations. It disbanded five air corps headquarters and nine corps-level naval bases and removed them from the chain of command.[74] For the PLA Air

Force, the CMC orders now would pass to a region command, the region's air branch, and combat air divisions, though in emergencies the CMC could issue orders directly to the divisions. Similarly for the navy, the CMC's orders would go to the coastal region commands, then to the fleets and flotillas, but again the CMC could bypass the regions and fleets to give orders straight to the flotillas.[75] As we shall discuss in the next chapter, moreover, the CMC can bypass the Second Artillery headquarters to issue operational orders to any missile launch brigade. Taking lessons from U.S. practice, the PLA continues to devise and test innovations in its command system.

RECOGNIZING THE SHORTCOMINGS AND ASSESSING THE PROGRESS

For whatever reason and despite some wrenching progress, the CMC directives have not yet energized the services to move quickly or resolutely, and one must wonder how much can truly be achieved in the future. Reorganizing command and control and future military operations to meet satisfactorily the requirements for conducting a high-tech local war remains a distant goal.[76] Only the pressing problem of Taiwan, which we address in the last chapter, may finally cause the PLA to fully embrace reform. Joint exercises in recent years, PLA planners acknowledge, have exposed "the low efficiency in command and control and the loose combination of the services."[77] These deficiencies can be summarized under six headings.

1. Duplicative command responsibilities.

Under the Mao-era organization formed to limit factionalism and ensure domestic stability, military departments exercised overlapping and often conflicting command and control. Elements of that organization still exist. Both Beijing and the region commands continue to conduct separate but parallel control over the military region units. The obsolescent checks and balances produced by this system have impeded command responsiveness and departmental initiative. Protected by culture and habit, that system still remains virtually impervious to radical changes.

2. Low quality of commanders.

The marginal fitness of PLA commanders continues to frustrate fundamental improvements in joint operations. Most senior officers are considered unqualified to fight a high-tech war. In the CMC's own authorized assessment, for example, only three of thirty-six corps-level officers from one region's five group armies were university graduates, and none of the region division commanders held a college degree.[78] All field commanders come from the ground forces, and most senior staff officers at the four general departments in Beijing and the seven region commands have never held assignments in services other than their own, again mostly the ground forces.[79] The careers of most corps-level commanders have been limited to a single region, peacetime duty, and single-service exercises. Few know how to write comprehensive reports for their senior commanders.[80] The situation is particularly acute for officers in the region and central-level operations departments, and few understand even the basic technologies required in joint operations. Conversely, the technical officers in the Intelligence, Technical (signals monitoring), Radar and Electronic Countermeasures, and Communications departments know little about operations. As a corrective, the CMC has highlighted the need to identify and promote commanding officers who understand the operational concepts of other services. In response, the National Defense University and other top military educational facilities have organized one-year advanced classes for training these staff officers, but the impact of the courses has yet to be widely felt.[81]

3. Bloated headquarters.

The overstaffing of headquarters units has inhibited well-organized command and control. More than three hundred personnel work at the "four departments" of a division, and comparable departments in a region command or group army are much larger. Some one hundred and twenty personnel are typically assigned to a division's main command post in peacetime but then reduced to about eighty during a conflict. An over-staffed structure undermines efficient operations and even jeopardizes a post's survivability. As a CMC leader put it, "[In a war,] it is not easy even to evacuate [headquarters] personnel, let alone exercise command and control."[82]

4. Uncoordinated regional organization and force structure.

When a conflict erupts, a theater joint command can directly issue orders to the region headquarters of the air force, navy, and Second Artillery conventional forces, but before then a region command cannot directly control those same services under its nominal authority. Even for the ground forces, the joint command can only control the subordinate group armies or in a few cases division-level units.[83]

It was not until the mid-1990s that regulations and communications were put in place to coordinate infantry regiments and armored and artillery battalions. They enabled PLA ground forces to perform combined-arms operations. The same lack of coordination plagued the air and ground forces, and only in the late 1990s were qualified teams of ground-air fire controllers created to solve the problem. The air force sent forward controllers to each joint command and most divisions (but not to battalions) to support close air-ground strikes.[84] Engineers are still developing interoperative communications for these missions, but serious training in this regard is years away.

5. Obsolete command-and-control technologies.

In our discussion of automated command-and-control networks above, we noted several outstanding deficiencies, and these remain the weakest links. In addition, recent PLA sources blame the air force for its inadequate use of China's satellite reconnaissance and surveillance systems, and accuse the other services of lagging ever farther behind.[85]

A special problem relates to the failure of the army to introduce the newest technologies and techniques to fight at night and in highly mobile situations. Where the People's War tradition lauded the PLA's ability to fight after dark or in fluid environments, China's potential adversaries now have the advantage in these operations. The military urgently needs fully automated and interoperable command and control within and among the services. Few space-borne and airborne sensors exist, computerized intelligence information is just coming on line, and all foreign-made communication equipment is considered suspect. In the final analysis, many PLA officers believe the changes in this area are coming far too slowly and blame the failures on resilient bureaucratic impediments.[86]

6. Questionable survivability.

Most PLA specialists fear that a dedicated information warfare attack would paralyze their communication networks.[87] They consider this a formidable challenge, and their concern could only have grown after U.S. operations against the Taliban in Afghanistan and the Iraqi army. Only a few PLA command centers and early-warning radars are located in hardened silos. Most Taiwanese airfields are 200 km from the mainland, and Taiwanese fighter-bombers could enter PRC airspace in less than fifteen minutes. PLA commanders worry most that when fighting a technologically advanced adversary, their command centers and radars would be primary targets, and few would survive.[88] Without them, the ability to wage a sustained high-tech local war would vanish.

The durability of the six deficiencies after a decade of dedicated efforts to remove them causes us to ask why the disparity between plan and reality has persisted and in some cases even widened. In addition to the ever-targeted bureaucratic impediments, three reasons, we believe, explain much of the gap. First, Deng Xiaoping made military modernization a distant objective, even though he acknowledged that the command system was "very backward."[89] With economic development the dominant goal, military budgets fell, forces were slashed, and weapons programs were delayed.

The second reason goes beyond the lack of funds or technical sophistication. In a word, that reason is corruption. During the years when the military engaged in business, the PLA's culture of sacrifice and devotion to duty waned, and the culture of making money led many in the PLA to misappropriate substantial funds for private use. Even the most critical projects succumbed to greed, and with this in mind one can better understand the Politburo's edict in 1998 to end military businesses and to launch a national campaign against corruption as the sine qua non for genuine change.

The third reason relates to the PLA's obsession with obsolete doctrines. Long isolated from foreign military debates and advances, the Chinese military resisted conceptual and doctrinal change, and Mao's outmoded dogmas endured. Only in the past decade has his influence eroded, allowing senior generals such as Liu Huaqing to acknowledge that the Americans "have averaged [new] developments in their operational doctrines every seven or eight years and have partially revised their regulations almost every year." China, he said, must now keep pace.[90]

If nothing else, the Chinese recognize clearly the wide gap between their weaponry and that of their potential adversaries, particularly the United States. Great controversy exists concerning Beijing's "real" military budget, but China commands far fewer resources than, say, Japan or the United States and has dedicated by far the largest part of its national spending to non-weapons-related needs, including the need to modernize and globalize its high-technology industrial base. What the CMC has done is to seek out a small number of highly effective weapons and to concentrate its limited financial and technical resources on their acquisition. These weapons cannot truly be called a deterrent because so little is known of them. If the deterrence fails, however, they theoretically would be used to inflict massive damage on an adversary.

The Chinese call these weapons *sashoujian*—literally "an unexpected thrust with a mace" or "trump cards"—and date the origin of the term to the late Sui dynasty, when two generals, Luo Cheng and Qin Qiong, fought using their best martial arts. Qin finally won the battle by throwing his mace (*jian*) against Luo at an unexpected moment. Though their details are kept secret, we can conjecture that sashoujian technologies or tactics may actually provide for genuine innovation or that they may become another elusive "magic" bullet in the PLA's arsenal. Either way, they suggest a note of desperation in Chinese military development. In Chapter 6, we shall return to the meaning of these "trump cards" for the Second Artillery.

We do know that by the early 1990s, the Politburo and CMC had opened a Sashoujian Bangongshi or Trump Card Office with Jiang Zemin as its director. The unit was renamed the High- and New-Technology Weapons Office (Gao Xin Jishu Wuqi Bangongshi) sometime after early 2002, and General Cao Gangchuan, then head of the General Armament Department and later the defense minister, became its first director. The "trump cards" reportedly included next-generation cruise and ballistic missiles, satellites, electronic countermeasures equipment, air defense weapons, and new-generation submarines.[91]

In 2003, Major General Dai Qingmin, the head of the General Staff Radar and Electronic Countermeasures Department, identified achieving information supremacy as the trump card most needed for genuine progress in "the establishment of information warfare command and control arrangements."[92] The Chinese acknowledge their deficiencies in command, control, communications, computers, and intelligence (C^{4}I), and the renaming of the Sashoujian Bangongshi undoubtedly reflects the goal of modernizing both weapons and C^{4}I. They reportedly link that goal of "seizing information control" to the ambitious national 863 and 973 programs' applied and basic research on advanced information technologies.[93]

To assess the current readiness of command and control and the overall capability of its forces, the CMC has scheduled a series of large-scale joint exercises, and we shall examine the biggest and most publicized of these, a four-month exercise started in mid-May 2001, in the final chapter. After completing such exercises, General Staff officers reevaluate their command-and-control capabilities and do so in the first instance by comparing them to those of the United States, and in that comparison the PLA comes off badly. Chinese strategists explain the disparity by pointing to the PLA's fewer battle engagements, its less-advanced equipment and intelligence means, and the Maoist legacy, and in doing so find it hard to return to the military fundamentals set forth by Sun Tzu so long ago.[94]

When comparing their army's C⁴I functions to those of their American counterparts, these military officers concentrate on the supposed environments determining the chief differences. Still mired in the cultural constraints with which we began the book, they routinely return to the purported differences in operational arts, operational concepts, force structure, and types of command. We should note that the term "operational arts" (*zhanyi fa*) refers to the most general approaches to combat, while "operational concepts" (*zhanyi gainian*) focuses on battlefield tactics, terms that PLA strategists are trying to root in traditional Chinese military concepts. PLA strategists hold that the salient differences between the U.S. and Chinese military concepts are these:

- Operational arts: America's military strategies are more adaptive and specific than China's. U.S. forces in battle stress offensive actions and trials of strength, while the PLA emphasizes flexible and innovative tactics, mixing defense and offense, to compensate for equipment deficiencies. Compared to the U.S. army, the PLA depends more on massed close-contact assaults designed to lure the enemy into complicated "jigsaw" warfare that can neutralize the enemy's technical superiority.
- Operational concepts: U.S. forces typically strive to deny an enemy the initiative by unremitting bombardment of its strategic strong points. The PLA, by contrast, usually attacks an enemy's weakest forces and avoids battles with the strongest ones.
- Force structure: The U.S. military normally creates flexible organizations that incorporate specific components depending on each campaign's requirements. Because it still lacks fully compatible combat units, the PLA in most cases cannot yet adopt a campaign-specific force structure and instead depends on a relatively fixed one for different engagements.

- Types of command: Consistent with its flexible approach, the American type of command is more decentralized than that of the PLA. The U.S. high command tends to focus more on the general mission and less, when compared to the Chinese, on battlefield tactics. The PLA relies less on lower-level initiative and interservice coordination and more on centralized command.

PLA leaders have studied the U.S.-run actions during and since the Gulf War of 1991, and know that they would receive heavy losses in any comparable conflict involving the PLA. They have concluded that should such a battle be inevitable, to succeed they must make thoroughgoing and lasting changes. The challenge, of course, is to incorporate new concepts and lessons learned into PLA battle planning and its modernizing command and control. The right mix of technologies and organization would come next, all Herculean tasks for the military and government in any nation.

Yet, few theater commanders have ever led troops in wartime, and one can wonder how this inexperience would affect their readiness. Senior PLA strategists, however, play down the decisive role of battlefield knowledge and cite the case of the founder of the modern Prussian army, Helmuth Karl Bernhard von Moltke. He and his colleagues had never exercised command in wartime, and their troops had not fought in decades. Nevertheless, they prevailed when war came because of the introduction of novel concepts and rigorous training.[95] The PLA high command also has concluded that the lack of combat exposure was not a deciding factor in the Sino-Vietnamese border war.[96] These examples encourage the Chinese to believe that they, too, will emerge victorious should war occur.

Decisiveness and endurance depend in the final analysis on effective and survivable command and the willingness of the Chinese people to pay the high price of modern warfare. The military high command appears to hold that the Chinese people will accept the costs of a prolonged war if they believe in the justness of the cause. For them, maintaining China's sovereignty over Taiwan represents such a cause, and that in turn helps increase the PLA's influence and budgets, especially in the military regions opposite the island.

The building of a modern military is an iterative process for any state, and for China the process is clearly in medias res. The most progressive generals now emphasize that achieving a consensus on strategic concepts must precede the selection of advanced hardware. Nonetheless, the revolution in foreign military hardware makes a mockery of the PLA's slow-motion pursuit of revolutionary military thinking, and its elite has become locked in a fruitless debate about ends and means.[97] No military thinker has yet emerged to move this debate to more productive ground.

Any more fundamental changes, should they be made, will require equally revolutionary political decisions. For example, the political departments throughout the military weaken the authority and smooth operation of command. These departments that once helped guarantee Party rule and internal stability have become an anachronism in modern warfare especially as the current reforms are raising the profile of the operational commanders. The CMC might, as a temporary expedient, retain the General Political Department but restructure the political departments of the regions and combat forces. Another proposal is for the CMC to rename these departments as teams or centers for political work.

Should such major restructuring occur, the entire underpinning of the military-political system must be transformed and that in turn depends on the future of the overall political reform. This broader reform will determine the so-called "major climate" (*da qihou*) within which to pursue a more thoroughgoing military reform. Until then, the upgrading of technologies and procedures is relegated to the "minor climate" (*xiao qihou*) and at best constitutes partial measures. Changing the major climate may come only when a new generation of leaders has consolidated its power.

Figure 1 Mao Zedong with senior Politburo members in 1950s (*from left*: Zhu De, Zhou Enlai, Chen Yun, Liu Shaoqi, Mao, and Deng Xiaoping)

Figure 2   Mao with senior leaders in 1960 (*from left*: Nie Rongzhen, Lin Biao, He Long, Zhou Enlai, Luo Ruiqing, Peng Zhen, Mao, Deng Xiaoping)

Figure 3 Soviet frontier troops attacking Zhenbao Island, March 2, 1969

Figure 4 Soviet tanks on frozen Ussuri River west of Zhenbao Island, March 15, 1969

Figure 5 A typical 1969 poster calling for preparations to meet Soviet invasion

Figure 6 A PLA armored force entering Vietnam, February 1979

Figure 7   A PLA tank detachment crossing a Vietnamese river, February 1979

Figure 8   Deng Xiaoping viewing a large north China exercise, September 1981

Figure 9   Jiang Zemin and Deng Xiaoping in 1989

Figure 10   Jiang Zemin and Hu Jintao at the Sixteenth Party Congress, November 2002

Figure 11   Six Politburo Standing Committee members (*from left*: Li Changchun, Jia Qinglin, Wu Bangguo, Wen Jiabao, Zeng Qinghong, Luo Gan) viewing shuttle launch

Figure 12   CMC Chairman Hu Jintao (*center*) with full CMC membership

Figure 13 Hu Jintao reviewing troops in Macao, December 2004

Figure 14 PLA command center during a large joint exercise

Figure 15　A mobile command post in field operations

Figure 16　Air force, navy, and army officers conducting joint logistical field exercise

Figure 17 Mobile communications unit in frontline operations

Figure 18 A Second Artillery communications regiment in mobile exercise

Figure 19   A DF-3A missile launch unit pledging political allegiance

Figure 20   A Second
Artillery launch battalion
fueling a DF-3A missile

Figure 21   A DF-3A missile erecting on TEL

Figure 22   A Second Artillery unit launching a DF-15 surface-to-surface missile

Figure 23   Possible maneuverable warhead and decoy-dispensing bus

Figure 24   Air combat unit testing surface-to-air missile

Figure 25 Surface-to-air missile unit in mobile exercise

Figure 26 An Su-27 squadron preparing for takeoff

Figure 27   B-6 bomber squadron crews scrambling

Figure 28   IL-78M tanker refueling Su-27s

Figure 29 A-50 AWACS outfitted with a new PRC-designed fixed active phased-array radar

Figure 30 Cruise missile fuselage in a stress-test rig

Figure 31   Sovremenniy guided missile destroyers of the East China Sea Fleet

Figure 32   Antiship missile being fired from 052-class missile destroyer *Harbin*

Figure 33   Sailors boarding a 035-class (Ming) attack submarine

Figure 34   039-class (Song) attack submarine

Figure 35　T-59 medium tanks in combined-service exercise

Figure 36　Fishing craft used to transport T-63A amphibious tanks in cross-Strait exercise

Figure 37 Amphibious tanks in Dongshan exercise, July 2004

Figure 38   An amphibious assault operation in Dongshan exercise

Figure 39   Troops storming beach in annual Dongshan exercise

Figure 40   Helicopter landing operations in Dongshan exercise

PART THREE

Modernizing the Main Arsenal

Redefining the Strategic Rocket Forces

Building on our discussion of national decisionmaking and military command and control, this chapter illuminates the history and contemporary evolution of China's strategic rocket forces, the Second Artillery. Long the primary strategic deterrent instrument of the Chinese military, these forces in the 1990s began to acquire new missions as Beijing concluded that Taipei's alleged moves toward independence and potential responses by the United States in a conflict over Taiwan constituted the greatest security threats. Those missions required more robust command, control, communications, and intelligence, and the retrofitting of some short- and medium-range missiles with conventional warheads.[1]

Today's missions are a far cry from those first envisioned by Beijing's leaders in the 1960s, though now as then their dream of great-power status rested on the military's acquisition of long-range missiles armed with nuclear warheads and on a modern economy. The organization, arsenal, and strategies for carrying out these missions thus have a forty-year tradition, a legacy that shapes the outlook, commitment, and competence of the Second Artillery's current generation of commanders. In examining that legacy as it affects the present-day strategic missile forces, we attempt to answer two principal questions. How have the politics and changing national priorities over the past four decades affected the fighting capacity of China's premier strategic deterrent force? Does the Second Artillery have the resources and support infrastructure to meet the requirements of the high command's ever evolving and more demanding grand strategy?

The brief review of the Second Artillery's history with which we begin shows how much the domestic political turmoil during the Cultural Revolution (1966–76) overwhelmed and perverted its purposes in the formative years. The corrosiveness of Maoist politics, moreover, coincided with the mounting challenges of Soviet and American satellite reconnaissance and more lethal long-range weapons. The PLA leadership had first to overcome outmoded thinking as well as the vulnerability of its strategic retaliatory forces and then to meet the changing requirements for nuclear deterrence and, more recently, for fighting a high-tech local conflict. This chapter examines how far China has come in achieving those goals.

ORGANIZING THE STRATEGIC ROCKET FORCES

On June 6, 1966, the Central Military Commission established the Second Artillery as an independent arm and assigned it to oversee and operate all ground-based strategic missiles.[2] "Independent" meant that these weapons, coming directly under the CMC's centralized control, did not fall under the jurisdiction of the army, navy, or air force. Only a small number of departments of the General Staff (such as the Operations Department) were given access to the Second Artillery or were in its chain of command.

Formative Years

By 1966, the plans for creating the Second Artillery were already well advanced. In 1957, the CMC had authorized its Artillery Corps to establish the 802nd Battalion and equip it with Soviet short-range missiles. By 1961, the Artillery Corps had organized four additional missile battalions and stationed them in the Shenyang, Beijing, and Ji'nan military regions. Three years later, the CMC reinforced the five original launch battalions and expanded them into five regiments.

On June 1, 1965, Premier Zhou Enlai assigned General Zhang Aiping, deputy chief of the General Staff and deputy director of the Defense Science and Technology Commission, to set up the headquarters for these strategic missile units, and on July 1 a year later, Zhou named them the Second Artillery (*Dier Paobing*) and presided over its formal inauguration. (Technically, the term Second Artillery *Corps* is a misnomer, though we will use it here because of its wide currency.) Zhou cobbled together the Second Artillery command by merging the headquarters of the Public Security Army and a department of the Artillery Corps in charge of strategic missiles.[3]

Mao Zedong ordered Deng Xiaoping, the CCP general secretary, to cooperate with Zhou in crafting the Second Artillery organizations.[4] In 1966, just as the first-generation 1,050 km DF-2s were being deployed, the strategic missile commanders were operating two bases, five launch regiments, five engineering regiments, and related educational and research groups.

The introduction of security army soldiers into the missile headquarters reflected the PLA's passion for secrecy and discipline that has continued to this day. For example, in its first decades, the strategic missile command was not allowed to recruit from the coastal areas. After an officer had reported to his assigned command billet, he had access only to the information and contacts indispensable to his own job. Each unit and its subordinate parts were compartmentalized. Without special approval, officers and men of one component were prohibited from visiting others or making unauthorized inquiries of them. On holidays, an officer could not enter his own office unless escorted by at least one other colleague.[5]

In this insulated and protected world, superior officers would often warn their subordinates not to mention their assignment to their family members. As an example, Xiang Shouzhi, twice commander of the Second Artillery, reportedly never revealed his assignment to his wife, who learned of it only from Red Guard posters attacking him. Wives visiting their soldier husbands were only permitted to stay in distant guesthouses and were cautioned never to disclose the guesthouse locations. These security measures followed the missile soldiers for the rest of their lives. Upon retirement, they had to return to their hometowns in the interior, and local governments could not reassign them to coastal areas.

In the initial years, the small number of missile units mostly adopted the army's hierarchical structure, although, unlike the ground troops, their original division-level organizations were called "bases" (*jidi*), and the base commanders reported directly to the Second Artillery headquarters in Beijing. While *jidi* is used internally, the more ambiguous term *budui* (unit) is more commonly found in unclassified media. Each base in turn contained two or three launch regiments and roughly the same number of engineering regiments. Five years after the initial deployment of the DF-2s in September 1966 and at the time of mounting tensions with the Soviet Union, the Second Artillery acquired the longer-range (2,650 km) DF-3s. By 1972, it ran six launch bases, fourteen launch regiments, and sixteen engineering regiments, with more than 115,000 officers and soldiers, or 1.9 percent of the total PLA manpower.[6] Yet, behind these impressive numbers on paper lay a force in disarray.

Power Struggle

Right after the formal launching of the Second Artillery in June 1966, the chaos of the Cultural Revolution engulfed the nation and the Second Artillery. Politics eclipsed military preparedness. R&D and the manufacturing of missile components and warheads became mired in the political swamp produced by rampaging radicals, and few weapons were arriving at the distant bases. According to Chinese sources, as of 1973, ten of the fourteen launch regiments were not equipped with missiles, and some of them had no weapons at all. Even the four "missile-equipped" regiments fielded incomplete or substandard systems.[7]

The debilitating power struggle plagued the Second Artillery throughout its first decade, and the timing of the "merger decision" creating the corps headquarters could not have been worse. By integrating soldiers of the Public Security Army and the Artillery Corps, the CMC had forced together two hostile factions just before Mao's call for rebellion and "bombarding the headquarters" magnified the internecine warfare.[8]

The rise and fall of Xiang Shouzhi, the first commander of the Second Artillery, illustrates the damage inflicted by the resulting dissension on the missile command. In its first year, the missile headquarters had no designated commander at all, and the CMC only formally appointed Xiang to that post on July 4, 1967. It took him some forty-three days to disengage from his post as deputy commander of the Artillery Corps and to report to his new assignment. By that time, however, the power struggle was escalating, and Lin Biao, Mao's chief lieutenant who then ran the CMC's daily affairs, labeled Xiang an enemy and plotted to disgrace him. Lin told his wife to phone Li Tianhuan, the political commissar of the Second Artillery, and to tell him, "Xiang Shouzhi is not our man. He came to the Second Artillery in order to gobble up your forces [that is, Li's supporters]. You should report to us. Chief Lin will append a note to his transmittal letter on your report to dismiss him from office."[9] Lin trusted only known veterans from his own revolution-era Fourth Field Army, while Xiang had been a division commander in the Second Field Army, once headed by Lin's rivals Marshal Liu Bocheng and Deng Xiaoping.

At the time of the July 1966 merger, Li Tianhuan and his closest associates had been transferred from the Public Security Army, and they suspected that Xiang would usurp the power they had surreptitiously accumulated during the corps' year without a commander. The message from Lin carried the news they had hoped for and the mandate to move against the hapless Xiang, who never quite knew what hit him. Xiang and his wife were detained, and the radicals at the Second Artillery headquarters accused him of "having betrayed China and defected to the Soviet Union." In the missile crisis of October 1969, Xiang and other senior figures were forced to leave Beijing. Soldiers took Xiang under guard to a military farm, where he spent the next three years raising pigs. After Lin Biao's death in 1971, Xiang's confinement was eased, but he was not allowed to rejoin his wife and children until 1972.

In the days leading up to his death, Lin allegedly had plotted to assassinate Mao, and the chairman retaliated with a ruthless purge of Lin's followers. This purge in turn prompted yet another round of factional strife within the Second Artillery that consumed its leaders for almost three more years, and only in early 1974 did the CMC order the Party leaders in the corps to compromise and end their bitter feuding. Backed by their patrons in the center, however, the two major factions refused reconciliation, and negotiations for a truce went on intermittently "without resolution" for another nine months. In November, an exasperated Marshal Ye Jianying, who had taken charge of the CMC's daily affairs, asked Xiang to return to head the Second Artillery. Having spent years tending pigs because of trumped-up charges, Xiang had little desire for command and sat on the proffered appointment for four months. Finally, on March 26, 1975, he yielded to Ye's overtures, thus making Xiang the only person to serve twice as commander of the strategic rocket forces.

As one of his first acts, Xiang transferred forty-eight technical officers from the Artillery Corps—his former unit—to the Second Artillery and sought to use their new assignments as a catalyst to produce a more professional missile force. Later, he dismissed the unfounded charges leveled by the radicals against many of his former comrades and announced their immediate "rehabilitation." The radicals in turn slandered Xiang's actions as a plot to "form his own faction," an accusation that coincided with Ye Jianying, Xiang's patron, being forced temporarily from his powerful position on the CMC.

Once again, radicals in the CMC meetings attacked Xiang, who responded by initiating private talks with Wang Hongwen, a Party leader and close ally of Mao's wife. After Mao's death and the purge of Wang and other members of the "Gang of Four" in 1976, Xiang's "secret" talks with Wang were interpreted as an effort to ingratiate himself with the gang. In 1977, the ever-suspicious CMC transferred Xiang to be deputy commander of the Nanjing Military Region. Three years later, when Ye Jianying, once more back at the CMC, asked him to return to the corps, the embittered Xiang said he would rather stay in Nanjing, and perhaps even the pigs looked more appealing at that moment.

Thus, throughout its first decade, the Second Artillery struggled in near chaos to establish its professional military credentials and become a viable strategic force. Its senior officers wasted these years mostly jockeying for survival or launching political attacks on their opponents, real or imagined. Even as Mao fretted about an "inevitable" war with the Soviet Union and pressed the military to build a powerful strategic arsenal, his policies fostered indiscipline and indecision. Caught up in destructive politics, the missile battalions conducted few flight tests, and Zhou Enlai warned them against becoming an "empty shell" (kong pao).[10]

CONSOLIDATING THE SECOND ARTILLERY

The first and only available evidence on how the Second Artillery operated in these tumultuous times or at any time thereafter is anecdotal information on the missile alert during the Sino-Soviet crisis of 1969, whose story we told in Chapter 3. In the immediate aftermath of the crisis and the continuing domestic chaos until Deng Xiaoping returned to power in 1977, little changed with the missile forces even as they deployed the first 2,650 km DF-3 missiles in 1971 and worked on the long-range (4,750 km) DF-4s and the intercontinental (12,000 km) DF-5s, both deployed in the early 1980s.[11] In 1970, as the Sino-Soviet-U.S. strategic triangle began to form with the steady improvement of Sino-American relations, the threat of a Soviet attack on China began to recede. Moreover, the outside world fixated on Beijing's nuclear tests and missile programs and was totally oblivious to the near anarchy in its strategic forces. As the survivors of the prolonged struggles faded away, the next generation enjoyed the luxury of a political environment in which it could begin the long process of forging an adequate strategic missile force in relative calm.

Organizational Purification

The process began with a series of organizational edicts, which enjoyed only a short lifespan while Mao was still alive but set the basis for longer-term modernization. In the summer of 1975, when Deng Xiaoping had briefly returned to the PLA high command, a conference of the CMC predicted that a full-scale war between China and any of its probable adversaries would not occur within the next five years. Thus Beijing would have time to reconstruct its military under peacetime conditions. Deng told the conference that the PLA must "reduce its size, improve its equipment, and strengthen its strategic research." Bloated military departments and combat units, including those of the Second Artillery, would be trimmed, and the meeting resolved to reduce the military from 6.1 to 4.5 million over the coming three years. As a result of this decision, the manpower of the Second Artillery was cut by 27.2 percent.[12]

Within a few months, however, Mao struck once again. He removed Deng from his offices and temporarily negated the positive effects of the CMC's decision. A concrete plan for downsizing the army, which the military had only just started drafting, was summarily shelved. Everything remained on hold until after Mao's death and Deng's final return to power in July 1977, when the reduction plan was completed and implemented.

Deng, of course, had been acutely aware of the fierce power struggle that had wrought havoc within the Second Artillery over the preceding decade.

He attached great importance to its recovery and sought to keep a tight rein on it. In May 1978, he summoned its senior officers and told them to enforce discipline and purge the radicals. He said, "Politically, the Second Artillery must be very reliable and pure," which these officers interpreted to mean rooting out any questionable elements, especially those who had long fragmented and radicalized the corps.[13]

Solving one problem, however, exposed a host of others. Reports from Second Artillery headquarters to the CMC cataloged the costs of the years of neglect and irrational decisionmaking, to say nothing of the hardships endured by its missile soldiers locked away in desolate mountain areas. Operating on survival budgets and often cut off from the basic support expected on ordinary military installations, their living conditions were far worse than those in any of the other services. For Deng, this was unacceptable, and he told the relevant departments of the CMC to devise immediate remedies. His orders energized the General Logistics Department to dispatch investigation teams to all missile launch sites, and much more promptly than was usual within the military, the CMC allocated additional funds to provide reliable electricity, purified water, livable barracks, and other improvements.

Having helped the Second Artillery deal with some of its most pressing subsistence and morale problems at the launch positions, Deng ordered it to concentrate on readiness and stressed the use of science and technology (S&T) to promote the mandated changes. Later in 1978, the missile headquarters held a conference that resulted in the formation of the Second Artillery's own science and technology committee and the issuance of an eight-year plan for S&T management and technical innovations.

Throughout the next seven years, the CMC continued to pursue the dual policy of cutting excessive manpower while increasing system capability. The nation's first priority was economic modernization, and the military had to endure the axing of what most in the Second Artillery command deemed essential personnel and funds.[14] In practice, building capability was put on hold. In 1985, the Second Artillery convened its second science and technology meeting and mouthed the same words as before about S&T being the miracle cure for the ailing service. Vacuous orders were issued to its fledgling research and educational groups to develop more advanced weapons and to streamline combat operations, and the technical sections attached to the launch battalions were told to "push forward mass technical innovations." Despite the torrent of words and edicts, only marginal advances were forthcoming.[15]

Meanwhile, behind the scenes, changes were beginning to come from within the corps itself, not from top-down decrees. The Second Artillery had earlier established its Research Academy to organize and manage six institutes dealing, respectively, with electronics and computation, equipment maintenance and innovation, command-control-and-communications technologies, weapons and equipment, strategies and operations, and engineering designs for constructing underground emplacements.

We know the most about the academy's Fourth Institute, which was founded on July 1, 1987. The Second Artillery headquarters assigned the institute the mission of helping develop procurement policies for the "trump card" (*sashoujian*) weapons that we introduced in Chapter 5.[16] The institute's R&D methodology, which would sound familiar to new-technology firms in Silicon Valley, was to develop weapons and equipment "from qualitative to quantitative verification, and then from the specification of [the tactical and technical] performance [of a single weapon or piece of equipment] to the specification of integrated performance of complete weapons systems, making frequent use of performance simulation, verification through demonstration, simulation prototypes, and other advanced measures." The institute utilizes the major weapons test bases and firing ranges on the "high plateau" in west China and elsewhere, and some eighteen years after its founding, it has been credited with sending hundreds of technologies to the missile battalions.

In order to step up their research output and meet the mandated quality standards, the Second Artillery headquarters increased the institutes' budgets for setting up laboratories and purchasing equipment. Some sources estimated the new budgets to be in the "tens of millions of yuan," but the actual amounts are classified.[17] The missile command funded two additional educational institutions—the Engineering Academy in Xi'an and the Command Academy in Wuhan—to meet its research and training requirements.

As a consequence of this reported budget bonanza, the corps signed hundreds of contracts with outside institutes for a wide range of important projects, such as one on the hardening of the launch silos against nuclear attack, and over the next four years it could claim significant progress as witnessed by the number of prestigious scientific prizes received by its members. Such results and associated training programs boosted the quality and readiness of the missile troops. According to often-exaggerated Chinese sources, from 1984 to 1989, the launch battalions test-fired "some tens" of liquid-propellant mobile missiles and had a success rate of 96 percent. From 1989 to 1991, these battalions boasted a success rate of 100 percent in firing their missiles in training, and kept 91 percent of their missiles and 96 percent of their support operations in full readiness.

In response to the CMC's repeated calls for greater war preparedness, the Second Artillery convened follow-on technical meetings in 1991 and 1996. These sessions focused on better command and control, and the second of them approved an outline for "scientific development" over the next fifteen years.[18] In 1997, the first-stage implementation of this outline coincided with the CMC's decision to further reduce the armed forces. The Second Artillery cut its manpower by an additional 2.9 percent and retired several thousands from its ranks over the next three years, but the percentage of its actual reductions was much smaller than that of the other services.[19]

Inventing the Modern Second Artillery

In 1982, as the rebuilding program was proceeding, the CMC set in motion a series of follow-on organizational changes that have given the Second Artillery its present-day unique force structure and simplified but rigorous command procedures. Two years later, the CMC adopted a "guiding principle" for these changes. It elevated the missile bases from division to corps level, reclassified the launch regiments as brigades, and placed them in command of the launch battalions. In 1985, the missile headquarters began increasing the number of its brigades and technical support groups. Conversely, with the completion of the planned fixed launch positions and the steady movement toward mobile missiles, the number of noncombat engineering regiments needed for construction was sharply reduced.[20]

The absence of the terms corps, division, and regiment within the Second Artillery's combat chain of command causes some confusion for those used to the terminology for the other PLA service arms. In the Second Artillery, the term "regiment," as we shall see, is reserved for specialized units within each missile base. Operationally, the missile bases are the warfighting organizations under the Second Artillery headquarters. Their administrative and command structure, which varies slightly from base to base, is illustrated in Chart 3.

As noted earlier, the base commander reports directly to the Second Artillery headquarters and the General Staff Operations Department in Beijing. Under the commander and his political commissar are four departments—Headquarters, Political, Logistics, and Equipment—each of which has a number of functional units. The Headquarters Department stands at the apex of the line chain of command leading from the Command Center (First Division) to the launch brigade headquarters and through the brigade command center (Operations and Training Section) to the launch battalions and companies. The base headquarters command hierarchy and its command center are backed by four divisions that deal with intelligence, signals monitoring, radar and electronics countermeasures, and communications. The typical base has regiments below the departments that deal with equipment overhaul, equipment technical services, transport, communications, electronic countermeasures, training, and engineering.

Each base currently has two to four launch brigades equipped with either nuclear or conventional missiles. A launch brigade contains three to five launch battalions and a variety of technical support teams. The number of launch brigades varies from base to base, as does the number of launch battalions under any given brigade. For internal use within the corps, the launch brigades and battalions are also called "detachments" (*zhidui*) and "groups" (*dadui*), respectively.[21]

As Chart 3 shows, each missile base is organized as a self-contained combat organization. In addition to the task-specific regiments noted above, each base has other specialized support units or troops stationed mostly at the brigade level for computing, weather forecasting, signals monitoring, survey and mapping, security, reconnaissance, camouflage, chemical defense, air defense, and maintenance.[22] By 1987, the Second Artillery had ordered its bases to reorganize their warhead sections (*dantou shi*) as a way of reinforcing the maintenance and safety of the nuclear warheads.[23] By this same year, it had established "mobile commands" at the base and brigade levels.[24]

In addition to its several subordinate launch battalions, each launch brigade has a command center, an equipment division, a technical battalion, a launch-site management battalion, and other support arms parallel to the organizations under the base. With semiautonomous logistics, a brigade if necessary can function as a survivable subunit, though always responsive to higher command authority. Each launch battalion is composed of launch

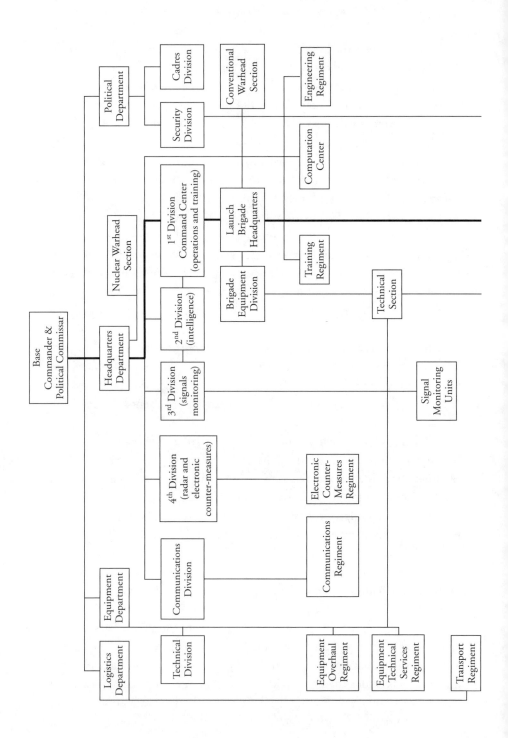

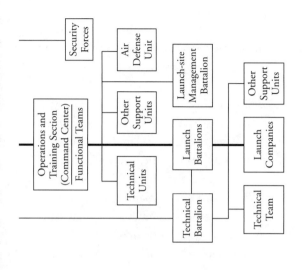

Security Forces

Operations and Training Section (Command Center) Functional Teams

Air Defense Unit

Other Support Units

Technical Units

Launch-site Management Battalion

Launch Battalions

Technical Battalion

Other Support Units

Launch Companies

Technical Team

——— Lines of administrative responsibility and reporting
━━━ The base-brigade-battalion combat chain of command

Chart 3. Organization of a Typical Second Artillery Base

companies, a propellant injection company (for liquid-propellant missiles), a technical team, and support teams for maintenance and security.

The operations of a mobile missile brigade reportedly cover an area of thousands of square kilometers, and the brigade is trained to fire its missiles at sites as far as 1,000 kilometers from their storage caves.[25] Each brigade travels with its own medical team, transport company, repair company, field warehouse (including fuel tanks), and several other teams.[26]

In addition to the Research Academy's six institutes noted above, the Second Artillery has set up separate bodies that can provide the entire corps with strategic guidance and operational analysis, logistical and communications support, launch site management, and R&D on the equipment needed for servicing the weapons systems. These facilities are not constituted as warfighting units and are not in the line chain of command.

As a technology-intensive military force, the Second Artillery has continuously sought to modernize its technical support organization and operations. It has charged its headquarters Technology and Equipment Department, now renamed the Equipment Department, with drafting the operational guidelines for all technical personnel assigned to the bases, brigades, and battalions.[27] In coordination with the command-and-control organs and other departments, the Equipment Department of each base and the technical, equipment, and maintenance support units of each brigade supply on-site services at their respective levels.[28]

The base Equipment Department directs an equipment overhaul regiment that sustains the launch-ready status of the brigades' missiles and other military equipment. This regiment boasts the highest concentration of engineers in the corps, and nearly 80 percent of its officers on average are university graduates. In a crisis or even to solve major equipment problems, this regiment can dispatch its engineers to a launch brigade on a temporary or semipermanent basis. Under normal conditions, however, the brigade's own equipment division tasks its technical section and coordinates the electronics and electrical engineers responsible for servicing the computerized equipment, troubleshooting, and preparing firing data.[29]

As part of the modernization process, the Second Artillery in the past decade has instituted a responsibility program for evaluating and certifying the preparedness of the launch battalions. Each base Equipment Department and the technical division, regiments, and other units below it have signed "contracts" with their respective levels for this management responsibility and for the strict adherence to readiness standards. How well the terms of each contract are fulfilled directly affects the promotions and assignments of individual technicians named in the contract. It is in this context, moreover, that we find the most extensive and more recent discussions of model launch brigades or battalions that have won awards as sashoujian units, thus extending the meaning of sashoujian beyond "trump card" weapons and equipment.[30]

MISSILE LAUNCH BASES

In June 1960, six years before the official creation of the Second Artillery, the CMC decided to build the first launch bases for its planned missile force. A year later, the General Staff assembled senior officers from the Artillery Corps, Engineering Corps, Railroad Corps, and the Shenyang Military Region Command to devise a preliminary plan for constructing the pioneer base in southern Jilin Province. They recommended the base consist of underground bunkers to house the DF-2 missiles, surface buildings for liquid propellants, and multiple presurveyed fixed launch positions. The finalization of this plan occupied the next four years.[31]

Base Construction

In February 1964, the General Staff assigned its deputy chief, Zhang Aiping, to head a special group to determine the Jilin base's location. Two months later, the CMC approved the group's recommendation and ordered the General Staff to transfer the troops needed to finish this base in the mountains near Tonghua. In December 1964, Nie Rongzhen, director of the Defense Science and Technology Commission (DSTC), ordered Zhang to build the base, code-named Base 51, for both DF-2 and DF-3 missiles. Building started the next year and was completed in mid-1966. The just-certified DF-2s were trucked to the base in September and were initially targeted at U.S. military bases in Japan. In mid-1965, while this base was under construction, the General Staff instructed another group, also headed by Zhang, to settle on the placement of a second base, code-named Base 52, in southern Anhui Province. The missiles of Base 52 would be targeted at U.S. bases in Southeast Asia.

In January 1966, Zhou Enlai, who secretly headed the Central Special Commission in overall charge of the strategic weapons programs, presided over the first in a series of meetings to review the plans for the next bases.[32] Zhou's goal was to complete them by the end of 1970, and he placed the General Staff in overall charge of the project. The relevant combat and military industrial organizations were ordered to draft the detailed construction plan, and in June 1966 the CMC endorsed the final version and authorized its execution.[33]

With the rapid deployment of foreign reconnaissance satellites and more accurate long-range missiles in the 1970s, assuring base survival from a nuclear assault became the most daunting challenge.[34] The best available option for the PLA in the latter half of the 1970s, when its DF-3 missiles had been readied, was to conceal the missiles in mountain caves. What the base engineers did not know in designing the caves was the structural-design criteria, the coefficients of safety, the potential for cave-ins, the drainage of underground water, and so on. A whole new generation of young engineers rallied to the task of solving these technical problems. They reportedly drew their inspiration from U.S. movies and from their colleagues engaged in related tunneling and drilling projects for the nuclear weapons test programs.[35]

Yet, even as they labored, the probability of destruction from a precision nuclear strike was outpacing their genius in designing viable defenses. In 1981, Zhang Aiping, by then the DSTC leader, conceded that the problem of survivability remained unsolved, if not unsolvable, but the CMC's only answer was to press the Second Artillery to design new types of missile launch silos and to reinforce the existing ones. In 1983, the CMC enlarged the budget for this effort, code-named it the Great Wall Project, and dispatched engineering regiments to this largest-ever building program in the history of the corps. The next year, the construction of underground bunkers and silos expanded, with orders placing some launch battalions on round-the-clock alert, but as each new generation of DF missiles came on line, their vulnerability increased.[36]

By 1988, the Second Artillery had deployed most of its first-generation missiles in hardened silos and caves. It had concealed its DF-5s in fixed reinforced-concrete silos and land-mobile DF-3s and DF-4s in mountainous areas and made them capable of rapid transport to presurveyed launch sites. Mobile commands had been formed at the base and brigade levels, and an

immense infrastructure of tunnels, hardened launch installations, troop barracks, highways, and underground communications cables had been
finished. Whether justified or not, PLA leaders confidently believed that the
overall concealment effort prevented detection of their missile complexes
throughout the 1980s and that most of them would ride out a counterforce
attack.[37]

Nevertheless, by the end of that decade, this confidence had waned because of the ever-greater capability of Soviet and American spy satellites and
counterforce missiles. As a result, the military reluctantly had to conclude
that survivability would depend more on mobility than on concealment or
hardening. The Second Artillery Survey and Mapping Department began
strongly promoting a "rapid joint surveying mechanism for missile positioning," an "integrated geodetic support technical system for mobile operation of missiles," and global positioning systems (GPS).[38] The missile battalions had already started testing their liquid-propellant rockets in mobile
operations, and a whole new generation of mobile solid-propellant rockets
was being tested or designed. The military traced this switch toward mobility to Deng Xiaoping's emphasis on "using modern weapons to wage a guerrilla war."[39] We now briefly review that shift.

As early as the 1970s, Chinese missileers were deciding that solid-
propellant rockets eventually would have to replace the first generation
liquid-fueled missiles, and much of the missile story for this and subsequent
decades is the building of submarine-launched and land-mobile solid-
propellant rockets. Their first attempt at mobile operations for liquid-
propellant rockets dates to March 1977, when a missile regiment moved out
of its fixed position to fire four DF-3 missiles as part of a mobile training exercise. The success of this exercise gave the military some hope that it could
prolong the survivability of its liquid-propellant rockets. The long road toward a primary reliance on mobile operations had begun. From that time
on, quick-reaction missile firings were practiced on highways and rail cars
and in all-weather conditions over different terrains.[40]

By the mid-1980s, however, the CMC slowly was coming to appreciate
that these were only stopgap and largely futile measures and that its fixed
missiles were almost totally vulnerable or soon would be. In an atmosphere
of crisis, the CMC ordered a more rapid changeover to mobile rockets and
flexible operations then under development. Until the changeover was realized, emphasis would have to be given to simplifying the preparations for

firing missiles and developing the rapid-deployment capabilities of the battalions equipped with liquid-propellant rockets. For example, one team worked on injecting the missile's fuel and oxidizer simultaneously, invented a new-type igniter, and designed a meter to test automatically the on-board electronics equipment. Another built a truck-mounted erector for rapidly loading and launching a missile in any terrain.[41]

Evidence for these changes was the sharp reduction in the number of engineering regiments whose job had been to build the concealed installations. By the late 1980s, a myriad of technical fixes had been tried, and from time to time the PLA temporarily convinced itself that the Second Artillery's "quick-reaction and nuclear counteroffensive capabilities" would work, only to have its doubts freshened with each publicized advance in U.S. and Soviet satellite surveillance and missile accuracy.

For Beijing's leaders, the dramatic use of U.S. air-delivered weapons in the 1991 Gulf War alerted them to the global revolution in air power. Even so, Iraq's ability to launch its Scud missiles throughout the war despite repeated U.S. air strikes to destroy them gave those leaders some confidence in the survivability of China's mobile missiles. That confidence in turn motivated the Second Artillery to concentrate ever harder on mobile operations.

By this time, as we have noted, the CMC had concluded that Western intelligence assets could locate most of the underground launch silos and that fixed missiles were obsolete. Moreover, cave-ins at underground missile storage sites had become more common, and the temporary solutions of the 1980s were looking less and less promising.[42] Mobile platforms and solid-rocket technology offered the only path to a survivable deterrent, and the foundation was being laid for a new strategic concept. However, we must first address the issue of missile basing as part of that foundation.

Test and Launch Bases

China has built these four bases for testing its strategic missiles:

- Base 20: Shuangchengzi, Gansu Province, for flight-testing the DF-2, DF-3, DF-5, and DF-15/M-9 missiles and launching satellites.[43]
- Base 25: Kelan, Shanxi Province, for flight-testing the DF-3, DF-5, JL-1/ DF-21, and JL-2/DF-31 missiles.

- Base 27: Xichang, Sichuan Province, for launching satellites, especially synchronous orbit communications satellites. The first launch from this base was in 1984.
- Base 28: Jingyu, Jilin Province, for flight-testing the DF-4 and JL-2/DF-31 missiles.[44]

Since the early 1960s, the staffs of these bases and three missile impact zones have reported to the DSTC and its successors, the Commission of Science, Technology, and Industry for National Defense (COSTIND) and now the General Armament Department (COSTIND's military successor). The DSTC constructed the three impact zones in Xinjiang: near Lop Nur and Minfeng for flight-testing the DF-2 and DF-3 missiles and near Korla for flight-testing the DF-4 and DF-5 missiles.[45]

From its central headquarters—now located in Qinghe in the northern suburbs of Beijing—the Second Artillery reportedly has planned and guided the construction of eight missile bases, which collectively field more than twenty brigades. The headquarters of these bases are located in Liaoning, Anhui, Yunnan, Henan, Hunan, Qinghai, Shanxi, and Hebei provinces,[46] though the brigades and their battalions assigned to the bases operate in a number of other provinces. The base in Qinghai may have been partially deactivated, and a noncombat base in Xinjiang reportedly is used only for training foreign tactical missile teams. A brigade generally is assigned a single type of missile in order to facilitate command, maintenance, and crew specialization.[47]

According to a Taiwanese report, the Second Artillery has active-duty billets for approximately 147,000 officers and men. This number includes those assigned to the missile bases and launch battalions, staff engaged in logistic and technical support, construction crews, and management personnel at the launch sites. Among those counted in the Taiwanese figure are special personnel stationed in hardened command-and-control centers separated for maximum survivability away from the base and battalion headquarters and, of course, from the Second Artillery's high command in Beijing.[48]

For internal use within the Second Artillery and General Armament Department, a two-digit code number has been given to each operational missile base. These base codes are thought to be numbers in the 50s—that is, 51 and above—but with discrepancies in the open sources concerning which numbers belong to which bases. At the same time, the CMC assigned each base a five-digit code number beginning with 80 (such as 80301 and above) but later may have given them new numbers. The following are launch bases on which we have information; the names of the cities and provinces in parentheses are the reported locations of the base headquarters, but all of this information (including the numbers above), of course, comes from un-classified sources and should be viewed with caution.[49] Furthermore, the op-erational status and specific missile deployments at each base have sometimes changed, as we shall observe later.

- Shenyang Base (Shenyang, Liaoning Province; moved in the early 1990s from Tonghua, Jilin Province; often referred to as the Tonghua Base): DF-3/DF-21
- Wannan Base (Jilingshan, Anhui Province): DF-3/DF-21/DF-15/DF-11/ DF-18
- Yunnan Base (Kunming, Yunnan Province): DF-3/DF-21
- Yuxi Base (Luoyang, Henan Province): DF-4/DF-5
- Xiangxi Base (Huaihua, Hunan Province): DF-4/DF-5
- Qinghai Base (Xining, Qinghai Province): DF-3/DF-4
- Jinbei Base (Taiyuan, Shanxi):[50] DF-3/DF-4
- Hebei Base (Xuanhua, Hebei Province):[51] DF-4/DF-5/possibly DF-31

For management convenience, the corps has given a three-digit code num-ber to each of the launch brigades.[52]

The missiles at each base are kept in places sometimes hundreds of kilo-meters from the base command center, and any mobile missiles in the base inventory, when exercised, are never in one spot for long. While the older missiles (DF-3, DF-4, and DF-5) use liquid propellants, the newer missiles (DF-15, DF-21, and DF-31) all use solid-propellant engines and can be fired from mobile transporter-erector-launchers. By the time of its well-publicized test in August 1999, the 8,000 km DF-31, the newest land-based ballistic mis-sile, had gone through a multiyear test phase, and its deployment could begin "during the first half of the decade," according to a CIA report of December 2001, but the Pentagon's 2004 report put the deployment later in the decade.[53]

The Second Artillery has worked hardest on the survivability of its under-ground command centers, missile storage bunkers, and missile silos. By the 1980s, Chinese sources acknowledge that U.S. reconnaissance satellites had located most, if not all, of these centers and structures.[54] In response, the CMC first ordered the PLA Engineering Corps to work out effective countermeasures but soon recognized that silo-based missiles and fixed installations, once detected, could not survive a direct hit. It therefore redefined the quest for survivability and began to explore novel modes of concealment.

Moreover, the introduction of side-looking radars, long-range infrared detectors, photoelectric sensors, and laser cameras negated each supposed invulnerable concealment mode and forced the Chinese to test electromagnetic decoys, multifunctional camouflage netting, special missile coatings, metal angle reflectors, and other such countermeasures, again without much success. Sometimes using their own reconnaissance systems and technicians, the engineers studied the limits and biases of satellite photography and photo-interpreters and attempted to identify and prove camouflage technologies that would fool the best of them. They came to believe that it would be more difficult to conceal their missiles from aerial infrared and microwave radars and telephoto cameras than from reconnaissance satellites.[55]

The Engineering Corps concluded, moreover, that certain advanced camouflage technologies could alter the appearance of the land around the missile emplacements and with high probability could effectively deceive the best intelligence experts. They applied "fuzzy theory" to topographic camouflaging, and the Engineering Corps formed and trained special camouflage teams that it sent to advise the Second Artillery on how to modify the surface areas of the newly built underground installations or just their appearance. By applying fuzzy theory, camouflage units visually merged those facilities into the surrounding landscape, and reportedly PLA reconnaissance aircraft equipped with telephoto cameras and infrared and microwave radars could not differentiate the missile positions from their neighboring landscape.

As the decade of the 1980s progressed and the vulnerability of the missiles technically increased, the perception of an immediate nuclear threat to the nation declined, which gave the PLA breathing room in the next decade to exploit the reduced risk and concentrate on enhancing the quality and survivability of the force. Recognizing the vulnerability of many, if not most, of the older missile sites, moreover, the Second Artillery in the late 1990s began a massive relocation and building project. It purchased top-of-the-line equipment from Europe and enlisted China's best engineering schools to train the corps engineers in advanced tunneling and construction methods in difficult mountainous terrain. As of mid-2002, the relocation effort was underway in nearly one hundred underground complexes scattered in nineteen counties in thirteen provinces.[56]

Although the PLA appears to be achieving its goals of greater concealment and enhanced survivability, the concurrent campaign to tighten the
security of classified information limits any outsider's access to data on the
actual progress toward those goals.[57] Nevertheless, Chinese specialists claim
that the new bases in mountain tunnels make it more difficult for the new-
generation missiles to be targeted and destroyed in a first strike.[58]

The Wannan Base

We can illustrate aspects of base development by examining the history of
the base in the mountains of Anhui and Jiangxi provinces.[59] Starting in
the mid-1960s and continuing into the mid-1990s, the Second Artillery
dispatched several engineering regiments to build the launch-site infrastructure. As noted for all bases, the Wannan Base (Base 52 or originally
numbered Unit 80302) reports only to Beijing, and the commander of the
Nanjing Military Region, where 52 is located, has no authority to supervise
the base's routine activities. By the early 1990s, the base contained at least
two brigades in Anhui's Qimen and Shitai counties,[60] and reliable evidence
suggests that the CMC had added another brigade to the base by the mid-
1990s. However, even the experts debate the actual number and composition
of the brigades currently under Base 52 because of their shifting assignments
and newly deployed conventionally armed missiles following the worsening
tensions in the Taiwan Strait in 1995–96 and in 2001.

Security is tight at the base, and contact with the local population is minimal. For example, the base mail cannot be delivered but must be picked up
from a nearby post office, and without special approval, no uncleared person
is allowed to visit the base's restricted military zones. No one, not even the
base commander, is permitted in any quarter without an authorizing stamp
on his identity card. More modern security measures were also gradually introduced. Around 2001, the Second Artillery installed electronic monitoring
units and alarms at this and all other bases and stationed many Special Service Teams with guard dogs to patrol the base areas.[61]

The restricted areas around the base are among the most closely guarded
military zones in the country. The nearby offices of state security have been
given precedence in obtaining money, personnel, and surveillance equipment, and base security measures include the use of informants recruited by
base security and the local state security offices. These citizen watchdogs

report on strangers loitering near restricted military areas, visiting local families, or taking pictures. Security guards are authorized to detain and interrogate such "intruders" and to hustle them out of the area for any reason or place them under arrest. On the other hand, base engineers have been allowed to provide TV and electronic repair services for nearby residents as a sideline business, and it is possible that the severe code of discipline breaks down in other informal ways.

Security procedures at the bases become especially demanding around the warhead storage depots. Only college graduates who are granted top-secret clearances can serve in the nuclear warhead sections, and special code locks are used on the depots and weapons themselves.[62] Once aboard, the soldiers assigned to these sections have accepted a lifetime commitment. Thereafter, they can never go abroad, and their domestic travel and communications even with relatives are rigidly monitored. The base commander once admonished them, "Your mission is glorious. . . . You must work and live at the base forever. Even your memorial services will be held here." This last sentence has special poignancy, because many of the underground warhead bunkers suffer from high levels of radiation contamination. It is said that over the years almost half of the warhead section members have died in their forties. As a partial remedy to counteract the effects of the radiation, each section member is given a special counter-radiation "nutrition allowance," though all reportedly believe the amount is inadequate.

The isolation of the original base headquarters in Qimen County also complicated the daily lives of the unit's officers. Security measures made their situation even worse. In some cases, the officers' families had to live in places nearly 100 kilometers away from Qimen, and, as is the case throughout the PLA, no enlisted personnel were (or are) allowed to live with their families. Moreover, during Base 52's first two decades, its officers regularly complained about such restrictions as their inability to send their children to universities or colleges and other personal hardships. Eventually, such hardships caused a sharp increase in the number of divorces.[63]

Still, security remained the absolute priority, and Beijing even worried about where to build the launch crew barracks because their concentration near the launch sites could reveal their location to foreign reconnaissance satellites. For this reason, in the latter half of the 1980s, the CMC told the Second Artillery to move most barracks farther from the launch areas, but as it turned out, this took them closer to the married officers' families.[64]

Nevertheless, such improvements, planned or not, did nothing to boost morale for other officers still living in substandard housing at the base head-quarters, and only in 1988 did Beijing approve their transfer from Qimen to newer quarters in Jilingshan, a suburb of Huangshan City.

Significantly, morale problems were not confined to Base 52. Throughout the Second Artillery, these problems festered and weakened the professional-ism of launch-site personnel. Faced with falling reenlistment rates of younger officers, the CMC authorized the corps to give them preferential treatment, including additional meal allowances, higher pay (a launch company captain's pay equals that of a colonel in the corps headquarters), and virtually certain admission for their children to military colleges. These and other steps helped stabilize the retention level of these officers, though in the final analysis, noth-ing could change geography and their lonely and monotonous life.

Despite these personnel problems, Beijing considered its elite Second Ar-tillery battalions fully ready by the mid-1990s. In June 1995 and again in March 1996, the CMC ordered Base 52 to conduct live conventional missile firings across the Taiwan Strait to influence political trends on the island, and in advance of the firings the base sent its mobile DF-15/DF-21 battalions from northern Jiangxi to Fujian Province.[65] After the second of these politi-cally inspired "exercises" ended, the commission hailed them as a success and awarded them high unit commendations.

Faced with the bitter confrontation across the Taiwan Strait, the CMC has backed up its policy of "generating pressure" (*baochi yali*) against the is-land with increased missile deployments to Base 52. The different types of conventionally armed missiles (DF-15/DF-15A/DF-11/DF-11A) at the base reflect the decision to prepare for a variety of contingencies from limited firings as warnings to full-scale combat and to deal with continuing tactical uncertainties. These missiles are now positioned in launch sites in Jiangxi, Fujian, and Guangdong provinces, and their number could reach 800 by the end of 2006, if not earlier.[66]

ENHANCING FIGHTING CAPACITY

PLA planners state that the Second Artillery's command-and-control proce-dures, compared to those of the other military services and reviewed in Chapter 5, are more explicit and inflexible. Applying these procedures in remote regions where the launch battalions are dispersed has been a major challenge for the command center's communications crews, and modernizing its telecommunications for real-time control has become a prime goal.[67]

Strengthening the Missile Command-and-Control System

In order to achieve that goal, the Second Artillery has given precedence to training and personnel performance, which it deems essential to achieving the absolute control needed for the missile bases to carry out their missions. Their stern discipline and remote locations perhaps make it easier to enforce their training regimens, but the proximity of nuclear weapons—the so-called national treasures—makes the high command ever wary of taking the results for granted.

The essence of command and control in the Second Artillery was always more a matter of personnel quality than of equipment improvements, although the latter also received high-level attention.[68] With the introduction of regular "advancement examinations" for all noncommissioned officers, for example, the Second Artillery has tried to come to grips with the "stagnant military technological quality" of these NCOs, and placed a number of them on probation for failing the exams.[69] All brigade personnel, like their fellow soldiers throughout the PLA, undergo annual evaluation according to the CMC's "Outline for Army Building at the Grassroots Level" and new directives from CMC chairman Hu Jintao.[70] Week by week, the PLA media report on new efforts to conduct operational training and to introduce such training technologies as a "launching simulation system" in order to reinforce each brigade's emergency response performance.[71]

Beijing's leaders in particular have attached great weight to the political reliability of the Second Artillery officers and men, and over the decades they have devised tests to measure that and other aspects of reliability.[72] To do so, they adopted screening procedures comparable to the Nuclear Weapons Personnel Reliability Program used in the U.S. military for selecting individuals to handle nuclear weapons, but for many years with a greater stress in China on a person's political background because neither drug addiction nor alcoholism appears to have been a significant problem as it is in the West and Russia.[73] From 1995 on, however, psychologists assigned to the Second Artillery began testing to identify "unstable soldiers" suffering from excessive "nervousness, ennui, and lack of focus." These maladies were deemed the cause of most missile test failures attributed to individuals, and by 1999, the tests were used to screen all officers and men participating in missile operations.[74]

All launch battalions of the Second Artillery are under the ultimate direction of the CMC and subject to its decisions on procurements, launch-site construction, deployment and employment, and exercises. Those decisions pass through the base headquarters, but never originate in those headquarters. During routine launches, the CMC issues the launch commands to the Second Artillery headquarters, which conveys them to the launch battalions via the combat chain of command given in Chart 3. The rules governing launch procedures are regularly reviewed and strictly enforced. The General Staff Operations Department plays a critical role in the communications chain from the CMC to the base headquarters. The CMC uses this department's command center to transmit and monitor all missile deployment and employment decisions. The CMC issues operational orders to this center for further transmittal to the Second Artillery and other services, and the center in turn relays the responses from all other senior military organizations to the leaders of the department for retransmittal to the CMC.[75]

Starting from the 1970s and continuing into the 1990s, the Second Artillery issued a number of directives to enhance the survivability of the command-and-control system and the second-strike capabilities of the strategic nuclear force. The corps has constructed its command centers in hardened underground bunkers that contain communications gear, drainage and decontamination equipment, and power generators. Commanders in these centers reportedly believe they could operate for long periods under nuclear, conventional, or chemical attack, but with no way to test this belief the more skeptical PLA officers fear the worst.

In addition to underground main command posts, the Second Artillery also has created alternative airborne and truck-mounted posts to communicate with its launch battalions. In some emergencies, the CMC and missile headquarters may bypass the base and brigade headquarters and issue launch orders directly to those battalions, and the headquarters' General Communications Station has tested a variety of alternative communications, including phones for individual soldiers, to ensure connectivity in wartime.[76] The center has devised special codes for preventing unauthorized or accidental launches and multistep procedures to transmit and verify orders. A launch will automatically be aborted if any step violates the verification requirements, and several steps depend on the coordinated action of at least two authorized officers.

Secure and uninterrupted communications are considered the key to success in any conflict, and over the past decades the PLA has concentrated on improving the survivability and reliability of its message networks. For enhanced security and effectiveness, the CMC has made the General Staff's Confidential Bureau, Communications Department, and Technical Department responsible for message encryption, deciphering, and traffic flow. Furthermore, the corps has constantly upgraded its own "nerve center," the General Communications Station in Beijing. This regimental-level unit has the special responsibility to receive and transmit all coded information delivered by phone, radio, fax, and e-mail, and its paramount task in recent years has been to defeat an enemy's monitoring and code-breaking efforts. To this end, the station has introduced such electronic countermeasures as rapid frequency changes, deceptive operations, and one-way communications, measures whose antecedents date back to the revolution.[77]

Since 1992, PLA organizations, including the Second Artillery, have purchased a large quantity of advanced fiber optics and specialized microwave, satellite, frequency hopping, scattering, cellular, and adaptive array equipment. These units have organized training courses and invited experts to help their officers gain the expertise needed for running sophisticated communications, and to this end, the Second Artillery's officers have been accorded the highest priority. The first fiber optics lines authorized in the PLA were laid at one of its missile bases, and in 1995, the corps approved a plan for replacing electric cables with fiber optic lines in all its bases. By 1998, for example, twelve separate fiber optic lines with a total length of 335 km had been laid at one missile launch base, and a network center was built at this base to provide digital communications and control for all its battalions.[78]

The same year, the General Staff Communications Department developed a "software radio technology" to connect the transceivers using different frequencies. This technology, PLA sources state, could integrate analogue and digital messages and digitize the signals to previously incompatible equipment. It could assure reliable and protected communications between the Second Artillery and the headquarters of the four general departments (General Staff particularly for the ground armies, General Political, General Logistics, and General Armament) and between the corps and the other PLA services in joint operations.[79]

The Communications Department also assigned a technical team to work on a blast- and jam-proof underground communications network. Specialists determined the optimum frequencies—said to be between 3 and 30 MHz—capable of penetrating hundreds of meters of hard rock and developed the equipment to operate on these frequencies. To do so, they needed to solve two key problems: signal weakness and weather interference. For the first problem, transceivers were designed to enhance signals as weak as one-fortieth of the ambient noise with an error rate as low as 0.04 percent. Thunder and lightening interference posed the second major challenge, and it was not until the late 1990s that they could boast to the high command that the newest equipment in the command centers had overcome the many problems and linked the CMC and the strategic missile bases under the most severe conditions. Short of its total destruction, they said, the center could provide "communications of last resort." [80]

With the current focus on high-tech warfighting, the Second Artillery's dominant post–Cold War concern has been on how to wage and win conventional battles, though in our final chapter we will suggest this overriding concern may be changing. The writings of senior PLA strategists, however, provide limited details on how the Second Artillery's control system would function in trans-theater joint operations that remained conventional. They state that in advance of an impending nonnuclear conflict, the CMC would transfer senior officers to the command center in the General Staff Operations Department from the headquarters of the four general departments, the navy and air force, and the Second Artillery. This joint command group would organize itself into a "combat-ready" structure. Under the CMC chairman as the designated national command authority, the chief of the General Staff would head the chain of command for this group. The senior commanders from the three services and the Second Artillery would organize joint operations and implement orders given to their own units and run the interservice structure during a conventional theater conflict. [81]

For conducting coastal theater operations, the CMC would transfer command to the head of the military region engaged in the conflict. If more than one region should become involved, a single trans-theater commander would be designated. The CMC also might dispatch senior officers from the four general headquarters, the navy and air force, and the Second Artillery to support this designated commander, and standing orders—all tested in the March 1996 missile firings into waters near Taiwan and the 2001 joint exercise near Dongshan Island, Fujian Province, discussed more fully in Chapter 8—would guide these officers in forming the ad hoc command organization as the conflict unfolds.

Should the senior commander assign nearby missile battalions to an independent mission, the Second Artillery has standing orders to mobilize a special conventional missile command headed by the closest base's deputy commander. This deputy has the duty to coordinate with local service commanders in carrying out their overall assignments. The CMC only slowly promulgated plans for control at the subregion level, and for years, PLA officers writing on the subject called this "a gap that quickly needs filling." That gap, it should be noted, has apparently now been removed.

Although most of the planning thus far has concentrated on integrating the air force, navy, and Second Artillery in combined operations, the PLA has begun to think through how to include the ground troops in those operations. At a minimum, commanders would have to coordinate the army's defensive fire against an attack on the Second Artillery's missile batteries and command centers, and that army mission reportedly includes the use of its short-range surface-to-surface missiles as well as cruise missiles, antiaircraft batteries, and artillery. The army missile force—called "operational tactical missile units" (*zhanyi zhanshu daodan budui*)—belongs to artillery units. It complements the conventional missile battalions under the Second Artillery but under actual wartime conditions the coordination between the two conventional missile organizations could become complicated. During 1998 and 1999, experts from the two missile groups worked on how to concentrate fire efficiently on enemy targets and focused on landing and counter-landing operations.[82]

Tightened Security

As China's opening-up policies over the past quarter century gained momentum, official and societal constraints on personal behavior weakened. The corruptive influences within the nation at large quietly spread to the military, including the barracks of the Second Artillery. Almost unheard of in the early years, violations of discipline within the corps multiplied, and the once strong bastion of security faced a host of novel threats. Though few in number, some officers and soldiers failed to return to their units after their vacations, and others "jumped into the sea" of business or took part-time jobs without authorization. As morale and "security consciousness" lapsed, the Second Artillery acted to restore discipline.[83]

Most threatening of all, the wall of secrecy around the rocket forces began to crumble, and classified information began to leak to the outside. As this problem worsened throughout the PLA, the CMC reissued the call to abide by its security regulations.[84] In line with these documents, the Second Artillery called for ensuring the security of key departments, core secrets, and trump card weapons, and ordered its security units to tighten control over confidential secretaries, guards, and typists who had access to classified materials and to protect secrets in the command-and-control centers and launch sites. It reached out to retired officers and routinely reminded them of their sworn duty to obey security regulations. Local security agencies were told to monitor these retirees and to report any possible violations.

In the winter of 2004–5, the Second Artillery further extended the surveillance measures over its officers and soldiers who were scheduled to leave the first-line service. Launch base security personnel conducted intensive prerelease education on how to keep secrets after their return home. Prior to their discharge, these retirees took a special oath of secrecy and signed contracts that reaffirmed their lifelong security obligations.[85] For the Second Artillery, the effectiveness of these security measures has yet to be tested.

Strategic Alerts

Even as it modernized its missiles and command and control, the Central Military Commission established and refined a four-stage alert system for the Second Artillery's nuclear missiles. (Parenthetically, we should note that the system and order sequence had not been perfected at the time of the 1969 missile alert discussed in Chapter 3.) From the lowest to highest, the four-stage system consists of Standing War Preparedness Alert, Class 3 Alert, Class 2 Alert, and Class 1 Alert.[86] The precise level of readiness, of course, varies as the alert level rises. Similarly, the exact preparations for each level differ for mobile and fixed installations and from base to base. For each stage in the alert process, unit and individual assignments will already have been minutely specified, precisely timed, and repeatedly tested in exercises. From the sources available to us, we do not know whether or how this rigid alert system might be modified in a nonnuclear crisis involving the Second Artillery.

In moving up the ladder of alerts toward the command to launch the nuclear-armed missiles, the CMC will issue three different orders: the Preparatory Order (*yuxian haoling*), Combat Order (*zuozhan mingling*), and Launch Order (*fashe mingling*). These orders may be preceded or accompanied by warnings from the General Staff and the military region. They may be terminated should the perceived emergency end, and the level of alerts may be increased, decreased, or put on hold. A Preparatory Order normally contains four main parts: a concise description of the enemy's status; a brief statement of the unit's assigned mission; the unit's required preparations with a precise schedule; and the timing and location of the operation.[87] This order is given by the CMC to initiate a Class 3 or Class 2 Alert and sets in motion actions for a higher-stage alert. In a confirmed emergency, the military commission, now operating as the national command authority, can bypass the Preparatory Order and directly tell the General Staff Operations Department to issue the Combat Order that initiates a Class 1 Alert. The sequence of alerts and orders is understood to involve the following:

Standing War Preparedness Alert (jingchang zhanbei zhuangtai). This routine or normal day-to-day readiness condition assumes that an enemy attack is possible but unlikely. To order any higher alert, intelligence must indicate a heightened threat level, and the next two higher alerts are initiated by a Preparatory Order unless the CMC decides to bypass either one and move quickly to the highest stage alert.

Class 3 Operational Preparedness Alert (san deng zhanyi zhunbei zhuangtai). Intelligence must indicate that an enemy attack is probable in order to justify the initiation of this alert. Upon receipt of a Preparatory Order from the CMC via the General Staff Operations Department, the Second Artillery sends the order to the missile bases, which must begin preparations for launching their missiles and for going to a higher-stage alert. During the preparations, base security is rapidly augmented. If the first Preparatory Order initiated a Class 3 Alert, a second Preparatory Order must be given to initiate a Class 2 Alert unless the emergency abates.

Class 2 Operational Preparedness Alert (er deng zhanyi zhunbei zhuangtai). To order this alert, intelligence must confirm that an enemy attack is underway, but the CMC in consultation with the Politburo Standing Committee has not yet decided on its response in accordance with a specific operations plan.

When a Class 2 Alert is sounded upon receipt of the encoded Preparatory Order, all bases begin shifting to the predetermined stage of high readiness, and the air defense and ground units assigned to missile bases become fully activated and move toward their own highest alert. All further actions must await the receipt of the Formal Order.

Class 1 Operational Preparedness Alert (yi deng zhanyi zhunbei zhuangtai). The issuance of the next order—a Combat Order, not a Preparatory Order—by the CMC via the General Staff Operations Department to the corps headquarters will cause the specifically named launch bases to go to a Class 1 Alert. The precise nature of the threat level required to reach this Class 1 Alert decision remains highly classified, and the range of possibilities and response options could be quite complex. For example, the initial enemy attack could be a nonnuclear assault on China's strategic targets such as the Second Artillery missile silos or command-and-control installations. In any case, when a threat reaches the point where the CMC decides a Class 1 Alert is warranted, the PLA equivalent of the Single Integrated Operational Plan (SIOP) that guides U.S. nuclear war plans would dictate the high command's possible prompt responses, including nuclear retaliation on the attacker's homeland.[88] The Class 1 Combat Order raises the readiness of the designated bases to the highest level and details the final action steps that must be taken by the missile battalions prior to the issuance of the Launch Order. The Launch Order sanctions the release of specifically named nuclear weapons and authorizes the action commanders to commence the nuclear counterattack.

By this time, the Standing Committee would have made its decision for nuclear war and transferred the national command authority to the military commission. The CMC in all but extreme cases will already have issued a Class 2 Alert and will have chosen the operations plan for initiating the war from among several rigidly rehearsed alternative plans that have been drafted and sanctioned to meet a range of high probability contingencies. It then promulgates the Class 1 Alert Combat Order, which is based on that plan, to the Second Artillery headquarters. In most cases the entire missile force by then will have gone to a Class 2 Alert, and when they move to a Class 1 Alert, the designated bases make ready to fire when the Launch Order comes. That latter order's content, the subject of the section below, constitutes a "core secret."[89]

In order to improve the alert system and firing order sequence, the missile high command over the years has conducted feasibility studies and many exercises to search for shortcomings. The CMC reportedly has great confidence in the corrective measures that have been taken to augment the quick-reaction capabilities of the strategic nuclear force and to prevent unauthorized or accidental launches.

Targeting and Command Procedures

Because of its limited number of nuclear warheads and missiles, the Second Artillery has selected a list of priority targets and ranked them for their perceived value to the overall war scenario.[90] The criteria for making the target list range from international security threats and a potential enemy's retaliatory capabilities and likely objectives to the availability of specific weapons against high-value targets, the assessment of each missile type's attack profile (such as survivability, penetrability, precision, and destruction potential), and the characteristics of each possible target.[91]

Using those criteria, the CMC has divided the targets of China's probable enemies into five categories:

1. Relationship of targets to overall war aims: strategic and tactical targets. Strategic targets include strategic missile launch bases, naval and air bases, central military and political headquarters, political and economic centers, industrial bases, and vital communications hubs. Tactical targets include presumed tactical nuclear weapons sites, tank formations, massed troops, and regional command-and-control centers.
2. Value of the target to the enemy: military, industrial, and transportation targets.
3. Vulnerability of the target to destruction: soft and hard targets.
4. Difficulty of destroying targets of different shapes: point, linear, and area targets.
   —Point target: Half of a target's maximum length is no greater than one-fifth of the radius of destruction from the nuclear blast; that is, a nuclear weapon can totally destroy the target.
   —Linear target: The length of a linear target is at least twice its width.
   —Area target: Half of the area's minimum length is larger than the radius of destruction from the nuclear blast.
5. Difficulty in finding the targets or the maneuverability of targets: fixed versus mobile targets.

In formulating its targeting policies and perfecting its operations plans, the Second Artillery has adopted the principle of cost-effectiveness; that is, use the fewest weapons for greatest effect. It regularly reruns its scientific calculations and computer simulations to test and refine those policies and has written "several tens" of operations plans for the CMC's use in a war crisis. These plans cover contingencies from warnings and alerts to escalation scenarios and full-scale nuclear war. Given China's vulnerability in today's nuclear environment, Beijing would activate any of these plans only as a last resort.

Because a nuclear conflict, however remote, could erupt quickly, the Second Artillery headquarters and its Operations Department have calculated the exact sequence of steps leading up to launching the missiles under different conditions. Prior to that conflict and long before moving from the first Preparatory Order to the Class 1 Alert and the Launch Order, officers in its Operations Department will have prepared and communicated sets of cards that list the key elements for each type of launch in accordance with the above-noted categories and tested policies. The most menacing crises themselves will have been typed, and each type will determine the content of a detailed operations plan. Each of these plans in turn is directly linked to a specific, numbered set of cards so that unwanted delays in decisionmaking can be eliminated. These cards thereby translate the operations plan chosen by the CMC into a specific sequence of precisely timed steps to be taken by each selected base commander and his launch crews.

The Launch Order activates the firing sequence. It dictates which battalions will launch, the precise timing for the mobile units to arrive at presurveyed launch sites and for them and officers in hardened silos to complete their prelaunch check lists, the exact timing for the designated battalions and companies to fire their missiles, and, most important, the number or numbers of the targeting cards to be used. The cards state the number of missiles and types of warheads to be launched, names of the targets with their geographical coordinates, types and heights of explosions (air, surface, underwater, or underground), evacuation routes for the launch units to take after firing their missiles, and other actions essential to the mission.

After receiving and authenticating the Launch Order from Second Artillery headquarters, the base commander will unseal the predetermined set of numbered cards that convey the CMC's political and military aims. When the command comes, his launch crews must follow the instructions on these cards and strictly pursue their prescribed procedures in a "timely, precise, and secret" manner.[92] At history's fateful moment, the CMC will trust a small deck of cards, not the computer, to guide the launch officers toward nuclear war.

DETERMINING STRATEGIC CONCEPTS

From the mid-1950s to his death in September 1976, Mao deemed the acquisition and deployment of strategic weapons essential to his grand strategy, but clung to the People's War concept in defining the PLA's military doctrines and operational tactics.[93] From its inception to the late 1970s, the Second Artillery concentrated exclusively on operating its small missile force, not on theories or doctrines. After Mao's death in 1976, however, Deng Xiaoping assumed the leadership of the army and directed each of the services to develop its own strategies and operational arts. He decreed that the rapid assimilation of advanced knowledge—not just new hardware—would help assure success in future crises or wars. In 1979, his slogan for this decree was "People's War under modern conditions," a formula attributed to Marshal Ye Jianying.[94]

Even before then, in November 1978, the Second Artillery Research Academy had opened an institute to formulate operational concepts for the corps, and the next year, Deng urged the academy to accelerate research on those concepts. In cooperation with other PLA think tanks, the institute began drafting guidelines for missile operations; command, control, and communications; and technical support. In the following years, the academy held three symposia to refine and finalize these drafts.[95]

Meanwhile, in October 1980, Yang Dezhi, then the chief of the General Staff, presided over an all-army meeting to extend the call for new guidelines to all services and issued an additional instruction to the Second Artillery. Moving away from Mao's long-standing policy of "active defense" within a People's War, Yang defined the essence of his instruction with eight Chinese characters (*yanmi fanghu, zhongdian fanji*), which translate as "strictly protecting [the missile forces] and carry out counteroffensives against key targets."[96] The guidelines, he implied, would emphasize survivability. Within a few years, the corps issued a series of classified documents for implementing Yang's eight-character instruction. These documents included "General Principles for Operations of the Second Artillery" and "Several Issues Concerning the Operational Employment of the Second Artillery." The missile

bases for the first time regularized and standardized the operational procedures of their widely dispersed brigades and battalions.

A remaining problem was how to clarify and perfect the combat chain of
command, and additional regulations were written to define the authority of
commands at all levels and their responsibilities to each other. In 1984, the
corps issued its "Operations Regulations for the Second Artillery," "Work
Rules for Commands at Various Levels of the Second Artillery," "Operations
Regulations for Missile Detachments [Brigades] and Launch Groups
[Battalions]," and a book, *Military Terms of the Second Artillery*. The most
noteworthy directive came the next year. This document, "Operational Concepts for the Second Artillery," provided the theoretical basis for all Second
Artillery operations. Step by step, a command structure and procedures for
all probable contingencies were being formalized. Those contingencies, it
should be noted, then postulated the likelihood of a limited nuclear strike
from the Soviet Union. In 1988, the CMC promulgated the doctrine of "limited nuclear retaliation" (*youxian he baofu*) to deal with this threat, though the
probability of such a strike occurring had significantly diminished by then.[97]

Throughout the 1980s, Second Artillery commanders gave precedence to
research on a nuclear strategy that would meet this and other assumed threats,
and many academies and institutes were being assigned to the research effort.
By 1988, for example, strategists from some twenty groups had published
nearly two hundred research papers, though we have learned little of their
content. We only know that these groups worked on scientific policy, management of science and technology, weapons development, selection standards for corps officers, simulation techniques, and enhancement of survivability and combat capabilities. We know few other details, but a central
theme of these studies was how to implement the official limited nuclear retaliation doctrine, and it was these studies that provided the foundation for
the CMC's deterrence doctrine and its policies on the deployment and use of
strategic weapons.

The origin of the 1988 deterrence doctrine could be traced to Deng Xiaoping's somewhat simplistic statement of 1983 to the effect "we [must] have
what others have, and anyone who wants to destroy us will be subject to retaliation." The Second Artillery's nuclear arms, he added, "had forced the
superpowers not to use" nuclear weapons against China.[98]

Beijing's leaders were in fact mimicking Western, especially French, deterrence theories that stressed the basic requirements needed by a small

nuclear power to survive a nuclear attack and to launch a second strike in defense of its "core values."[99] They also adopted the principle of strategic uncertainty concerning any public disclosure of the nature and timing of specific responses to an attack in contrast to the greater definitiveness of their actual war plans. Even before issuing the highly classified 1988 doctrine, the CMC had directed its strategic missile command in peacetime to "maintain nuclear deterrence, dissuade the enemy from launching a nuclear war against our country, and serve our country's peaceful foreign policy."[100]

In wartime, the surviving missiles would prevent, if possible, "the escalation of a conventional war to the nuclear level, contain any further escalation of the nuclear war, and [be ready to] conduct a nuclear counterattack to destroy the enemy's strategic targets and weaken its military potential and strategic capability." According to the then prevailing line, the first phase of a war with the Soviet Union would open with a conventional attack on China and, if the war could be kept conventional, Mao's dogma of People's War under modern conditions would continue to apply.

In 1985, balancing the growing vulnerability of his retaliatory forces and the reduced probability of war, Deng Xiaoping slowed the quest for missile survivability when he decreed that China no longer had to prepare to fight an early, large-scale nuclear war, even though meetings throughout the late 1980s continued to assume that nuclear war could not be completely ruled out.[101] Like all leaders in the nuclear age, he had to weigh the level of risk against the unimaginable disaster should deterrence fail. Gone was Mao's slogan about the inevitability of an all-out nuclear war, and the vaunted Great Wall Project launched in 1983 lost momentum. The debates about nuclear policy continued, but they did so increasingly in a vacuum as China's strategic programs and military industry suffered severe budget cuts and neglect.

The CMC's long-standing no-first-use policy remained intact, to be sure, and was still defined as "conducting centralized command and gaining mastery by striking only after the enemy has struck" (*jizhong zhihui, houfa zhiren*).[102] This policy, which could be changed at any time, had been the hallmark of China's nuclear doctrine since its first atomic explosion in October 1964.[103] According to PLA writers, the high command would not be caught by surprise from a nuclear first strike, because it could always detect signs of an immediate attack by a careful analysis of political, diplomatic, and military intelligence. When a nuclear confrontation seemed certain, the CMC would finalize the target list for a limited retaliation against the enemy's cities and bases and proceed up the ladder of alerts. It would be up to the CMC chairman to decide whether and when to retaliate and how to coordinate the actions of his nuclear and conventional forces.

Despite the more relaxed strategic climate of the late 1980s, the small number of China's missiles and their increased exposure to satellite detection and a surgical strike caused some PLA planners to reexamine the traditional no-first-use policy. That policy stressed flexible retaliation after a nuclear assault, and the assumed survivability of a sufficient number of strategic missiles appeared to justify that policy. The issue for the planners was the lack of enough warning time, and they began to recommend changes to compensate for the ever-greater vulnerability of their deployed missiles. The original policy authorized the Second Artillery to launch a nuclear counterstrike immediately after ascertaining that incoming missiles were nuclear-armed but before the first nuclear explosion. By the late 1990s, however, it had become manifestly impossible to determine whether or not the incoming missiles were nuclear, and the CMC was forced to choose between launch on warning or waiting out the actual hit. It chose the latter. Missile units would only be allowed to "launch the first counteroffensive after the first nuclear explosions but before the second-wave nuclear strike." [104] The fact that the initial "explosions" might not be limited or even anticipated continued to haunt the planners, but the no-first-use policy remained fundamentally intact.

The specter of an actual nuclear attack directly affects Second Artillery recruitment and assessments of personnel reliability discussed earlier. Simply stated, for a small nuclear power the psychological demands of waiting out and responding to a nuclear attack are far greater than those required of personnel who can launch a first strike. In our history of China's early nuclear program, a commander of a missile launch brigade is quoted as saying "I am often lost in thought. Can our country survive a first strike inflicted by our adversaries? We put ourselves in a passive position because of our strategic principle." [105]

A senior PLA general put the psychological dilemma of the missileers in even starker terms. Because China's no-first-use policy dictates that its missile battalions can only launch after surviving the initial nuclear explosions, they must be ready to act at a moment of "extreme psychological pressure." As a result, special attention has been paid to the "psychological quality" of Second Artillery commanders to make sure they will act in a disciplined and predictable way when the Launch Order comes. [106]

After the first nuclear counterattack, the CMC would reassess the strategic balance, the changed war situation, the size and condition of its surviving nuclear arsenal, and the ability to prevent the further escalation of the conflict before ordering subsequent nuclear rounds. The CMC would not set a timetable for those follow-on strikes, and Chinese sources suggest that any retaliation would be more dependent on the surviving nuclear-armed weapons of the navy and the air force because few warheads would remain in the Second Artillery's inventory.[107]

This current policy is based on the assumptions that an enemy would launch only a limited nuclear first strike and that a sufficient number of nuclear weapons and the essential command structure for a second strike would survive. Despite arguments challenging these assumptions, Beijing's leaders have still not adopted or even seriously considered detailed measures for responding to the worst case, an enemy's all-out nuclear attack that would destroy virtually all retaliatory nuclear missiles and their command infrastructure. So far, the policy is to make an immediate response to a nonfatal nuclear attack. The dangers in delaying a decision to retaliate until "after the first nuclear explosion" are readily apparent to China's military commanders, and some of them have long pushed for a less-restrictive response policy.

Should a conflict erupt with the United States, for example, the use of conventionally armed precision-guided munitions would perhaps pose the most likely threat to China's strategic missiles. Until recently, the PLA had no comparable conventional capability to hit back at U.S. strategic targets, because the Second Artillery had deployed only short-range conventionally armed missiles to help fight a high-tech local war. By the late 1990s, however, the vulnerability of the nation's strategic missiles to a conventional bombardment caused alarm in the CMC. Should U.S. high-tech weapons destroy those missiles and their command infrastructure, the PLA could make neither a nuclear nor a conventional response, rendering its deterrence policy worthless. Its leaders thus were being driven to choose between launching their nuclear weapons before the first explosions, which might not be nuclear, and equipping their launch battalions with medium-range conventionally armed missiles that could be launched on warning in response to any incoming attack. By choosing the latter, they added a strategic mission to the Second Artillery's conventionally armed missile battalions and thereby strengthened the no-first-use policy.[108] Their presumed targets would be Taiwan and U.S. assets or allies in Asia.

Although the CMC had decided that a powerful conventionally armed missile capability should become an indispensable component of its overall deterrence policy, its foremost concern was the global trend toward more frequent and deadly high-tech wars. Based on a review of those wars in the 1990s, senior PLA officers concluded that "strategic missiles had not played their predicted deterrent role in local wars," and the burning question for them was how to prevent or conduct a high-tech local war.[109] After investigating the outcome of recent armed conflicts, they understood that revolutionary increases in the destructive power and operating ranges of modern air-delivered conventional weapons could cripple an adversary's command-and-control system and destroy its warmaking potential. A state with such power, they held, could "attain its war goals in a single campaign."[110] In time, some of the PLA's top commanders equated this deadly campaign to a nuclear attack and the crossing of the nuclear threshold.

However, China's plans for a high-tech local war contain a major flaw, the failed modernization of the PLA Air Force (PLAAF), to which we turn in the following chapter. Its planes cannot match those of Japan or Taiwan let alone the United States, its pilots lack combat experience, and the onboard equipment and weaponry of its aircraft are at least a generation behind those of its potential adversaries. Despite a guiding principle that calls for air dominance, the PLAAF falls far short of its implementation even on its own territory. For the PLA, therefore, the only alternative is to adapt its strategic missiles to fight a conventional war. Caught between doctrine and reality, the CMC has been forced to bet on the short- and medium-range missiles of the Second Artillery to fight and win a high-tech local war.[111] Whether the logic of this decision will stand the test of battle has yet to be demonstrated.

Dictated by the requirements for winning a high-tech local war, the CMC has begun redefining the Second Artillery's missions and armaments. Many PLA officers now hold that while the Second Artillery's nuclear-armed missiles can prevent the outbreak of a nuclear war, only a large and well-defended force of modern conventionally armed missiles (including cruise missiles) could defeat China's most likely regional foes and cause Washington to think twice about entering any fray against China.[112]

This shift in thinking became official in 1998, when the Second Artillery issued a document entitled "Employment of Conventional Missiles by the Second Artillery in an Assault Campaign." According to the document, the threats that justify the use of these missiles include "separatist" actions to split China and foreign military assaults against key infrastructure (including nuclear power plants and large water reservoirs) and large cities. In these cases, conventional missiles rather than the air force and navy would be the first to be employed.[113]

The 1998 document and subsequent directives highlight the absolute requirement to protect those missiles against enemy air strikes in a military showdown. Other key requirements for the Second Artillery to achieve its objectives are equally demanding. The CMC has called on its missile designers to speed up the miniaturization of reentry vehicles on the new generation of long-range nuclear missiles and the conversion to more lethal conventional warheads on an increased number of ballistic and cruise missiles. It has equated nuclear-armed missiles to a "shield" and conventional missiles to the "sword." Gradually, Chinese strategists have begun to echo their counterparts in the West on the complementary roles of nuclear and conventional missiles in modern warfare. In our final chapter we will trace the course of their search for a viable strategy to the more public debate beginning in 2004 on the possible early use of nuclear weapons. In Chapter 7, by connecting that search to the long-frustrated effort to build a modern air force, we identify one of the strategy's most persistent weak links.

SEVEN

The Quest for a Modern Air Force

For more than fifty years, China has sought to build a combat-ready air force. First in the Korean War (1950–53) and then again in 1979 after Deng Xiaoping's becoming the supreme leader, Beijing's leaders accorded urgency to this goal, but it was the demonstration of air power during the conflicts involving the United States since the Gulf War in 1991 that most alerted them to the global revolution in air warfare and prompted an accelerated buildup.[1]

As a consequence of appraisals of U.S. air operations in those conflicts, the modernization of the air force began to bear fruit, though slowly and in an unexpected direction: away from self-reliance toward increased foreign procurements. This was the time that the People's Liberation Army began the shift to a "two-legs" policy of producing its own planes while stepping up purchases of aircraft from Russia. In the same period, PLA theorists inched closer to Western concepts of the role of air power in warfare, a movement that influenced fundamental modifications in the nation's overall defense strategy.[2]

In the 1980s, China's single-minded pursuit of economic progress coupled with the general downsizing of its military forces and defense industry had sapped air force construction programs. In the next decade, however, as the PLA was becoming ever more fixated on the necessity of future air dominance over the Taiwan Strait, the nation's economic growth and reacquisition of Hong Kong helped underwrite and advance those programs. China's gross domestic product grew at an average annual rate of 11.7 percent from 1991 to 1995 and 8 percent from 1996 to 2000,[3] and that growth, which continues, helped the aviation industry procure more sophisticated aircraft and related weaponry. The large-scale infusion of Su-27SK and Su-30MK fighters (as well as related training aircraft) from Russia in recent years is only one example of the growing commitment of money and personnel to the construction of the PLA Air Force (PLAAF).[4]

The presumed—and feared—high probability of conflict in the Taiwan Strait along with the parallel reassessment of American air power and strategy uniquely dictated the direction of revisions in China's force posture and defense strategy. The contention for the island's sovereignty quickened the pace of planning and preparations intended to diversify Beijing's political and military options should tensions increase in the strait.

This brief overview of the history of China's efforts to create a modern air force suggests the two principal questions to be addressed in the sections that follow. Why did those efforts, which enjoyed the highest priority, repeatedly fail? The air force programs could not claim the center's unequivocal endorsement after 1949 and especially after Mao committed his country to building nuclear weapons and their delivery systems, but PLA commanders did make ever-higher demands on those programs even as they held back the necessary resources to achieve their success. Available Chinese military writings on the history of the air force suggest that the reasons for the failure varied markedly from period to period. That variation itself prevented the military and political leaderships from forming a powerful consensus about policies that could work.

The sources become even richer during and since the decade of the 1990s, in which the air force fashioned both a more effective R&D and procurement policy and a more comprehensive doctrine for the PLAAF in future conflicts. When viewed from the perspective of past failures and how far the air force must go just to catch up with the enemies that it one day may face, a second question must be addressed: How do the Chinese justify the search for an advanced air arm, and does that justification make sense in the contemporary world? The final sections of this chapter examine the elements of the new policy and doctrine and set forth the rationale for this priority mission.

MARCHING IN PLACE

Mao Zedong first assigned precedence to his air force in the early stages of the Korean War. In 1951, faced with mounting casualties from U.S. air strikes, he called for the formation of a national aviation industry, and in October, his diplomats inked an accord in Moscow on technical support for that industry. Within weeks, Soviet experts began heading to China to help construct assembly plants for planes and jet engines.[5]

Formative Years

Mao had negotiated a pledge of $300 million in credits during his journey to Moscow in the winter of 1949–50. The Chinese at first resolved to devote the bulk of this sum to buying Soviet naval equipment for an invasion of Taiwan planned for the summer of 1950. The staggering losses from U.S. air raids in Korea changed his mind, however, and in February 1952, Mao redirected half of the credits intended for the navy to the air force. Over time, virtually all these credits flowed to the purchase of planes and aviation ordnance from Moscow.[6] Thereafter, China manufactured Soviet-designed jet fighters and then bombers under license.

Poor planning, lack of a sufficient industrial base, misguided bureaucratic meddling, Nikita Khrushchev's denigration of air power at a time of Soviet influence within the PLA, and the ever-greater importance attached to the strategic forces interrupted progress toward a battle-ready air force for the next quarter century. Chief of the General Staff Luo Ruiqing did try again to accelerate the aircraft program in 1964,[7] and by 1966, China had begun making light and medium bombers as well as fighters based on leftover Soviet blueprints. In the latter year, Mao also approved construction of an assembly center and other pioneering facilities in Shaanxi Province for manufacturing parts for the Soviet-designed bombers, and for most of the 1960s, he gave budgetary precedence to the production of bombers over all other aircraft.[8] Because of the large cost differential, we should note, only a few hundred bombers were produced in comparison to a much larger number of fighters.

The mistakes and missteps extended well beyond the pace of production. Dictated by the PLA's traditional active defense strategy, including the protection of its big cities and industrial bases, China should have assigned high urgency to R&D programs on fighters, radars, surface-to-air missiles, and electronic countermeasures for strengthening air defense. But that decision, too, was not forthcoming. Decades later, PLA historians would blame Beijing's senior leaders for their failure to grasp the need for such protection.

Mao was also mired in outmoded concepts about the nature of warfare. Even as he was expressing his fear of imminent global conflict in the 1960s and was pushing the nuclear weapons and long-range missile programs, he impeded all conventional weapons procurement programs by launching massive industrial construction in China's interior or "third line," as discussed in Chapter 3. In these remote bastions, primitive factories would manufacture the tools of war for the survivors of the predicted nuclear holocaust. Just at the moment violent clashes broke out on the Sino-Soviet frontier in March 1969, Mao stayed so committed to this construction program that most of the money for the aviation industry was poured into projects that were doomed from the outset (93.4 percent of the total in 1966–70, 83.2 percent in 1971–75). Official investigations conducted later in Sichuan and Shaanxi provinces, for example, revealed that almost half their third-line enterprises operated below capacity or had not even begun operation.[9]

The fault lay with form as well as substance. To succeed, any R&D program on advanced aircraft and their armaments must be minutely planned and take into account technological uncertainties, long lead times, and the vagaries of political commitment. However, the Central Military Commission, in a near frenzy caused by the mounting Sino-Soviet border tensions and the general mood of the times, ruined the possibility for the success of any long-term development effort. In 1971, it ordered the aviation ministry (Third Ministry of Machine Building) to commence R&D programs on twenty-seven new types of aircraft, including a long-range bomber, a long-range transport, and a vertical-takeoff fighter.[10] By starting everything at once, nothing truly got underway.

Years of Chaos

During the Cultural Revolution (1966–76), factional pressures and simplistic slogans paralyzed the air force, causing it to slight pilot training and flight operations. For example, many pilots had only thirty to forty flying hours a year, some even fewer than twenty, and plane crashes came with tragic regularity. Because of chaotic training and poor maintenance, the rate of fatal accidents for military aircraft soared to 0.6 accidents per 10,000 flying hours in 1974 from 0.249 in 1964. By 1972 only 6.2 percent of pilots could fly safely at night in good weather, and a mere 1 percent could do so under marginal night conditions.[11]

For a while, nothing seemed to go well. In 1973, for example, Zhou Enlai called on the air force to heighten its fighting skills within two and a half years.[12] However, the lack of well-trained pilots was so consequential that the air force could not assign a single organic squadron to provide air cover during the Sino–South Vietnamese armed conflict of January 15–20, 1974. As an emergency measure, the air force had to transfer qualified commanders from different squadrons on an ad hoc basis to fly these missions. By the mid-1970s, as a prelude to taking more substantial upgrading measures, the air force had also reorganized its combat units as follows: air corps (*kongjun jun*), air division (*kongjun shi*), air regiment (*kongjun tuan*), and air squadron (*feixing dadui*).[13]

Meanwhile, Mao's radical bannermen launched large-scale persecution of designers and engineers, and technical and logistics bugs continued to plague aircraft production. A typical case was the J-6 fighter, a version of the Soviet MiG-19. In 1971, seven of the forty J-6s built for foreign sale proved defective, and when Zhou Enlai halted the delivery of the J-6s on December 15, 1971, he issued a directive to warn senior officials about the low quality of military hardware.[14] Hundreds of the J-6c's were built before the design was finalized, and millions of yuan had to be budgeted to have them dismantled and rebuilt. In this and similar ways, the aviation ministry wasted 65.8 percent of its R&D funds. In 1972, Marshal Ye Jianying, who had replaced Lin Biao to oversee CMC operations, told the ministry never to "give birth to a child before giving birth to its father," but to no avail.[15]

What is more, the institutes under the Aviation Research Academy (or Sixth Academy) made sorry headway in their efforts to develop new designs.[16] The academy had been set up in June 1961, to supervise various facilities for carrying out R&D programs on military aircraft and airborne weapons, but the standard of its work was deeply affected by the country's political climate and remained low. For example, its engineers could not finish the designs for the J-7 and J-8, two fighters then under development, until more than ten years after the inaugural test flights of their prototypes. Not until 1979, thirteen years after the test flights of a prototype J-7, did the ministry approve the J-7 to replace the J-6.[17] This was the same for air-launched weapons and avionics, which fell far short of minimal requirements and firm deadlines.

By the end of the Cultural Revolution in 1976, the aviation industry was reeling from the decade of neglect, and from the perspective of the CMC, the air force was in a doom loop. Examples abounded. Quality problems occurred on the vanes of the J-6c turbojet engines. Rivets on the Q-5 attacker (fighter-bomber) were found loosened. Rotary wings dropped from Z-5 helicopters. Engineers found flaws endemic in the J-6c fighter and Q-5 attacker as well as the Z-5, and shipped 1,050 of these aircraft back to the factories where technicians hunted down thousands of defects. In typical bureaucratese, the air force summarized these faults as "backward equipment, poor-quality products, and inadequate components." Moreover, it could not break free from its reliance on the Soviet aircraft introduced in the 1950s and 1960s, and PLAAF leaders concluded that the revolutionary advancements in foreign aviation technologies had increased the inequality between China and other military powers.[18]

After years of fruitless striving, repeated examinations exposed unresolved failures of leadership and training. Fifty percent of pilots could not accurately land by instrument. Most fighter pilots had failed to master the art of hitting targets from a wide angle of attack. Some fighter squadrons had hits in mock dogfights as low as 1.7 percent of total engagements, and most attacker and bomber pilots had equally dismal records on the target ranges. Many pilots had few, if any, opportunities to fire a gun or make a bombing run. To make matters worse, a third of their commanders were deemed incompetent.

Redefining the Problem in the Early Deng Years

By 1977, the air force began to comprehend the costs of these failures and drafted a Three-Year Plan for Constructing the Air Force (1978–80) for the CMC's approval. It would take years, however, for the aviation sector to understand fully and accept the causes of the underlying dysfunctions. With a focus on pilot training and new weapons, the air force launched some sixty projects and a fresh attempt to end the confusion and deadlock. The favored remedies dealt with command and discipline at the regiment level and above.[19] The key, the CMC proclaimed, lay in organizational and leadership reforms.

In line with these reforms, which were mostly completed by the following year, the air force began assigning pilots many more flying hours, and compared to 1974, the serious aircraft accident rate dropped sharply from 0.62 to 0.3 per 10,000 flying hours by 1978. And after air units at the division level and above formed safety committees to oversee the training programs in 1984, the rate dropped to 0.182 within six years.

What happened after Deng Xiaoping took charge of the CMC in 1977 interests us most, because of China's dramatic national turnaround associated with his name. In August, he ordered the air force to shape up, saying, "the frequent and recent plane accidents were the result of inadequate training and aircraft quality."[20] Again, little happened immediately, and not until a year later did the air force with some fanfare begin to rectify equipment defects and beef up pilot training. When it came to the PLA's most intractable problems, Deng's influence was proving to be marginal.

At about the same time, Deng began pressing the bureaucratic aviation ministry to finalize the J-7b as a replacement for the J-6. Some months later, in early 1978, the CMC announced a new guiding principle: "The air force must enhance domestic air defense by concentrating on the defense of strategic points and strengthen its capability to provide support in land and naval battles." In response, the ministry called a meeting in June to rethink its R&D programs. This session ended with an order to concentrate on the J-7b and to begin planning for follow-on generations to replace it.[21]

Convinced that the air force would play a decisive part in any future large conflict, Deng publicized his general conclusions about its role. He wrote: "The army and navy both need air cover. Otherwise, the enemy air force will run rampant. . . . We must possess a powerful air force to guarantee air superiority [in a future war]." He told the CMC to "attach primary importance" to the pursuit of air dominance. On January 18, 1979, Deng, who by then had become China's "paramount leader," elevated his perspective on air power to official CMC doctrine:

> Without the air force and the domination of the skies, winning a future war is out of the question. The army needs air support and air cover. Without air cover, winning a naval battle is also out of the question. . . . Give priority to the future development of the air force. Stress investment in the development of the aviation industry and the air force to ensure control of the skies.[22]

Deng's secondary, though unstated, purpose in concentrating on the air force was to assert his authority over what was generally regarded as the most potentially dangerous service. The new leadership attached special political weight to the air force because Lin Biao had seized control of the PLAAF at the onset of his abortive coup against Mao in 1971. As a result of such power struggles during the Cultural Revolution, Party leaders thereafter sought to keep a much tighter rein over the air force than the other services. Later, PLA officers credited Deng's action to "removing a sword of Damocles" over his head.[23]

So the question is: With so much emphasis given to the air force after 1977, what happened next? Herein lies a puzzle coming at a turning point in the evolution of the PLAAF.

CHOOSING PRIORITIES: THE AIR FORCE IN THE 1980s

What we again see here is a case of "small politics" operating in the context of "large politics," as the Chinese say. While Deng was taking charge of the air force and raising its ranking in his security equation, his overriding goal was to consolidate his power base as the nation's supreme leader. From late 1977 on, Beijing became enmeshed in the grand leadership realignment, and Deng wanted time for his supporters to regain the authority wrested from them during the Cultural Revolution. In need of "soldiers" who would man their coalition, Deng and his associates assigned top priority to reversing "unjust verdicts" on loyalists. It was a matter of numbers. He had to rehabilitate the more than six thousand senior officials who would become his main foot soldiers.[24] From 1979 to 1981, power politics caused a slowdown in most military programs, including those designed to revitalize the air force.

Deng's Orders

Only in 1981 did the air force begin executing its second and third three-year plans for training and readiness. Fundamental changes to be carried out by the air force were announced, and Deng as CMC chairman singled out his air force commanders, praising them for "strict enforcement of orders and prohibitions." "The air force has a good style of work," he said, and "has made great achievements in training, style of work, and discipline."[25] Blessed by Deng, the PLAAF headquarters once more urged the aviation industry to gear up for high production and enhanced performance.

For their part, the leaders in the defense industry echoed Deng's directive giving precedence to the air force. Still in 1981, the director of the Defense Science and Technology Commission (DSTC), Zhang Aiping, conceded that the air force was one of the military's two weak links (the other being the Second Artillery) and once more prodded the aviation industry to produce more advanced weaponry.[26] But, once more actions did not match the official word.

In March 1983, presumably in a mood of frustration but technically with orders and organizations in place, the Commission of Science, Technology, and Industry for National Defense (COSTIND), which had replaced the DSTC, convoked a national defense-industry conference. At this gathering, the CMC demanded that the aviation ministry clarify its approach to "renewing a generation, developing a generation, and conducting a preliminary study on a generation [of new weapons and aircraft]." Yang Shangkun, the CMC's executive vice-chairman, directed COSTIND to "revitalize the aviation industry," and Zhang Aiping, then minister of defense, for good measure added that the ministry should "streamline R&D programs, assure success in essential systems, attach greater importance to scientific research, and replace obsolete weapons with new types."[27]

The message and its urgency appeared clear, but in fact the defense industry was receiving mixed messages. For a quarter century, the industry's overriding target continued to be the building of nuclear weapons and their delivery systems, and everyone knew that goal took primacy over all others. Money, expertise, and political backing told the actual story, and promotions went to those who had made their mark in the strategic programs.

By the mid-1980s, the CMC had to face facts and revisited its policy goals and finally revamped its weapons procurement plans. We briefly noted the resulting doctrinal changes earlier. First, holding that the most likely future armed conflicts would be local wars under nuclear deterrence, the CMC determined that R&D programs on conventional weapons should take priority over those on strategic weapons. Second, the military was enjoined to augment the existing conventional force and to fashion new weapons. Third, whereas ground weapons originally claimed precedence, the navy and the air force now were given pride of place. Compared to the other services, the air force was awarded a higher priority, the reasons for which could be traced more to Deng Xiaoping's political-strategic assessment than any specific threats at that time.[28]

In the meantime, the CMC prescribed these wartime tasks for the air force: defend strategic points and provide air cover for strategic deployment of massed troops; maintain air supremacy in the main theaters of operation in support of the army and the navy; launch surprise attacks on high-value targets of the enemy; participate in nuclear counterattack; and conduct strategic aerial reconnaissance. The CMC further directed the PLAAF to prepare defenses against air raids and support the other services opposing a ground invasion or launching counteroffensives.[29] The effect of this directive, almost unnoticed at the time, was to give the air force license to fashion its own strategy, a strategy that was to become full-blown in the coming decade.

One reason for the failure to notice the doctrinal change was the flurry of activity on the procurement front. In line with its newly defined strategic missions and weapons priorities, the air force began drafting a series of directives and multiyear plans on weapons development. These plans emphasized domestic air defense and listed a number of high-priority projects: surface-to-air missiles, medium/long-range all-weather interceptors, early-warning aircraft and technologies, electronic countermeasures equipment, and automatic command-and-control systems. The air force was also to undertake research on space defense weapons and long-range bombers that could launch cruise missiles. Yet, most R&D programs centered on fighters and fighter-bombers, the HQ-7 surface-to-air missile, a precision-guided bomb for the H-6 medium bomber, new-type radars, unmanned reconnaissance aircraft, and avionics for fighters.[30]

In response to reports on revolutionary changes in Western military aviation, the PLAAF found itself caught between the leadership's demand for immediate improvements and the Maoist-era insistence on self-reliance. The compromise was to extend the meaning of Deng Xiaoping's Open Door policy to permit foreign assistance in the acquisition of advanced air-launched weapons and avionics. The most dramatic evidence of the compromise came in 1986, when a consortium of U.S. companies as part of a group led by Grumman signed an ill-fated deal to install avionics on fifty-five J-8b fighters under the so-called Peace Pearl program. Other Western countries and Israel also signed contracts for both avionics and weapons.[31]

At about the same time, Deng made what was to be his last genuine attempt to adhere to self-reliance in building the air force. His initial solution: The air force must clean house. "The total number of our air personnel is perhaps the largest in the world," he said, and only after deep reductions in personnel and outdated planes could the air force "significantly raise its efficiency." Deng blasted those officers who sought remedies in foreign purchases: "How many advanced airplanes can you afford to purchase? . . . We will become poor soon after we have bought a few airplanes."[32] The emphasis on efficiency simply masked the underlying compromise. Self-reliance was still the avowed policy, but it merely precluded the purchase of foreign aircraft.

Giving Air Power National Priority

Even that exception proved short-lived. Rapid obsolescence was moving faster than paced acquisitions and rendering the self-reliance policy unworkable. By 1988, 48.8 percent of aircraft, 53.9 percent of aircraft engines, 42 percent of radars, 50 percent of HQ-2 surface-to-air missiles, and 42 percent of HQ-2 missile guidance sites were not operational. This state of disrepair restricted pilot training and further degraded combat readiness.[33]

For these and other reasons, the CMC finally was forced to face these failures, but it could not directly blame the policy or its assumption that the PLAAF could modernize quickly on its own. As it had done so often in the past, the high command sidestepped the real causes of the failures and proclaimed that management and budget deficiencies were at fault. Obediently, the PLAAF called for "reducing equipment, readjusting flying hours, differentiating the first-line units from others, and replacing obsolete equipment," and for a time, carrying out these changes seemed to make a difference.

Compared to 1989, readiness in 1990 increased in most key sectors: aircraft, engines, radars, and surface-to-air missiles and related missile guidance sites.

Following suit, COSTIND pushed the aviation ministry to expand aircraft acquisitions, but it had limited funds at best and remained focused on the strategic weapons programs. The revised wish list was defensible but overly ambitious: five types of replacement fighters, three new fighter-bombers, five aircraft under development or under study, and new types of ground-attack aircraft. The aviation ministry directed work to proceed on the next-generation surface-to-air and air-to-air missiles.[34] By the early 1990s, initial replacements had begun to enter the inventory, and the high command for a time seemed to relax.

With all the apparent progress, PLA strategists and intelligence specialists began calculating the strategic balance. They weighed the chances of a super-power surprise attack against China's coastal areas and proposed a coordinated response with the air force playing the pivotal part. Decades hence, the United States or another military power, even Japan or India, might pose such a threat, they argued, and the danger of a lightning or surgical strike against strategic Chinese targets would be particularly acute during escalating crises.[35] They also warned their commanders about the transfer of advanced airborne weapons from the West and Russia to China's neighbors and potential adversaries. They believed that these weapons outclassed China's, and cited India as an example of a military power making the transition from a defensive to an offensive air power. China, they maintained, had only a defensive air force, and a weak one at that.[36]

In May 1990, at the high tide of assessments focusing on the air force, Yang Shangkun chaired a conference to discuss the acquisition of air combat systems and once more issued directives echoing those of the past. He said: "Accelerate the development of the air force equipment. We are determined to revitalize the aviation industry. . . . Short service life and high fuel consumption characterize our aircraft engines. We must build our own aircraft engines even if we have to risk our old lives." The CMC in turn reissued a near-meaningless decision to give the first preference to the development of aircraft weapons and equipment and prepared the budget to implement it.[37] For all practical purposes, Yang's directive duplicated Deng's of a decade earlier. Despite the rush of activity in the decade of the 1980s, the result, in short, was an air force weaker in comparative terms than the one that began the decade.

The questions are why, and what led to a turning point in the history of the PLAAF?

THE TURNING POINT AND THE EMERGENCE OF AN AIR FORCE STRATEGY

The search for an answer takes us back to the mid-1950s. From then to the 1980s, Mao Zedong and his heirs were embarked on a crusade to create a nuclear and missile arsenal, and, as we have noted, that goal blunted any sustained push for PLAAF modernization. Even in the Cultural Revolution, Mao attempted to protect his strategic programs from the turmoil,[38] but R&D on conventional weapons was mostly shut down.

When they did worry about conventional arms in the 1960s and 1970s, Mao and his lieutenants in practice were bound to the revolutionary culture that favored the ground forces and confined the navy and the air force to a subordinate status.[39] When conventional weapons did rise to priority status in the mid-1980s, the conflict in the South China Sea cast a shadow on all planning, and naval equipment for a brief time went to the top of the list.[40]

In addition to a lack of focus on the air force because of strategic and naval priorities, the Chinese military had to cope with the overriding redirection of policy in the early 1980s that turned the nation's energies to civilian production and rapid modernization. Shortly after his return to power, Deng had dismissed the likelihood of a major war (though he was soon to become obsessed by Vietnam) for decades to come and ordered a near-total shift to activating industry and agriculture.[41] Sharp reductions in the defense budget followed, and the PLA's share of the annual state budget dropped from 18.5 percent in 1979 to about 8 percent in 1989.[42]

For a few years, the defense industry sold a large number of weapons abroad, and much of the state budget supported the growth of the nation's dual-use infrastructure.[43] Some idled workers, moreover, moved to civilian production and assembly lines under joint-venture contracts with Western firms.[44] The downward spiral of defense orders in turn undermined morale in a labor force feeling ever more insecure in the increasingly idle defense factories. The most qualified workers and staff began scouring the non-state sector for higher pay and better career opportunities. Some Chinese officers compared the increased priority for the air force in a declining military to filling a bathtub on a sinking ship.

The revolution in air-delivered weapons dramatized by the United States in the 1991 Gulf War shattered Beijing's complacency. Time was no longer an ally, for delay would bring the danger of total, perhaps permanent obsolescence. China's air defenses could not prevent surprise attacks deep into the nation's heartland.[45] Some strategists analyzed the possibility of such attacks in the context of a future confrontation between Beijing and Taipei, and assigned a greater probability to future hostilities with the United States should cross-strait tensions increase.[46]

As reports of Iraq's defeat poured into his office, Yang Shangkun attempted to deflect the psychological blow to his army produced by the U.S.-led victory: "The model [of the Gulf War] is not universal. It cannot, at least, be applied in a country like China, which has a lot of mountains, forests, valleys and rivers. Another characteristic of this war is that the multinational forces faced a very weak enemy."[47] Few military officers took his Panglossian words seriously.

For the air force, the Gulf War came as an especially rude wakeup call. For decades, the air force had only been given operational and tactical assignments to provide air cover and fire support for the other two services in combined operations. It had no identifiable strategy of its own, though it did sponsor strategic studies and seminars on its missions in a "People's War under modern conditions." In the latter half of the 1980s, the CMC had begun to give the air force more defensive assignments, but these assignments only further forced the PLAAF planners to extend their research to encompass foreign air strategies. They resolved that their service would have to establish its own strategic doctrine and that the central condition for its successful implementation lay in "technology," meaning the constant incorporation of advanced knowledge, not just new hardware.[48]

From the late 1970s on, Deng Xiaoping had issued a series of directives defining the PLAAF's wartime missions. "Active defense itself," he argued, "is not necessarily limited to a defensive concept.... Active defense also contains an offensive element.... The bombers of the air force are defensive weapons." The recurring message in Deng's directives called for the air force to switch from a purely defensive to a combined defensive-offensive posture. Freed from the shackles of the more traditional interpretation of People's War, PLA strategists began a systematic refinement of "China's concept" of deterrence. They pored over the West's writings on high-tech warfare, and concluded that in order to move toward a combined-forces posture the PLAAF must add more offensive forces.[49]

This conclusion in turn spurred further research on air strategy. Air force researchers assumed that China would continue to face regional military threats. Operating within the prescribed but malleable military strategy of active defense, they began elaborating the nation's first air strategy to meet those threats. They reviewed global politics and military relations, potential combat scenarios, current missions and assignments, China's economic and industrial capacity, and existing PLAAF capabilities.[50] These strategists further assumed that the most likely wars in the foreseeable future would be limited, that wars would "always" begin with air strikes, and that control of the air was "a prerequisite" for victory.[51] Within a decade, their special pleading on behalf of the air force would seem justified by U.S. air actions in the 1991 Gulf War.

The emerging air strategy emphasized both the requirements and tactics of air power and deemed the two interrelated and interactive. Echoing the strategists' sense of urgency, the CMC in a 1986 order declared that by the end of the century the air force must be able to "cope with local wars and contingencies of various types and make preparations for rapid expansion in case of a full-scale war."[52] Heralding this decision, the air force issued its own slogan calling for "quick reaction, integrated coordination, and combat in depth (*kuaisu fanying, zhengti xietiao, zongshen zuozhan*)." "Quick reaction," "integrated coordination," and "combat in depth" sounded like textbook phrases from a U.S. defense paper, but when taken together and compared to previous policy statements, they obviously were intended to infuse the new PLAAF doctrines with greater substance and the rhetoric needed to claim precedence for the air force in grand strategy.

That position, when fully elaborated, modified the then prevailing interpretations of active defense. The PLA still ruled out preemptive air strikes, especially against more powerful opponents, and held to the declared policy of retaliation only. Yet, the air force recognized its fate if forced to remain totally passive in a first strike.[53] Once hit, there would be little left for a second-strike response, and herein began the modification.

"Quick reaction" would provide part of the mandate to launch the instant second blow as a prerequisite for deterrence, even survival. Moreover, "integrated coordination" would begin at first warning and give the air force access to and even control over various high-tech arms in conventional war. This "coordination" would continue throughout the entire course of the conflict and include collecting and analyzing intelligence information; conducting command, control, and communications; organizing various arms in combined operations; and guaranteeing sustained logistical support.

By calling for "integrated coordination," the CMC intended to redefine and expand the limited power of the region commander over the air force in his region. Unless otherwise directed by the CMC, the air units had reported to the local air command posts (*kongjun zhihuisuo*) in a command chain that led directly to central air force headquarters.[54] Under implementing directives that followed the 1986 order, the CMC placed the fighter and fighter-bomber squadrons under the dual control of the air force and the region command. However, the air force headquarters still controlled the long-range bomber groups, coordinated the air combat units stationed in different military regions, and for large-scale air operations could take command of all required aircraft. The CMC itself would issue orders through a dual control system for employing fighter and fighter-bomber units; that is, these units would come under both their region commander and the region's air force commander.[55]

At the same time, the probable requirement to conduct operations over a wide geographical area led the PLAAF to embrace the concept of "combat in depth," and it was the realization of this concept that most tested the operational limits of the hallowed no-first-strike inhibition. It should be noted at the outset that the PLAAF has not adopted nor is it considering a forward strategy and that many of the elements of the traditional "active defense" doctrine remain untouched. Rather, it adheres to the principle of "light deployment in the frontier and massive deployment in the rear." According to the early formulations of this combat-in-depth principle, the military still would not be allowed to retaliate until the enemy had inflicted the initial blow, and the doctrine implied that in that first engagement the frontier forces would be sacrificed. The air force would have redeployed all its bombers, transport planes, and most attackers to the rear, and only the frontier-based fighters would be lost.[56]

However, even these fighters were to be stationed for maximum survivability. Fighter air groups would be dispersed throughout the nation, while bombers and attackers would be concentrated in the rear as a second-strike deterrent.[57] To facilitate this deployment policy, air units were divided into three types: quick reaction air groups (*kuaisu fanying budui*), alert air groups (*zhanbei zhiban budui*), and strategic reserves (*zhanlüe yubeidui*).[58]

As a stopgap measure, the frontier air groups were ordered to camouflage their aircraft and place them in semi-hardened shelters even though their commanders realized the futility of such measures in surviving a sustained attack by advanced precision-guided munitions. Other measures quickly followed to increase survivability and readiness. The air force selected highways and other alternative sites as emergency runways for the dispersion of frontier planes, and designed special equipment for the refueling of fighters on freeways in emergencies. Alert fighters could refuel and take off in twenty minutes at these sites, and the PLAAF adopted other quick-reaction measures that required early warning.[59]

As a result of the transition to a combined offensive-defensive posture, the balance steadily tilted toward the offense. This ongoing shift was quickened by tactics to defend against attacks on theater targets and by the reassignment of air groups as shock units against the enemy's rear areas.[60] Step by step but without fanfare, basic changes were occurring in Chinese military doctrine, and the clarity between an actual hit and a warning of an attack as the cause for launching the rear-based bombers and attackers began to blur.

Moreover, the changes continue. Some strategists still doubt the soundness of a strategy for fighting a limited war that depends on high-tech defensive weapons. They belittle the wisdom of a mere partial shift toward an active offensive strategy. Precision-guided bomber weapons and cruise missiles, they argue, could inflict devastating surprise attacks deep inside China, and despite the latitude implied by combat in depth, these attacks could well wipe out any retaliatory forces and countermeasures and leave the leadership without viable options in an escalating crisis.[61] The argument about the essential importance of high-tech weapons remains unsettled and has become a focal point in the PLA's strategic studies since the late nineties.

By 2002, the CMC had restructured and modernized the command-and-control system in the air force bringing it into line with the overall reconfiguration needed to fight a high-tech local war. It disbanded five air corps headquarters and removed the corps-level combat forces from the command chain. In theater operations, CMC directives would now pass directly to a region command, the region's air branch, and combat air divisions, though in emergencies CMC orders could go straight to the divisions.[62]

IMPACT ON PROCUREMENT

PLA analysts have concluded from their studies and debates that the force structure must be revamped. The total number of air force personnel within the PLA must be reduced, and the composition and size of the main PLAAF units and their arming must be reviewed. Along with its preoccupation with enhanced air defenses, the air force fretted about its puny ground attack capability. For decades, more than 70 percent of the PLA's military aircraft were fighters, while bombers, attackers (fighter-bombers), helicopters, and transport planes made up the balance.[63] In line with the new strategy, the air force began to adjust the mix of its order-of-battle. Although fighters still far outnumber attackers and bombers, the ratio is reversing, and increasing numbers of reconnaissance planes, electronic countermeasures aircraft, early-warning aircraft, air refueling aircraft, and transport planes are entering the force.[64]

The strategists particularly have applauded the greater attention given to attackers. They maintain that all leading military powers including the United States, Russia, and other European countries have mandated such a priority. They argue that attackers, air refuelable and equipped with precision-guided cruise missiles, match bombers in range and destructiveness. With greater maneuverability, attackers could help repulse an aggressor. While a certain number of strategic bombers could reinforce deterrence and complicate an enemy's strategic calculus, attackers could do both and in the future should far outnumber deployed bombers. This planned reversal in plane ratios also has a political rationale. Any marked growth of China's strategic bomber fleet might aggravate suspicions among its neighbors and fuel an arms race.[65] The nuclear-capable attacker is considered the near-perfect plane to obscure the boundary between offense and defense and between retaliation and first strike. Accusations about the "China threat" are having an effect.

Thus, changes in strategy increasingly interacted with weapons procurements. The air force earlier had worked out short-term (five years), medium-term (ten years), and long-term (twenty years) procurement programs,[66] but almost before they were ready for promulgation, they had to be redrafted. Finally, in 1992, a new ten-character weapons procurement policy was adopted: *duo yanzhi, shao shengchan, zhongdian zhuangbei.* Loosely translated, this new policy assigned a greater role to indigenous R&D and temporarily settled for supplying most of the forces with little up-to-date matériel, while only selected units would be singled out to receive newly produced arms. In an attempt to upgrade its weaponry, the air force stressed surface-to-air missiles; long-range, all-weather fighters; command, control, and information equipment; early-warning and air-refueling aircraft; and air-to-ground attack weapons with an emphasis on airborne precision-guided cruise missiles. Simultaneously, the air force also began upgrading its technical and strategic knowledge or what it called its software base.[67] Chinese commanders had absorbed the lesson from the West: construct the technical and industrial infrastructure first and then concentrate on step-by-step technology testing and manpower training.

In early 1993, following a prolonged review of the Gulf War's "lessons," the CMC called for two cardinal changes by the year 2000: Change the military from dependence on manpower and People's War to greater reliance on science and technology; and switch plans for military preparedness from winning a conventional local war to winning a high-tech local war.[68] PLA strategists downgraded the likelihood of regional or global wars and acknowledged that the two changes magnified the gap between Chinese and Western air forces.

This was a sobering finding because in earlier decades they had consistently belittled the idea that a decisive inequality even existed. In self-defense, the strategists claimed that the gap was of recent origin and had not always existed between China and the West. They held that J-6 fighters of the 1960s were comparable then to fighters anywhere in the world, but that China's less advanced fighter-engine designs and superior avionics in Western countries had created what they called "short legs" (*duantui*). PLA aircraft, they said, had short ranges and were short on avionics.[69]

The shadow of a coming crisis in the Taiwan Strait made these short legs especially dangerous. Should a conflict occur there, the PLAAF would now expect to be defeated because of the enemy's better air force. Any domestic program to correct this weakness, moreover, would require the creation of a much more sophisticated industrial base and a huge investment and faced long lead times. Even before the 1993 decision, the choice had become clear: total self-reliance would have to be abandoned.[70] The planes for the next decade would have to come from foreign countries. Although PLA strategists deemed such purchases to be "mutually complementary" to the dogma of self-reliance,[71] everyone in the high command had come to recognize that Mao's dictum for military modernization again must be set aside in practice.

Once more the supplier would have to be Russia, whose arsenals were becoming available for a price and where many senior Chinese leaders had been trained in the 1950s.

In November 1992, shortly before the "two cardinal changes" decision, senior Russian and Chinese military officials began annual meetings on military-technical cooperation and signed a so-called Protocol I to formalize their commitment to long-term ties.[72] During his visit to Beijing that December, Russian president Boris Yeltsin signed a "Memorandum of Understanding on Sino-Russian Military Equipment and Technology Cooperation," the origins of which could be traced to a similar, though largely unfulfilled, agreement dated December 28, 1990. Protocol I included provisions for the sale of twenty-six Su-27SK fighters and jet engines as well as the training of Chinese pilots. The second annual meeting, which took place in Moscow in June 1993, led to the conclusion of Protocol II in May 1994. Inter alia, this document simplified the approval procedures endorsed in 1990.

Even before the signing of Protocol I, the PLAAF had concluded its own agreement with the Russians, signed on August 3, 1992, for delivery of an advanced air defense system, and the contract for its delivery was finalized in July 1993. Protocol II added to the list of air defense equipment and itemized areas for further defense industrial and technology cooperation, especially the areas of communications and advanced countermeasures. Consistent with the protocol, the CMC told the PLAAF to reinforce its "shield" while sharpening its "spear" and to purchase Russian air defense technologies, including S-300 and TOR-M1 surface-to-air missile systems.[73]

Within a decade, China had purchased enough Su-27s for four squadrons, and of these, three fighter squadrons were based in Huhu, Anhui Province, Suixi, Guangdong Province, and Anshan, Liaoning Province, respectively, and a trainer squadron in Baiduo near Chongqing. China signed a contract to pay Russia a $2.5 billion license fee for manufacturing 200 Su-27SKs (code-named J-11) over fifteen years, and its engineers modified the SK models by replacing the radar and engines with equivalent Chinese models.[74] The PLAAF reportedly will deploy 373 Su-27SKs by 2010.[75]

The PLAAF also expressed a strong interest in the Su-30MK, a highly capable fighter-bomber. Beginning in 1999, China began importing eighty Su-30MKs in two batches, for which it paid $1.8 billion per batch. In 2003, Russia reportedly supplied a naval version of this aircraft and licensed the production of additional Su-30MKs in Chinese factories.[76]

While the magnitude and pace of Russian aircraft imports have been repeatedly reported in the world's press, the principal emphasis from the mid-1990s was on pilot training as well as aircraft and air traffic control upgrades. Even earlier in the decade, the PLAAF began sending its most experienced pilots to Russia for advanced flight training and schooling in tactical techniques and operations.[77] Prior to 1999, the pilot training programs concentrated on how to fight conventional local wars, although they also dealt with waging a high-tech war. In 1997, the PLAAF drafted a new training program for the latter, but in carrying it out encountered an unexpected personnel problem because only 20.7 percent of air officers were college graduates. Quick fixes or short-term training classes could not solve the lack of qualified technical personnel to operate high-tech air weapons in an environment that attracts the best to civilian occupations.[78]

The senior officers slowly came to recognize that the real costs could be the price tag to attract and hold skilled men and women, and following the issuance of the "Strategy on Developing Professionals in the Air Force" in 1999, the PLAAF inaugurated special programs for advanced college-level training of pilots at China's best universities. Technical backgrounds were stressed for postgraduates sent to the PLAAF Engineering University, Radar College, and Logistics College. Special training classes for selected "technical professionals" were organized at civilian and military university "bases," and top experts were recruited to assist these bases. At the same time, the PLAAF devised specialized courses for its air and surface-to-air missile units and gave top priority to the ones that had been equipped with new aircraft and weapons. It posted more technical professionals to these in comparison to other units.[79]

Upgrading all air force planes and installations thus ran parallel with personnel training. Russian and other mostly non-U.S. technology was being introduced because many senior leaders had concluded that China by itself could not reach the goal of rapid, high-quality development. An indication of a possible shift toward alternative suppliers was a deal with Hughes Aircraft of Canada, Ltd., to build seven en-route air traffic control centers for the PLAAF. Three of these centers are level-one or military region-level centers, three are level-two centers at the provincial level, and one is a demonstration center. The contract for this project was signed on December 30, 1994, and was run by a former U.S. air attaché to China. During the Ninth Five-Year Plan (1996–2000), the air force budgeted for an additional sixty-four level-three centers, one at each of the major PLAAF airfields. These projects were all under the PLAAF Air Traffic Control Department, headed by a senior colonel. This officer also completed deals for advanced primary surveillance radars from French and German suppliers.[80]

China also urgently sought to purchase airborne early warning capabilities for its air force and navy. It contracted with Israel Aircraft Industries, Ltd. (IAI), for a prototype Phalcon over-the-horizon surveillance system and advanced electronics subsystems for the PLAAF and with Britain's Racal Electronics to purchase Searchwater radar systems for the Chinese navy. Phalcon was designed to detect fighters at ranges of more than 200 nautical miles, while aircraft equipped with Searchwater can cover the seas from Taiwan to the Spratlys in the South China Sea.[81] When the U.S. Department of Defense forced IAI to cancel the Phalcon deal, the Chinese accelerated the building of their own early warning plane.[82] By late 2004, the PLA scheduled the deployment of this plane with advanced radars within the coming months. According to Taiwanese sources, Taipei feared this deployment would alter the air balance over the strait in favor of the mainland.[83]

Moreover, China's aviation industry made slow but steady progress in designing and building its own fighter-bombers and fighters. The Chengdu Aircraft Industry Company, for example, developed the J-10, a single-seat, light multi-role fighter based heavily on the canceled Israeli Lavi program. Earlier, the Chinese had obtained an F-16 from Pakistan as a desired prototype of their new-type fighter-bomber. From Russia the company imported the Su-27SK turbofan engine for the J-10, and from Israel it bought optical and telecommunications equipment and radar and fire-control systems. The Xi'an Aircraft Industry Company, as another example, designed and built the JH-7 (code-named FBC-1 for sale abroad), a twin-engine, two-seat, supersonic fighter-bomber, for the navy. The company equipped the JH-7 with two British Spey turbofan engines and advanced avionics. The J-10 and JH-7 are said to have longer operating ranges, bigger bomb-carrying capacities, and much greater precision air-to-ground attack capability than all other PLAAF fighters and attackers.[84] The industry also built two additional advanced fighters, the FC-1 (Super-7) and J-7MF, and the results apparently exceeded the designers' expectations.[85]

On balance, the Chinese believe that through purchases of foreign aircraft and avionics and new indigenous designs the PLAAF has slowly narrowed the gap with the world's most advanced air forces. For example, Senior Colonel

Lei Qiang, one of the nation's top test flight pilots, stated that the FC-1's horizontal maneuverability was "as excellent as that of Su-27," though we would have preferred to see an independent validation of Lei's exuberant claim. A Pakistani air officer helps a little in this respect by stating that the FC-1's "flight performances should be better than those of the F-16A aircraft now in service in the Pakistani Air Force." [86] None of these claims, however, has yet been independently verified or tested in actual air engagements.

Moreover, despite all the effort and steady progress, significant inequalities still exist between the performance of Chinese and Western military aircraft, especially with respect to engines, radar and fire-control systems, air-borne missiles, and counter-electronic equipment. The continuing deficiencies in these areas, many Chinese aircraft designers believe, result primarily from starkly different design cultures. For its part, the PLAAF rewards excellence in engineering of aircraft and air-delivered weapons and proudly displays its trophies based on engineering standards from foreign and domestic air shows. It gives second place to the combat performance of its own aircraft, but at the same air shows PLAAF officers flock to the foreign products that have been combat tested. [87]

A second problem results from the tendency of the PLAAF to drop its support for a project whenever it meets setbacks or it can procure better weapons abroad. The fate of the FBC-1 fighter-bomber is an example of the air force abandoning a project in trouble, though its cancellation was halted just as the navy was readying to take over the project from the PLAAF. A third problem results from the industry's failure to give priority to advanced engines, making them the greatest bottleneck in the design cycle. Finally, the Chinese government has failed to promote competition when developing its next-generation aircraft and has allowed mediocre performers to stay in business.

We should note that many of the problems impeding the modernization of the air force mirror those that we encountered in our discussion of command and control and the Second Artillery. A senior PLAAF officer listed these as his service's most glaring deficiencies: "electronic warfare, automated command and control, simulated operations, employment of new-type weapons, and [hardware] maintenance and management." As so often before when confronted with such a list, the high command's "solution" is the call for more advanced technology and personnel, but the air force is only one claimant on a tight budget and limited manpower pool. [88]

Nevertheless, the significant augmentation of air power in China has influenced the PLAAF's strategy and operational tactics. Just as the weapons procurement policy has shaped the nation's arsenal, so, too, has the buildup of the arsenal influenced the PLA's operations and strategies. With Israel the supplier of choice for refurbishing China's existing air fleet, the PLAAF has modified a few of its Il-76 and H-6 aircraft as tankers and has installed equipment on its J-8b fighters for aerial refueling. In this way, the military has added to its air power projection capability and its ability to provide air cover for PLA ground and naval forces operating in a wide circle beyond China's shores.[89] The extended-range capabilities or "long legs" (*changtui*) have enabled the transition from a purely defensive to a combined defensive-offensive posture. By 2001, the PLAAF theoretically could engage hypothetical enemies out to the second island chain (from China to the west of Guam and from the northern sea areas to the South China Sea).[90]

OFFENSIVE AIR DEFENSE

Woven into the new operational directives are lessons drawn from the 1991 Gulf War. General Liu Jingsong, former president of the Academy of Military Science, said what was on the minds of many of his comrades: "A key mistake made by Iraq was to sit by idly waiting at the initial stage of the Gulf War and thus to lose a favorable opportunity" to strike while the anti-Iraq mobilization was underway. Speaking more generally, he stressed that the very assembly and positioning of coalition forces constituted the "first firing" and justified preemptive military action. Such preemptive action might "postpone or even deter the outbreak of a war," reflecting the revised no-first-strike and deterrence doctrines.[91] Liu ended by commenting on a possible confrontation over Taiwan between China and the United States.

Lessons from the wars that occurred in the past decade have prompted Beijing's leaders to adopt a new operational concept that mandates preemptive assaults as an integral part of air defense and the coming air battles. In the 1991 Gulf War and subsequent conflicts, the United States and its allies steadily mobilized their armies, while their adversaries waited passively and hoped for rescue from the international community. In each case, the coalition mustered its forces with impunity and then struck, and PLA generals now say, "The lessons from the Gulf War and the Kosovo War have told us: Passive air defense cannot change the outcome of a war."[92] The lesson is: Do not wait for the enemy to strike first.

By the mid-1990s, a turning point in China's military thinking, that lesson helped shape the CMC air defense doctrine and was built into the plans for a national air defense network. Those plans called for military and civilian co-operation to minimize and recover from the destructive effect of air raids, and preparations began for the drafting of a new National Air Defense Law, which was adopted in 1996.[93] Like the combat units, air defenses would be deployed "lightly" at the frontier and "massively" in designated rear areas. The CMC later in the decade called for further beefing up the air defense network at strategic points and airfields in theater and multi-theater zones.[94]

Senior military planners stressed that preemptive actions against troop assembly and logistical targets in any military showdown across the Taiwan Strait would require China's defenses against air-delivered munitions.[95] In response to the persuasiveness of their arguments, the CMC revised its strategic and operational air defense concepts, and the new concepts in turn made the nation's air defense strategy more compatible with the CMC's operational guidelines for conducting a high-tech conflict.

At the strategic level, the CMC endorsed "offensive air defense" (*gongshi fangkong*) as the future air defense doctrine. As the guiding principle for air defense, if war becomes inevitable, the "offensive air defense" doctrine directs the PLA to "take resolute and forceful offensive operations" and directly engage the opponents' air forces. The doctrine ended the passive posture of China's air defenses prior to the outbreak of war.[96] As we have seen in Chapter 6, the CMC has included in its target lists many air and naval bases that could be used for launching air raids against China.

Speaking of air defense when he was CMC chairman, Jiang Zemin declared, "Ours is such a large country with so many important points to defend. Pure air defense will make it very hard for us to guard against [air raids]." He equated the establishment of offensive air defense as a guiding principle to the "concrete application" of Mao's doctrine of "active defense." He concluded, "We must pursue the principle of offensive air defense in operations to gain air dominance efficiently through actions taken both from the air and ground in order to seize the strategic initiative."[97]

The offensive air defense doctrine not only incorporates lessons from the U.S.-led conflicts from the Gulf War to the 2003 Iraq invasion but also recognizes that China's air groups and conventional missile battalions would be the only effective arms available to the PLA in a major military confrontation. For the coming decades, moreover, China could not change the basic military equation: it would remain vulnerable to a combined air-missile attack and would face the classic use-it-or-lose-it dilemma. In a military showdown, the only rational choice left to the CMC would be to order its air force and conventional missile forces to attack first.[98] This choice echoes the Chinese saying: "He who strikes first prevails, he who strikes late fails" (*xian xiashou wei qiang, hou xiashou zaoyang*).

The PLAAF, of course, keeps secret the operational tactics based on the new doctrine. Our own analysis suggests that if, say, U.S. military involvement should become inevitable in an escalating military conflict over Taiwan and under conditions that China itself would become the target, the PLA would designate the air and sea area between the first and second island chains as the main battle zone and assign its Su-27SK and Su-30MK groups as well as its submarines to attack U.S. carrier battle groups. The J-10 and JH-7 groups and conventional missiles would engage incoming U.S. planes and would attack U.S. bases in Okinawa, Japan, and South Korea, should they allow their use by U.S. forces. The FC-1, J-8b, and J-7MF groups would be launched to defend China's coastal areas, provide air cover for local army and naval units, and carry out land attack against invading units. Considered flexible and mutually supportive, these preassigned wartime missions would be expected to determine the course of the battle as the balance of losses shifted against the enemy.[99]

At the operational level, the CMC has embraced a new guiding concept for domestic air defense: "Mobile joint air defense over a large area" (*da quyu dongtai lianhe fangkong*). The military had pursued a concept of "point defense" (*yaodi fangkong* or *yaodian fangkong*) before the mid-1990s, but the CMC then decided to adopt the new operational concept because it recognized that "point defense" would no longer be effective against a modern air campaign.[100]

Taking the next steps, the CMC began promulgating revised instructions and making organizational changes in PLA operations. The instructions highlighted the value of multiple air defense spheres in much larger areas because of the greater maneuverability and operating ranges of the most advanced foreign aircraft. It also emphasized the mobile deployment of surface-to-air missile and antiaircraft gun battalions and radar units and promulgated measures for integrated command and control that would coordinate all joint operations. With regard to organizational changes, it ordered the General Staff and the seven region commands to set up independent air defense commands for national and theater air defense, respectively. Each region air force command was expected to train all air defense units in peacetime and take control of them in wartime.[101] Under the General Staff, the national air defense command was tasked with drafting the guidelines for establishing and training all air defense units and coordinating all trans-theater joint air defense operations.

Moving further, the CMC singled out the adversary's airborne warning and control system (AWACS), early warning aircraft, and other electronic warfare support aircraft as its number one target in future air operations, once more mimicking U.S. practices in the opening stages of an air offensive. Since 2003, the air force has assigned the task of destroying these targets to selected Su-27SK and Su-30MK squadrons.[102] Furthermore, the missile industry manufactured several surface-to-air anti-radiation missiles (ARMs) for intercepting and downing those targets. Of these missiles, the FT-2000 surface-to-air ARM with a maximum range of 100 kilometers is designed to force enemy aircraft to keep their distance from China's coast.

It is in the context of early warning and the defense of coastal areas that a priority for naval construction and foreign purchases, especially from Russia, began to appear from 2000 on. Many of the newer-generation guided-missile destroyers and frigates, for example, have entered the fleet to provide advanced air warning and defense, and much of the fleet modernization, including the newest nuclear- and diesel-powered submarines, suggests an expanded effort to deal with U.S. naval deployments in the Pacific. Moreover, Jiang Zemin's call in 2002 "to place the construction of the Naval Air Force in an important strategic position" helped lift it out of the decades-long state of disrepair, eventually leading to the purchase of twenty-four Su-30MK2s and MK3s and the introduction of advanced indigenous fighters and bombers that would complement the more modern PLA Air Force divisions.[103]

Thus in the space of less than a decade, the air force (along with the Second Artillery and to a certain extent the navy) had assumed a privileged place in operational planning and procurements at the expense of the ground forces. People's War as a unifying doctrine had given way to service-specific doctrines. As Taiwan became the focal point of Chinese military planning, the purchase of Russian aircraft, presumably a stopgap measure, had qualified

Deng Xiaoping's call for self-reliance. With the shadow of a threatened U.S.-Chinese confrontation over Taiwan looming larger, some PLA senior generals advocated scrapping the no-first-strike doctrine in favor of retaliation on warning. As we shall see in the next chapter, reinterpretations of "combat in depth" also signaled a fundamental change in the Chinese military strategy of active defense toward a more proactive strategy to fight high-tech wars. The review of China's security interests had spawned an ongoing debate and re-formulation within the military and political hierarchies.

In that process, the die is already cast concerning the future of the air force. The CMC knows that it must rely on the country's conventional forces once deterrence fails. In any military showdown across the strait, air power and de-fense against air strikes hold the key to victory or defeat in today's warfare.[104] In 1997, the former PLAAF commander Liu Shunyao told his units that they would be "the first to be attacked" at the onset of the conflict and "employed from the beginning to the end" of the war.[105] Seven years later, General Qiao Qingchen, Liu's successor, echoed that judgment and once more urged his officers to meet the challenge.[106]

THE CASE FOR THE QUEST

Our examination of the shift away from the antiquated thinking of People's War and of the strategic reasoning underpinning the search for a modern air force leaves a central question unanswered: Is that goal realistic? All of China's potential adversaries have the advantage in producing or importing ever more advanced fighters and bombers, and several have employed those aircraft in combat and repeated exercises. There is no near- to medium-term likelihood that China's air force could match those of its possible foes.

Beijing's leaders do not dispute this. Rather, they justify the development of the nation's air power as a necessary condition for China to become a ma-jor military power and a technological competitor in defense and commercial aerospace. The dominant position of the air force in contingency plans for conflict in the Taiwan Strait helps focus on and mobilize resources to meet that condition, but the priority would remain even if Taiwan were not in the calculus. Four arguments provide the core of the Chinese rationale for the pri-ority and the policies sustaining the quest. We will focus on the fourth of these arguments, which relates to Taiwan, because it has the overriding impact on current military thinking in China and it will strengthen our discussion of changes in military policy in the next chapter.

The first argument simply echoes the Chinese belief that all nations, regardless of size, must prepare for war and that recent large-scale wars have demonstrated the deadly destructiveness of air power. To the Chinese, the proposition is self-evident: the contemporary state requires a combat-ready air force. Put another way, the development of the state requires the acquisition of competitive defense technologies, and the sine qua non of those technologies is advanced aircraft.[107] Speaking as the CMC's chairman, Jiang Zemin told his commanders that the nation would "bitterly suffer" if it did not strive to create a powerful air force, an oft-repeated view that he also extended to the Second Artillery.[108]

The Chinese military makes a second argument that the most likely threats to its security will come first from the air, especially from Taiwan or the United States. From the Korean War to the Iraq War, China has drawn the lesson that conceding control of the air to an adversary can lead to political intimidation and humiliation, not to mention huge losses. General Liu Yazhou has put that lesson more simply: "A destructive air strike could ruin a country."[109] China, he implied, could be that country. Its national security and diplomatic influence thus require that it demonstrate the will and the commitment to challenge any would-be attacker from the air even as its leaders acknowledge the PLAAF's current weaknesses.

The third argument links the deterrent force of advanced aircraft to nuclear deterrence. PLA strategists hold that the revolution in conventional weapons has increased the need for air power in reinforcing nuclear deterrence. A deputy commander of the PLAAF has said, "nuclear deterrence might not work without a high-tech air force especially in the post-nuclear era," and many of his colleagues have expressed doubts whether nuclear weapons could protect against a devastating conventional attack. Because the essence of the revised PLA strategic guidelines is to "prevent the outbreak of a war and prevail after its outbreak," a powerful air force has become an indispensable component of nuclear deterrence and all probable steps on the escalation ladder.[110]

The PLA's doctrine on the likelihood of future wars being local and high-tech supports a fourth argument: A nation cannot plan to fight a high-tech war without having an effective air arm. In assessing two hundred local wars and border conflicts since 1945, the Chinese have determined that the combatants employed air power first 90 percent of the time and that the chances are China will face the same odds in any of its future conflicts.[111] China's potential foes have advanced air forces, and most of them stress the first use of air power when hostilities erupt.

This fourth argument applies with special force to any future military showdown over the Taiwan Strait caused by the island's declaration of independence. As in the past, the CMC would prefer to threaten or "blockade" Taiwan by the use of missiles fired in measured numbers close to but not on the island itself. PLA generals hold that for such a calculated demonstration of force to work, the missile bases would have to be protected. That military requirement in turn would make the PLAAF Taipei's first target. If Taiwan's planes could easily destroy the air bases protecting China's missile bases, the missile forces would face the fearsome use-it-or-lose-it predicament, and not surprisingly, Taipei's public statements concerning its war plans appear consistent with this PLA assessment.[112] Thus, the anticipated outcome of the battle for air dominance would determine the ultimate political and military effectiveness of the missiles as a weapon of choice to threaten or blockade the island.

However, the Chinese analysis of such a conflict with Taiwan does not end there. Beijing knows that halting Taiwan's move toward independence could spark a U.S. military response in an escalating cross-strait crisis. In the worst case, which neither side wants, the United States might be faced with the choice of intervention or a Taiwanese defeat. A critical element in the fourth argument is the assumption that formidable Chinese air power could cause Washington to pause. The very possibility of that hesitation per se could inhibit Taipei's taking irreversible steps toward independence in the first place because Taiwan would not be sure it could prevail in the air. A PLA officer puts it this way:

> The Taiwan issue involves the territorial integrity and national sovereignty of China. It is our vital security interest to prevent Taiwan from drifting toward independence. In contrast, the future of Taiwan does not involve U.S. vital interests. If Beijing copes with the Taiwan issue properly and demonstrates resolve at the decisive moment, Washington will probably keep its hands off the issue.[113]

Operationally speaking, the ability to execute a policy of missile intimidation and air defense has necessitated carrying out carefully planned exercises.

The purpose of these exercises is both to enhance and publicize the PLA's readiness for conflict in the strait. At the end of 1996, following the well-advertised issuance of CMC directives, a group of specialists from the PLAAF and the other services completed the operational rules for coordinating combined-services campaigns across the strait and carrying out exercises to validate them.[114]

Arguments based on national stature, threat assessments, deterrence, and sovereign independence, of course, are neither new nor unique to China. What is relatively new is the centrality given to the air force in Beijing's formulation of those arguments, particularly as they apply to Taiwan and the United States. China's search for an effective air force also reaches back to the foundations of the People's Republic and the Korean War. Although the recent formulations giving saliency to the air force make military and political "sense" at least to senior PLA commanders, the question still remains: Can China actually build the credible air power that will deter both foreign aggressors and separatists alike?

Embedded in the policy are assumptions concerning the directions of technology, the nature of future conflicts, the behavior of foreign states, and the sustainability of current defense programs. After examining the security implications of the PLAAF's buildup in the decade ahead, we conclude that the answer to that question is far from clear even to the Chinese who have placed their bets on the air force. Many decades have passed since then chief of the General Staff Luo Ruiqing called for a change in priorities from strategic to conventional weapons with the emphasis on the air force. A victim of the Cultural Revolution, Luo fell from power and his call vanished with him. The challenge of an emerging independent Taiwan appeared to resurrect Luo's dream of a world-class air force. Standing in the way are competing demands and policies beyond the military's, even China's, control. After decades of false starts, the realists know that the dream could fade once again.

PART FOUR

National Strategy and Uncertain War

EIGHT

Sun Tzu's Pupils and the Taiwan Challenge

In December 1936, just at the time that the nation's leader Chiang Kai-shek was being kidnapped by two of his own generals and forced to forge a united front with the Communists against the invading Japanese, Mao Zedong lectured his officers on the study of war.[1] Revolutionary war, he said, had its own basic nature and laws, but those laws could only be understood in the context of laws of war in general. The differences in time, place, and circumstances between China's revolution and other wars were the place to start, not like Aristotle whose monumental writings in fourth-century Greece seem eerily detached from the confused and cheerless period in which he lived.

Today Mao's "circumstances" are relegated to history, taught to generations whose youth and inexperience make even the Vietnam War of 1979 seem lost in legend. The peasant warrior of the 1930s had little use for copying texts or "cutting the feet to fit the shoes," and because he had witnessed war firsthand he both wished "this monster of mutual slaughter among men" would be finally eliminated and often scoffed at its cost.

The place for his student fighters to start was with Sun Tzu's dictum "know the enemy and know yourself." This was easier said than done, Mao warned. "Some people are good at knowing themselves and poor at knowing the enemy, and some are the other way round; neither can solve the problem of learning and applying the laws of war." [2] The most important knowledge drew on theoretical principles and had been tested in battle. Politics, economics, and "the art of direction" or tactics had practical consequences for the commander, and the essence of tactics was maintaining freedom of action.

Yet, the commander must always operate under the political direction of the supreme ruler, and Sun Tzu defined politics "as the thing which causes the people to be in harmony with their ruler so that they will follow him in disregard of their lives and without fear of any danger." [3] The successful warrior leader must create situations that produce this harmony, and deception, treachery, exploiting personality weaknesses, innovation, opportunism, and espionage all mark the commander cum statesman for greatness. Sun Tzu cautioned:

> Therefore, analyze the enemy's plans so that you will know his shortcomings as well as strong points. Agitate him in order to ascertain the pattern of his movement. Lure him out to reveal his dispositions and ascertain his position. . . . When a victory is won, one's tactics are not repeated. One should always respond to circumstances in a variety of ways. [4]

In short, be smart, informed, creative, devious, and flexible. Rare qualities indeed, and often missing in military command centers.

Let us, nonetheless, imagine such a command center in Beijing and ask "Sun Tzu's" not-so-hypothetical questions, "Do senior Chinese officers really know their adversaries?" In seeking an answer to this question, a move by Taiwan toward independence looms as the most significant threat with Taipei's "separatists" becoming the principal enemy. Second, "How has the PLA changed its strategic direction to cope with that threat?" Here, we will examine how the civil-war era active defense strategy has been revamped in light of modern warfare and Taiwan's political and military actions. Third, "How has that strategy been tested in large-scale military exercises?" The review of these exercises, especially the one in 2001, will reveal the degree to which modern information technologies and Taiwan's reliance on the United States now shape China's battle plans. And, finally, to the extent that the United States has become China's would-be enemy, "How does the American factor alter some of the long-standing Chinese inhibitions against preparing to fight a nuclear war? Do Chinese officers know themselves, their capabilities, and their limitations?"

The answers to these questions may illuminate the strategies that still lie hidden in the hard data that have preoccupied us to this point and will help refine our analysis of Chinese concepts of war with which we began. That more nuanced analysis will reveal the direction of Beijing's military plans and the potential dangers and opportunities they present.

IMAGINED ENEMIES IN
A MODERNIZING WORLD

True to their tradition, Chinese military planners have long attached importance to the identification and analysis of friends and enemies before taking decisive actions. In the opening page of his *Selected Works*, Mao Zedong echoed Sun Tzu's call to distinguish friends from enemies, and much of his writings over the years examined how to differentiate "contradictions" within the "people" and those between friends and foes.[5] Mao studied this problem from a philosophical as well as practical perspective. He believed that inherent conflict in all relationships was permanent but its form and content were constantly changing, and that "each of the two contradictory aspects transforms itself into its opposite" under knowable conditions.

The essence of command for Mao was to understand those conditions and take advantage of the inevitable changes. As an example, Mao cited a Chinese legend in which a Song dynasty military leader defeated the opposition by breaking up his rival's alliance. The key to the victory lay in winning over one of his adversary's allies, and his strategy maximized both the contradiction in that alliance and the opportunity it provided.[6]

Mao further connected his beliefs and conclusions to the origins of war and peace. He asked: "War is not brewed in peacetime. Why does a war break out all of a sudden? Peace is not fermented in wartime. Why is peace suddenly achieved?" He concluded that it was a rule that war definitely would break out after a long period of peace, and peace would inevitably be achieved after a long, drawn-out war (*jiu he bi zhan, jiu zhan bi he*).[7] By the "law of contradictions," states had neither permanent friends nor enemies, and the foreign policies of Mao and his successors historically reflected this philosophy of flexible, conditional commitments.

After assuming power in the late 1970s, Deng Xiaoping made a series of dramatic changes in the nation's foreign and domestic policies. These policies were highlighted by reform and opening to the outside world. Economic progress quickly became his priority, and rapid, continuous development would require external policies to ensure peace and stability. Deng mandated these policies as the Party's basic line for the next century and enshrined them in three of his best-known principles:

1.   China's economic development requires a peaceful international environment. China must foster that environment by making as many friends and as few enemies as possible. "We are afraid of nobody, but we offend nobody as well," Deng said.

2.   China must never head an alliance that could become the target of international contention. Deng regarded this principle as a "fundamental state policy."

3.   China must maintain a low profile and meet foreign challenges with great self-constraint. Deng said, "Coolly observe [the outside world], secure your own position, and cope with [challenges] calmly."

Deng's three principles remain in force to this day as Beijing seeks to balance its goal of enhanced global status with the reaction of its concerned neighbors to China's surge toward greatness.[8]

Significantly, Deng differed with Mao's approach to the evolving relationships with China's foes and friends. Mao laid far greater emphasis on real and imagined foes and considered friends chiefly as instruments for coping with his enemies. By contrast, Deng stressed improving the nation's relationship with friends while he concentrated on reducing the number and influence of adversaries as a way to increase and consolidate those friends.

In identifying and prioritizing foes and friends, Deng's successor, Jiang Zemin, went even further than his mentor because of his even greater preoccupation with economic modernization and domestic stability. Jiang proclaimed, "Of all matters, economic development claims precedence over all others," and made economic security the foundation on which to build state security.[9] Jiang's was a "win-win" concept that typically underplayed China's enemies and somewhat naively expected that the "adoption of actions with good intention would no doubt receive an appropriate response."[10]

Seeking to remove or invalidate U.S. excuses to pressure or threaten China, Jiang actively developed cooperative ties with Washington and used regional security issues, such as the North Korean nuclear crisis, to forge a closer relationship with the Clinton and Bush administrations. In his strategy, moreover, such a relationship could help prevent Taiwan's steady drift toward independence and make it far less likely that the United States would intervene forcibly in the event of a cross-strait conflict.

Through compromise with potentially hostile neighboring countries and continued cooperation with Western nations, war, Jiang apparently believed, could be avoided indefinitely and, in the end, even imagined enemies would fade away. His guiding principle in international relations reaffirmed the traditional view that "peace claims precedence" (*he wei gui*). He wei gui could be invoked to justify policies toward the United States that some in Beijing deemed appeasement.[11]

Even without this criticism at home, balancing hostile external pressures and concentrating on the economy proved daunting for Jiang's Politburo. Mao had proclaimed a line that categorized others on the basis of their treatment of China: those who *acted* like competitors or enemies were almost automatically deemed to *be* competitors or enemies.[12]

For Jiang, the world was far too complex to endorse Mao's simplistic tit-for-tat strategy. Chinese security and development demanded the strategy's modification. Nevertheless, within the global environment of economic growth and interdependency, the ultimate fate of Taiwan and its ties with the United States clouded the clarity of the friends-enemies dichotomy. Simply put, Taiwan housed both Chinese "brothers" and enemy separatists, and while the United States would long remain an indispensable economic partner it would also continue to be a protector of Taiwan.

Thus, in the special case of Taiwan and its relations with America, no obvious way existed to distinguish friends and enemies, and over time each would have to be treated as a necessary friend and possible foe. When setting its security objectives vis-à-vis the United States, Beijing has thus attempted to perfect and implement twin tactics, termed "using [our] two hands to deal with the two hands [of the other party]" (*yi liangshou dui liangshou*). In practice, this has meant that U.S. policies of peaceful engagement would be met with policies in kind, but its acts to contain China or support Taiwan independence would be forcibly confronted. One "hand" assumes that cooperation and flexibility could mitigate if not halt acts of hostility, but the other "hand" would stand ready to defeat containment or separatism. When implementing this dual policy, moreover, Beijing typically employs multiple diplomatic, economic, and military means in order to moderate risk and provide fallback options.[13]

If implemented successfully, this policy can neutralize or deter China's presumed adversaries and their threatening actions.[14] Should an unwanted conflict become unavoidable, Beijing's leaders would follow Mao's instruction to "prepare for the worst."[15] Under the leadership of Jiang and his successors, the Taiwan issue has repeatedly forced Beijing to face the worst.

The priority given to the first of the five strategic goals discussed in Chapter 2, moreover, has reflected the deepening concern about Taiwan's uncertain future. It will be recalled that these goals are: safeguard territorial sovereignty and "rights"; maintain domestic stability and a stable environment in the Asian-Pacific region; promote economic development; oppose hegemony and power politics; and build a new international political and economic order.[16]

The primary mission assigned to the Chinese military is, as with defense establishments everywhere, to safeguard territorial sovereignty and "rights," and so it is that the specter of a sovereign Taiwan has strengthened the military's hand despite the absence of genuine threats to China's security. The crises and conflicts of the People's Republic of China (PRC) since 1949 have, to be sure, shaped the definition of national sovereignty and the rights to be defended and made the leadership vulnerable to particular perils of which the status of Taiwan has touched the nation's most sensitive political nerve. So, while mainland leaders more often than not prefer compromise and accommodation, their one-China policy and Taiwan's independence moves continue to thwart lasting reconciliation across the strait. Taiwan's problematic future constitutes the PLA's recurrent nightmare.

Contention over the status of Taiwan, moreover, transcends national pride. From the purely military vantage point, an independent Taiwan would place China at a strategic disadvantage in any future great-power contest. As a senior PLA naval officer has put it, Taiwan constitutes the central link in the "first island chain" and a key access to the "second island chain" in the northern Pacific, which seems to contradict Beijing's long-standing pledge not to send troops to Taiwan if Taipei willingly accepts the one-China policy. By controlling Taiwan, the PLA could hope to defend China's coastal sea lanes and access to the vast ocean area to the west of the second island chain including the Marianas, Guam, and the Carolines. Taiwan would serve as a springboard to project Chinese power to the east and south.[17]

By the same logic, with the "loss" of Taiwan, China would be forever confined to a continental status west of the first chain and deprived of the requisite "strategic space" required by a great power.[18] Within the nation, moreover, a declaration of independence by Taipei could easily produce a domino effect that would threaten the long-term unity of the Chinese nation and thereby its very survival.[19] Thus, Beijing sees a direct link between the nation's territorial sovereignty and its security and ambitions, and few in China would question that link and the priority decisions that follow.

This priority runs headlong into the national policy to avoid war. Both are important, and somehow the preservation of the one-China policy must be worked into the strategic framework of war avoidance. The key is to separate the protection of national unity from the possibility of a war with the United States as Taiwan's protector. The dilemma is how to appear tough on Taiwan but compromising toward Washington. While seeking to prevent war, the Chinese military must accelerate its preparations for fighting the most powerful military force in the world. The goal is to "fight a small war to avert a big war," a strategy that looks good on paper but is virtually impossible to implement in practice.[20]

The small war refers to Taiwan and the big war to the United States. That all sides want to avoid conflict may not be enough to halt the slow drift to a showdown on the future of Taiwan. China's overriding security objective in the event of such a showdown is to avoid war with the United States, and the enduring challenge is to refine the active defense strategy to achieve that objective.

THE EVOLUTION OF THE ACTIVE DEFENSE STRATEGY AND THE EMERGENCE OF CONTEMPORARY DOCTRINE

Active defense has constituted the nation's military strategy since Mao first decreed it during the revolutionary years.[21] The most elementary principle of the active defense strategy is: Gain mastery by striking only after the enemy has struck first (*houfa zhiren*). Over the past five decades, only this simple statement of principle has stayed unaltered in the codification of active defense. As we have noted elsewhere, almost everything else in the strategy has changed since Mao first enunciated it in the 1930s, when he proclaimed, "If we are attacked, we will certainly counterattack." Before the Chinese People's Volunteers (CPV) entered the Korean War, for example, he devised a plan to wage positional warfare to check the United Nations' advance. Shortly thereafter, before putting the plan into effect, he changed his mind and decided to engage the enemy in mobile warfare. In June 1951, Mao again reversed himself. He ordered the CPV to adopt temporarily a different guiding principle characterized by wearing down the enemy's effective strength in positional warfare.[22]

After the Korean armistice in 1953, Mao and the high command made a number of significant changes in the content of the active defense strategy.[23] Mao first ordered Peng Dehuai, the vice-chairman in charge of the CMC's daily affairs, to accentuate research on the impact of a modern war on the established military strategy.[24] In the winter of 1953–54 at a high-level military conference, Peng and his fellow officers, in an attempt to adjust their forces to the coming age of intercontinental warfare, made a series of decisions on creating a regularized and modern army.[25] They clung closely to Moscow's "historical experience" and advice and bought its weapons.

The army was reorganized largely along Soviet lines. With an eye to strengthening the leadership of the Party in military affairs, the Politburo, in September 1954, adopted a resolution to redefine the Central Military Commission's authority and its relations with top-level Party organizations. As we have stated earlier, it put the commission under the Politburo and Central Secretariat.[26] Thereafter, the commission expedited the overhauling of military strategy.

From March 6 to 15, 1956, a commission meeting debated a range of issues on strategy and the buildup of national defense.[27] It affirmed the revolutionary-era active defense strategy but rewrote its substance. Preoccupied by the lessons of Korea, Peng Dehuai told the gathering that the "combination of positional defensive warfare with mobile offensive warfare" would become the PLA's operational doctrine.[28] He emphasized that future wars must be fought on the Maoist principles of strategic defense and operational offense, protracted warfare and battles of quick decision, and positional warfare and mobile warfare.[29] Opportunistic attacks and counterattacks would erupt following relentless battles of attrition and the enemy's inevitable mistakes.

The meeting's participants further reinterpreted the PLA's guiding principle in future wars: After the outbreak of a war, Chinese troops would check the enemy's advance in prepared fortified zones in order to thwart its plan to wage a war of quick decision. The initial battles would buy time to stabilize the battlefield and convert the national economy to a wartime footing. After waging a protracted struggle, the army would move from active defense to strategic offense.[30] This new strategy had obvious implications for "luring in deep," and in 1962, in anticipation of a possible Nationalist invasion from Taiwan, the commission ordered the PLA to resist all landing operations at the invasion beachheads.[31]

In the spring of 1969, the rapidly escalating Sino-Soviet border conflicts prompted Chinese leaders once more to adjust their guidelines for waging war. In April, Mao, fearing a full-scale Soviet armored campaign, pointed out, "I stand for giving up land in an all-out war."[32] With the nation facing a showdown with the Soviet Army, Mao returned to the revolutionary-period notions of "luring the enemy in deep" and mobile warfare. Mao's statements greatly influenced the adjustment of the PLA's strategic guideline, which was reaffirmed after his death. In 1977, on behalf of the military commission, Ye Jianying announced that the PLA's new eight-character guiding principle would be active defense (*jiji fangyu*) and luring the enemy in deep (*youdi shenru*). This principle, simplified into a few characters and invariably referred to by the number of characters, was to continue in force throughout the rest of the decade.

Under Deng Xiaoping, the content of jiji fangyu underwent another mutation. In the autumn of 1980, the commission resurrected the 1956 concept, which stipulated that at the onset of a full-scale war frontline troops would fight from prepared fortifications. They would absorb the brunt of the attack in order to delay the enemy's advance and to allow time to complete other strategic deployments and the conversion of the national economy from a peacetime to a wartime footing. Compared to the previous guideline, "luring the enemy in deep" was shelved and mobile warfare downgraded.

The new guideline highlighted, for the first time in the PLA's history, the dominance of positional warfare in Chinese strategy. General Song Shilun, president of the Academy of Military Science, submitted a report to Deng Xiaoping recommending the formal abandonment of "luring the enemy in deep." Deng accepted Song's advice and removed the doctrine from the official definition of active defense.[33]

PLA theorists and planners in the 1990s then began considering how to cope in the twenty-first century with sudden attacks from multiple directions and on targets deep inside China.[34] They identified four possible scenarios: small wars (presumably at the frontiers), medium-sized conventional wars, full-scale conventional wars under the condition of nuclear deterrence, and nuclear war.[35] Deng Xiaoping's adoption of a peacetime strategy in 1985 was based on the premise that the third and fourth of these would not occur in that century, and thus investments in forces for "limited retaliation" against a nuclear first strike could be lowered and the people's militia (essential for waging a People's War) substantially reduced. Some PLA strategists, however, determined that China could confront direct military threats of the third kind should mainland-Taiwan relations deteriorate, and the head of the National Defense University ordered his officers to conduct research on such a conflict, the most likely form of the next world war.[36]

Still, the debate about strategy converged on scenarios one and two, small- and medium-sized wars, neither of which was considered probable in the 1990s.[37] Reflecting the regime's general optimism about reaching an accommodation with Taiwan early in the decade, PLA analysts worried most about how to win local wars between China and its neighbors.[38] They deemed Vietnam and India to be their most probable future adversaries, a judgment that was to change radically in just a few years.[39] Twelve Chinese characters summarized the approved policy toward these regional conflicts: adopt every diplomatic means to check the outbreak of war (*lizheng zhizhi*); assure victory if war is inevitable (*quebao dasheng*); and quickly end the war on favorable terms after the predetermined goals have been achieved (*jianhao jiushou*).[40]

Despite the decision and the thousands of pages of detail (all classified) on the policy, some Chinese strategists still voiced concern about the danger of a lightning or surgical strike against strategic targets inside China during escalating crises.[41] Twenty years hence, they said, the United States or another superpower, even Japan, might pose such a threat. The strategists weighed the chances of a superpower surprise attack on the country's coastal areas and proposed an integrated response in which the navy's role would be indispensable.[42] They mostly put the possibility of such a U.S. attack in the context of a future confrontation between the PRC and Taiwan. Some apparently assigned a greater probability to future hostilities with the United States after the deterioration of U.S.-China relations in June 1989.

As China's search for more appropriate strategic concepts continued, the emphasis fell on developing advanced technologies that would lessen both the threats to the nation and its weaknesses. Yang Shangkun, China's president and a senior leader on the military commission, told his colleagues in late 1986: "The principal contradiction in our army building is the contradiction between the objective requirements of modern warfare and the low level of modernization of our army." To resolve the contradiction, the leadership determined that "army building should be aimed at promoting the modernization of equipment and man. Particular attention should be paid to . . . the modernization of defense science and technology, weapons and equipment, management, and military thinking."[43]

The military began formalizing its views on strategy in army-wide symposia that ran from 1986 to early 1990.[44] Experts systematized military terminology and worked out the principles of the PLA's own military science on the nature and laws of war and how to prepare for and conduct it. While there are some aspects of this "science" unique to China, the Chinese made no claim to originality.

Specifically, the high command ordered research to be undertaken on defense strategy, operations or campaigns, and tactics. Its directive quoted Mao as saying, "the science of strategy deals with the laws that govern the war situation as a whole. The science of campaigns deals with the laws that govern campaigns and is applied in directing campaigns. The science of tactics deals with the laws that govern battles and is applied in directing battles."[45]

In concrete terms, strategy was defined as encompassing the use of forces at the front and included what Western and Russian military specialists call theater operations. In times of peace, the group army (*jituanjun*) is the largest independent operational unit, while in a war the front army (*fangmianjun*) comprising several group armies would conduct military operations at the theater level.[46] During those operations, as noted in Chapter 5, each of the nation's seven military regions could be deemed a separate theater. The Chinese held that the philosophical foundations for their perspectives on strategy were laid down in ancient military treatises, particularly those of Sun Tzu, Wu Qi, and Sun Bin.[47]

In the late 1980s, the Politburo Standing Committee reaffirmed the prime responsibility of the CMC in formulating national security strategy and, as discussed in Chapter 4, began to establish new security-related groups and research organs to devise innovative strategic options and contingency plans for peace and war.[48] They complied by directing the strategists in various institutes to delineate the new strategy within four parameters: the state's overall goals, military theories based on Mao's military thought, the status of China's power, and an assessment of foreign threats.[49] They were told to set a definite time frame as a part of each strategy; ten years was to be considered normal for implementing a short-term strategy. The actual time limit set would define the period required for mobilizing the nation to meet any major probable threat.[50]

Some defense strategies were given life cycles longer than ten years. In December 1986, Yang Shangkun, vice-chairman of the military commission, pointed out that "the modernization of our country's national defense and military equipment will have approached those of the world's first-class powers" by the year 2050, thus solidifying China's international position as a world power.[51] The setting of such a distant time limit caused PLA strategists to reconsider the short- and medium-term horizons. Nevertheless, in 1986 the military considered 1986–95 and 1996–2005 as its frames of reference for short- and medium-term policies. The PLA judged it feasible to modernize its armory by 2005, when the level of military sophistication should have reached that attributed to the United States and the Soviet Union in the 1990s. As we have seen, those set milestones steadily slipped after 2000, and the commitment to a fixed timetable gradually faded away.

Having defined the relevant time periods, however, the strategists concentrated on the contents of a short-term defense strategy, which soon became the permanent present. They endeavored to work out a consensus on the goals for the buildup of national defense and on ways to achieve them. The agreed goals were general: "The country must possess powerful defensive capabilities and counterattack capabilities that should be able to deter enemy states, play an important role in maintaining global equilibrium, and ensure the implementation of our independent and peaceful foreign policy."[52] PLA planners then captured the means to achieve these goals in a new set of widely promulgated eight Chinese characters (*zhongti fangwei zhongdian fazhan* or "comprehensive defense, key-item development") whose meaning was widely discussed but misunderstood by all but ranking insiders.[53]

The CMC also changed its weapons procurement policy, which, loosely interpreted, would now emphasize *sashoujian*, or trump-card weapons. These weapons, it was argued, would help the PLA attain superiority across the Taiwan Strait by the secret introduction of high-impact arms. Within the limited military budget, the defense industry could develop these selected weapons or other technologies that would help achieve victory. Assuming the sashoujian technologies could be developed and built, China could thereby meet wartime emergencies without getting caught up in a dangerous cycle of arms races and perpetual insecurity.[54] That assumption, of course, masks an illusion: all rivals seek their own sashoujian in a technology race that dates back to the dawn of man.

TRANSLATING STRATEGIC CONCEPTS INTO OPERATIONS

So far we have dealt with the arena of the mind. Traditions, philosophies, doctrines, and plans are routinely debated within China's high policy councils and military think tanks, but we must now consider, partially as a summary of the ideas we have explored, how these matters of concept translate into a changing pattern of military operations. It is those patterns, dialectically balancing dreams of greatness and genuine security and the costs involved, that can now be used to illuminate the PLA in action.

Over the past decade, the military commission has struggled with a dazzling array of operational questions. As we have seen, it has completed a series of reviews and forecasts on the kaleidoscopic nature of modern war. The revolution in weaponry has an overlay of knowledge assets and ways to display and manipulate them. The bewildering flood of new acronyms that defy easy translation into Chinese and the language of high-tech defense can no longer be consigned just to armchair officers far from the fields of combat. Furthermore, the new terminologies do foster more precise intellectual exchange, and help promote the rigorous understanding needed to forecast budgets, design and deploy advanced systems, train and promote officers, and cross the barrier between novel doctrines and the brutal logic of the war room.

Officers in these war rooms must daily ponder two interrelated questions: Can we fight and win a war against Taiwan should it declare independence? Could China deter the United States from entering that war, and if not, could the expanded conflict be kept limited and conventional? We have touched on these questions before, but now we must face them directly if we are to grasp what the national command authority, the command-and-control officers, the Second Artillery, and the PLA Air Force have been doing and must do to survive modern warfare. These are the topics of the preceding chapters, but now we must attempt to explore the contemporary version of Sun Tzu's commandment to his generals: "Attack the enemy's strategy!"[55]

On May 3, 2000, the widely read *Zhongguo Xiaofeizhe Bao* (China Consumer Newspaper) published a report on questions raised not in the war rooms but by the "Chinese people" on estimates of a war across the Taiwan Strait should Taipei declare its independence. Several senior colonels at the PLA Academy of Military Science attempted to answer such questions as: Will the state order a general mobilization should war break out across the strait? Is it possible for a war across the strait to become a protracted war? Will Taiwan launch missiles against Shanghai and Beijing? Will the United States intervene? How long would a war last? Hard questions, and we should note that these PLA officers strongly disagreed in their answers. Their differences highlight how complex and contentious their debates had become.

Addressing the first question, a senior colonel said, "Generally speaking, local mobilization will be carried out in the southeastern coastal areas. . . . The state would not proclaim a state of emergency throughout the nation [unless] the war expanded or the U.S. militarily intervened."

One of his colleagues, Senior Colonel Peng Guangqian, whose work we have cited in previous chapters, said the mainland would impose a blockade on the island, and "Taipei would yield after 270 days [because] our true purpose would be to force Taiwan to accept negotiations." Another officer answered that the war "would be a political battle, and before we calculate the losses, we first must settle a political score. But, the war would surely result in losses in lives and to the economy." Finally, yet another academy colleague added, "The United States will not stand by with folded arms [should a war break out], [but] the United States would not lose China just to support the 'independence of Taiwan.'"

A few months later, a PLA officer reflected on the actual tactical operations needed to prevent Taiwan's move toward independence. He told us:

> We can accomplish the mission to unify our country. For this purpose, successful amphibious operations will be indispensable. We can perform landing operations if the navy can convoy our armored divisions, and our

naval officers say they can provide escort forces for amphibious flotillas if our air force dominates the air over the strait. To this our air force has replied, "We can maintain air domination if the strategic rocket forces can paralyze the enemy's air force and naval aviation." Of course, we can succeed if we have enough precision-guided munitions. The strategic rocket forces are now the focal point.[56]

The elements of expected operations, so conceived, were becoming clearer and had begun to coalesce into a war plan. All invasion units assigned to the amphibious assaults would function as integrated trans-theater forces, but their very interconnectedness, of course, complicated the assessment of any single capability in the heat of battle. The time had come to test how such interconnected forces would work together.

From 1996 to 2000, the PLA had already conducted annual tests on and near Dongshan Island in Fujian Province with Taiwan the "imagined target." These annual exercises continued through 2004, though the outbreak of SARS caused their cancellation in 2003. In most of these years, the exercises were relatively small, and as a PLA officer put it, "The exercise is part of the PLA's annual training, but its political significance is greater than its military significance."[57] In 2004, Party newspaper *Renmin Ribao* once again stressed the underlying purpose of the exercises was to warn the "'Taiwan independence elements' [should they] dare to dismember the country someday that the PLA is capable and confident of settling the Taiwan issue by military force."[58]

The Dongshan exercise held in 2001 by contrast was several orders of magnitude greater than the ones before or after. It became the largest military exercise since the founding of the People's Republic.[59] The first stage of the exercise, which began in early May, stressed "information warfare," with PLA-initiated electronic warfare against a not-so-hypothetical Taiwan. Its aim was to paralyze Taipei's communications and command systems. Taking a page from U.S. military operations, the PLA would launch electronic offensives and thereby test how far it had gone toward reaching its objective of information modernization. The second stage employed "the combined forces of the navy, army, and air force crossing the strait and carrying out landing operations," which used actual cruise missile launches and multiple aircraft sorties. According to the Chinese press, this stage illustrated the fact that the PLA's plan of attack on Taiwan had switched from a direct "sea-borne landing" to an "airborne assault." Preemption had been operationalized because of the need for quick and decisive results before America entered the battle. The third stage would require engaging the "counterattacking reinforcements," which would consist primarily of U.S. carrier battle groups.[60] No consideration, it seems, was given to the possible involvement of the United States virtually from the outset as opposed to providing reinforcements during the course of the campaign.

Each of these three overlapping stages of the Dongshan exercise constituted distinct scenarios that were planned in accordance with the most realistic and current thinking about war and, when considered together, would validate the PLA's most advanced high-tech weapons, programs, and techniques. The three stages were considered the most likely sequence of any probable high-tech local conflict. The weapons used in these stages—though greatly exaggerated in Chinese press accounts—included Su-27 and Su-30 fighters, Sovremenniy-class destroyers, and on-board anti-ship missiles purchased from Russia, and reportedly involved simulated or actual launches of the DF-15 and other missiles.[61] According to one source:

> The exercise drew on troops under the Nanjing, Guangzhou, Ji'nan, Beijing, Chengdu, Shenyang, and Lanzhou military regions; ship units, naval air forces, and marines of the East Sea, South Sea, and North Sea fleets; the First, Sixth, Seventh, and Eighth air corps, and airborne brigades from South, East, North, and Southwest China; conventionally armed missile units from the Second Artillery; and national defense reserve units. . . . Seven class-A group armies rated as the mainland's best rapid reaction troops sent field units.[62]

The overall commander of the exercise was CMC vice-chairman Zhang Wannian. Most of the troops taking part in the exercise came from the Nanjing Military Region, and Lieutenant General Liang Guanglie, then the region commander, served as commander-in-chief of the Fuzhou Theater Joint Command. More than one hundred of the PLA's highest-ranking officers flew to Dongshan to "concretely plan" the exercise and, in some cases, assumed roles in the joint command.

Though the exercise was concentrated near Dongshan, combat units in other parts of the country simultaneously carried out specialized and complementary exercises. Because the troops participating at Dongshan were deployed from throughout the country at the same time, part of the exercise was to evaluate the national highway, communications, and logistical networks

under emergency conditions. Advance PLA units guarded crossroads in ur-
ban areas such as Fuzhou City and throughout Fujian, and directed the as-
semblage of large truck convoys carrying troops and their gear. Hotels and
hostels on Dongshan Island were commandeered by the PLA to accommodate high-ranking military officers and their staffs.

Stage 1 (Early May–Late July)

In the month prior to this stage, which started in early May, troops began to
bivouac in Fujian.[63] In this kick-off phase, recently formed PLA information
warfare and air force counter-radar units played a pivotal role in both the offensive and defensive operations and training.[64] On the offense, the PLA reportedly employed hitherto unused weaponry, technologies, and tactics, such
as the application of electronic devices to emit dummy signals, electronic jamming, and precision strikes against command and communications centers.
Communications technicians operated their networks in joint operations,
practiced coordination among leading organizations, and worked to integrate
the missile forces into attacks on the enemy's command, control, communications, and intelligence (C^3I) centers.

At Dongshan, the PLA on both the offense and defense relied for the first
time on military satellites and early-warning aircraft to conduct regionwide
reconnaissance, bringing "the Taiwan Strait under the surveillance and control of the PLA troops."[65] Two communications satellites launched in 2000
were tied into the exercise, and communications companies in each military
organization carried out separate C^3I drills. For example, *Liberation Army
Daily* reported the following mock engagement by a Second Artillery launch
brigade under attack:

> At midnight, the "enemy's" airborne force attacked a command center of our
> brigade. The troops needed to move quickly and asked the [center's] com-
> munications squad to ensure unobstructed contacts. At that time, unex-
> pected situations such as the breakdown of the radio vehicle followed. Under
> a blackout condition, the officers and men speedily overcame the troubles,
> adjusted radio frequencies, and laid cables to set up the communications net-
> work for a new command post.[66]

Just how realistic these "attacks" and "troubles" were cannot be verified,
but every effort was apparently made to cover the "terrain" with the fog of

war. In the final assessment, the command center and its launch brigade comrades were judged to have survived and continued to function, though those PLA officers who earlier had witnessed the relentless NATO air campaign against Iraq and Serbia may well have reached a less sanguine conclusion.

Stage 2 (Early June–Late August)

The aim of this stage was to simulate the attack on and seizure of the Penghus (Pescadores) with emphasis on sea-crossing and landing operations.[67] The exercise did not plan the occupation of the offshore islands of Jinmen (Quemoy) or Mazu (Matsu), which are considered irrelevant to an assault on Taiwan. As an article put it: "The strategic Penghu archipelago is situated midway in the Taiwan Strait. Because of the islands' level terrain, it is relatively easy to take them tactically. For Taiwan, losing the Penghus would mean the loss of a vital strategic protective screen and shipping lifeline. Taiwan is bound to collapse without a fight."[68]

In this stage of the exercise, both special forces and some of China's elite troops drawn from several military regions took part in the mock landings. Rapid-reaction forces were used for the first time in this exercise.[69] With the Penghus as the chosen target, this stage focused on an invasion described as follows:[70]

> The army, navy, air force, and Second Artillery launched shells, missiles, and bombs. Landing craft hit the beaches, and hovercraft and aircraft covered the attack. Tens of thousands of civilian ships, including container ships armed with artillery, transported supplies and rescued injured servicemen. Electronic jamming and countermeasures were carried out. On one mission, medium- and intermediate-range missile units simulated the first wave of attacks, some launched because of their threatened loss to Taiwan's attack aircraft.[71]

Afterward, the report continued, the air campaign started, and commando units seized strategic targets as a prelude to the second-wave landing assault. In florid language typical of the Chinese media, the report gushed: "Shielded by destroyers, landing-craft vessels, submarines, and armored helicopters, tens of thousands of field army troops, the naval marine brigade . . . and amphibious tanks fiercely attacked the islands off Dongshan Island and Zhaoan Bay," simulating an attack on the Penghu Islands and Taiwan.

Stage 3 (Early to Late August)

After July, the United States was assumed to have intervened, and the mock conflict escalated. In essence, the exercise switched to engaging targets at sea and in the air and focused on attacking and neutralizing aircraft carriers and their support ships. These engagements took on a great air of realism when, by chance and at the same time the PLA exercises were being conducted, two U.S. carrier battle groups were staging their own exercises in the South China Sea.[72] For its part, the PLA's actions were designed to measure its still-limited offshore capabilities. As one source put it:

> Besides, the PLA also carried out training in new tactics for three offensives [san da] and three defensives [san fang], such as fighting stealth aircraft, cruise missiles, and armed helicopters and defending against precision attacks, electronic jamming, and reconnaissance and surveillance. . . . Fighting aircraft carriers, cruise missiles, stealth aircraft, and armed helicopters is an effort that the PLA will make . . . to forcefully prevent the United States from intervening in China's local war.[73]

According to another report, "[Our] advanced weapons, effective training, and favorable terrain are sufficient to deter or destroy two to three carrier battle groups."[74] Deterring and preparing to engage U.S. forces would proceed in tandem.

Moreover, in this phase of the exercises, special emphasis was given to a possible "succession of attacks with no advance warning." Recognizing that an enemy would not "give notice" and then attack, the military region air force declared: "Old-style methods of . . . combat readiness work must change!" In response, the air force increased the frequency of no-notice attacks and made them more complex and intense. Attacks came from all altitudes and directions and under all conceivable conditions, using a variety of aircraft when communications interference was the greatest.[75]

On balance, these exercises had both propaganda and training purposes. From the military perspective, they tested the ability of the high command and all services from several military regions to conduct rapid-reaction

combat in joint operations. In each of the three stages, the recently restructured command-and-control system faced the challenges expected in high-
tech action against Taiwan and U.S. carrier battle groups. Assuming that the
nuclear threshold would not be breached, the joint operations in the exercise were restricted to a simulated conventional conflict where the "adversary" was expected to employ its most technologically advanced weaponry.

From the CMC's perspective, it had devised a most difficult and exhaustive exercise and staged it over four grueling months. For what was probably
the first time, preemption, joint operations, and launch-on-warning were
being operationalized and tested in a full-scale exercise. In time, the results
on these tests would drive China's own revolution in military affairs, a revolution that not so strangely reflected the CMC's conclusions on how U.S.
military doctrine and deployments would affect China.[76]

DETERIORATING CROSS-STRAIT
RELATIONS AND THE NEW
STRATEGIC DEBATE

From the conclusion of the Dongshan exercise to the Taiwanese presidential
election in March 2004, the leadership in Taipei under Chen Shui-bian accelerated the movement toward de jure independence. This change and
Taipei's open defiance of Beijing convinced both the leadership and the general Chinese populace that in all likelihood there could be no political solution to the cross-strait impasse. Moreover, the infusion of sophisticated U.S.
weapons and other equipment to Taiwan measurably strengthened the island's military and forced the Central Military Commission to reevaluate
the very plans for a full-scale amphibious landing that had been tested at
Dongshan. The result was a deepening debate on how to stage a successful
invasion in the foreseeable future and how to force an acceptable outcome.

Authoritative evidence that Beijing may have despaired of a lasting political compromise came on May 17, 2004, the first such official indication
since the issuance of a White Paper on February 21, 2000.[77] In contrast to
the 2000 White Paper, the CCP leadership in 2004 authorized the Central
Taiwan Work Office and the State Council's Taiwan Affairs Office to issue
jointly the statement on the deteriorating cross-strait relations. The joint release of the statement, the Beijing press emphasized, was an indicator of the

document's importance. The statement alleged that the actions taken by Taiwan president Chen over the previous four years constituted a breach of faith. Despite an avowed interest in a peaceful solution and its benefits for Taiwan, the final paragraph stressed that such a "win-win scenario" was likely to evaporate. The choice between "two roads" fell exclusively to Taiwan's leaders: "One is to pull back immediately from their dangerous lurch towards independence" and the "other is to keep following their separatist agenda . . . and, in the end, meet their own destruction by playing with fire."

At this same moment, Beijing accelerated preparations for the passage of an Anti-Secession Law, an approach reportedly endorsed by Premier Wen Jiabao on May 10, 2004.[78] Chinese scholars had long been working on draft legislation to bind Beijing's leaders to an attack on Taiwan should Taipei formally declare the island's statehood or otherwise grasp what the Chinese call the "high-tension wire" (*gaoya xian*). In response to such drafts, the Taiwan Affairs Office invited scholars to discuss its main points. Of relevance here, a scholar had highlighted three conditions under which the PLA would be legally bound to launch a war against Taipei without the approval of the National People's Congress: Taipei declares independence or takes substantive steps toward independence; a foreign army invades Taiwan; or Taipei indefinitely postpones or obstructs peaceful reunification. A related article on this draft law noted that the Chinese military would "not be limited to conventional weapons in attacking Taiwan."[79] This proviso was soon dropped, but it reflected internal debates on the possible use of nuclear weapons in an invasion of the island.

Once called the National Reunification Law, the Anti-Secession Law was officially debated for the first time by the Standing Committee of the National People's Congress in late December 2004. The name change marked a subtle but crucial retreat from aggressive measures to promote reunification. The new title presaged a shift toward modest efforts at cross-strait accommodation while still drawing a bright line against Taiwan's independence. Slowly but surely, Beijing was abandoning the rigid policy announced in the 2000 White Paper, including the threat to use force if reunification was indefinitely delayed. The renamed law was scheduled for final passage at the next plenary session of the congress in March 2005.

The debate about weaponry, moreover, was consistent with the rising tide of mainland press coverage on the growing military threat caused by the introduction of U.S. arms into Taiwan under the Bush administration. This coverage dramatically increased in 2002, in response to Jiang Zemin's judgment that "a war across the Taiwan Strait is unavoidable" and when the General Staff Operations Department convened a meeting to consider plans for an amphibious campaign against Taiwan. One of the topics was whether U.S. forces would participate in the war. Based on America's proclaimed geostrategic interests and recent military actions, the prevailing opinion was that U.S. forces would undoubtedly intervene.

Having reached that consensus, the military officers in the meeting then asked: When and how would U.S. intervention start? Many officers believed that U.S. forces would wait until about 200,000 PLA troops had landed on the island. At that point, U.S. forces would pounce with their superior air and sea power and quickly cut off the invasion force from its lines of supply and tactical support, despite the planned infusion of equipment and personnel using fishing and commercial vessels as well as regular air and sea craft.[80] Together, the U.S. and Taiwanese units would systematically annihilate the exposed PLA troops and thereby break the will of the Chinese army to continue the fight.[81] Nothing in this debate confirms the view sometimes expressed by American specialists that the PLA has repeatedly misestimated U.S. capabilities and commitment to the defense of the island.

The debates among senior PLA military officers so evident in 2002 continued and expanded in the months and years that followed. Some senior PLA officers cautioned their colleagues not to underestimate the resistance spirit of the Taiwanese army or the American's combat capabilities. They stressed the unfavorable conditions that seemed almost immutable: the dependence of any amphibious campaign on air and sea domination, the likelihood of strong local resistance from the Taiwanese army and people defending their homes, and the proven skill and capacity of the U.S. military in conducting wars of attrition. These officers noted the PLA's lack of preparations for a war with the United States and claimed that all of the bravado about a quick victory had failed to take into account the realities of a battle fought across a formidable sea barrier.

For the CMC, the specter of a coming crisis loomed ever larger as Taipei intensified its drive toward independence and as the international community was becoming more vocal in its backing for Taipei. As the mood of pessimism grew, so too did the search for a viable alternative strategy and ways to lessen the confrontation with Taiwan expand.

SCENARIOS OF A FUTURE WAR

Beginning in the late 1980s and for years thereafter, PLA strategists faced the question: "What can the Second Artillery do when [waging] a conventional local war?" At that time the threat from the Soviet Union was being replaced by growing military challenges from China's neighbors, especially Japan, India, and Vietnam, three countries that had begun introducing advanced conventional weapons into their order of battle.[82]

The contention for the sovereignty of the Spratly Islands in the South China Sea added to the threat and to the rationale for the creation of a conventional missile force within the Second Artillery. Senior PLA officers maintained that a "huge psychological impact on the enemy" would result from even a conventional missile attack and that a conventional missile force could "deter the outbreak of a conventional local war in time of peace and contain the expansion and escalation of a conventional local war after it had broken out." To wage future wars, they ordered the acceleration of R&D on medium- and intermediate-range conventional missiles and a strengthening of their launch unit cadres.[83]

By the early 1990s, the CMC had authorized the corps to set up a trial conventional missile unit under the Wannan Base in southern Anhui and then formalized it as the First Conventional Missile Brigade. Within a short time, these so-called quick-action "fists" proliferated throughout the Second Artillery's coastal bases. Their primary purpose was to provide a strong military response short of nuclear war, and their employment would occur under the prevailing condition of nuclear deterrence.[84] Indeed, when used, they would help ensure victory without forcing a nuclear exchange. According to the PLA's current doctrine, the "fists" could silence an enemy's command centers and cripple its logistics.

Armed with antiquated air, ground, and naval forces to fight in combined-services engagements, conventional missiles were believed to be one of the few means available to the Chinese military to destroy high-tech weapons and infrastructure.[85] Facing threats from advanced adversaries, the planners assumed that their ground troops would have little or no time to reach the battlefield in most fast-moving joint operations. The air force, Second Artillery, and navy would most likely be the first to engage, and their effectiveness would determine the outcome.[86] Yet, how to conduct such campaigns against a superior adversary such as the United States proved to be the most daunting challenge in planning for a future cross-strait conflict, and the PLA's task was being further complicated by the CMC's great uncertainty and a continuing debate about what the U.S. role in that conflict might be.[87]

We should digress briefly to note that the sources for a future conflict with the United States multiplied in 2003 with the growing crisis on the Korean Peninsula. In that year, for example, the North Koreans reprocessed the spent fuel rods at their nuclear facility in Yongbyon and by 2004 were estimated to have enough plutonium for several atomic devices. That dramatic change raised the specter of a U.S. attack on North Korea, and senior PLA officers told us that their two greatest fears stemmed from the increased possibility of a direct American attack on the DPRK or a war resulting from "falling strategic dominoes" whereby Japan and Taiwan would acquire nuclear arms. In the first case, we were told, Beijing would not tolerate an American occupation of North Korea and would fight the United States to prevent it. The second case as it concerns Taiwan would constitute "a fatal act of independence" that would justify a PLA invasion of the island.

In their exercises, military journals, and internal debates, PLA officers clearly show an understanding that any engagement with U.S. forces for whatever reason would, as a minimum, pit their entire arsenal against American carrier battle groups, and as a consequence they recognize the urgent need to modernize and restructure their forces, strategy, and command and control. Many senior naval officers continue to call for China to build a small number of naval battle groups of its own, or as one PLA author put it: "This is not a question of what we want or whether this can be done, but a requirement of China's national interest."[88]

In one of the most detailed, authoritative analyses of how to meet the U.S. carrier threat, another PLA writer emphasized the urgent need to acquire a vast array of land, sea, air, and space assets and to forge them into an integrated, information-age strike force that would utilize advanced "target detection and assessment measures; sneak and powerful attack [technologies]; jamming and deception; concealment . . . ; stealth and disinformation tactics; and tri-service joint operations."[89] Few if any knowledgeable PLA strategists underestimate, let alone dismiss the extraordinary steps that must be taken to "reign victorious" in the feared and perhaps inevitable "anti-carrier struggle."[90] All recognize that the battle for Taiwan must be won quickly and decisively, before the carriers could enter the fray.

Should a cross-strait confrontation escalate and draw in the United States, the PLA strategy that prevailed until at least 2004 would be a modern version of active defense. Yet, the most likely scenarios of a future war highlight just how contingent these estimates can be, how dependent they are on whether and how Taiwan resists and how much and how quickly the United States would be prepared to act, if at all.

According to the now-modified active defense strategy, a high-tech conventional war with the United States would probably become large-scale and employ the most sophisticated nonnuclear weapons of each side. During the active fighting, the foremost mission of the Second Artillery and air force would be to maintain the integrity of the nuclear deterrent and secondarily to wear down the fighting will of Taiwan's military through conventional means. In addition to Taiwan itself, the main battles would be inside China, with U.S. allies in the region participating indirectly. Throughout the conflict, the United States would possess superior arms. Moreover, the war could be prolonged, and both sides would take significant casualties. Again according to the doctrine, especially by the mid-phase of the war, public opposition in the United States and Asia to the fighting would grow, even as the economy on Taiwan would be destroyed; conversely, domestic support for Beijing's "just war against American aggression" would mount.

As senior PLA planners dissected the American strategy from the Gulf War of 1991 to the lightning war against Iraq in 2003, however, it was to become painfully evident that no war with the United States could be won or even brought to a reasonable draw if the United States were able to buy time to mobilize and deploy its superior combat forces and seize the initiative early in the conflict. Waiting for a U.S. response and a cautious, staged engagement with the Americans by the PLA would be a certain recipe for defeat.

It was in this mood that those responsible for devising the new contingency plans began to pay close attention to and take into account the U.S. *Nuclear Posture Review* (January 8, 2002)[91] and *The National Security Strategy of the United States of America* (September 17, 2002) on the preemptive use of nuclear weapons.[92] These sentences in the *Review* struck the Chinese as especially ominous:

> In setting requirements for nuclear strike capabilities, distinctions can be made among the [nuclear] contingencies for which the United States must be prepared. Contingencies can be categorized as immediate, potential or unexpected.

> Immediate contingencies involve well-recognized current dangers. . . .
> Current examples of immediate contingencies include . . . a military con-
> frontation over the status of Taiwan. . . .
> Due to the combination of China's still developing strategic objectives
> and its ongoing modernization of its nuclear and non nuclear forces, China
> is a country that could be involved in an immediate or potential contingency
> [requiring the use of U.S. nuclear weapons].

The Americans had always rebuffed demands that they embrace a nuclear
no-first-use doctrine, but possible nuclear preemption against "a military
confrontation over the status of Taiwan" without mentioning the type or
level of the confrontation opened up entirely new threats and risks. Given
the American mentality after September 11, 2001, the Chinese had to reappraise their plans to recover Taiwan by force should it become necessary.[93]

It was against this background that the authors discovered eleven articles
that most challenged our understanding of Chinese military policy and how
to evaluate information published in unofficial journals. We had been searching for signs of how the military commission would weigh its response should
deterrence against Taiwan's independence fail. In 2004, a discussion of the
possible use of nuclear weapons on China's "sovereign territory" finally surfaced in the year-long series of articles that described a PLA "invasion" of an
unnamed island. Published in *Jianchuan Zhishi* (Naval & Merchant Ships), a
widely circulated monthly with apparent ties to the PLA Navy, these articles
and another in *Bingqi Zhishi* (Ordnance Knowledge) examined nuclear preemption and justified it in operations that would determine the "nation's destiny" and where defeat would be unacceptable.[94]

In the discussion of sources for the book in our Introduction, we said that
existing analytical tools make it possible to "sift through so much information, to identify possible nuggets of potentially useful evidence, and to subject that evidence to extensive reliability tests, including multiple sourcing,
which can never be perfect." Still, there are limits to any outsider's ability to
make those tests, especially when such highly suspect and controversial information comes from one source, as is the case with the *Jianchuan Zhishi*
articles. The impulse to include the detailed operational plans in these sen-
sational articles was, of course, extremely tempting.

After all, there were traces of the possible use of nuclear weapons against
Taiwan that came long after Beijing's first official statements on its projected
nuclear arsenal. Ever since it conducted its initial atomic test on October 16,

1964, China had proclaimed a no-first-use of nuclear weapons policy, and with respect to international conflicts that declaration remains in force, though under pressure. A little-noticed change, however, occurred when the high command apparently came to regard the policy as inapplicable to its own territory, a change kept secret though hinted at when a Soviet armored invasion was considered probable in the late 1960s and 1970s.[95] Always adhering to the conviction that Taiwan was part of China, moreover, "well-informed" but unofficial mainland sources began to hint in the mid-1990s that the no-first-use policy applied only to international conflicts. On August 4, 1996, for example, Sha Zukang, the PRC disarmament representative to the Geneva arms control talks, told *Newsweek* magazine, "China promises no-first-use of nuclear weapons to any country, but this does not apply to Taiwan, because Taiwan is a province of China."[96] A few articles repeated Sha's line as recently as 2004, though none carried the official seal of the Central Military Commission.[97]

Most troubling of all was the specificity of the *Jianchuan Zhishi* articles. They treated the global and domestic repercussions of a nuclear assault against the island, the coordination of nuclear and conventional operations, the types of the nuclear weapons to be employed, and the issues of psychological warfare, civilian casualties, and mass evacuations. Moreover, PLA and Taiwanese officers confirmed the *Jianchuan Zhishi* claim that Taiwan has "mass destruction" weapons—such as fuel air explosives—that could wipe out an entire invasion force and should be considered equivalent to tactical nuclear weapons. The several different *Jianchuan Zhishi* authors appeared to have had access to data that could only have been declassified at a high level. Could it be that the not-so-theoretical island was Taiwan and that *Jianchuan Zhishi* had been selected as the outlet because the navy would carry the brunt of an invasion?

There were many possible answers to this question. We, of course, could not simply dismiss the military arguments for the use of tactical nuclear weapons in an attack on Taiwan. It was also possible that the articles could be surrogates for hidden political debates, not genuine invasion plans, and several other nonmilitary reasons for a threatened use quickly come to mind. Other, perhaps more plausible reasons might include the scare factor as Beijing seeks to intimidate pro-independence activists on Taiwan.

By raising the specter of the nuclear sword at the moment a new mainland Party and military leadership was galvanizing its power and debating the use of "non-peaceful means and other necessary measures to protect China's sovereignty and territorial integrity" in the Anti-Secession Law, Beijing might well have been attempting to raise the stakes of a showdown with Taipei to convince its own people, including the PLA, of its determination to block the island's independence. If challenged, moreover, as we have done, military officers could dismiss the articles as "laughable," as indeed one PLA officer did.

Keeping all these possibilities in mind, we came down on the side of great caution in view of the extraordinary consequences of giving credence to Beijing's alleged plans to use nuclear weapons against Taiwan. In our earlier discussion of sources, we noted the tendency of mid-rank officers to advocate positions that "prove their mettle as trusted warriors, only to become more seasoned and realistic about the efficacy of military force as they rise through the ranks." Even worse, the bona fides of the authors of the *Jianchuan Zhishi* articles were completely unknown to us, and we could not even verify that they had ever held any military or other security-related positions. So, we repeatedly asked ourselves, Why would Beijing tolerate the open publication of its military secrets, even as a trial balloon, in a popular journal? Simply put, this would be totally inconsistent with the way the PLA protects its military plans and operations. Furthermore, the year-long release of apparently classified information is also inconsistent with the way security-conscious censors would normally react. So, could this be a deliberate leak through an unofficial source, an act similar to the "unauthorized" leak of portions of the *Nuclear Posture Review* in the United States?

In our effort to evaluate these 2004 articles during the months that they were appearing, we spoke to well-informed Chinese who flatly denied that the PLA would ever use nuclear weapons first or against Taiwan. One official said:

> Those who say that we might be the first to use nuclear weapons against Taiwan don't know anything about our military thinking or plans. There is zero—repeat zero—chance that we would use them first against Taiwan. If we did so, our relations with our brothers on the island would never again be the same. If we intentionally threatened to do this, this would also end the cooperation we have received from the international community to sustain the one-China policy and oppose the separatists from crossing the red line.

Another official echoed the point we made in our Introduction when he said: "At the fringes of the military, especially among some inexperienced junior officers, there are debates about using nuclear weapons against your carrier battle groups. But no one in the General Staff Operations Department has ever taken them seriously." A knowledgeable scholar in Beijing made this comment more general when he asserted, "These days anyone can publish anything sensationalistic just so it doesn't criticize the government."

Although we wrestled with how to weigh these articles on the possible first use of nuclear weapons against Taiwan, we had no such difficulty with the evidence on their use after a nuclear attack against China in the course of a conflict in the strait. Should a country such as the United States launch the first preemptive strike, the PLA would carry out tit-for-tat nuclear retaliation in accordance with the alert, targeting, and launch policies discussed in Chapter 6. In 2004, then CMC chairman Jiang Zemin told China's warriors: "Modern war is close to us. . . . If war occurs on our land, sea, or air, the territory of the aggressors will suffer our counterattack and strikes. . . . It is impossible for China to make a commitment not to resort to military means, including nuclear counterattack and strikes." [98] Consistent with Jiang's edict, PLA planners explained how China would retaliate. In one scenario, both nuclear and conventionally armed missiles would attack the foe's carrier battle groups if "the enemy" had used nuclear weapons against the PLA invasion fleet in the strait. In a second scenario, nuclear missiles would hit the enemy's overseas military bases if nuclear weapons had struck the landing forces on Taiwan or military bases inside China. As a third scenario, should that enemy attack the mainland of China, one of the *Jianchuan Zhishi* articles declared, the Second Artillery would launch against that enemy's homeland. [99]

Although the Chinese military acknowledges that it could not match U.S. technology in the war we have been describing, it rejects any suggestion concerning its inferiority in the realm of strategy and fighting spirit. Its guiding principle for waging war is: "You fight your way. I will fight mine and strive for total initiative." [100] Loosely interpreted, this adheres to Sun Tzu's injunction to anticipate and defeat the enemy's strategy and means that the PLA would launch surprise and diverse offensives or "resort to offensives to defeat offensives." [101] Its soldiers would not hunker down in a defensive posture against heavy air strikes but would instead draw on their sashoujian or "trump cards" to destroy the enemy's bases. The threatened use of nuclear weapons could be one of those cards.

Even the possibility of using nuclear weapons to "resolve" a political confrontation that had escalated to war between China and the United States, of course, sounds so preposterous that accepting that possibility seems almost beyond comprehension. When so many years ago, world leaders spoke of letting time heal the wounds of civil war and end its legacy, few realized that buying time fundamentally contradicted the law of changing generations and national interests. For many on both sides of the strait, the status quo has worn out its welcome, and now the leaders in Taipei are demanding the very movement that could set in motion chaos. For the PLA, prudent planning for that moment of chaos requires the stepped up procurement of advanced arms and the search for "trump card" weapons that could help attain rapid victory. Should a challenge to that victory involve a showdown with the United States and the threat to use nuclear weapons, the enduring logic of deterrence perpetuates a continued not-so-delicate balance of nuclear terror.

The well-publicized CMC guideline for a full-scale amphibious campaign against Taiwan is: "Strive for quick resolution, prepare for a sustained war."[102] This guideline may help explain the CMC's apparent interest in employing nonconventional weapons, because no other weapons in the PLA arsenal could achieve a "quick resolution" given the large influx of U.S. weapons into Taiwan since 2001. Nevertheless, U.S. reconnaissance satellites and Taiwanese long-range radars provided by the United States could easily detect significant military movements on the mainland, and a major Taiwan spy network exposed in April 2004 revealed how deeply Taiwan intelligence had penetrated the PLA high command and compromised its secret war plans.[103] Given all this, major questions would remain unanswered until the test came on the battlefield.[104]

IRRATIONAL WAR AND
THE LOGIC OF PEACE

Thus, as we come to the end of our history of China's military modernization, we end up with the decades-old Taiwan crisis. Without that crisis looming ever larger, Beijing's military preparations would undoubtedly atrophy, much as they did in the early and mid-1990s, and its national programs and social energies would concentrate almost exclusively and quite probably successfully on China becoming a global economic and political power. While the skeptical will continue to divine threats in the so-called peaceful rise of China, none of those threats would lead us to the potential tragedy of nuclear war and the long-term destruction of tranquility in the Pacific. The most salient issue then is not how can we understand and deal with China as a military power. The question is: What can be done to end Taiwan as China's putative enemy and Beijing's preparations for an uncertain war that could well engulf the United States?

Our story of the transformation of Chinese military power and its focus on Taiwan may be the logical—and tragic—conclusion to Beijing's main security dilemma, but it has also linked righteous national purpose to the stark realities of weapons of mass destruction. As Samuel Johnson, the author of the first great English dictionary, once said, "the prospect of hanging clears the mind, wonderfully," and the prospect of the nuclear option may do just that. In this vein, Chinese strategists have cited the Iraq War as an example of a great power strategically losing a war while winning all the battles and by analogy to Taiwan they recognize that this may turn out to be the same for China.[105] Beijing might achieve a Pyrrhic victory for that outcome would stigmatize Beijing as a global pariah. The decision to rekindle the long-dormant civil war might seem justified by political necessity, but the consequences of the conflict could be an unmitigated disaster.

The destiny of Taiwan has baffled and frustrated the best minds and leading statesmen for more than half a century. Settling the island's future is a story of failed "solutions" from Yalta in 1945 and Mao's aborted invasion plans of 1950 to cross-strait agreements in the early 1990s and the rapid economic integration and social interaction ever since.[106] Each of those solutions has failed both for grand reasons of revolution and war and because of higher priorities accorded Cold War hostilities, local nationalism, and hidden fears of a united, strong China. The background to the present predicament is long and complex. What is new in the tense cross-strait relations is the direction and character of the military preparations that have preoccupied us to this point.

In the final analysis, the Taiwan issue is a political one. Its solution depends on the wisdom of the leaders in Beijing, Taipei, and Washington rather than the military might on the two sides of the strait and the United States. The leaders in the three capitals have stood witness to the bitter disagreement across the strait, and most acknowledge the mounting danger. Although none so far has demonstrated the political wisdom and courage to act, let alone the will to compromise, there is still time. Few comprehend the history of the crisis from the others' perspective; standing in the others' shoes is not part of China's grand tradition.

Beyond the direct mainland-Taiwan confrontation over the sovereignty of the island, any effort to resolve the Taiwan issue would have to include several parties with conflicting security interests, legal connections, and historical memories. Coping with the complexity of this issue would require genuine knowledge, committed leadership, and seasoned diplomatic statesmanship. What we have addressed in this volume is one of the most consequential dimensions of that complexity, the dimension of war and peace in the nuclear age.

In the end, of course, for Beijing and Taipei to pursue a peaceful solution, each must be willing to weigh realistic and mutually beneficial alternatives to achieve it. Clearly a long cooling-off period would be required if war is to be avoided, and one can imagine ways to define and guarantee a standstill agreement that would deepen and ramify the benefits of economic integration and other confidence-building processes and that would run parallel to the internal political changes already underway on both sides of the strait.

For such changes to happen, there must be a major modification in political direction, and as of this writing, few appear willing to risk making such a move. Those seeking independence on Taiwan have long depended on American political and military support to underwrite their pursuit, and that support has undoubtedly contributed to the drift toward a showdown and possible war. But, so too have Beijing's preparations for battle and its threats of hostile action exacerbated the tensions and justified Taipei's plea for assistance.

To be sure, any major effort to achieve a peaceful accommodation or even to buy a long-term commitment to the status quo would have to be embraced by the international community, but this would not seem to be a major obstacle. The nationalism that drives so much of the crisis could be tempered by the global community's aversion to a cross-strait conflict and by its most cherished jointly held values. International cooperation based on the near-universal commonality of interests and concerns, be they economic prosperity or antiterrorism, appears to unite all but the direct parties to the Taiwan problem. The tragedy is that the only important players—the People's Republic, Taiwan, and the United States—are at an impasse.

At the strategic level, the mainland leadership has increasingly understood that it probably will need third-party mediation to prevent the war that we have been describing and that no one wants. Given its part in the entire postwar history of Taiwan, that third party would undoubtedly be the United States. Moreover, Washington often does understand and respond to its need for Beijing's support on such crucial issues as terrorism, the proliferation of nuclear weapons, the North Korean nuclear crisis, trade competition, drug smuggling, and so on. On these issues, Taipei is far less involved. Taiwan depends on the mainland for its economic well-being and competitiveness and to maintain a climate of peace for its domestic political stability, and it needs Washington to guarantee its survival in case of unprovoked war. And Beijing must work with Washington and Taipei on a range of issues as part of its grand strategy to achieve national unity and complete its quest to become an international power. War would destroy all of these strategic imperatives, and its staggering costs in lives and treasure would poison the regional and international climate for the coming century.

Nevertheless, the common goals of peace and stability and the well-understood risks of moves toward war have not yet determined or even significantly informed the most critical policies of the three major actors. Despite routine statements heralding the benefits of compromise and caution, the ongoing political dynamic leads Beijing to deploy missiles and make threats, causes a growing part of the Taiwanese leadership and populace to press somewhat recklessly for independence, and emboldens Taiwan's strongest advocates in the United States to supply it with more and more sophisticated weapons. The vicious cycle of recriminations and hostile actions justifies risking war, not peace.

At the same time, each side has underestimated the resolve and influence of the most provocative elements within the other two and has dismissed as crisis mongering the likelihood of war. Each wants it both ways: to be the champion of peace and the messenger of war. The three publics, moreover, are not operating from the same database or sense of urgency. The Chinese public focuses mainly on the Taiwanese independence activists, and its leadership has failed to divorce its public message on the benefits of accepting the one-China policy from its hard-line war preparations and contradictory policies toward Hong Kong. The public on Taiwan is split between those who primarily see dangers coming from across the strait and those who would pursue the economic and societal cross-strait opportunities. Few in the American public have any substantial knowledge about Taiwan and could care less about its trials or its hopes. As the climate of hostility worsens and the tide shifts toward war, no stream of concern and no search for peace have appeared to meet the shifting tide of hostility.

Years ago, Taiwan defense minister Tang Yao-ming proclaimed, "Making a cross-strait war impossible is Taiwan's best military strategy." [107] Yet, this is more a vain plea than a valid strategy. In the final analysis, the "best" strategy for all would be to temper extremist pronouncements and actions and redirect national policies to avert the final confrontation. Failing that, imagined enemies will become real, and China's war preparations will no longer posit an uncertain conflict.

Notes

For complete authors' names, titles, and publishing data on works cited in short forms, see the References Cited section, pp. 313–347.

CHAPTER I

1. Lewis and Xue, "Social Change."
2. Xinhua, November 15, 2004.
3. Xinhua, November 23, 2004.
4. On the question of costs of a cross-strait war, see Scobell, *Costs*, esp. chap. 7 by Ellis Joffe.
5. Information Office, State Council, *China's National Defense in 2004*.
6. A major effort to examine how this occurred is provided in Lewis and Xue, *China Builds*; Lewis and Xue, *China's Strategic Seapower*; and Feigenbaum, *China's Techno-Warriors*.
7. Mao Zedong, "Problems of War," pp. 224–25.
8. The best study of this linkage between the military-industrial programs of the 1950s and 1980s is Feigenbaum.
9. The literature on this subject is too extensive to cite fully here. We have found most useful Johnston, "Is China," pp. 5–56; this article cites much of the burgeoning list of publications on this subject.
10. For an excellent summary analysis of this crisis, see Scobell, *China's Use*, chap. 8.
11. In addition to our *China's Strategic Seapower* and the many secondary sources on the navy cited there, see Cole; Allen; and Kamer. On the ground and other general purpose forces, see the sources cited in Chapter 5, Note 3, esp. Shambaugh.
12. McDevitt, p. 1.
13. Xu and Sha.
14. Yu Yongbo, pp. 135–43.
15. See, for example, the "Note on Sources" in Shambaugh, which includes extensive references to a number of important bibliographical compilations and assessments of materials and studies on the PLA.

16. For a well-informed analysis and compilation of Internet sources on the PLA, see Fravel.

CHAPTER 2

1. Li Jijun, "On Strategy," p. 23. General Li is the former vice president of the PLA Academy of Military Science.

2. Ba Zhongtan, *Zhongguo*, pp. 3, 5. General Ba was commander of the People's Armed Police and now is a senior adviser to the Central Military Commission.

3. Ibid., p. 164.

4. Liu Bingchen, p. 78.

5. Li Jijun, "On Strategy," p. 23.

6. Wu Jiulong, p. 2. We have used the translation by General Tao Hanzhang. Most earlier histories date Sun Tzu's life much later, but Tao's dates are based on exhaustive research.

7. Quoted in Bloodworth, p. 284.

8. Wu Jiulong, pp. 37–38.

9. Tao Hanzhang, p. 100.

10. Bloodworth, p. 285.

11. Tao Hanzhang, p. 104.

12. Guangdong, p. 784.

13. Ba Zhongtan, *Zhongguo*, p. 2.

14. Shi Dongbing, *Xumu*, p. 160.

15. Li Jijun, "On Strategy," pp. 22–24. Quoted from p. 23.

16. Unless otherwise cited, the information in this and the next two paragraphs is from Guo Ping, pp. 26–27; Li Jijun, *Junshi*, pp. 60–62, 175; and Li Jijun, "On Strategy," pp. 20–24.

17. See also Gong Yuzhen.

18. See, for example, Bao Guojun, p. 28; and Li Jijun, *Junshi*, p. 239.

19. Quoted from Li Jijun, "On Strategy," p. 23.

20. The information in this paragraph and the next is from Ba Zhongtan, *Zhongguo*, p. 7; and Li Jijun, "On Strategy," p. 23.

21. Guo Ping, pp. 26–27; Li Jijun, *Junshi*, p. 62.

22. Unless otherwise cited, the information in this paragraph and the next is from Li Jijun, *Junshi*, p. 61.

23. For a description that Beijing's leaders always give top priority to domestic security issues rather than international crises, see, for example, Wang Li, Vol. 2, pp. 1086, 1088.

24. Lin Boye et al., pp. 240–42.

25. Peng and Yao, pp. 118, 188–89. See also Shang Jinsuo et al., p. 241.

26. On Beijing's tendency toward worst-case planning, see Yuan Zhengling, p. 23.

27. For further explanation of a cautious attitude toward the first battle in the CMC's war planning, see, for example, Peng and Yao, pp. 121, 256–57.

28. Unless otherwise cited, the information in this paragraph and the next is from Li Jijun, *Junshi*, pp. 60–62, 74–75, 175, 227–28; and Li Jijun, "On Strategy," pp. 20–24.

29. See Ba Zhongtan, *Zhongguo*, pp. 65, 66, 120, 121.

30. For the PLA's judgment of the need for readjusting the weapons procurement policy, see, for example, Peng and Yao, pp. 437–38.

31. Most of the information in this paragraph and the next two is from Ba Zhongtan, *Zhongguo*, pp. 152, 153, 154, 161.

32. Interviews with Chinese air traffic control specialists and PLA Air Force officers, 1994–96.

33. Ba Zhongtan, "Opening," p. 1.

34. Mi Zhenyu, pp. 4–5, 19. Lieutenant General Mi Zhenyu is vice president of the PLA Academy of Military Science.

35. "Deng Xiaoping Talks About," p. 9; "Deng Xiaoping Talks Freely," pp. 9–10.

36. Peng and Yao, pp. 462, 477.

37. Zhao Li, pp. 5, 6.

38. For a systematic analysis of this issue, see, for example, Peng and Yao, pp. 470–72.

39. Zhou Enlai, "Several," pp. 327–28.

40. Mao Zedong, "On People's," p. 416.

41. Deng Xiaoping, "Speech," pp. 132–33.

42. Deng Xiaoaping, "Task," p. 34.

43. Deng Xiaoping, "Speech," pp. 131–32, 133.

44. Yu Zemin, p. 28.

45. This paragraph and the next are based on interviews with senior military officers in Beijing, April and July, 1998.

46. Peng and Yao, pp. 117–18.

47. For an analysis of the background for Beijing's decision to give priority to domestic issues, see Lewis and Xue, "Social," pp. 24–40, passim.

48. Cao Yingwang, p. 19.

49. Wang Wenrong, p. 276.

50. Peng and Yao, p. 238. For the background of Mao's decision to prepare for "an early war, an all-out war, and a nuclear war," see Lewis and Xue, *China's Strategic Seapower*, pp. 211–13.

51. Unless otherwise cited, the information in this paragraph and the next is from Wang Wenrong, p. 276.

52. See, for example, Saiget; and "Reduced Growth Rate."

53. Sagan and Waltz.

54. See United States, Department of Defense, *Nuclear*; the quote is from p. 16. For a Chinese assessment of the *Nuclear Posture Review*, see Shang Jinsuo et al., pp. 489–90.

55. Bao Guojun, p. 28.

56. Wang Wenrong, p. 352. On Chinese assessments of the potential U.S. use of tactical nuclear weapons against China in a "conventional" conflict, see Peng and Yao, p. 477.

57. Bao Guojun, p. 29.

58. See, for example, Jiang Zhengming, pp. 14–15; Xiong Yuxiang, pp. 16–17; and Su Bei, p. 12.

59. United States, Department of Defense, *Nuclear*, p. 7.

60. The New Triad set forth in the *Nuclear Posture Review* would be composed of offensive strike systems, active and passive defenses, and a "revitalized defense infrastructure," all "bound together" by enhanced command, control, and intelligence systems. United States, Department of Defense, *Nuclear*.

61. See, for example, Lü Qiang et al., p. 1. This paragraph is also based on interviews with strategic specialists in China in January, March, and August 2002 and February 2003. For a scholarly view of the changes in U.S. nuclear strategy by a member of the Arms Control Research Division, Institute of Applied Physics and Computational Mathematics, see Tian Jingmei.

62. Tian Yi, p. 9.

63. Sun Yamin, pp. 37–38; Peng and Yao, pp. 340–41. Quoted from Sun Yaomin, p. 37.

64. Peng and Yao, pp. 340–41.

65. Shang Jinsuo et al., p. 348.

66. Tian Yi, p. 9.

67. Li Jiqing, p. 59.

68. See, for example, Wang Yusheng.

69. Peng and Yao, p. 122.

70. Unless otherwise cited, the information in this paragraph is quoted from Peng and Yao, pp. 122, 124, 126.

71. Shang Jinsuo et al., p. 243.

72. Ibid., pp. 123, 127. Quoted from p. 123.

73. Wang Wenrong, p. 287.

74. Ibid., pp. 287–88.

75. Shang Jinsuo et al., p. 244.

76. Peng and Yao, p. 491.

77. Chen Yilin.

78. Wang Wenrong, pp. 287–88.

79. Gao Shangrui.

80. Bao Guojun, p. 29.

81. Peng and Yao, pp. 453–54, 490–91. The quotes are from pp. 454 and 491, respectively.

CHAPTER 3

1. The authors have reviewed these efforts in Lewis and Xue, *China Builds*; Lewis and Hua, pp. 5–40; and Lewis and Xue, *China's Strategic Seapower*.

2. These documents are found in *Polemic*.

3. CCP Central Document, p. 426.

4. Huang and Zhang, pp. 471–72, 476–77.

5. Quan Yanchi, *Zhenshi*, p. 101.

6. Li Zhisui, p. 115.

7. For a discussion of the "third-line" program, see Lewis and Xue, *China's Strategic Seapower*, pp. 88–99.

8. Ren and Chen, p. 27.

9. Zhou and Luo, p. 493.

10. Xu Kui, p. 53.

11. Zhang Xiaogang, p. 32.

12. Zheng Qian, p. 205.

13. Zhou Enlai, "We," p. 520 (note 8).

14. Le Duan.

15. Liu Zhinan, pp. 41–42.

16. Xiao Xinli, p. 389.

17. Zheng and Han, p. 318. See also Xu Kui, p. 51.

18. General Wang, p. 565; Zheng Qian, pp. 210–11.

19. Liu Zhinan, pp. 41–42; Xu Kui, p. 53. In September 1955, Mao had promoted ten generals from the revolutionary years as marshals, emulating the ranks of the most senior officers in the Soviet Army. By 1966, nine were still living: Chen Yi, *He Long, Lin Biao, Liu Bocheng, Nie Rongzhen, Xu Xiangqian, Ye Jianying*, and Zhu De; Peng Dehuai had been purged, and Luo Ronghuan had died. The six chosen by the CMC are in italics; Chen, Nie, Xu, and Ye—the four marshals—prepared major reports on July 11 and September 17.

20. Editorial Departments of *Renmin Ribao* and *Hong Qi*, p. 8.

21. For a brief discussion of this purge, see Lewis and Xue, *China's Strategic Seapower*, pp. 33–39.

22. For a detailed description of the Standing Committee's decision to participate in the CPSU's Twenty-third Congress, see Wang Li, Vol. 2, p. 581–83; and Shi Dongbing, *Feng*, p. 36.

23. The quotes in the rest of this paragraph are from Gao Wenqian, p. 104. Gao had access to the CCP classified documents before he wrote this book.

24. Yang Zanyu, p. 31; Xu Kui, pp. 50–51.

25. Shi Dongbing, *Feng*, p. 279.

26. See the useful analyses of Chinese security thinking in the 1960s by Goldstein, "Do Nascent" and "Return."

27. The Inner Mongolia Military District earlier was parallel to the Beijing Military Region. Li and Hao, pp. 354, 365–66.

28. Qiu Shi, p. 629.

29. See, for example, Zheng Qian, pp. 208–9.

30. Examples of Western accounts of this highly studied border conflict can be found in Ostermann, pp. 186–201; Robinson, pp. 1178–82; Cohen, pp. 269–96; National Security Archive, p. 286; Gelman, pp. 47–103; Gobarev; and Goldstein, "Return." Our analysis cites the most important Chinese sources on the 1969 border conflict.

31. Unless otherwise cited, the information in this paragraph and the next is from Yang Kuisong, pp. 492–93; Xiao Xinli, p. 396; and Liu Zhinan, p. 43. The quote in the next paragraph is from Yang Kuisong, p. 493.

32. Li Lianqing, *Da*, p. 134.

33. Throughout much of its history, both the Party and government have had these commissions, though only the Party organization has held real power. In September 1954, when the CCP created its own military commission, Zhou Enlai was not a member of that commission. Zhang Zhen, *Zhang Zhen*, Vol. 1, pp. 432, 485. We discuss the tortuous history of the military commissions in Chapter 4.

34. For a discussion of Mao's reliance on intermediaries and advisers during the revolution, see Goncharov et al., pp. 14–22.

35. From the early years of the strategic weapons program, Zhou headed the Fifteen-Member Special Commission in charge of the program. See, for example, Lewis and Xue, *China Builds*, pp. 131–34.

36. Cohen, p. 278.

37. Unless otherwise cited, the information in this paragraph and the next is from Li Lianqing, *Da*, pp. 137–39; and Li Lianqing, *Lengnuan*, pp. 354–57. Quoted from the former source, p. 138. Li was then a senior official in the Foreign Ministry.

38. Zhang Yunsheng, "Talk."

39. On Mao's directive, see his "Remarks on Zhou," p. 21.

40. Wu Xujun, p. 249. Wu was Mao's chief nurse. Although some Chinese scholars do not believe that Mao would have discussed critical decisions with Wu (Yang Kuisong, p. 507), Xiong Xianghui, deputy head of the PLA Second Department, states that Mao did discuss major decisions with her. Xiong, "Mao," p. 347. See also Wu Miaofa, p. 173.

41. The text of Lin's report and the Party constitution are found in *Peking Review*, Vol. 12, No. 18 (April 30, 1969), pp. 16–39. According to Chen Boda, Zhang Chunqiao and Yao Wenyuan, Mao's subordinates and subsequently condemned as two of the Gang of Four, drafted this report on orders from Mao, and Lin reportedly did not like it. Chen Boda, pp. 113–14.

42. Lin Biao, p. 24. We have used the pinyin spelling of Mao's name.

43. "Constitution," p. 36.

44. The quotes are from Li and Ma, p. 290; and Han Suyin, p. 357, respectively.

45. Mao Zedong, "Speech," p. 38.

46. Han Suyin in *Eldest Son* details the story of Zhou's efforts to keep control of these ministries at the onset of the Cultural Revolution; see Han Suyin, pp. 326–27, 344–48.

47. Quan Yanchi, *Weixing*, pp. 27–28, 136–37, 175, 228–29; Gao Wenqian, p. 261. The quote is from Quan Yanchi, p. 137.

48. Xiao Sike. On the evolution of the group, see Lewis and Xue, *China's Strategic Seapower*, pp. 85, 108, 279.

49. Wang Li, Vol. 1, p. 343.

50. The information in the rest of this paragraph and the next is from Li Jian, p. 172.

51. Huang Yongsheng and Wu Faxian were the Administrative Group's chief and deputy chief, respectively. Other members were Ye Qun (Lin's wife), Li Zuopeng, Qiu Huizuo, Liu Xianquan, Li Tianyou, Li Desheng, Wen Yucheng, and Xie Fuzhi. The group was under the control of Ye Qun as well as Generals Huang, Wu, Qiu, and Li Zuopeng. Mao Zedong, "Transcript"; *New China Monthly*, p. 351.

52. Gao Wenqian, p. 275.

53. Unless otherwise cited, the information in this paragraph and the next is from Zheng Qian, pp. 211–12.

54. Xiong Xianghui, "Prelude," pp. 64–65; for the Chinese response to the Soviet statement that the Great Wall was China's real boundary, see also Chi Zehou. The Russian quote is from Gobarev, p. 46.

55. Qiu Shi, p. 661.

56. Liu Zhinan, p. 44

57. Zheng Qian, pp. 212–13.

58. Li Jue et al., pp. 74–75. We tell some of this story in Lewis and Xue, "Chinese Strategic Weapons," pp. 12–14.

59. Yuan Wei, p. 956.

60. Yang Kuisong, p. 498.

61. Li and Hao, p. 351.

62. Zheng Qian, p. 213.

63. Goncharov et al., p. 204.

64. Gao Wenqian, p. 410.

65. Li and Ma, pp. 307–8; Li and Hao, p. 351.

66. Zhao Dexin, pp. 181–82.

67. Shan Lan, Vol. 2, p. 739.

68. Zhao Dexin, pp. 181–82; Liu Jingzhi and Wang Zhongyu, p. 325.

69. "Struggle," p. 100.

70. Li Zhisui, pp. 513–14.

71. Li and Ma, pp. 311, 313.

72. The translation of a partial text of the report is in *Cold War Bulletin*, No. 11 (Winter 1998), pp. 166–68. For the names of the four marshals, see Note 19, above.

73. Liu Zhinan, p. 44.

74. The information in this paragraph is from United States, Department of State, docs. 14, 21, 24, 29, and 33. The online edition is not paginated.

75. See Xiong Xianghui, "Prelude," pp. 76–79. Xiong was then deputy head of the General Staff Second Department.

76. Ibid., p. 65.

77. Li Jian, pp. 172–73; Gu Baozi, *Jingtou*, p. 53.

78. Mao Zedong, "Remarks on the CMC's," pp. 57–58.

79. For the Chinese response to these events, see Xiong Xianghui, "Prelude," p. 80.

80. Unless otherwise cited, the information in this paragraph is from ibid.

81. Zheng Qian, p. 214.

82. Reproduced in *Cold War Bulletin*, No. 11 (Winter 1998), pp. 168–69; the Chinese text can be found in Mao Zedong, *Jianguo Yilai*, Vol. 13, pp. 59–61.

83. Li and Ma, p. 317; a translation of the text of this order is in *Cold War Bulletin*, No. 11 (Winter 1998), pp. 168–69.

84. Yang Kuisong, p. 499.

85. Zheng Qian, p. 216.

86. "Review."

87. Liu Zhinan, p. 45.

88. Yang Kuisong, p. 498.

89. Gu Baozi, *Jingtou*, pp. 144–45; Li and Ma, p. 319.

90. Zhang Yunsheng, "Talk"; Gao Wenqian, p. 411.

91. Gao Wenqian, p. 411.

92. Li Lianqing, *Lengnuan*, pp. 367, 376. For a detailed description of the Kosygin-Zhou talks, see ibid., pp. 367–76; Li Lianqing, *Da*, pp. 144–45; and New China Monthly, p. 355.

93. Li Lianqing, *Da*, p. 411.

94. Xiong Xianghui, "Prelude," p. 83.

95. A translated text of Zhou's letter to Kosygin outlining the points agreed to in their talks is in "Letter, Zhou Enlai to Alexei Kosygin (18 September 1969)," in *Cold War Bulletin*, No. 11 (Winter 1998), pp. 171–72. For Zhou's comment on this point, see Zhou Enlai, "Zhou Enlai's Talk," pp. 172–73.

96. The information in this paragraph is from Yang Kuisong, p. 501; and Xiong Xianghui, "Prelude," pp. 83–84.

97. On the timing of the negotiations, see Li Lianqing, *Lengnuan*, p. 375.

98. The translated text of excerpts from this report is in "Report by Four Chinese Marshals . . . (17 September 1969)," in *Cold War Bulletin*, No. 11 (Winter 1998), p. 170. In an addendum to this report, Marshal Chen Yi discussed the resumption of the Sino-American ambassadorial talks; for the translated text, see ibid., pp. 170–71.

99. Liu Zhinan, p. 46.

100. Ibid., pp. 47–48.

101. Zhang Yunsheng, *Maojiawan*, p. 312; Zhang Yunsheng, "Talk."

102. Li and Hao, pp. 365, 367, 375.

103. Qiu Shi, pp. 644–45.

104. Mao Zedong, "Remarks on and Revision of the Draft," p. 66. The English text of the twenty-nine slogans is found as a flyer in *Peking Review*, Vol. 12, No. 39 (September 26, 1969).

105. Yang Kuisong, p. 501; Liu Zhinan, pp. 46–47.

106. In the reply letter, Kosygin did say that the Soviet frontier forces had been ordered to prevent border clashes. Li Lianqing, *Da*, p. 156. The Kremlin's position further aroused Beijing's vigilance. Chi Zehou.

107. Unless otherwise cited, the information in the rest of this paragraph and the next is from Liu Zhinan, p. 47.

108. The quotes are from the test announcement found as an insert in *Peking Review*, Vol. 12, No. 40 (October 3, 1969).

109. Li Shenming, p. 21.

110. Unless otherwise cited, the information in this and the next two paragraphs is from Li and Ma, pp. 323–25; Yang Kuisong, p. 502; and Liu Zhinan, p. 48.

111. Chi Zehou.

112. Zhang Yunsheng, *Maojiawan*, p. 306.

113. Yang Yinlu, pp. 161–63.

114. The classic study of this phenomenon is Leon Festinger et al.

115. Zhang Yunsheng, "Talk."

116. Li and Ma, pp. 324, 327.

117. Wang Chao-chün, pp. 193–94.

118. Chi Zehou. This source is based on information from General Yan Zhongchuan, whose story is told below.

119. Yuan Wei, p. 957.

120. Liu Zhinan, pp. 48, 49.

121. The information in this paragraph is from Chi Zehou; and Zhang Yunsheng, "Talk."

122. On Jiang Qing's role in the crisis, see Yang Yinlu, p. 163.

123. Chi Zehou. See also Zheng Qian, pp. 219–20; and Su Caiqing.

124. Liu Zhinan, pp. 48, 49.

125. Li and Ma, p. 329.

126. Unless otherwise cited, the information in this paragraph is from Chi Zehou.

127. For the location of the underground shelters built for the State Council and the central leadership, see Quan Yanchi, *Weixing*, p. 79.

128. Li and Wanyan, pp. 418–19; Qiu Shi, p. 644.

129. Zhang Yunsheng, *Maojiawan*, pp. 316–22; Chi Zehou; Li and Hao, pp. 124–25.

130. Interview with a former senior officer in the Russian Strategic Forces, December 10, 2002. According to this officer, the Soviet Strategic Forces were only twice (1962 and 1968) placed on the second stage of alert (*povyshennaya*), and never placed on either of the next highest stages (*voyennaya opasnost'* and *polnaya*).

131. Zhang Yunsheng, "Talk."

132. Unless otherwise cited, the information in this paragraph is from ibid.

133. On the formal title of Lin's directive, see Li and Ma, p. 329.

134. Mei and Gao, p. 320.

135. Zhang Yunsheng, "Talk."

136. Xiao Sike.

137. Chi Zehou.

138. Unless otherwise cited, the information in the rest of this section is from Chi Zehou; Xiao Sike; and Yan Mingzai. Yan Mingzai is Yan Zhongchuan's son.

139. The Beijing, Shenyang, Lanzhou, and Xinjiang region commands constituted the four commands in *san bei*.

140. See, for example, Suo Li Weng; and Xiao Sike.

141. Suo Li Weng.

142. Yan Mingzai.

143. See CCP Central Party History Research Section, *Zhonggong Dangshi Dashi Nianbiao* [Chronological Table of Major Events in CCP History] (Beijing: People's Press, 1986), quoted in Yan Mingzai.

144. Zhang Yunsheng, "Talk."

145. Wen Feng; Mei and Gao, p. 322. For data on the PLA missile deployments, see Lewis and Hua, esp. pp. 9–12.

146. Zhang Yunsheng, *Maojiawan*, p. 320; Chi Zehou.

147. Yang Kuisong, pp. 502–3.

148. Chi Zehou.

149. Liu Zhinan, p. 49.

150. Zhang Yunsheng, "Talk"; Zhang Yunsheng, *Maojiawan*, p. 324.

151. United States, Department of State, doc 24, Editorial Note.

152. Wang Chao-chün, p. 194. The story of this extraordinary event is told by Sagan and Suri, pp. 150–83.

153. Sagan and Suri, p. 174.

154. Unless otherwise cited, the information in this paragraph is from Gao Wenqian, pp. 413–14. Zhou's statement is on p. 414.

155. The story of the developments in U.S.-China relations in October and November is told in Tyler, pp. 74–75.

156. Ibid., pp. 74–75. The two Americans were released on December 7; Stoessel to Rogers, December 7, 1969, National Archives and Records Administration, RG 59, Central Files, PolChiCom-US, Box 1973, Folder: Political Affairs and Relations.

157. Unless otherwise cited, the information in the rest of this paragraph is from Gao Wenqian, pp. 410–11.

158. Quoted from Li and Ma, pp. 340, 349, respectively.

159. Yang Kuisong, p. 508.

160. Chi Zehou.

161. Jiang Fangran, pp. 53–54.

162. For Chinese comment on this "lesson," see Shang Lin, p. 22.

163. For the seven principles setting boundaries on the PRC nuclear arsenal, see Lewis and Xue, *China's Strategic Seapower*, p. 232. For one of Mao's earliest references to the atom bomb as a "paper tiger," see his "Talk," p. 100.

CHAPTER 4

1. Cai Renzhao, pp. 73, 74.

2. Research Section, pp. 118, 119.

3. "Decisions," p. 345; Xiao and Shi, pp. 31, 32. Quoted from "Decisions," p. 345.

4. Li Jue et al., pp. 13–14. The story of the decision is found in Lewis and Xue, *China Builds*, chap. 3.

5. Gao Wenqian, p. 73. On the evolution of the Central Secretariat, see He Fang.

6. Wu Lengxi, pp. 2–3; Yue and Chou, pp. 24–25.

7. Sun Daluo, pp. 175, 180–81.

8. Wang Li, Vol. 2, pp. 668, 716.

9. See the constitution adopted by the Sixteenth Party Congress (November 2002), in *Documents*, esp. pp. 97–99. The change in the relationship between the Secretariat and Standing Committee occurred in 1987. "Revision," p. 33.

10. Yang Qinhua, p. 14.

11. Quoted from Wang Li, Vol. 2, pp. 1069, 1228, respectively.

12. Based on a record of a conference of the CCP Politburo (November 3, 1935), quoted in Gao Wenqian, pp. 63–64.

13. Mao Zedong, "Problems of War," pp. 224–25.

14. The information in this paragraph is from Huang Yuzhang et al., p. 83.

15. Gittings provides a useful overview of the history of the Military Commission from 1931 to 1965 in *Role*, pp. 282–91.

16. Information Office, State Council, *China's National Defense in 2002*.

17. Zhang Wannian, pp. 213–14.

18. "Revision," pp. 33–34.

19. Han Gang, pp. 3, 5.

20. Most of the information in this and the next two paragraphs is from Zhang Zhen, *Zhang Zhen*, Vol. 1, pp. 507–8; Shan Lan, Vol. 1, pp. 94–95, 108, 109, 202–5.

21. "Doubts"; Bo Yibo, pp. 1083–87, 1128–34. Quoted from "Doubts."

22. Zhu Zhongli, pp. 299–300.

23. CCP Central Party History Research Section, *Zhonggong Dangshi Dashi Nianbiao*, p. 186; CCP Central Party History Research Section, *Zhonggong Dangshi Dashi Nianbiao Shuoming*, p. 198.

24. Wen An, p. 26; Quan Yanchi, *Weixing*, p. 22.

25. Wang Nianyi, pp. 173, 180, 181; Shi Dongbing, *Fengbao*, p. 259.

26. For a comment on the character of central decisionmaking and the command apparatus in the Cultural Revolution, see, for example, Wang Li, Vol. 2, p. 951; and Dong Jianwen, "Unknown."

27. "Inner-Party political life meetings" were used to resolve serious factional disputes especially from the mid-1960s and continuing into the late 1980s. See, for example, Shui Gong, pp. 373–74.

28. Most of the information in this paragraph is from Luo Bing, "CCP Plans," pp. 6–7.

29. Yao Jianping; Wang Li, Vol. 2, p. 945.

30. The quote is from Wang Li, Vol. 2, p. 668.

31. On the CMC's leadership, see "Comrade," p. 1.

32. Luo Bing, "CCP Plans," pp. 6–7.

33. Li Zijing.

34. Unless otherwise cited, this paragraph and the next three are based on Luo Bing, "CCP Plans," pp. 6–7; Su Xin et al.; and Lei Yingfu, pp. 182–83.

35. Michel Oksenberg examined the different types of meetings, documents, and personal communications networks in China in his "Methods," pp. 1–39.

36. A useful American study of this event is provided by Keefe. For the relevant Chinese sources, see "An Article by the *China Daily* Commentator"; Ren Yujun; and "Legal Principles," p. 1.

37. On the Party's preoccupation with domestic problems, see, for example, Liu Bingrong, p. 16.

38. Quoted from Su Xin et al.

39. Most of the information in the rest of this section is from Su Xin et al.; Luo Bing, "CCP Plans," pp. 6–7; and Deng Wen, pp. 14–16.

40. The information in this paragraph is from Deng Wen, pp. 14–15.

41. The six members of the Shanghai Cooperation Organization are China, Kazakhstan, Krygyzstan, Russia, Tajikistan, and Uzbekistan.

42. Interview with the office's executive vice minister, August 2003.

43. For details on the creation of the SARS leading group, see Xinhua, April 23–24, 2003. Part of this information is based on interviews with senior Chinese health officials, August 2003.

44. For a relevant comment of a well-informed Japanese security specialist, see "Shortcomings."

45. One of the best analyses of the NSC system is Alexander L. George, esp. chaps. 4, 5, 11, and 12.

46. On Jiang's resignation of his position of CMC chairman, see "Decision Made," p. 1.

47. Mao Zedong, "Get Organized!" pp. 153–61. The best study of the Chinese approach to organizations is Harding.

48. On the assignment of the General Office's director to supervise all intelligence agencies, see, for example, Li Xin, "Yang Shangkun," No. 4, p. 105; and Yang Shangkun. The information in this and the next paragraph is from Su Ha, pp. 145–46; Li Xin, "Yang Shangkun," No. 4, pp. 96–108; and ibid., No. 2, pp. 104, 105, 107.

49. For the location of the General Office, see Shi Dongbing, *Lushan*, p. 48.

50. Quote is from a senior informationization official interviewed in June 2003. This paragraph and the next are based on this interview.

51. On the codename of the Telephone Bureau, see Yang Yinlu, p. 50; and excerpts from Zhu Yu et al.

52. Shi Dongbing, *Duanzan*, p. 176.

53. Wang Li, Vol. 2, p. 764; Shi Dongbing, *Huairen*, p. 481.

54. Yang Yinlu, p. 50.

55. Huang and Zhang, p. 416; Shan Lan, Vol. 2, pp. 509, 625.

56. Wang Li, Vol. 2, p. 590. The information in this paragraph is from "Wang Gang"; Su Ha, pp. 145–46, 178; Li Xin, "Yang Shangkun," No. 4, pp. 96–108; and ibid., No. 2, pp. 104, 105, 107.

57. Unless otherwise cited, the information in this and the next two paragraphs is from Wang Fan, *Muji*, pp. 22–23; Wu and Han, pp. 220–22; Li Xin, "Yang Shangkun," No. 2, 2001, pp. 105, 106–7; and ibid., No. 4, 2001, pp. 95, 97–106.

58. Quan Yanchi, *Weixing*, p. 42; "Lei Feng's Diary."

59. Ding Shu.

60. This is based on interviews with PLA air force and civilian aviation air traffic controllers, February–March 1996.

61. For information on the regulation to return secret documents within two months, see Yang Yinlu, p. 146. The information in this paragraph is from "Wang Gang."

62. United States Congress, chap. 2.

63. Most of the information in this paragraph and the next is from Li Xin, "Yang Shangkun," No. 4, 2001, pp. 97–100, 102, 104, 96–108; ibid., No. 2, 2001, pp. 100–102, 105, 107.

64. Shan Lan, Vol. 2, p. 509; Ma Yongshun, pp. 250–53. Quoted from Shan Lan.

65. Yang Yinlu, p. 73.

66. Li Xin, "Yang Shangkun," No. 4, p. 107.

67. Xiong Lei, "[Recollection of] an Event," p. 395; Xiong Lei, "Mao," p. 251.

68. Unless otherwise cited, the information in this paragraph is from Su Ha, pp. 110, 194–95; Li and Jin; and Zhu Wenyi.

69. Lewis, *Political Networks*, esp. pp. 5–15.

70. Unless otherwise cited, most of the information in this and the next paragraph is from Su Ha, p. 178; Li Xin, "Yang Shangkun," No. 2, pp. 104–5; and ibid., No. 4, p. 106.

71. For the evolution of this CCP main think tank, see Gao Xin; Jin Shi, p. 29; and Yu Ruxin.

72. "Wang Gang."

73. Unless otherwise cited, the information in this paragraph and the next is from Wang Dongxing, p. 93; and Wu Jicheng and Wang Fan.

74. On the Guards Bureau Transportation Division, see Yang Yinlu, pp. 28–29.

75. "CMC Holds," p. 1.

76. For the history of the Central Guards Regiment, see Quan and Huang, p. 140; Li and Ji, pp. 53–54; and "Why Should."

77. Fu Chongbi, "Major Events," p. 78; Wang Dongxing, p. 93.

78. Shan Lan, Vol. 1, pp. 203–4; Wang Fan, "Former Deputy Commander."

79. Quan Yanchi, *Weixing*, p. 263.

80. "Hu [Jintao]."

81. Quan Yanchi, *Weixing*, p. 50.

82. Gu Baozi, "Mao," p. 115.

83. Yu Guangyuan, p. 12; Wu Jianhua, p. 13. Wu Jianhua was commander of the Guards Division.

84. Quan and Huang, p. 140; Wang Dongxing, p. 73.

85. Dong Jianwen, "Unknown"; Wu Jicheng and Wang Fan.

86. Chen Yangyong, pp. 231–33; Quan Yanchi, *Weixing*, p. 79.

87. Dong Jianwen, "Hatch Door."

88. For example, before the Cultural Revolution, Mao Zedong had placed Liu Shaoqi, the PRC president, under "observation." Shi Dongbing, *Feng*, p. 242.

89. Lewis and Xue, "Social Change," p. 934.

90. The text of this speech is found in Xinhua, May 31, 2002.

91. Jiang's statement to the congress (November 8, 2002), in *Documents*, p. 1, says of the "three represents," "The Party must always represent the requirements of the development of China's advanced productive forces, the orientation of the development of China's advanced culture, and the fundamental interests of the overwhelming majority of the people in China." For an analysis of the "three represents," see Lewis and Xue, "Social Change."

92. On the statement in the constitution's "General Program," see *Documents*, p. 76; Jiang's statement to the congress (November 8, 2002) is in ibid., pp. 14, 59.

93. Ibid., p. 15.

94. Deng Xiaoping made the need for foreign expertise and ideas explicit in his "Use," p. 43.

95. See Deng's "We" and "Urgent Tasks," pp. 288–93, 300–304.

96. Deng Xiaoping, "With Stable Policies," p. 308.

97. The quotes are from the "General Program" of the Sixteenth Party Congress constitution in *Documents*, pp. 78, 80.

98. For example, for almost two hours on December 23, 2003, Foreign Minister Li Zhaoxing exchanged views with an estimated twenty thousand online Internet users. Li Zhaoxing; French, p. A4.

99. Su Xin et al.

100. Deng Xiaoping, "Address," pp. 294–99.

101. Deng Xiaoping, "Crack Down," pp. 44, 45.

102. Deng Xiaoping, "With Stable Policies," pp. 305, 306.

103. The quotes from this lecture can be found in Liu Shaoqi, "On Inner-Party Struggle," pp. 209, 215.

104. See, for example, Ding Guoqiang; and "Academic Corruption."

CHAPTER 5

1. We are indebted to John Shalikashvili for clarifying this distinction between command and control and for calling our attention to the formal definition of command and control in the *DOD Dictionary*. According to the *Dictionary*'s explanation, "command and control functions are performed through an arrangement of personnel, equipment, communications, facilities, and procedures employed by a commander in planning, directing, coordinating, and controlling forces and operations in the accomplishment of the mission."

2. On the evolution of the Central Military Commission, see Lei Yuanshen, pp. 218–35.

3. For our understanding of the more general issues raised in this section, we have drawn on Johnston, "China's Militarized"; Lampton; Lieberthal and Lampton; Mulvenon; Pillsbury; Scobell, *China's Use*; Shambaugh; Stokes; Swaine; Whiting, pp. 202–3, 233; and Wortzel.

4. In September 2004, the Fourth Session of the Sixteenth Central Committee elected eleven members of the CMC: Hu Jintao, Guo Boxiong, Cao Gangchuan, Xu Caihou, Liang Guanglie, Liao Xilong, Li Ji'nai, Chen Bingde, Qiao Qingchen, Zhang Dingfa, and Jing Zhiyuan. Liao and Wang, p. 1. For the CMC's membership, see also "Comrade," p. 1.

5. The PLA's first-grade greater units include the four general departments, the air force, the navy, the Second Artillery, the Armed Police, the Academy of Military Science, the National Defense University, the National University of Defense Technology, and the seven greater region commands.

6. Most information in this paragraph and the next three is from Wang Shangrong, pp. 279, 285, 291; Fu Chongbi, "Divergence," pp. 26–27; and Li Xin, *Da*, pp. 11–13. The Joint Operations Bureau, it should be noted, is sometimes given different names.

7. As noted in Chapter 4, the Politburo, CMC, and government have separate confidential units with complicated organizational histories. See also Shan Lan, Vol. 2, pp. 94–95.

8. "Public Notice"; Ling Xiang, pp. 29–30; "China's Military Colleges."

9. "General Staff Operations Department," p. 25.

10. For a description of these silos, see Fu Chongbi, "Divergence," pp. 26–27; and Shu Yun.

11. For the information on the CMC's task teams in the three locations, see Jin Liren.

12. As discussed in Chapter 3, in 1969, the CMC designated the hardened silos under the Western Hills as the "advance command post." See also Liu Tianye et al., p. 418.

13. These terms and their formal translation are from Zhu Rongchang, p. 70.

14. Liu Tianye et al., p. 387.

15. Currently, there are seven "military regions" (*da junqu* or literally "greater military region"), all of which have undergone a complex evolution.

16. Wang Shangrong, pp. 252–53.

17. The information in this paragraph and the next is from Yuan Wenxian, "Challenges," pp. 91–94; and Yuan Wenxian, "Several," pp. 60–64.

18. Zhang Aiping, *Zhongguo*, p. 350.

19. The predecessor of the Strategic Committee was the Strategic Research Team, established in September 1959 and led by Marshal Liu Bocheng. Gu Yue, p. 725. On October 8, 1977, the committee replaced the team and named Marshal Xu Xiangqian director. General Wang, p. 651; Zhang Zhen, *Zhang Zhen*, Vol. 2, p. 194.

20. The General Staff established the International Situation Research Team on February 17, 1975. General Wang, 471, 576, 601–5. Unless otherwise cited, the information in this and the next two paragraphs is from ibid., pp. 442, 471, 576.

21. Liu Tianye et al., p. 418.

22. Zhang Zhen, *Zhang Zhen*, Vol. 1, p. 432.

23. Most information in this paragraph and the next five is from General Wang, pp. 450, 471–73, 475, 574, 576, 615; Lei Yingfu, pp. 145–46; Shan Lan, Vol. 2, p. 630; and Wang Shangrong, pp. 248, 251, 282, 285.

24. We will discuss the Joint Operations Bureau in the following sections. On the Bureau of Strategic Forces, see Yang Dezhi, p. 542. "Regional" (*fangxiang*) should be translated as "Directional," but the term simply refers to different geographical regions.

25. For a description of the command center inside the Operations Bureau, see General Wang, p. 478.

26. Information Office, State Council, *China's National Defense in 2000*; Information Office, State Council, *China's National Defense in 2002*. The 1998 and 2004 versions of the defense white paper do not mention how nuclear weapons are controlled; Information Office, State Council, *China's National Defense*, issued on July 27, 1998; and Information Office, State Council, *China's National Defense in 2004*.

27. On the differences between a military region and a theater of operations, see, for example, Zheng Wenhan, *Junshi*, p. 27. For a more complete, though brief history of the military regions, see Xu Ping, pp. 6–7.

28. Information in this and the next paragraph is from Zhang Zhen, *Zhang Zhen*, Vol. 1, pp. 501–9; Wang Shangrong, pp. 248, 251, 263, 282, 285; and Lei Yingfu, pp. 145–46.

29. See, for example, Whiting.

30. See, for example, Li Zhisui, pp. 105–6, 532, 566.

31. Wu Xujun, pp. 240–41; Gu Baozi, "Indissoluble Bond," pp. 152–52.

32. Fan Jiabing, p. 49.

33. Li Cheng et al., p. 9.

34. Unless otherwise cited, the information in this paragraph is from Wu De, p. 131; Dong Baocun, pp. 40–41; and Li Weisai, p. 47. For a comparable case whereby

the navy attempted to bypass the Operations, General Staff, and CMC in the 1980s, see Huang and Zhang, pp. 607–8; and Yi Ming, "Xiao Jingguang."

35. "General Staff Operations Department," p. 25.

36. Li Shenzhi; "Liu Yazhou's Presentation"; Zhou Deli, p. 245.

37. There is a small but important Western literature on this war, most of which regards the outcome as a Chinese defeat except for its successful discrediting of the Soviet treaty commitment to Vietnam. See, for example, Segal; King Chen; Jencks; Man Kim Lin; Scobell, *China's Use*, chap. 6; and Tretiak. The citations that follow give the relevant Chinese sources.

38. Zhou Deli.

39. The three documents are Cadres Department; and Office, Vols. 1, 2.

40. Unless otherwise cited, the information in this section is from Zhou Deli, pp. 246–60, 273–75; Zhang Zhen, *Zhang Zhen*, Vol. 2, pp. 165–73; Qu Aiguo; and Quan Yanchi, "Xu Shiyou."

41. The information in this and the next paragraph is from Cadres Department, pp. 1–3, 76, 85, 93–97; Office, Vol. 1, p. 8; and Office, Vol. 2, pp. 224–26.

42. For Beijing's estimate of the possibility of a Soviet armed intervention in the Sino-Vietnamese War, see, for example, Jin Hui et al., p. 27; and Office, Vol. 2, pp. 299–302.

43. Zhou Deli, p. 245; Li Shenzhi.

44. The PLA uses "directional teams" to apply to strengthening a command's control of combat forces that operate in different areas during theater operations. Zhou Deli, pp. 253, 275.

45. While each region command has an operations department, each corps-level or division-level combat unit has an operations and training division (*chu*) or section (*ke*).

46. On the adjustment of the CMC's operations plan, see Zhang Zhen, *Zhang Zhen*, Vol. 2, p. 171.

47. Han Weiguo, p. 50.

48. Fan Jiabing, pp. 46–47.

49. Tan Ren, pp. 44–45; Yu and Liu, p. 202.

50. Liu Yang, p. 119.

51. Institute 28 belongs to the Ministry of Information Industry; Institute 63 is under the PLA General Staff; and the College of Computation and Command Automation is affiliated with the PLA University of Science and Engineering. Ling Xiang, pp. 29–30.

52. Unless otherwise cited, the information in this paragraph is from Zhang Weiping, pp. 626–27; Liu Zhengwu, p. 13; Huang Dong, p. 73; and Ding Jie, p. 78.

53. Ling Haijian, p. 386.

54. Liu Huaqing, pp. 608–9.

55. "Capability."

56. "China's C³I."

57. Yang and Zhou, p. 11.

58. Wang Jianyun, pp. 4–5; Chen and Zhu, pp. 35–36.

59. Liu Huaqing, pp. 614–18.

60. Liu Yang, p. 121.

61. Huang Bin, pp. 19, 195, 197.

62. The document is titled "Outline of the Construction of an Automated Command System." Yuan Jun.

63. "Comparison."

64. Jiang Shui.

65. Information in this paragraph and the next two is from Zhang Aiping, *Zhongguo*, pp. 360–61; Ding Jie, p. 77; and Huang Bin, pp. 7, 21.

66. Li Qianyuan, p. 34.

67. Yang Yongmei, p. 72.

68. Zhang Peigao, "Summary," p. 16.

69. Yuan Wenxian, "Several," pp. 60–64.

70. Yang and Huang, p. 33.

71. Previously, regiments rather than battalions were responsible for training and the management of combat companies. Zhang Lianyin, pp. 47–48.

72. Sha and Min, pp. 261–62.

73. Information in this paragraph is from Ge Chengwen, p. 70; and Yang and Huang, p. 160.

74. For detailed information on the roles and functions of these naval bases, see Lewis and Xue, *China's Strategic Seapower*, pp. 124–25, 294.

75. Wang Wenjie, p. 1; He Liangliang, p. 26.

76. Zhou Baoyi, p. 234.

77. Sun Zhenjiang, p. 79.

78. Dai Xu, "Iraq War." The results of this assessment were released by Lieutenant General Liu Yazhou in 2003.

79. Han Weiguo, p. 51. For a case study of Lanzhou region commanders, see Guo Boxiong, p. 97; and Wang Zhicheng, p. 98.

80. Huang Bin, p. 27.

81. An Weiping, pp. 259, 260; Ding Jie, p. 77.

82. Huang Bin, p. 24.

83. Ibid., p. 21.

84. The air force dispatches forward controller "command teams" to the units at and above the corps level and forward controller "target guidance teams" to the units at and below the division level. Liu Zhengwu, p. 375. The information in this paragraph is from Yu Shusheng, p. 59; and Zhang Peigao, "Summary," p. 18.

85. Hao and Zhang, p. 89; Chen and Zhu, p. 36.

86. Yang and Huang, p. 263.

87. Yuan Jin, p. 78; Jiang Jianjun, p. 117; Ding Jie, p. 77.

88. Cui Yansong et al., pp. 110, 168.

89. Yuan Wenxian, "Challenges," p. 94.

90. Quoted from Liu Huaqing, pp. 644–45.

91. In classical Chinese, *sashoujian* literally means "an unexpected thrust with a mace." Authoritative Chinese sources now stress that the term is not *shashoujian* ("thrust with an assassin's mace"), as often stated in Western and even Chinese sources; Zhu Hongsheng. For a discussion of the concept, see, for example, Ma Baoan, p. 71; Wang and Cui, pp. 642–44; and Bruzdzinski.

92. Dai Qingmin, "On Seizing," p. 17. For Dai's other important writings on information warfare, see Dai, "On Four Abilities"; Dai, "On the Development"; Dai, "On Integrating"; and Dai et al.

93. Wen Tao, p. 46; Xinhua, October 15, 2004. Information on the National Basic Research Program (973 Program) can be found at www.973.gov.cn/English/Index.aspx. On the 863 Program, see Feigenbaum; and www.china.org.cn/english/features/China2004/107131.htm.

94. Most information in the rest of this section is from Wang and Sun, pp. 85–86.

95. Li Jijun, *Junshi*, p. 59.

96. Cadres Department, pp. 15–16; Office, Vol. 1, p. 8.

97. Dai Xu, "Considerations," pp. 9–13; Dai Xu, "Iraq War."

CHAPTER 6

1. Xiao Yusheng, p. 22.

2. Dongfang He, p. 813.

3. Ibid.; Chen Chuangang, p. 685.

4. The information in this paragraph is from Zhang Aiping, *Zhongguo*, pp. 109–11; and Li and Hao, p. 358. On the history of the early DF missiles series, see Lewis and Hua, pp. 7–19.

5. The information in this and the next paragraph is from Tao Dazhao, pp. 18–19; and Gu Baozi, "Xiang," p. 1018.

6. Li and Hao, pp. 282, 359, 363.

7. Ibid., p. 282; Zhang Aiping, *Zhongguo*, p. 125.

8. Unless otherwise cited, the information in the rest of this section is from Gu Baozi, "Xiang," pp. 1012, 1013, 1020–29.

9. The quotes in this paragraph and the next three are from ibid., pp. 1022, 1023, 1026, 1027, respectively.

10. Quoted from Xu Jian, p. 123.

11. Lewis and Hua, p. 6, gives the Chinese terminology and ranges for the PLA missiles: short-range (*jincheng*), less than 1,000 km; medium-range (*zhongcheng*), 1,000–3,000 km; long-range (*yuancheng*), 3,000–8,000 km; and intercontinental-range (*zhouji*), over 8,000 km.

12. The information in this and the next paragraph is from Li and Hao, pp. 147–50, 161. The quote is from ibid., p. 149.

13. Quoted from Yang Guoliang, p. 96. The information in this paragraph and the next two is from ibid.; and Chen Chuangang, pp. 685–87.

14. By 1987, the PLA had been reduced to 3.235 million and by 1990, to 3.199 million; in September 1997, China announced an additional cut of 500,000 military personnel; in September 2003, it decided on another cut of 200,000 troops by the end of 2005; the planned size of the PLA's manpower is about 2.3 million. The figures are from the sections on manpower reductions in Information Office, *China's National Defense*, for 1998, 2000, and 2004.

15. Chen Chuangang, pp. 687–88; quoted from p. 688.

16. Most of the information in this paragraph is from Fang and Chen, p. 1. Articles in some specialized military journals until recently used *shashoujian* (thrust with an assassin's mace), but for consistency we will use the currently approved *sashoujian* (trump card), as noted in Chapter 5.

17. Quoted from ibid., p. 688. The information in this paragraph and the next is from ibid., pp. 688, 689, 691; and Zhang Aiping, *Zhongguo*, pp. 119, 122.

18. Chen Chuangang, pp. 689–90.

19. Wang Fa'an and Zhang Jie, p. 4.

20. Zhang Aiping, *Zhongguo*, p. 112.

21. For the use of the terms of groups and detachments, see ibid., p. 120. The information in this paragraph and the next is from Wang Houqing and Zhang Xingye, p. 367; Wang Min, pp. 17, 18; and Yang Guoliang, p. 96.

22. Propaganda Department, pp. 392–93.

23. Guo Qingsheng.

24. Unless otherwise cited, the information in the rest of this paragraph and the next two paragraphs is from Li and Yang, p. 44.

25. Xue Xinglin, p. 150; General Logistics Department, pp. 356–57.

26. General Logistics Department, pp. 358, 359, 365.

27. The Second Artillery created its Science and Technology Department in December 1975 and later renamed it the Technology and Equipment Department. Li Cheng et al., p. 227.

28. Technology and equipment divisions (*chu*), sections (*ke*), and units (*shi*) were originally established in all launch bases, brigades, and battalions. As a result of the creation of the General Armament Department in 1998, the Second Artillery has upgraded these to technology and equipment departments, divisions, and sections.

29. The information in this and the next paragraph is from Wu Xudong et al., pp. 37, 38.

30. "PLA Second Artillery."

31. The information in this and the next paragraph is from Zhang Jiajun, p. 2; Lewis and Xue, *China Builds*, p. 212; Dongfang He, pp. 809–13; and Zhang Aiping, *Zhongguo*, pp. 113–14.

32. For background on the Central Special Commission (Fifteen-Member Special Commission), see Lewis and Xue, *China Builds*, pp. 131–34.

33. Zhang Aiping, *Zhongguo*, Vol. 2, p. 114.

34. Lewis and Hua, pp. 23–26.

35. Liu Ruishao, pp. 154–56.

36. Unless otherwise cited, the information in this paragraph and the next is from Zhang Aiping, "Speech," pp. 371, 374; Chen Chuangang, pp. 691, 698; Zhang Aiping, *Zhongguo*, p. 115.

37. See also Zhang Aiping, *Zhongguo*, pp. 114, 115; Liu Ruishao, p. 154.

38. See, for example, He Tianjin.

39. Zhang Aiping, *Zhongguo*, p. 118. For an early study of the shift to mobility and solid rocket technology, see Lewis and Hua, pp. 25–31.

40. Zhang Jiajun, p. 6; Zhang Aiping, *Zhongguo*, pp. 111–12, 118–19.

41. The information in this paragraph is from Chen Chuangang, pp. 112, 118.

42. Liu Ruishao, p. 156.

43. A history of this Jiuquan Satellite Launch Center is found in Li Fengzhou, pp. 38–42.

44. On the early history of Bases 25 and 28, see Liang Dongyuan, p. 250.

45. Cheng Qiuqing, pp. 4–6.

46. The information on China's missile bases is based on *1997 Chung-kung Nien-pao*, pp. 9–44; *2001 Chung-kung Nien-pao*, pp. V-185–V-187; and Wang Yufang.

47. Xue Xinglin, p. 152.

48. "Taiwan's Defense Minister." Unless otherwise cited, the information in this paragraph and the next is from ibid.; Li Rongming; and "List."

49. For example, there is great uncertainty about the numbers 57 and 58 and 80307 and 80308.

50. For information on the Jinbei base, see Liu Ruishao, p. 155; and "What Should," p. 46.

51. On the location of the Hebei base, see Li Rongming; and a *Jiefangjun Bao* report cited in "Some Assumptions."

52. Tao Dazhao, pp. 59, 60.

53. Zhong Min; United States, Central Intelligence Agency, p. 8; United States, Department of Defense, *Annual Report*.

54. See Lewis and Hua, which discusses the technical responses to the vulnerability as the solid-rocket program gained momentum. For Chinese sources, see Yang Baoshun, p. 10; Zhang and He, p. 2; and Bi Yongjun, p. 1.

55. The information in this and the next paragraph is from Cui Yansong et al., pp. 25, 107, 333, 334; and Yang and Chen, pp. 387–89.

56. Yang Baoshun, p. 10; Zhang and He, p. 2. For an earlier discussion of R&D on missile site environmental systems needed for deep underground living and survival under attack, see, for example, the article by Zhang Jiajun and Sun Jinhan in Xinhua, November 18, 1997.

57. "Unit," p. 3.

58. Interviews with a knowledgeable Chinese specialist, February 2000.

59. Unless otherwise cited, the information in this section is from Tao Dazhao, passim; Xu Jian, passim; and Dongfang He, pp. 811, 813.

60. *1997 Chung-kung Nien-pao*, pp. 9–44.

61. See, for example, Liu and Li, p. 2; He and Zhao, p. 1; and the text accompanying a picture in JFJB, November 1, 1998, p. 1.

62. In conversations with U.S. specialists, the Chinese have insisted that they have installed "devices" to prevent accidental or unauthorized launches and to promote safety.

63. Liu and Jiang, p. 3; Tao Dazhao, p. 245.

64. Xu Jian, p. 211.

65. Central News Agency (Taipei), February 24–25 and March 3, 1995; China Broadcasting News Network (Taipei), March 13, 1996.

66. Wen Zhi, p. 58; Central News Agency, October 18, 2004.

67. Zhang Peigao, *Lianhe*, p. 176; Li Guangrong and Bi Yongjun, p. 1.

68. The Second Artillery Military Representative Office places its inspectors in all missile-related production plants. Li Zubin and Bi Yongjun, p. 10. See also Zhan and Zhao, p. 1.

69. *Jiefangjun Bao* (Internet version), December 3, 2004. On the evaluation of officers and the use of electronic systems for evaluation, see, for example, ibid., November 11 and 18, December 15 and 17, 2004.

70. Ibid., November 18, 2004.

71. See, for example, ibid., August 24, November 5, 24, 25, and 29, December 2, 8, 9, 23, and 27, 2004.

72. Bi Yongjun, p. 1; *Jiefangjun Bao* (Internet version), December 10 and 23, 2004.

73. See Abrams, pp. 325–49, esp. p. 339.

74. Song and Wang, p. 5; Wang and Xia, p. 2.

75. Most of the information in this paragraph and the next two is from Liu Zhengwu, pp. 392–94.

76. Bi Yongjun, p. 1.

77. Sun and Song, p. 23.

78. Zhang and Ma, p. 2; Chen Chuangang, p. 693; Hu Yanning et al., p. 1.

79. Cheng and Zhang, p. 1.

80. Zeng Youqing, pp. 34–40. The quote is from p. 34.

81. Most of the information in this and the next two paragraphs is from Ge Zhenfeng, pp. 68, 69, 71, 72; and Wang Jianghuai, p. 75. The quote in the paragraph after next is from Ge Zhenfeng, p. 69.

82. Hu Xiaomin, pp. 59–60; Zhang Peigao, *Lianhe*, p. 176. The quote is from Hu, p. 59.

83. He Liangping et al.

84. These regulations include the "Regulations on Maintaining Secrets in Work at PLA Headquarters," "Law on Maintaining Secrets," "Regulations on Maintaining Secrets," and "Outline of the Work on Maintaining Secrets." The information in this paragraph is from a knowledgeable Chinese source, December 2002.

85. Wang and He, p. 1.

86. Unless otherwise cited, the information in this paragraph and the next seven is from Xue Xinglin, pp. 389–92.

87. Liu Huimin et al., p. 445. This volume instructs senior PLA staff officers on how to write official documents for their headquarters.

88. In a speech reportedly delivered by Jiang Zemin in June 2004 and a related CMC document, this possibility is specifically mentioned. Luo Bing, "To Oppose," pp. 9–10.

89. Quoted from Xue Xinglin, p. 390.

90. Wang Houqing and Zhang Xingye, p. 372.

91. The information in the rest of this paragraph and in the next four is from Liu Zhengwu, pp. 404–6.

92. The information in this and the next paragraph is from ibid., p. 404; Xue Xinglin; and Wang Houqing and Zhang Xingye, p. 374. The quote is from Liu Zhengwu, p. 404

93. One of the most important Western analyses of Chinese nuclear doctrine that we have used is Alastair Iain Johnston, "China's New 'Old Thinking,'" pp. 5–42.

94. Wang Fulin, p. 11; Wang Houqing and Zhang Xingye, p. 369.

95. The information in this paragraph and the next three is from Zhang Aiping, *Zhongguo*, pp. 119, 121, 122. Zhang uses the terms *zhanlüe xue* and *zhanyi xue*, which translate as "strategies" and "operational arts."

96. Quoted from ibid., p. 121.

97. Of all published materials, this source confirms for the first time that "limited nuclear retaliation" had become China's nuclear strategy. The quote is from ibid., p. 119.

98. Lewis and Xue, *China's Strategic Seapower*, p. 233.

99. The classic statement on a nuclear strategy for small or medium nuclear powers is Beaufre. See also Kemp.

100. The information in this paragraph and the next is from Gao Rui, pp. 95, 115. The quote is from p. 115.

101. See, for example, the discussion of Deng's strategic decision" in Johnston, "China's New 'Old Thinking,'" p. 9.

102. Quoted from Gao Rui, p. 115. The information in this paragraph is from ibid., pp. 95, 115–16, 235–36; and Wang Wenrong, pp. 355–57.

103. See Lewis and Xue, *China Builds*, p. 1 and appendix (which gives the Chinese statement of October 16, 1964).

104. Quoted from Wang Wenrong, p. 355. Most of the information in this paragraph and the next two is from ibid., pp. 355–56.

105. Yin Weixing, p. 21.

106. Liu Zhengwu, p. 398.

107. Ibid., pp. 403, 412; Wang Houqing and Zhang Xingye, pp. 374–75.

108. On the proposal to build a conventionally armed ICBM, see Zhao and Wang, p. 63.

109. Luo and Shi, p. 11.

110. Zhan Xuexi, pp. 26–29. The quote is from p. 26. We discuss the Chinese assessment of modern air power and the PLA Air Force in the next chapter.

111. Wang Zhenping, p. 298.

112. Most of the information in this and the next paragraph is from Lu Haozhong et al., pp. 287–92.

113. See also Wang Houqing and Zhang Xingye, pp. 369, 376, 379.

CHAPTER 7

The authors acknowledge with thanks the permission of *International Security* to re-print most of Lewis and Xue, "China's Search," and the contributions made by three anonymous reviewers and by Kenneth Allen, William J. Perry, and Dean Wilkening to this chapter. Two English-language studies, though now dated, provide the foundation for any understanding of this subject: Allen, Krumel, and Pollack; and Duan Zijun, *China*.

1. Zhang and Xu, p. 3.

2. See, for example, Dai Xu, "Considerations," pp. 9–13.

3. "Comment"; Gao Xinmin, p. 4.

4. "Russia"; "Liu Huaqing," p. A10.

5. Duan Zijun, *Dangdai*, pp. 18–19.

6. *Haijun Shi*, p. 37; Yang Guoyu, p. 687.

7. Huang and Zhang, pp. 398–99.

8. Unless otherwise cited, the information in this paragraph and the next is from Duan Zijun, *Dangdai*, pp. 131–37, 171–75; and Song Yichang, pp. 102–6.

9. Peng Min, pp. 159–60; Duan Zijun, *Dangdai*, p. 73; Yan Fangming, p. 73.

10. Lin Hu, "Development," p. 784; Duan Zijun, *Dangdai*, pp. 95–96, 100, 136, 145.

11. See, for example, Lin Hu, *Kongjun*, p. 246. The information in this paragraph is from ibid., p. 197.

12. Zhang and Gao, p. 620.

13. Lin Hu, *Kongjun*, pp. 98–100, 197, 202–3.

14. Zhao Dexin, p. 110.

15. Yao Jun, p. 710; Lin Hu, *Kongjun*, p. 200; Duan Zijun, *Dangdai*, pp. 95–96, 100, 136, 145.

16. Duan Zijun, *Dangdai*, pp. 66, 385, 677. Unless otherwise cited, the information in this paragraph is from ibid., pp. 82–84; and Xie Guang, p. 191.

17. Pilots conducted test flights on prototypes of the J-7 and J-8 in 1966 and 1969, respectively. Duan Zijun, *Dangdai*, pp. 100–101, 139, 158.

18. The information in this paragraph and the next is from Wang Dinglie, pp. 545–46; Lin Hu, *Kongjun*, pp. 236–37; and Zhang and Gao, pp. 621–22, 625, 628–29.

19. The information in this and the next paragraph is from Zhang and Gao, pp. 622–23; Wang and Zhu, pp. 622–23, 628; and Wang Dinglie, p. 515.

20. Zhang and Gao, p. 621.

21. Duan Zijun, *Dangdai*, pp. 83, 95–96, 100–101, 136, 145.

22. Shao Zhenting et al., pp. 43, 44, 45; Wang Dinglie, pp. 550–51; Hua Renjie et al., p. 307.

23. Information from a Chinese senior colonel, 1997.

24. Quan and Huang, pp. 1–3; Shi Dongbing, *Duanzan*, pp. 193, 203–4.

25. Zhang and Gao, pp. 622–24, 631, 637–38.

26. Zhang Aiping, "Speech," pp. 371–74.

27. Unless otherwise cited, the information in this and the next paragraph is based on Yao Jun, pp. 712, 715; and Duan Zijun, *Dangdai*, pp. 100–104.

28. Liao Guoliang et al., p. 600.

29. Gao Rui, pp. 113–14.

30. Zhang and Gao, pp. 628–29; Gao Rui, p. 114; Lin Hu, *Kongjun*, pp. 239–41; Yao Jun, p. 715.

31. "China's F-8II," p. 529; "Grumman," p. 1261; "Asia," p. 11. The Peace Pearl deal was put on hold in the summer of 1989 as a result of the Tiananmen crisis and then cancelled in 1990.

32. Shao Zhenting, pp. 45, 47.

33. Unless otherwise cited, the information in this paragraph and the next two is from Lin Hu, "Development," pp. 789–91. The quote in the next paragraph is from ibid., pp. 789–90.

34. For information on the R&D on the HQ and PL missile series, see Xie Guang, pp. 14–39, 47–61. The LY-60 is designed to process up to forty targets, track twelve, and distinguish the three that present the highest threat. For information on the LY-60, FM-60, and KS-1 surface-to-air missiles, see Mecham, p. 61; "China Exhibits," p. A12; and "Chinese Mainland Is Developing," p. 2.

35. For a discussion of the types of war that might involve China, see Long Jize, pp. 139–40; and Zhang and Zhu, pp. 21–24.

36. Peng Guangqian et al., pp. 146–47; Teng and Jiang, p. 148; Yu Guantang, pp. 181, 195.

37. Lin Hu, "Development," p. 784.

38. Lewis and Xue, *China Builds*, chap. 3; Lewis and Xue, *China's Strategic Seapower*, chaps. 3, 6.

39. See, for example, Su Kuoshan, p. 31.

40. Luo and Shi, p. 11; Liao Guoliang et al., pp. 600–601; Chen Weijun, p. 12.

41. In 1985, Deng Xiaoping predicted that China could focus on economic construction in a peaceful environment for the next fifty years. "Deng Xiaoping Talks Freely," p. 10.

42. Qi Miyun, p. 20; Yuan Jiaxin, p. 10.

43. For a comprehensive discussion of budget and finance in the defense sector, see Shambaugh, chap. 5; Lewis, Hua, and Xue; and Feigenbaum, esp. chap. 5.

44. As examples during the 1980s and early 1990s, McDonnell Douglas began building nose sections, landing gear doors, and horizontal stabilizers for its MD-80s

and 90s and then assembling MD-80s from kits in Shanghai; and Boeing contracted with two major aircraft factories to build vertical fins and horizontal stabilizers for the B-737. "Boeing."

45. For a Chinese estimate of the penetrability of modern bomber weapons capable of launching deep surprise attacks, see Chen Hongyou, pp. 54–56; and Hua Renjie et al., p. 273.

46. Hua Renjie et al., pp. 357–58.

47. "United States Also," p. 44.

48. Gao Rui, p. 114; Peng Guangqian et al., pp. 150, 152–53; Teng and Jiang, pp. 147, 151; Yu Guantang, pp. 25, 30.

49. Shao Zhenting, pp. 44, 46–47.

50. Yu Guantang, pp. 49, 55–56, 196.

51. Liu Yichang, p. 225; Teng and Jiang, pp. 81, 98, 142; Yu Guantang, p. 98.

52. Wang Dinglie, pp. 649–50. Unless otherwise cited, the information in this paragraph and the next two is from Peng Guangqian et al., p. 151; Teng and Jiang, pp. 126–51; and Yu Guantang, pp. 39, 43, 163.

53. See also Teng and Jiang, p. 260.

54. Wang Kexue, p. 30.

55. Yu Guantang, pp. 25, 79, 86, 163; Hua Renjie et al., p. 324.

56. Peng Guangqian et al., p. 151; Yu Guantang, pp. 25, 39, 43, 79, 86, 163; Hua Renjie et al., p. 324; Teng and Jiang, pp. 126–51, 260.

57. Teng and Jiang, pp. 186–87, 258.

58. The information in this paragraph and the next is from "Support System," p. 2; and Yu Guantang, pp. 75, 81, 82, 86, 228.

59. For the measures the PLAAF takes to increase survivability and readiness, see also "Support System," p. 2.

60. In the Chinese military lexicon, campaign coordination (*zhanyi xietong*) and tactical coordination (*zhanshu xietong*) mean coordination carried out among the services in a campaign and a battle, respectively. Hua Renjie et al., p. 319. The information in this paragraph is from ibid., pp. 312–13, 318–19, 323.

61. Zheng and Zhang, pp. 84–85; Teng and Jiang, pp. 101–2; Liu Yichang, pp. 226–35.

62. Wang Wenjie, p. 1; He Liangliang, p. 26.

63. Hu Guangzheng, p. 124; Yu Guantang, pp. 28, 68, 220; Hua Renjie et al., pp. 311, 312.

64. The information in the rest of this paragraph and the next is from Yu Guantang, pp. 211–12, 220; Hu Guangzheng, p. 124; and Teng and Jiang, pp. 296–98.

65. Information from a senior Chinese security specialist, 1997.

66. Yu Guantang, p. 193.

67. Gao Rui, p. 114; Peng Guangqian et al., p. 150; Teng and Jiang, p. 151; Yu Guantang, pp. 25, 30.

68. Hu Changfa, p. 30; "Communist Army," p. A13; "Strategic Changes," p. A4.

69. Peng Guangqian et al., pp. 142, 149, 151–52.

70. Teng and Jiang, p. 300.

71. See, for example, Yu Guantang, p. 226.

72. Unless otherwise cited, the information in this paragraph and the next is from interviews with a knowledgeable Russian official in 1993 and 1994.

73. See also "Communist China Is Reportedly Negotiating," p. A12; and "Communist China Is Reportedly Purchasing," p. A2.

74. "Su-27/J-11"; "J-11."

75. Ma and Ch'iu, p. 47; "Liu Huaqing," p. A10; "Mainland," p. A10; "Many," p. A12; "Communist China Will," p. A10.

76. "Russia"; "Su-27/Su-30/J-11."

77. "Air Force Sends," p. A12.

78. "It," p. A12.

79. Air Force Political Department, p. 3.

80. This information is based on an interview with a Hughes Aircraft of Canada official in 1997.

81. Opall and Witt, p. 1.

82. For a description of the PLAAF's early warning plane, see Li and Zhang, p. 11. Photograph 29 in this volume shows this plane.

83. ZT; "China Has Developed."

84. For specifications of the J-10 and JH-7 aircraft, see "China Air Force"; "Israel's Role"; "JH"; "Chinese Super-Sonic Bomber."

85. "China Makes"; "China's Super 7"; "Having."

86. "PRC."

87. The information in this paragraph and the next is from "Why Does"; and "What Problems."

88. Xu Minjie, Part 2, p. 23. Xu is deputy chief of the PLAAF's Military Training Department.

89. Opall and Witt, p. 19; "J-8," p. A12; "Chinese Mainland Is Building," p. 2.

90. For the extension of the PLAAF's combat radius, see "Presentation."

91. Liu Jingsong, p. 41. On Liu's views as perceived by the Pentagon, see Opall, p. 10.

92. Shang Jinsuo et al., p. 248.

93. The People's Air Defense Law of the PRC was adopted on October 29, 1996.

94. Hua Renjie et al., pp. 320–22; Yu Guantang, pp. 102, 112–13, 115; Teng and Jiang, pp. 158–59, 187.

95. Pan Shiying, *Xiandai*, pp. 128–29.

96. Shang Jinsuo et al., p. 249.

97. Ibid., p. 248.

98. Ding Chong, pp. 39, 40.

99. For a similar description, see Ying.

100. Unless otherwise cited, the information in this and the next paragraph is from Min and Han; and Shang Jinsuo et al., pp. 464–82.

101. On the region air force's responsibility for the air defense units under its control, see Xu Minjie, Part 1, p. 15.

102. "Air Force Studies."

103. This paragraph and the next are based on Allen; Kamer; and Allen, Krumel, and Pollack. On Jiang's statement in 2002, see Xu and Sha. For a more complete study of the development of the PLA Navy and naval doctrine, see Lewis and Xue, *China's Strategic Seapower*; and Cole.

104. Pan Shiying, *Xiandai*, pp. 128–29.

105. Quoted in "Air Force Will," A10.

106. "CMC Confers," p. 4.

107. Unless otherwise cited, the information in this paragraph and the next three is from Jing Xueqin, pp. 40–41; and Zhang Changzhi, p. 14.

108. Liu Taihang, p. 46.

109. Dai Xu, "Iraq War."

110. Zhang Changzhi, p. 14.

111. Ding Budong, p. 49.

112. A Taiwanese military officer has asserted, "As a last resort, we can carry out air raids against strategic targets in sixteen provinces of the Chinese mainland including coastal areas and interior provinces." Conversation with a Taiwanese army officer in Taipei, 1996.

113. Interview with a PLA senior colonel, 1997.

114. See, for example, Liu Shunyao, p. 90; and Zheng Shengxia, p. 46.

CHAPTER 8

1. Mao, "Problems of Strategy," pp. 179–254. This and the paragraph that follows are based on chapter 1 of "Problems."

2. Ibid., p. 190.

3. Tao Hanzhang, p. 94.

4. Ibid., pp. 106–7.

5. Mao, "Analysis," p. 13; see especially "On the Correct Handling," pp. 384–421.

6. Mao, "On Contradiction" pp. 324, 328, 337.

7. Wu Donghai and Wang Guangxian, p. 698.

8. The information in this paragraph is from Chinese Communist Party Central Document, pp. 435, 452, 459. The quotes are from pp. 435, 452, respectively.

9. The quote is from Men Xiangqing, p. 38. The information in the rest of this paragraph is from ibid., pp. 38–40.

10. Quoted from Shi Baodong, p. 30. The information in this paragraph and the next is from ibid., pp. 30, 35.

11. See, for example, Liu Bingchen, p. 78.

12. Ba Zhongtan, *Zhongguo*, pp. 150–51.

13. Men Xiangqing, p. 41.

14. Yu Qifen, p. 11.

15. For Mao's instruction to "strive for the best and prepare for the worst," see Mao, "Faith."

16. Mi Zhenyu, p. 19.

17. Li Jie, pp. 13–16. For a discussion of the island chains and their strategic role, see Lewis and Xue, *China's Strategic Seapower*, pp. 229–30.

18. Peng and Yao, p. 471.

19. Wang Guozhong, p. 353.

20. Quoted from Liu Xiaowu, pp. 34, 35, respectively.

21. This section is drawn from Lewis and Xue, *China's Strategic Seapower*, pp. 214–19. It is reproduced here with permission of Stanford University Press.

22. The twelve–character guiding principle for the CPV was: wage a protracted war (*chijiu zuozhan*), adopt an active defense strategy (*jiji fangyu*), and send fresh troops to Korea in rotation (*lunfan canzhan*). The principle remained in force until the Korean armistice. Tan Jingqiao, pp. 436–37; Yang Chengwu, p. 50; Shi Yan; Han and Meng, pp. 629–31; Duan and Jiang, p. 1218.

23. Based on Jiang Kejun, p. 310.

24. On October 19, 1949, the military commission put Zhou Enlai in charge of its daily affairs. Because Mao Zedong apparently became dissatisfied with his increasing stature in the army, Mao removed Zhou from this role and assigned Peng Dehuai to replace him in July 1952. Deng Lifeng, pp. 7, 262; Qi Shengping, p. 3.

25. Unless otherwise cited, this paragraph is based on Zheng Wenhan, "Chief," p. 3.

26. Lei Yuanshen, p. 226; Zhi Shaozeng, p. 52; Yan Jingtang, p. 58. The CCP Central Secretariat became the Politburo Standing Committee after 1956.

27. Lin Yunhui et al., p. 449; Zheng Wenhan, "Chief," p. 3; Fu Shangkui, p. 10.

28. Jiang Kejun, p. 310.

29. Zhang Zongxun, pp. 444–45.

30. Lin Yunhui et al., p. 451.

31. Zuo Ying, pp. 8–9.

32. Mao's statement reportedly was issued in April 1969 at the first session of the Ninth CCP Central Committee. Unless otherwise cited, this paragraph and the next two are based on Liao Guoliang et al., pp. 591–92; and Jiang Kejun, pp. 310–11.

33. The Chinese defined "fortifications" as fortified cities, and from studies of Soviet actions in the early phase of World War II, attached greater importance to defending their principal cities. See Lin Boye et al., pp. 240–42.

34. Luo and Fan.

35. Mi and Chen, pp. 93, 96; Zhang Chengang et al., pp. 46, 47, 48.

36. Liao Guoliang et al., p. 600. Many recent sources bring the still-relevant debates of the 1980s and early 1990s up to date; see, for example, Liu Huaqing, pp. 636–38; and Zhang Wannian, pp. 19–20, 26–28. Unless otherwise cited, this paragraph and the next are based on Zhang Zhen, "Several," pp. 76–77.

37. Nie Quanlin, pp. 158, 159; Liao Guoliang et al., p. 600.

38. Liu Jushao, p. 25; Liu Shengjun and Wang Fengju; Wang Yuxiang et al., pp. 75–78; Zhang Qinsheng et al., pp. 15–16. For a discussion of the weapon requirements for border wars and medium-scale conventional wars, see Liu Huaqiu.

39. For Chinese strategists' estimation of future conflicts with Vietnam and India, see, for example, Chen Kehou, pp. 109–10; Si Yanwen; Tang Fuquan; Wei Chuan; and Xin Si, pp. 26–27. See also Goncharov, "Chinese," p. 56.

40. Chen Kehou, pp. 115–17.

41. For a discussion of the types of war that might involve China, see Long Jize, pp. 139–40.

42. See, for example, Zhang and Zhu, pp. 21–24.

43. Quoted in Pan Shiying, "Have."

44. See, for example, "Strategic Research"; Li and Zeng; Qi Changming; Zhu Songchun, pp. 6–8; Xu Jingyue; and Wu Chunqiu, *Zhanlüe*, p. 6.

45. Mao Zedong, "Problems of Strategy," p. 145 (note 1).

46. On the relations between the group army and front army, see, for example, Han and Yu.

47. See, for example, "International"; She and Xiao, pp. 19–23; Xie Guoliang; Huo Yinzhang, pp. 45–46; Li and Sun; and Sun Kaitai, pp. 20–24.

48. Wu and Dong, pp. 471–72.

49. Information from a Chinese specialist, 1988.

50. Nie Quanlin, p. 162.

51. This paragraph is based on Li and Hou, pp. 9, 10.

52. Zhang Qinsheng et al.

53. Wu and Dong, pp. 471–72.

54. Zhang and Liao, p. 34–36. Quoted from p. 36. For literal meaning of *sashoujian*, see Chapter 5.

55. Tao Hanzhang, p. 99.

56. Information from a Chinese specialist, 2001.

57. Quoted in Wu Ke.

58. "Three Purposes."

59. Xinhua, May 30, 2001.

60. This paragraph and the next two are principally based on "Military"; and Chin Shao-yang, "Areas," p. A1. The quote in the next paragraph is from the latter source.

61. As an example of the hyperbole published by the PRC media on the Dongshan exercise, see Yun Zhen.

62. Chin Shao-yang, "Field." *Wen Wei Po* in July and August gave the most extensive coverage to the Dongshan and other exercises, though much of this coverage greatly exaggerated the capabilities and weapons demonstrated in these exercises.

63. "China Prepares." Unless otherwise cited, the information in this paragraph is from Chin Shao-yang, "Areas," p. A1.

64. For a description of a simulated attack on an "enemy" radar station, see "Air Force Conducts." As is the case with *Wen Wei Po*, *Ming Pao*'s reporting is highly

unreliable but is useful for what the general public was being told about the Dong-shan exercise.

65. AFP, August 12, 2001, states, "Covering an area of 350 nautical miles, the exercise is the first to utilize three China-launched military satellites." A number of sources refer to the use of reconnaissance satellites in the exercises, but it is not clear which satellites were used. Many of China's communications, earth resources, and meteorological satellites have military uses.

66. Tang and Wu, p. 2.

67. On the timing of the start of Stage 2, see the articles on the exercise in "Military."

68. "Curtain," p. A1.

69. "Military."

70. Chin Shao-yang, "Areas," p. A1.

71. For a description of these and other missiles, see Lewis and Hua, pp. 5–40.

72. *Renmin Wang* (Internet version), August 19, 2001.

73. Chin Shao-yang, "Areas," p. A1; on *san da san fang*, see Chap. 2, pp. 38–39.

74. "Long-Range Precision Missiles."

75. Wang and Chen, p. 3.

76. As an example of the hundreds of articles of this genre, see the military's September 2004 analysis of the U.S. doctrine of rapid response and preemption as applied to Pacific region operations in Wu and Xie.

77. Taiwan Affairs Office; "Taiwan Affairs Office."

78. Comment by Wen Jiabao in Zhongguo Xinwen She, May 10, 2004, as confirmed in Wang Te-chun. See also Li Jiaquan; Huang Zhihui; and "Unification Law."

79. "A Draft (Reunification Law)."

80. On various forms of landing support, see "Preliminary Discussion"; and Guo Yike, pp. 46–47. For pictures of regular landing-craft and beach operations, see *Jianchuan Zhishi*, No. 2 (2004).

81. Most of the information in this and the next paragraph is from Liu Yazhou.

82. The quotations in this paragraph are from Wang Zhenping, pp. 297, 298, respectively.

83. From 2001 on, the emphasis on these conventional missile units steadily increased. For example, in March, the Second Artillery issued the "Criteria for the Quality Assessment of Scientific and Technological Cadres in Conventional Missile Brigades." The purpose of the document was to "regularize its contingent of scientific and technological cadres" in these brigades. Li Guangrong and Bi Yongjun, p. 1.

84. Qiu Yiwu, p. 7; Second Artillery Team, p. 51; Yang Guoliang, p. 93. The quote is from the former source.

85. Second Artillery Team, p. 51; Dong Xuebin, pp. 47, 48.

86. Zhang Jiechuan, p. 58; Zheng Shengxia, p. 46.

87. On the debate concerning the U.S. role, see, for example, "Will the U.S."; and Bi Lei.

88. Lou Dou Zi.

89. Liu Dingping, p. 22. In 2004, two new deputy chiefs of the General Staff, Xu Qiliang and Wu Shengli, were said to be antiaircraft-carrier warfare experts having special knowledge of Taiwan.

90. Ibid.

91. Authoritative excerpts from the United States, Department of Defense, *Nuclear*. The quotations in this paragraph are from this document, pp. 16–17.

92. United States, White House, p. 15.

93. For a sample of contemporary Chinese responses to the *Nuclear Posture Review*, see Zhou Jianguo, p. 12; Li Bin, pp. 16–17; Mei Zhou, p. 3; Zhu Qiangguo; and Chen Xiaoping et al., pp. 34–36;

94. An Jing; Xi Wang; Chang Feng; Yun Hai; Chang Ying; Zhu Fei; Han Yang; Liu Hua; Zeng Tai; Shang Lin; He Shui; Fang Cheng; Du Xuesong.

95. One of the authors' conversations with senior Chinese military officers during arms control conferences in Beijing, 1981 and 1982.

96. "Beijing Claims."

97. See, for example, Chang Ying.

98. Luo Bing, "To Oppose," pp. 9–10.

99. Shang Lin, p. 24.

100. Bao Guojun, pp. 28–29. Quoted from p. 29.

101. Ma Baoan, p. 268.

102. Bao Guojun, p. 29.

103. Some of the main press coverage on this spy network allegedly headed by Major General Liu Guangzhi can be found in "PLA Air Force"; "Beijing Arrests"; and "Jiang Orders." The exposure of this network helps explain the creation of the Three-Anti Leading Group mentioned in Chapter 4. See Li Zijing.

104. Quoted from An Jing, p. 11.

105. Wu Chunqiu, "Iraq War," p. 6.

106. We deal with some of the relevant history from 1945–1950 in Goncharov et al., chaps. 1–3.

107. Information from a Taiwanese colonel, October 2002.

References Cited

Chinese romanizations are not provided for newspaper or journal articles. English names are given in brackets for all journals and newspapers except the most frequently cited ones:

GFDXXB   *Guofang Daxue Xuebao* [National Defense University Gazette]
JCZS   *Jianchuan Zhishi* [Naval & Merchant Ships]
JFJB   *Jiefangjun Bao* [Liberation Army Daily]
JSLS   *Junshi Lishi* [Military History]
JSSL   *Junshi Shilin* [Military History Circles]
RMRB   *Renmin Ribao* [People's Daily]
SJRB   *Shijie Ribao* [World Journal] (New York)
ZGJSKX   *Zhongguo Junshi Kexue* [China Military Science]

Unless otherwise stated, all Chinese-language journals and newspapers are published in Beijing.

Abrams, Herbert L. "Human Reliability and Safety in the Handling of Nuclear Weapons," *Science & Global Security*, Vol. 2, 1991.

"Academic Corruption in China Is Approaching the Last Moral Line of Defense," excerpt from an article in *Zhongguo Qingnian Bao* [China Youth Newspaper], http://book.peopledaily.com.cn/gb/paper250/1/class025000002/hwz190823.htm.

"Air Force Conducts Drill of Long-Distance Changed-Location Raid," *Ming Pao* [Mingpao] (Hong Kong) (Internet version), June 27, 2001.

Air Force Political Department. "Accelerate Training Professional Personnel in Those Units That Have Been Equipped with New-Type Weapons," *JFJB*, June 5, 2003.

"The Air Force Sends Elite Pilots to Russia to Test-Fly Su-27s," *SJRB*, February 4, 1997.

"The Air Force Studies How to Attack Early Warning Aircraft . . . ," reprinted from *Kongjun Bao* [Air Force Newspaper], http://jczs.sina.com.cn/2004-01-09/1004176315.html.

"The Air Force Will Soon Deploy Over-the-Horizon Fighters," *SJRB*, July 22, 1997.

Allen, Kenneth W. "The People's Liberation Army Naval Aviation: Status, Relationship with the PLA Air Force, and Prospects for the Future," unpublished paper (Alexandria, Va.: Center for Naval Analysis Corp, April 2003).

———, Glenn Krumel, and Jonathan D. Pollack. *China's Air Force Enters the 21st Century*. Santa Monica, Calif., 1995.

"An Article by *The China Daily* Commentator: None Can Benefit from the Crisis," www.huaxia.com/zt/2001-07/16870.html.

"An Article Written by a Famous Taiwan Watcher in the Chinese Mainland: How to Face the Deep-Rooted Contradictions across the Strait," www.phoenixtv.com/home/news/ review/200404/03/233732.html.

An Jing. "An Amphibious Campaign of a Front Army under Nuclear Conditions," *JCZS*, No. 2, 2004.

An Weiping. "New Requirements for Staff Officers to Exercise Command and Control in High-Tech Operations," in Wen and Fang.

"Asia Watch; Military A-5M Fantan," *Asian Aviation*, November 1988.

Ba Zhongtan. "An Opening Speech at the Symposium of State Security Strategy," in Ba Zhongtan, *Guojia Anquan*.

———, chief ed., *Guojia Anquan Zhanlüe Lunwen Ji* [A Collection of Essays on the Strategy for State Security]. Beijing, 2001.

———, chief ed. *Zhongguo Guojia Anquan Zhanlüe Wenti Yanjiu* [A Strategic Study of China's State Security Issues]. Beijing, 2003.

Bao Guojun. "What Kind of a High-Tech Local War Will China Face? An Interview with Major General Peng Guangqian, a Research Fellow at the Department of Strategic Studies of the Academy of Military Science," *Huanqiu Junshi Banyuekan* [Global Military Semi-Monthly], latter half of June, 2002.

Beaufre, Andre. *Deterrence and Strategy*. New York, 1996.

"Beijing Arrests Military Officers on Spy Charges," *China Post* (Taipei), April 17, 2004.

"Beijing Claims: 'Taiwan Is a Province of China,'" [Thirty-five Cases (November 15, 1971–August 31, 2000)], www.mac.gov.tw/english/english/macpolicy/bj8906-1.htm.

Bi Lei. "Sending an Additional Aircraft Carrier and Stationing Massive Forces: The U.S. Military's Adjustment of Its Strategic Disposition in the Asia-Pacific Region," *Renmin Wang*, [People's (Daily) Internet], August 23, 2004.

Bi Yongjun. "The Second Artillery's General Telecommunications Center Focuses Efforts on Solving Problems in 'Mobile Telecommunications,'" *JFJB*, May 20, 2001.

Bloodworth, Dennis. *The Chinese Looking Glass*. New York, 1966.

Bo Yibo. *Ruogan Zhongda Juece yu Shijian de Huigu* [A Review of Several Major Decisions and Events], Vol. 2. Beijing, 1993.

"The Boeing Company and China," www.boeing.com/ companyoffices /aboutus /
    boechina.html.

Bruzdzinski, Jason E. "Demystifying *Shashoujian*: China's 'Assassin's Mace' Con-
    cept," in Andrew Scobell and Larry Wortzel, eds., *Civil-Military Change in
    China: Elites, Institutes, and Ideas after the 16th Party Congress.* Carlisle, Penn.,
    2004.

Cadres Department of the Advance Command Post of the Guangzhou Greater
    Military Region, ed. *ZhongYue Bianjing Ziwei Huanji Zuozhan Ganbu
    Gongzuo Ziliao Huibian* [Compilation of Materials on Cadres Work in the
    Sino-Vietnamese Border Self-Defense Counterattack]. Guangzhou, 1979 (Se-
    cret document for circulation above the division level).

Cai Renzhao. "On 'Dual' Military Talents," *GFDXXB*, No. 3, 2000.

Cao Yingwang. *Zhongguo Waijiao Diyi Ren Zhou Enlai* [Zhou Enlai: China's
    Number One Diplomat]. Taiyuan, 2000.

"The Capability to Engage in Electronic Warfare Has Become Our Army's
    No. 1 Combat Capability," http://mil.eastday.com/eastday/ mil /node3509/
    userobject1ai34997.html.

CCP [Chinese Communist Party] Central Document Research Section, ed. *Deng
    Xiaoping Sixiang Nianpu (1975–1997)* [A Chronicle of Deng Xiaoping's
    Thought]. Beijing, 1998.

CCP Central Party History Research Section. *Zhonggong Dangshi Dashi Nianbiao*
    [Chronological Table of Major Events in the History of the CCP]. Beijing, 1981.
————. *Zhonggong Dangshi Dashi Nianbiao Shuoming* [Explanation of the Chro-
    nological Table of Major Events in the History of the CCP]. Beijing, 1983.
————, ed. *Zhongguo Dangshi Ziliao* [Materials on CCP History], Vols. 34, 41, 42.
    Beijing, 1990, 1992.

Chang Feng. "The Employment of Neutron Bombs in an Amphibious Campaign,"
    JCZS, No. 4, 2004.

Chang Ying. "Elementary Introduction to the Two Roles of Nuclear Deterrence,"
    Bingqi Zhishi [Ordnance Knowledge], No. 4, 2004.

Chen Boda. *Chen Boda Yigao Yue zhong Zishu ji Qita* [Chen Boda's Unpublished
    Manuscript: An Account of My Own Words Written in Jail and Other (Papers)].
    Hong Kong, 2000.

Chen Chuangang. "The Rise of the Strategic Missile Forces," in the Military
    History Department of the Academy of Military Science, ed., *Junqi Piao Piao*
    [Flying Military Flags], Vol. 2. Beijing, 1999.

Chen Hongyou, chief ed. *Xiandai Fangkong Lun* [On Modern Air Defense].
    Beijing, 1991.

Chen Kehou, chief ed. *Zhanzheng Heping yu Guofang* [War, Peace, and National
    Defense]. Beijing, 1989.

Chen, King. *China's War with Vietnam, 1979: Issues, Decisions, Implications.*
    Stanford, Calif., 1987.

Chen Shuiquan and Zhu Renyuan. "The Issues with Our Army's Joint Operations and Countermeasures," *GFDXXB*, No. 12, 2000.

Chen Weijun. "Jiang Zemin and Li Peng Support Generals' Request for a Large Increase in the Military Budget in Preparation for Any Contingency," *Guangjiaojing* [Wide-Angle Lens] (Hong Kong), No. 2, 1991.

Chen Xiaoping et al. "Is the Nuclear Target List Intended to Frighten China?" *Zhongguo Xinwen Zhoukan* [China News Weekly], March 25, 2002.

Chen Yangyong. *Kucheng Weiju Zhou Enlai zai 1967* [Zhou Enlai Made Extraordinarily Painstaking Efforts to Cope with a Dangerous Situation in 1967]. Beijing, 1999.

Chen Yilin. "Mao Zedong's Last Housekeeper," www.langsong.net/lstd/wxshk/htm/xiandai/xiandai2/js/dp/354.htm; www.kanzhongguo.com/news/articles/3/4/24/40650.html.

Cheng Gang and Zhang Dongwen. "Our Army Has Made a Breakthrough in Coordinated Communications," *JFJB*, November 11, 1998.

Cheng Qiuqing. "Reminiscences of the Construction of the '935' Impact Area," *Shenjian* [Magic Sword], No. 6, 1997.

Chi Zehou. "[Major Events] around the Issuance of Lin Biao's 'No. 1 Order,'" excerpt from *Zhonghua Renmin Gongheguo Shilu* [True Record of the People's Republic of China]. Changchun, 1994, reprinted by *Huaxia Wenzhai* [China Digest], supplementary issue (No. 327),www.cnd.org/HXWZ/ZK03/zk327 .gb.html.

Chin Shao-yang. "Areas within the Circumference of 350 Sea Miles under Reconnaissance and Control," *Wen Wei Po* [Encounter Newspaper] (Hong Kong) (Internet version), August 12, 2001.

———. "Field Armies of Seven Military Regions Practice Fighting in Rotation" *Wen Wei Po*, August 27, 2001.

"China Air Force Equipped with J-10 Fighter-bomber," http://english.people .com.cn/200212/13/eng20021213_108423.shtml.

"China Exhibits Its Surface-to-Air Missiles," *SJRB*, November 6, 1996.

China Forum on Future Military Studies, ed. *YaTai de Xuanwo* [Eddies in the Asian-Pacific Region]. Beijing, 1989.

"China Has Developed 'Air Force Early Warning 2000' with Better Radar Technology Than the United States and Russia," http://jczs.sina.com.cn/2005-03-01/ 0917269635.html.

"China Makes Known the F-7MF, Its Most Recently Developed Warplane," www.chilicity.com/publishhtml/1/2/2002-09-18/20030918103214.html.

"China Prepares for 'Largest Ever' Military Exercise Simulating Taiwan Invasion," AFP (Hong Kong), August 10, 2001.

"China's C³I and C⁴I Command Systems for Theater Operations," http://bbs3 .xilu.com/cgi-bin/bbs/view?forum=emas&message=41329.

"China's F-8II Upgrade to Include Litton Navigation System," *Jane's Defence Weekly*, March 19, 1988.

"China's Military Colleges (Colleges Affiliated with the Armed Services)," www
.cetcn.com/www/college/college5.htm-c0504.

"China's Super 7 Warplane First Flight-Tested with Missiles," www.chinanews
.com.cn/n/2003-07-10/26/322633.html.

"The Chinese Mainland Is Building Aerial Refueling Tankers to Strengthen Its
Capability to Attack Taiwan," *Guoji Ribao* [International Daily News] (Los
Angeles), March 13, 1996.

"The Chinese Mainland Is Developing the KS-1 Surface-to-Air Missile to Replace HQ Series Gradually," *Qiao Bao* [China Press] (New York), November 12,
1996.

"Chinese Super-Sonic Bomber," www.software.net/fh7.html.

"The CMC Confers the Honorary Title 'Pioneer Air Group in Applying Science
and Technology to Training Pilots' to a Certain Air Group in a Ceremony
Held in Beijing," *RMRB*, January 9, 2004.

"The CMC Holds a Grand Ceremony to Promote Military and Police Officers to
General," *Guofang Bao* [National Defense Newspaper], June 21, 2004.

Cohen, Arthur A. "The Sino-Soviet Border Crisis of 1969," in Alexander L. George,
ed., *Avoiding War: Problems in Crisis Management*. Boulder, Col., 1984.

Cold War International History Project Bulletin [hereafter *Cold War Bulletin*],
No. 6/7 (Winter 1995/96), No. 11 (Winter 1998), No. 12/13 (Fall/Winter 2001).

Cole, Bernard D. *The Great Wall at Sea: China's Navy Enters the Twenty-first
Century*. Annapolis, Md., 2001.

"A Comment on China's Economic Growth That Attracts Worldwide Attention,"
www.ccec.com.cn/news/news/cjzx/guon/gn000930-1.html.

"The Communist Army Will Pursue Two Fundamental Changes by the Beginning of the Next Century," *SJRB*, September 15, 1996.

"Communist China Is Reportedly Negotiating to Purchase Russian High-
performance Weapons," *SJRB*, September 3, 1996.

"Communist China Is Reportedly Purchasing Antiaircraft Missile Systems from
Russia," *SJRB*, January 16, 1996.

"Communist China Will Build an Improved Version of the Su-27," *SJRB*,
October 21, 1996.

"A Comparison of the Command Systems of the U.S. Army and the Chinese
Liberation Army," http://club.backchina.com/htm/2004_08_25/88230.html.

"Comrade Hu Jintao Chaired the First Plenary Session of the Sixteenth Party's
Congress and Central Leading Bodies Established at the Session," *JFJB*,
November 16, 2002.

"The Constitution of the Communist Party of China" (April 14, 1969), *Peking
Review*, Vol. 12, No. 18 (April 30, 1969).

Cui Yansong et al., chief eds. *Lianhe Fangkong Xinxi Zuozhan* [Information Warfare in Air Defense in Joint Operations]. Beijing, 1999.

"The Curtain Is Raised on the Combined Military Exercise on Dongshan Island,"
Wen Wei Po (Internet version), August 10, 2001.

Dai Qingmin. "On the Development of Army Informationization Warfare,"
    ZGJSKX, December 20, 2002.

———. "On Four Abilities for Informationized Warfare," *JFJB*, July 1, 2003.

———. "On Integrating Network Warfare and Electronic Warfare," *ZGJSKX*,
    February 1, 2002.

———. "On Seizing Information Supremacy," *ZGJSKX*, April 20, 2003.

Dai Qingmin et al. *Wang Dian Yitizhan Yinlun* [Introduction to Integrated
    Network and Electronic Warfare]. Beijing, 2002.

Dai Xu. "Considerations Concerning the Iraq War: A Simplified Record of an
    Interview with Lieutenant General Liu Yazhou," *Xiandai Junshi* [Conmilit],
    September 2003.

———. "The Iraq War Viewed by a Chinese General One Year Ago: Air
    Lieutenant General Liu Yazhou Talks about the Iraq War," *Kongjun Junshi
    Xueshu* [Air Force Military Studies], excerpt of this article reprinted in www7
    .chinesenewsnet.com/gb/MainNews/Opinion/2004_4_7_15_1_24_581.html.

"The Decision Made by the Fourth Plenary Session of the CCP Sixteenth Central
    Committee on the Agreement Concerning Comrade Jiang Zemin's Resignation
    as CMC Chairman," *JFJB*, September 20, 2004.

"Decisions on the Adjustment and Simplification of the Central Organizations
    (Adopted by the Politburo on March 20, 1943)," in Teaching and Research
    Section on Political Work for Party History and Party Construction of the Na-
    tional Defense University, ed., *Zhonggong Dangshi Jiaoxue Cankao Ziliao* [Ref-
    erence Materials for the Teaching and Study of CCP History], Vol. 17. Beijing,
    1985.

Deng Lifeng, ed. *Xin Zhongguo Junshi Huodong Jishi (1949–1959)* [The True
    Records of New China's Military Affairs (1949–59)]. Beijing, 1989.

Deng Wen. "China Activates the Counter-terrorism Mechanism," *Guojia Anquan
    Tongxun* [National Security News Report], No. 1, 2003.

Deng Xiaoping. "Address to Officers of the Rank of General and Above in
    Command of the Troops Enforcing Martial Law in Beijing" (June 9, 1989),
    in *Selected Works of Deng Xiaoping (1982–1992)*, Vol. 3. Beijing, 1994.

———. "Crack Down on Crime" (July 19, 1983), in *Selected Works of Deng Xiao-
    ping (1982–1992)*.

———. "Speech at an Enlarged Meeting of the Military Commission of the Cen-
    tral Committee of the Communist Party of China" (June 4, 1985), in *Selected
    Works of Deng Xiaoping (1982–1992)*.

———. "The Task of Consolidating the Army" (July 14, 1975), in *Selected Works
    of Deng Xiaoping (1975–1982)*. Beijing, 1984.

———. "Urgent Tasks of China's Third Generation of Collective Leadership"
    (June 16, 1989), in *Selected Works of Deng Xiaoping (1982–1992)*.

———. "Use the Intellectual Resources of Other Countries and Open Wider
    to the Outside World" (July 8, 1983), in *Selected Works of Deng Xiaoping
    (1982–1992)*.

————. "We Must Form a Promising Collective Leadership That Will Carry Out Reform" (May 31, 1989), in *Selected Works of Deng Xiaoping (1982–1992)*.

————. "With Stable Policies of Reform and Opening to the Outside World, China Can Have Great Hopes for the Future" (September 4, 1989), in *Selected Works of Deng Xiaoping (1982–1992)*.

"Deng Xiaoping Talks About Preserving World Peace," *Liaowang* [Outlook], September 16, 1985.

"Deng Xiaoping Talks Freely about the Situation at Home and Abroad," *Liaowang*, September 16, 1985.

Ding Budong. "Employment of the Air Force in Modern Combined-Services Campaigns," *Xiandai Junshi*, No. 5, 1998.

Ding Chong. "Experience and Lessons of Air Defense Operations by the [Chinese People's] Volunteers in the War to Resist U.S. Aggression and Aid Korea," *JSLS*, No. 4, 2003.

Ding Guoqiang. "Who Will Come to Oppose Academic Corruption?" www .people.com.cn/GB/wenyu/68/20030422/977641.html.

Ding Jie. "The Main Problems We Will Face in Command and Control of Armed Forces under High-Tech Conditions and Our Countermeasures," *GFDXXB*, No. 6, 2000.

Ding Shu. "Mao Zedong and His Female Cryptographer," http://members.lycos. co.uk/sixian001/author/D/Dingshu/Dingshu013.txt.

Documents of the Sixteenth National Congress of the Communist Party of China. Beijing, 2002.

Dong Baocun. "An Interview Regarding '[Mao's Comment:] Wu Zhong Is Loyal,'" *Renwu* [Personages], No. 6, 2000.

Dong Jianwen. "The Hatch Door of the [CCP] General Secretary's Special Airplane Found Open: The Whole Story of the 'Special Airplane Incident' during Hu Yaobang's Visit to Britain," *Baokan Wenzhai* [Newspapers and Periodicals Digest] (Shanghai), No. 1825 (September 26, 2003), www.jfdaily.com.cn/gb/node2/node17/node161/node19831/index.html.

————. "Unknown Historical Facts of the 'Cultural Revolution' Disclosed in the Memoir of Wu Jicheng, Former Deputy Director of the Central Guards Bureau," *Baokan Wenzhai*, June 27, 2003, www.jfdaily.com.cn/gb/node2/node7/node161/node14541/index.html.

Dong Xuebin. "Questions on the Employment of the Second Artillery in Countering the Enemy's Joint Operations," *GFDXXB*, No. 5, 1997.

Dongfang He. *Zhang Aiping Zhuan* [The Biography of Zhang Aiping]. Beijing, 2000.

"Dongshan Island Exercise Aims to Seize Air Control over the Taiwan Strait," *Ta Kung Pao* [Impartial Newspaper] (Hong Kong) (Internet version), July 16, 2004.

"Doubts about the 'Four Clean-ups Movement,'" *Baokan Wenzhai*, No. 1500 (November 2, 2000), p. 1, excerpts of Liu Yuan and He Jiadong, *Ni Suo Bu Zhidao de Liu Shaoqi* [The Liu Shaoqi Whom You Do Not Know].

"A Draft (Reunification Law): The System of Confederation Adopted for the Two Sides of the Strait, Punishment of Separatists Valid for 100 Years, and Three Cases to Activate the Use of Force," www.backchina.com/news/2004-05-20/36304.html.

Du Xuesong. "The Taiwanese Army's 'Small Atomic Bombs,'" *Bingqi Zhishi*, No. 8, 1998.

Duan Suquan and Jiang Renguan. "Strategies in China's Revolutionary Wars," in Song Shilun, Vol. 2.

Duan Zijun, chief ed. *China Today: Aviation Industry*. Beijing, 1989.

———. *Dangdai Zhongguo de Hangkong Gongye* [Contemporary China's Aviation Industry]. Beijing, 1988.

Editorial Departments of *RMRB* and *Hong Qi* [Red Flag]. *Refutation of the New Leaders of the CPSU on "United Action."* Beijing, 1965.

Fan Jiabing. "Several Issues on Operation Planning for Joint Operations," in Wen and Fang.

Fang Bing and Chen Zhenzhong. "The Fourth Institute Provides Support for 'Achieving Victory' through Powerful Verification of Weapons and Equipment Procurement," *Huojianbing Bao* [Rocket Corps Newspaper], July 2, 2002.

Fang Cheng. "Civilian Air Defense and Nuclear Protection," *JCZS*, No. 10, 2004.

Feigenbaum, Evan. *China's Techno-Warriors: National Security and Strategic Competition from the Nuclear to the Information Age*. Stanford, Calif., 2003.

Festinger, Leon, Henry W. Riecken, and Stanley Schachter. *When Prophecy Fails*. Minneapolis, Minn., 1956.

Fravel, Taylor. "The Revolution in Research Affairs: Online Sources and the Study of the PLA," in James C. Mulvenon and Andrew N. D. Yang, eds., *A Poverty of Riches: New Challenges and Opportunities in PLA Research*. Santa Monica, Calif., 2003.

French, Howard W. "China Opens a Window on Really Big Ideas," *New York Times*, June 2, 2004.

Fu Chongbi. "The Divergence between Me and Xie Fuzhi in the 'Cultural Revolution,'" *Zhonghua Ernü Zazhi* [The Magazine of China's Sons and Daughters], No. 4, 1999.

———. "The Major Events, Minor Matters, and Troubles I Met When I Was the Beijing Garrison Commander," *Zhonghua Ernü Zazhi*, No. 5, 1999.

Fu Shangkui. "An Exploration into the Development of Our Country's Active Defense Thought in Peacetime," *JSSL*, No. 4, 1991.

Gao Rui, chief ed. *Zhanlüe Xue* [Strategy]. Beijing, 1987.

Gao Shangrui. "Chinese Air Force Expert on Air Defense: Antiaircraft Guns Are Effective Weapons for Fighting Cruise Missiles," *JFJB*, March 26, 2003, www.pladaily.com.cn/gb/pladaily/2003/03/26/20030326001189_TodayNews.html.

Gao Wenqian. *Wannian Zhou Enlai* [Zhou Enlai's Later Years]. New York, 2003.

Gao Xin. *Lingdao Zhongguo de Xin Renwu* [New Figures in the Chinese Leadership]. www7.chinesenewsnet.com/gb/MainNews/Forums/Backstage/2003_10_28_9_4_6_107.html.

Gao Xinmin. "China: State Information Center Director on the State Economic Information System," *Beijing Keji Ribao* [Beijing Science and Technology Daily], April 1, 1996.

Ge Chengwen. "The Stability of Command Should Be Strengthened in Mobile Operations," in Wen and Fang, *Zhongguo Dangdai Guofang Wenku*.

Ge Zhenfeng. "Preliminary Ideas on Setting Up a Joint Command in Subregional Operations," *GFDXXB*, Nos. 2–3, 1997.

Gelman, Harry. *The Soviet Far East Buildup and Soviet Risk-Taking Against China*. Santa Monica, Calif., 1982.

"The General Staff Operations Department Undergoes Organizational Readjustment," *Guangjiaojing*, No. 3, 2004.

General Logistics Department, ed. *Bianjing Fanji Zuozhan Houqin Baozhang* [The Logistics Support for Counterattack on the Frontiers]. Beijing, 1997.

General Wang Shangrong Editing and Writing Team. *Wang Shangrong Jiangjun* [General Wang Shangrong]. Beijing, 2000.

George, Alexander L. *Presidential Decisionmaking in Foreign Policy: The Effective Use of Information and Advice*. Boulder, Col., 1980.

Gittings, John. *The Role of the Chinese Army*. London, 1967.

Gobarev, Viktor M. "Soviet Policy Toward China: Developing Nuclear Weapons, 1949–1969," *Journal of Slavic Military Studies*, Vol. 12, No. 4 (December 1999).

Goldstein, Lyle J. "Do Nascent WMD Arsenals Deter? The Sino-Soviet Crisis of 1969," *Political Science Quarterly*, Vol. 118, No. 1 (Spring 2003).

———. "Return to Zhenbao Island: Who Started Shooting and Why It Matters," *China Quarterly*, No. 168 (December 2001).

Goncharov, Sergei. "The Chinese Concept of National Security," in *New Approaches to Security in the Asian-Pacific Region*. Stanford, Calif., 1990.

Goncharov, Sergei, John W. Lewis, and Xue Litai. *Uncertain Partners: Stalin, Mao, and the Korean War*. Stanford, Calif., 1993.

Gong Yuzhen. "The Limitations of the Times on the Mainstream of Western Strategic Cultures," excerpts from Gong Yuzhen, *Zhongguo Zhanlüe Wenhua Jiexi* [An Analysis of Chinese Strategic Culture], *Baokan Wenzhai*, No. 1763, April 30, 2003, www.jfdaily.com.cn/gb/node2/node7/node61/index.html.

"Grumman in Chinese Fighter Deal," *Jane's Defence Weekly*, November 19, 1988.

Gu Baozi. "An Indissoluble Bond between Mao Zedong and Tiananmen," in Gu Baozi et al., Vol. 1.

———. *Jingtou xia de Zhongnanhai* [Zhongnanhai in the Camera Lens]. Hong Kong, 1993.

———. "Mao Zedong on the Move in Zhongnanhai," in Gu Baozi et al., Vol. 1.

———. "Xiang Shouzhi Twice Appointed Commander of the Missile Forces," in Gu Baozi et al., Vol. 2.

Gu Baozi et al. *Texie Zhongnanhai* [Feature Stories That Occurred in Zhongnanhai]. Vols. 1, 2. Beijing, 1999.

Gu Yue. *Da Yunchou Gongheguo Yuanshuai Zhongda Juece* [Grand Strategy: Key Decisionmaking of the Republic's Marshals]. Beijing, 1999.

Guangdong, Guangxi, Hunan, and Henan Team to Revise *Ciyuan* and Commercial Publishing House's Editorial Department, eds. *Ciyuan* [Big Dictionary]. Beijing, 1998.

Guo Boxiong. "Exploration of the Training Issues Regarding Joint Operations," *GFDXXB*, No. 11, 1999.

Guo Ping. "A New Trend in the Employment of Military Strategies," *Xiandai Junshi*, No. 7, 1996.

Guo Qingsheng. "The Second Artillery Has Formed a War Preparedness System to Meet the Requirements during Peacetime and in War," *JFJB*, December 16, 1987.

Guo Yike. "Civilian Ships: A Paranaval Force from among the People," *Dangdai Haijun* [Contemporary Navy], February 1, 2004.

Guoji Xingshi yu Guofang Zhanlüe [The International Situation and Defense Strategy]. Beijing, 1987.

Haijun Shi [The History of the (Chinese) Navy]. Beijing, 1989.

Han Gang. "Main Features of the Evolution of Our Country's Political System in the Ten-Year Period before the Cultural Revolution," *Dangshi Yanjiu yu Jiaoxue* [Studies and Teachings on the Party's History] (Fuzhou), No. 2, 1989.

Han Suyin. *Eldest Son: Zhou Enlai and the Making of Modern China, 1898–1976*. London, 1994.

Han Weiguo. "Prediction of the Status Quo and Characteristics of Our Army's Joint Operations and Their Developing Tendencies," *GFDXXB*, No. 5, 1999.

Han Xianchu and Meng Zhaohui. "The War to Resist U.S. Aggression and Aid Korea," in Song Shilun,, Vol. 1.

Han Yang. "Airborne Operations in an Amphibious Campaign under Nuclear Conditions," *JCZS*, No. 6, 2004.

Han Yongfa and Yu Guidong. "The Shenyang Military Region Command Strengthens Theoretical Study on Defensive Warfare under Nuclear Conditions," *JFJB*, Aug. 22, 1987.

Hao Yukun and Zhang Weiping. "Modernization of Command Means Is an Objective Requirement for Winning a Joint Campaign," *GFDXXB*, No. 9, 1999.

Harding, Harry. *Organizing China: The Problem of Bureaucracy 1949–1976*. Stanford, Calif., 1981.

"Having Stealthy Functions, the Combat Capabilities of the Super-7 Warplane's No Worse Than F-16," www7.chinesenewsnet.com/gb/MainNews/SocDigest/Technology/2003_7_9_23_59_15.713.html.

He Fang. "History Must Be True: On the Party's Central Leadership Established at the Zunyi Conference," www.cass.net.cn/webnew/chinese/s30_rbs/files/kycg/hefang1.htm.

He Liangliang. "PLA's Additional Grand Disarmament," *Fenghuang Zhoukan* [Phoenix Weekly] (Hong Kong), No. 121.

He Liangping et al. "How Can Personnel Be Prevented from Losing Control?" *Huojianbing Bao*, November 10, 2001.

He Shui. "Psychological Warfare in Landing Operations under Nuclear Conditions," *JCZS*, No. 9, 2004.

He Tianjin. "Our Strategic Missile Unit Greatly Improves Its Surveying and Mapping Capabilities—All-Weather, High Accuracy, High Mobility," *Keji Ribao* [Science and Technology Daily], January 17, 2002.

He Tianjin and Zhao Fengyun. "Gao Guoqian, a Senior Engineer at a Missile Component Warehouse Who Has Stayed on a Plateau for Third Years and Made Contributions to Protecting the 'Magic Sword,'" *JFJB*, June 17, 2001.

Hu Changfa. "Some Theoretical Issues in Operational Command under Hi-Tech Conditions," *GFDXXB*, No. 4, 1997.

Hu Guangzheng. "Drawing Lessons from the Development of the Military Establishments in the Twentieth Century," *ZGJSKX*, No. 1, 1997.

"Hu [Jintao] and [His] 'Bodyguards in Zhongnanhai': Disclosure of the Secret Guard Unit for China's Authorities," reprinted from *Beijing Qingnian Bao* [Beijing Youth Newspaper], www.chilicity.com/publishhtml/3/2004-05-03/20040503084037.html.

Hu Xiaomin. "A Study on Certain Questions Related to Artillery Engagements in Joint Operations," *GFDXXB*, Nos. 2–3, 1998.

Hu Yanning et al. "The Consideration Resulting from the Building of a Fiber Optical Network for Digital Communications and Command at a Certain Base of the Second Artillery," *JFJB*, December 25, 1998.

Hua Renjie et al., chief eds. *Kongjun Xueshu Sixiang Shi* [The History of the Academic Thinking of the Air Force]. Beijing, 1992.

Huang Bin, chief ed. *Lu Hai Kong Jun Gao Jishu Tiaojian xia Zuozhan Zhihui* [Command and Control of the Three Services under High-Tech Conditions]. Beijing, 1993.

Huang Dong. "The Current Status of China's Digital Forces," *Guangjiaojing*, No. 4, 2004.

Huang Yao and Zhang Mingzhe. *Luo Ruiqing Zhuan* [A Biography of Luo Ruiqing]. Beijing, 1996.

Huang Yuzhang et al. *Jundui Jianshe Da Cidian* [The Big Dictionary on Military Buildup]. Beijing, 1994.

Huang Zhihui. "Beijing Obstructs 'Taiwan Independence' in All Directions," *Qingnian Cankao* [Youth Reference] (Internet version), May 26, 2004.

Huo Yinzhang. "Ancient Military Strategist: Sun Bin," *JSSL*, No. 2, 1986.

Information Office, State Council. *China's National Defense*. Beijing, 1998.

———. *China's National Defense in 2000*. Beijing, 2000.

———. *China's National Defense in 2002*. Beijing, 2002.

———. *China's National Defense in 2004*. Beijing, 2004.

"International Symposium on Sun Tzu's Art of War Will Be Held Next Year in Linyi, Shandong," *SJRB*, April 24, 1991.

"Israel's Role in China's New Warplane," www.atimes.com/atimes/China/DL04Ad0.html.

"J-8 Fighters Can Now Provide Air Cover over the South China Sea," *SJRB*, March 15, 1996.

"J-11 [Su-27 Flanker]," www.fas.org/nuke/guide/china/aircraft/j-11.htm.

Jencks, Harlan. "China's 'Punitive' War on Vietnam," *Asian Survey*, Vol. 19, No. 8 (December 1979).

"JH-7 [Jianhong Fighter-Bomber] [B7]," www.fas.org/man/dod-101/sys/ac/row//jh-7.htm.

Jiang Fangran. "The Theoretical Development of Antagonism of Command and the Main Academic Disputes," *GFDXXB*, No. 11, 1997.

Jiang Jianjun. "Preliminary Exploration of Our Army's Capability of Conducting Information Warfare," in Wen and Fang.

Jiang Kejun. "On the Features of the Past Shifts of Our Army's Strategic Guiding Principles," in Shao Chengye, chief ed., *Huigu Zhanwang Tantao* [Retrospect, Prospect, and Exploration]. Chengdu, 1987.

"Jiang Orders Strict Investigation of Taiwan Spy Case," *Hsiang-kang Shang Pao* [Hong Kong Commerical Newspaper] (Internet version), April 18, 2004.

Jiang Shui. "An Overall Review of the Development of Our Army's Command-and-Control Systems by the Federation of American Scientists," www.laocanmou.com/ShowArticle.asp?ArticleID=465.

Jiang Zhengming. "The United States Is Infatuated with Nuclear Blackmail," *Huanqiu Junshi Banyuekan*, latter half of April, 2002.

Jin Hui et al. *ZhongYue Zhanzhen Milu* [A Secret Record on the Sino-Vietnamese War]. Changchun, 1990.

Jin Liren. "Hu Jintao Has a New Residence on Mount Yuquan as Jiang Zemin's Neighbor," www.kanzhongguo.com/news/articles/3/8/8/48807.html.

Jin Shi. "Escorting Peng Dehuai Back to His Hometown for Investigation in 1961," *Bainian Chao* [Hundred-Year Tide], No. 7, 2002.

Jing Xueqin. "Make a Thorough Implementation of the Military Guiding Principle in the New Era and Make Great Efforts to Promote the Modern Construction of the Air Force," *GFDXXB*, Nos. 8–9, 1997.

Johnston, Alastair Iain. "China's Militarized Interstate Dispute Behaviour, 1949–1992: A First Cut at the Data," *China Quarterly*, No. 153 (March 1998).

———. "China's New 'Old Thinking': The Concept of Limited Deterrence," *International Security*, Vol. 20, No. 3 (Winter 1995/96).

———. "Is China a Status Quo Power?" *International Security*, Vol. 27, No. 4 (Spring 2003).

Kamer, Rick. "China Naval Air Force's Re-Emergence," *RUSI China Military Update*, Vol. 2, No. 3 (Sept./Oct. 2004).

Keefe, John. *Anatomy of the EP-3 Incident, April 2001*. Alexandria, Va., 2001.

Kemp, Geoffrey. *Nuclear Forces for Medium Powers.* International Institute for Strategic Studies, Adelphi Papers 106 and 107. London, 1974.

Lampton, David M., ed. *The Making of Chinese Foreign and Security Policy in the Age of Reform, 1978–2000.* Stanford, Calif., 2001.

Le Duan. "Comrade B on the Plot of the Reactionary Chinese Clique against Vietnam" (trans. and annotated by Christopher E. Goscha), in *Cold War Bulletin*, No. 12/13 (Fall / Winter 2001); for a Chinese version, see *Beijing zhi Chun* [Beijing Spring], No. 11, 2003, www.rainbowsoft.org/jzt/ARTICLE/000309.asp.

"Legal Principles Do Not Tolerate Hegemony," *JFJB*, April 8, 2001.

"Lei Feng's Diary," http://soyoung1999.nease.net/leifenghewo/lfrj.html.

Lei Yingfu. *Zai Zuigao Tongshuaibu Dang Canmou Lei Yingfu Jiangjun Huiyilu* [A Staff Officer in the Supreme Headquarters: General Lei Yingfu's Memoirs]. Nanchang, 1997.

Lei Yuanshen. "The Evolution of the Central Military Commission," in CCP Central Party History Research Section, *Zhonggong Dangshi Ziliao*, Vol. 34, 1990.

Lewis, John W. *Political Networks and the Chinese Policy Process.* Stanford, Calif., 1986.

Lewis, John W., and Hua Di. "China's Ballistic Missile Programs: Technologies, Strategies, Goals," *International Security*, Vol. 17, No. 2 (Fall 1992).

———, and Xue Litai, "Beijing's Defense Establishment: Solving the Arms-Export Enigma," *International Security*, Vol. 15, No. 4 (Spring 1991).

Lewis, John W., and Xue Litai. *China Builds the Bomb.* Stanford, Calif., 1988.

———. "China's Search for a Modern Air Force," *International Security*, Vol. 24, No. 1 (Summer 1999).

———. *China's Strategic Seapower: The Politics of Force Modernization in the Nuclear Era.* Stanford, Calif., 1994.

———. "Chinese Strategic Weapons and the Plutonium Option," *Critical Technologies Newsletter*, April / May 1988.

———. "Social Change and Political Reform in China: Meeting the Challenge of Success," *China Quarterly*, No. 176 (December 2003).

Li Bin. "Are U.S. Nuclear Weapons Aimed at China?" *Shijie Zhishi* [World Knowledge], April 1, 2002.

———, and Zhang Yuwen. "Zou Yanling: As Heroic as Before," *Zhongguo Kongjun* [Chinese Air Force], No. 5, 2000.

Li Bingyan and Sun Jing. "Lay Stress on Tactics: The Character of the Ancient Oriental Art of War," *JFJB*, April 21, 1989.

Li Bingyan and Zeng Guangjun. "Our Army's Strategic Studies Become Active," *JFJB*, May 10, 1986.

Li Cheng et al., chief eds. *Jianguo Yilai Junshi Bai Zhuang Dashiji* [One Hundred Major Events in Military History since the Founding of the Republic]. Beijing, 1992.

Li Fengzhou. "Western China's Developing Space City," *Zhongguo Hangtian* [China Aerospace], No. 11, 1992.

Li Guangrong and Bi Yongjun. "The Second Artillery Issues Criteria for the Quality Assessment of Its Scientific and Technical Cadres," *JFJB* (Internet version), March 18, 2002.

Li Haisheng and Wanyan Shaoyuan. *Juntong Ju Xiao Mao Renfeng* [Mao Renfeng: Chief of the Bureau of Military Investigation and Statistics]. Shanghai: 1995.

Li Honggu and Jin Yan. "A View the Corruption of Secretaries from the 'Case of Li Zhen,'" www.hubce.edu.cn/jwc/jwc5/messages/18511.html.

Li Jian, ed. *Taiwan yu Qian Sulian Jiaowang Milu* [A Secret Record on the Exchange between Taiwan and the Ex-Soviet Union], Vol. 1. Beijing, 1995.

Li Jianghe and Hou Aiping. "What We Think about Our Country's Defense Developmental Strategy," *JSSL*, No. 5, 1987.

Li Jianjun and Ji Hongjian. "The Mysterious '8341' [Unit]," *JSLS*, No. 3, 2004.

Li Jiaquan. "China Must Wield Legal Weapons and Enact a National Unification Law to Fight Against 'Taiwan Independence' and U.S. Interference in China's Internal Affairs," *Wen Wei Po* (Internet version), May 19, 2004.

Li Jie. "The First and Second Island Chains: 'Two Impediments' in the West Pacific Ocean," *JCZS*, No. 2, 2004.

Li Jijun. *Junshi Zhanlüe Siwei* [Thinking of Military Strategy]. Beijing, 2001.

———. "On Strategy: A Dialogue Concerning Strategy," *Shijie Junshi* [World Military Affairs], No. 8, 2002.

Li Jiqing. "Enhance Land-Based Air Defense to an Extremely Important Strategic Position to Dominate the Air: An Interview with Zhang Peigao, A Research Fellow from the Academy of Military Science," *Guoji Zhanwang Banyuekan* [International Forecast Semi-monthly], supplemental issue in June 2000.

Li Jue et al., chief eds. *Dangdai Zhongguo de He Gongye* [Contemporary China's Nuclear Industry]. Beijing, 1987.

Li Junting and Yang Jinhe, chief eds. *Zhongguo Wuzhuang Liliang Tonglan* [A Survey of China's Armed Forces]. Beijing, 1992.

Li Ke and Hao Shengzhang. *Wenhua Da Geming zhong de Renmin Jiefangjun* [The People's Liberation Army in the Great Cultural Revolution]. Beijing, 1989.

Li Lianqing. *Da Waijiaojia Zhou Enlai* [Zhou Enlai, a Great Diplomat (Diplomatic Negotiations in the Whirlpool of the Cultural Revolution)], Vol. 6. Hong Kong, 2002.

———. *Lengnuan Suiyue Yi Bo San Zhe de ZhongSu Guanxi* [Warm and Cold Years: One Trouble Followed Another in Sino-Soviet Relations]. Beijing, 1998.

Li Ping and Ma Zhisun, chief eds. *Zhou Enlai Nianpu (1949–1976)* [A Chronicle of Zhou Enlai (1949–1976)]. Beijing, 1997.

Li Qianyuan. "Exploration of Command and Control in Joint Operations in an Independent Direction of a Theater," *GFDXXB*, No. 5, 1998.

Li Rongming. "China's Mysterious Strategic Missile Forces," www.guangzhou
.gov.cn/node_559/note_562/2005-08/112433581165128.shtml.

Li Shenming. "Several Analyses, Concise Descriptions, and Considerations of
Mao Zedong's Thinking on War and Peace after the Founding of New China,"
Dangdai Zhongguo Shi Yanjiu [Studies on Contemporary Chinese History],
No. 3, 2004.

Li Shenzhi. "Talk About the PRC's Diplomacy," www.usc.cuhk.edu.hk/wk_
wzdetails.asp?id=2200.

Li Weisai. "Wu De, Wu Zhong, and the Complete Collapse of the Lin Biao and
Jiang Qing Cliques," *JSLS*, No. 3, 2004.

Li Xin, ed. *Da Yanxi* [A Grand Exercise]. Beijing, 1998.

———. "Yang Shangkun: A Transgenerational Director [of the CCP Central
Committee's General Office]," *Baogao Wenxue* [Reportage], Nos. 2, 4, 2001.

Li Zhaoxing. "China Diplomatic Forum [*Zhongguo Waijiao Luntan*]" of the Foreign Ministry's website, www.fmprc.gov.cn/.

Li Zhisui. *The Private Life of Chairman Mao*. New York, 1994.

Li Zijing. "Beijing Reportedly Has Created a 'Three-Anti' Leading Group," *Cheng
Ming* [Contention] (Hong Kong), No. 6, 2004.

Li Zubin and Bi Yongjun. "Secrets That Can Be Made Public," *JFJB*, April 25,
2001.

Liang Dongyuan. *Tian Xiao Zhongguo Guofang Jianduan Jishi* [The Roar from
Heaven: A True Description of China's Sophisticated Defense]. Beijing, 1997.

Liao Guoliang et al. *Mao Zedong Junshi Sixiang Fazhan Shi* [The Development of
Mao Zedong's Military Thinking]. Beijing, 1991.

Liao Yiwen and Wang Wenjie. "Jiang Zemin and Hu Jintao Attended the CMC's
Enlarged Meeting and Delivered Important Speeches," *JFJB*, September 21,
2004.

Lieberthal, Kenneth, and David M. Lampton, eds. *Bureaucracy, Politics, and
Decision Making in Post-Mao China*. Berkeley, Calif., 1992.

Lin Biao. "Report to the Ninth National Congress of the Communist Party of
China," *Peking Review*, Vol. 12, No. 18 (April 30, 1969).

Lin Boye et al. *Mao Zedong Junshi Bianzhengfa Sixiang Xintan* [Explorations of
Mao Zedong's Dialectical Thinking on Military Affairs]. Beijing, 1987.

Lin Hu. "The Development of Air Force Equipment in the Seventh Five-Year
Plan Period (1986–90)," in Wang Runsheng, chief ed., *Kongjun Huiyi Shiliao*
[The Air Force: Historical Materials on Recollections]. Beijing, 1992.

———, chief ed. *Kongjun Shi* [The History of the Air Force]. Beijing, 1989.

Lin, Man Kim. *The Sino-Vietnamese War*. Hong Kong, 1981.

Lin Yunhui et al. *1949–1989 Nian de Zhongguo Kaige Xingjin de Shiqi* [China's Tri-
umphant March from 1949 to 1989]. Zhengzhou, 1989.

Ling Haijian. *Zhonggong Jundui Xin Jiangxing* [Profiles of New Chinese Communist Generals]. Hong Kong, 1999.

Ling Xiang. "A Description of the Five PLA Comprehensive Universities (A Series of Visits to Military Colleges, Part 4)," *Xiandai Bingqi* [Modern Weaponry], No. 4, 2002.

"A List of Our Senior [PLA] Officers," http://cache.baidu.com/c?word=%B4%F7%3B%C7%E5%3B%C3%F1&url=http%3A//www%2Eblogdriver%2Ecom/njhsyj/&b=0&a=3&user=baidu.

Liu Bingchen. "A Strategy Shifting from 'Subduing the Enemy's Army without Battle' to 'Winning by All/Mutual Benefit,'" in Ba Zhongtan, *Guojia Anquan*.

Liu Bingrong. "Marshal He Long and the Defense Industry," *Shen Jian* [Magical Sword], No. 4, 2001.

Liu Dingping. "Topics Concerning Anti-Carrier Operations," *Junshi Wenzhai* [Military Digest], No. 7, 2004.

Liu Hua. "Talk Once Again about the Use of Neutron Bombs in Landing Operations," *JCZS*, No. 7, 2004.

Liu Huaqing. *Liu Huaqing Huiyilu* [Liu Huaqing's Memoirs]. Beijing, 2004.

"Liu Huaqing Signs a Contract in Moscow and Discusses Military Cooperation," *SJRB*, August 28, 1997.

Liu Huaqiu. *China and the Neutron Bomb*. Stanford, Calif., 1988.

Liu Huimin et al., chief eds. *Siling Jiguan Gongwen Xiezuo Daquan* [A Complete Collection on the Writing of Official Documents at (PLA) Headquarters]. Beijing, 2002.

Liu Jingsong. "Key Principles for Waging Combined Operations against Invading Enemies in a Theater," *GFDXXB*, No. 5, 1997.

Liu Jingzhi and Wang Zhongyu, chief eds. *Dangdai Zhongguo de Jilin* [Contemporary China's Jilin]. Beijing, 1991.

Liu Jushao. "At Recent Top-Level PLA Meeting, Zhao Ziyang Urges Vigilance against Partial War," *Wen Wei Po*, May 11, 1988, in *FBIS*: China, May 11, 1988.

Liu Ruishao, ed. *Zhongnanhai Gui Ke* [Distinguished Guests in Zhongnanhai], Vol. 2. Hong Kong, 1997.

Liu Shaoqi. "On Inner-Party Struggle," in *Selected Works of Liu Shaoqi*. Beijing, 1984.

Liu Shengjun and Wang Fengju. "A Symposium Held in Chengdu to Discuss [How to Strengthen] Logistic Support for Local Wars," *RMRB*, May 24, 1988.

Liu Shunyao. "Follow the Direction Given by Our Party's Third-Generation Collective Leadership in Building a Powerful Modern People's Air Force," *ZGJSKX*, No. 3, 1997.

Liu Taihang. "Strengthen Studies on Air Force Military Theory to Guide the Quality Construction of the People's Air Force," *ZGJSKX*, No. 4, 1997.

Liu Tianye et al. *Li Tianyou Jiangjun Zhuan* [A Biography of General Li Tianyou]. Beijing, 1993.

Liu Wei and Li Honglin. "Resolute Invention and Innovation," *JFJB*, January 8, 1993.

Liu Xiaowu. "On the Major Issues Required for Containing and Winning a War," *GFDXXB*, No. 2, 1999.

Liu Yang. "An Elementary Introduction to Command Confrontation in a High-Tech Local War," *ZGJSKX*, No. 4, 1997.

Liu Yaoxian and Jiang Wanliu. "Help Young Officers Establish Stable Marital Relationships," *JFJB*, November 27, 1998.

Liu Yazhou. "A Review of the Jinmen [Quemoy] Campaign," www.cnd.org/my/modules/wfsection/article.php%3Farticleid=6241.

"Liu Yazhou's Presentation: Faith and Morale," http://bbs.yannan.cn/viewthread.php?tid=42520&sid=OeAOeELD.

Liu Yichang, chief ed. *Gao Jishu Zhanzheng Lun* [On Hi-Tech War]. Beijing, 1993.

Liu Zhengwu, chief ed. *Xiandai Jundui Zhihui* [The Command of a Modern Army]. Beijing, 1994.

Liu Zhinan. "The Year of 1969: China's War Preparedness and Studies and Adjustment of Its Relations with the United States and Soviet Union," *Dangdai Zhongguo Shi Yanjiu* [Studies on Contemporary Chinese History], No. 3, 1999.

Long Jize. "Thinking and Experiment on Military Strategy," in *Guoji Xingshi yu Guofang Zhanlüe* [The International Situation and Defense Strategy]. Beijing, 1987.

"Long-Range Precision Missiles of the Liberation Army Can Destroy Aircraft Carrier Battle Groups as Seen in the Large-Scale Dongshan Island Exercises," Zhongguo Tongxun She, August 27, 2001.

Lou Dou Zi. "Looking at the Disposition of the Navy and Air Force after Restructuring the Establishment (1)," *JFJB*, July 14, 2004.

Lu Haozhong et al. "Assessment of the Military Situation in the Asian-Pacific Region in the Early Twenty-first Century and Its Impact on the Construction of Our Country's Strategic Nuclear Forces," in China Forum.

Lü Qiang et al. "A New Trend in U.S. Nuclear Weapons Programs: Importance Attached to Low-Yield Nuclear Weapons," *Guofang Bao*, May 20, 2003.

Luo Bing. "The CCP Plans to Set Up a National Security Council," *Qianshao* [Advance Guard] (Hong Kong), No. 6, 2001.

———. "To Oppose Sharply Hu [Jintao] and Wen [Jiabao], Jiang Zemin Ceaselessly Clamors for War," *Cheng Ming*, No. 8, 2004.

Luo Ping and Shi Keru. "Enhancing Air Offensive Capabilities," *Zhongguo Kongjun*, No. 3, 1997.

Luo Tongsong and Fan Hao. "An Interview with Wang Chenghan, Political Commissar of the Academy of Military Science," *RMRB*, July 30, 1988.

Ma Baoan, chief ed. *Zhanlüe Lilun Xuexi Zhinan* [A Guide to Strategic Theoretical Studies]. Beijing, 2002.

Ma Chih-chün and Ch'iu Ming-hui. "Exclusive Interview with Commander in Chief of the [Taiwanese] Air Force Huang Hsien-jung," *Hsin Hsin-wen* [The Journalist] (Taipei), May 31–June 6, 1998.

Ma Yongshun, ed. *Renmin Gongpu Zhou Enlai* [Zhou Enlai: A Servant of the People]. Beijing, 1991.

"Mainland China Reportedly Will Start Building Su-27s Next Year," *SJRB*, October 8, 1997.

"Many Su-27s Damaged by the Chinese Air Force," *SJRB*, April 15, 1997.

Mao Zedong [Mao Tse-tung]. "Analysis of the Classes in Chinese Society" (March 1926), in *Selected Works of Mao Tse-tung*, Vol. 1. Beijing, 1964.

———. "On Contradiction" (August 1937), in *Selected Works of Mao Tse-tung*, Vol. 1. Beijing, 1964.

———. "On the Correct Handling of Contradictions among the People" (February 27, 1957), in *Selected Works of Mao Tse-tung*, Vol. 4. Beijing, 1977.

———. "Faith in Victory Is Derived from Struggle" (October 20, 1965) [This is the major part of Mao Zedong's talk with a Party and government delegation from North Vietnam], http://english.pladaily.com.cn/special/mao/txt/w20.htm.

———. "Get Organized! (November 29, 1943)," in *Selected Works of Mao Tse-tung*, Vol. 3. Beijing, 1965.

———. *Jianguo Yilai Mao Zedong Wen'gao Di Shisan Ce (1969.1–1976.7)* [Mao Zedong's Manuscripts after the Founding of the Republic, Vol. 13: Jan. 1969– July 1976]. Beijing, 1998.

———. "On People's Democratic Dictatorship" (June 30, 1949), in *Selected Works of Mao Tse-tung*, Vol. 4. Beijing, 1961.

———. "Problems of Strategy in China's Revolutionary War" (December 1936), in *Selected Works of Mao Zedong*, Vol. 1. Beijing, 1964.

———. "Problems of War and Strategy" (November 6, 1938), in *Selected Works of Mao Tse-tung*, Vol. 2. Beijing, 1965.

———. "Remarks on the CMC Administrative Group's Draft to Strengthen Army-Wide Organization and Discipline (August 1969)," in Mao Zedong, *Jianguo Yilai*.

———. "Remarks on and Revision of the Draft of the Slogans for the Twentieth National Day Anniversary for Examination (August 1969)," in Mao Zedong, *Jianguo Yilai*.

———. "Remarks on Zhou Enlai's Report Regarding the Soviet Request to Communicate with Us by Telephone (March 1969)," in Mao Zedong, *Jianguo Yilai*.

———. "A Speech at the First Plenary Session of the CCP Ninth Central Committee (April 28, 1969)," in Mao Zedong, *Jianguo Yilai*.

———. "Talk with the American Correspondent Anna Louise Strong" (August 1946), in *Selected Works of Mao Tse-tung*, Vol. 4. Beijing, 1961.

———. "A Transcript of Mao Zedong's Speech as Chair to the Ninth CCP Congress (Part 2)," reprinted by *Huaxia Wenzhai*, supplementary issue (No. 349), www.cnd.org/HXWZ/ZK03/zk349.gb.html.

McDevitt, Michael. "Ruminations about How Little We Know about the PLA Navy," paper presented to the Conference on Chinese Military Affairs, October

10, 2000, www.ndu.edu/inss/China_Center/CMA_Conf_Octoo/paper14
.htm.

Mecham, Michael. "China Displays Export Air Defense Missile," *Aviation Week & Space Technology*, December 2, 1996.

Mei Xinsheng and Gao Xiaoling. *Wo Lin Fu Yinsi Mujizhe* [I Was an Eyewitness to Vice-Chairman Lin's Residence and Private (Matters)]. Beijing, 1988.

Mei Zhou. "The World Does Not Need a Nuclear Overlord," *RMRB*, March 19, 2002.

Men Xiangqing. "A Preliminary Study of Jiang Zemin's New Security Standpoint," *GFDXXB*, No. 2, 1999.

Mi Zhenyu. "The Basic Category of State Security and Our Country's State Security Strategy," in Ba Zhongtan, *Guojia Anquan*.

Mi Zhenyu and Chen Weimin. "The Determination of Military Strategic Goals Is a Question of the First Importance for Studying the Strategy for Defense Development," in *Guoji Xingshi yu Guofang Zhanlüe*.

"Military Exercises on Dongshan Island Use Russian-made Destroyers," *Sing Tao Jih Pao* (Star Island Daily) [Hong Kong] (Internet version), June 2 and 5, 2001.

Min Zengfu and Han Jibing. "The Basic Model for Air Defense in the Twenty-first Century," *Dangdai Kongjun* [Contemporary Air Force], No. 4, 1998.

Mulvenon, James C. "Chinese C4I Modernization: an Experiment in Open-Source Analysis," in James C. Mulvenon and Andrew N. D. Yang, eds., *A Poverty of Riches: New Challenges and Opportunities in PLA Research*. Santa Monica, Calif., 2003.

National Security Archive, ed. *Presidential Directives on National Security from Truman to Clinton*. Alexandria, Va., 1994.

New China Monthly Editorial Department. *Xin Zhongguo Wushi Nian Dashiji* [A Chronicle of Events in the New China over Fifty Years], Vol. 1. Beijing, 1999.

Nie Quanlin, chief ed. *Guoji Huanjing yu Weilai Guofang* [The International Environment and Future National Defense]. Beijing, 1989.

1997 Chung-kung Nien-pao [Yearbook on Communist China 1997]. Taipei, 1997.

Office of the General Political Department of the Chinese People's Liberation Army. *ZhongYue Bianjing Ziwei Huanji Zuozhan Zhengzhi Gongzuo Jingyan Xuanbian* [Compilation of Experience in Political Work in the Sino-Vietnamese Border Self-Defense Counterattack], Vol. 1. Beijing, 1980. (For internal circulation above the regimental level.)

———. *ZhongYue Bianjing Ziwei Huanji Zuozhan Zhengzhi Gongzuo Jingyan Xuanbian* [Compilation of Experience in Political Work in the Sino-Vietnamese Border Self-Defense Counterattack], Vol. 2. Beijing, 1980. (For internal circulation above the company level.)

Oksenberg, Michel. "Methods of Communications within the Chinese Bureaucracy," *China Quarterly*, No. 57 (January/March 1974).

Opall, Barbara. "Study Pits PLA Nukes against U.S., Taiwan," *Defense News*, Vol. 11, No. 38, September 23–29, 1996.

Opall, Barbara, and Michael J. Witt. "China Pits U.K. vs. Israel in AEW Quest," *Defense News*, Vol. 11, No. 31, August 5–11, 1996.

Oral Accounts of the Republic's Major Events Compilation Team of the Institute for Contemporary China Studies. *Gongheguo Yaoshi Koushu Shi* [Oral Accounts of the Republic's Major Events]. Changsha, 1999.

Ostermann, Christian F. "New Evidence on the Sino-Soviet Border Dispute, 1969–71," "The Cold War in Asia," in *Cold War Bulletin*, Nos. 6–7 (Winter 1995/1996).

Pan Shiying. "Have a Sober Understanding of the Principal Contradiction in Army Building," *JFJB*, Sept. 11, 1987.

———. *Xiandai Zhanlüe Sikao* [Considerations of Modern Strategies]. Beijing, 1993.

Peng Guangqian et al., eds. *Junshi Zhanlüe Jianlun* [Concise Studies on Military Strategy]. Beijing, 1989.

Peng Guangqian and Yao Youzhi, chief eds. *Zhanlüe Xue* [Studies of Strategy]. Beijing, 2001.

Peng Min, chief ed. *Dangdai Zhongguo de Jiben Jianshe* [Contemporary China's Capital Construction]. Beijing, 1989, Vol. 1.

Pillsbury, Michael, ed. *Chinese Views of Future Warfare*. Washington, D.C., 1997.

"PLA Air Force Officers Arrested for Spying for Taiwan," *South China Morning Post*, April 16, 2004.

"PLA Second Artillery Augmented a Railroad Mobile Missile Division," www.epochtimes.com/gb/1/4/8/n74185.htm

The Polemic on the General Line of the International Communist Movement. Beijing, 1965.

"PRC Pilot Lei Ch'iang Discusses Chinese Jet Fighter's Capabilities, Tactics," *Ch'uan-ch'iu Fang-wei Tsa-chih* [Global Defense Magazine] (Taipei), October 1, 2003.

"A Preliminary Discussion Regarding Organizing Fishing Craft for Sea-Crossing Operations," *JCZS*, No. 1, 2002.

"The Presentation Given by Li Wenzheng, Director of Institute 611, at the Beijing Aerospace University [November 25, 2003]," www.omnitalk.com/miliarch/messages/1917.html.

Propaganda Department, Political Department, People's Liberation Army General Staff, ed. *Junshi Jiyao* [A Major Collection of Military History]. Shanghai, 1997.

"A Public Notice of the General Staff's Institute 51 on Vacancies to Be Filled," http://stu.henu.edu.cn/jyzx/read.asp?newsclass=%D5%D0%C6%B8%D0%C5%CF%A2&offset=390&newsid=773.

Qi Changming. "Strengthen Strategic Studies, Deepen Military Reform," *JFJB*, May 8, 1988.

Qi Miyun. "The Shift of the Guiding Principle for Army Construction Judged by [the Decrease in] Military Funds," *JSSL*, No. 4, 1987.

Qi Shengping. "A Description of Marshal Liu Bocheng: The Prime Mover of the Military Academy [in Nanjing]," *Xinghuo Liaoyuan* [A Single Spark Can Start a Prairie Fire], No. 2, 1985.

Qiu Shi, ed. *Gongheguo Zhongda Shijian he Juece Neimu* [Inside Stories of the Republic's Major Events and Decisionmaking], Vol. 2. Beijing, 1997.

Qiu Yiwu. "The 'Great Wall Sword' Forged by Hot Blood: A Major and His Team Assembled for Training," *RMRB* (Overseas ed.), August 15, 1994.

Qu Aiguo. "General Wu Zhong Fought His Last Battle in 1979," in Qu Aiguo, *Baizhan Jiangxing Wu Zhong* [Wu Zhong: A General Who Has Fought One Hundred Battles]. Beijing, 2000. http://jngs.3322.org/mymemo/war79/file/136.htm.

Quan Yanchi. *Weixing Yang Chengwu zai 1967* [Traveling Incognito: Yang Chengwu in 1967]. Guangzhou, 1997.

———. "Xu Shiyou, Lin Biao, Zhu De, and Dong Biwu: Notable Figures in the Eyes of a Bodyguard in Guangzhou," www.shuku.net.8080/novles/zhuanji/wtgpuggtvyn/zisj61.html.

———. *Zhenshi Mao Zedong* [The True Mao Zedong]. Huhhot, 1998.

Quan Yanchi and Huang Li'na. *Tian Dao Zhou Hui yu Lushan Huiyi* [Heavenly Principle: Zhou Hui and the Lushan Conference]. Guangzhou, 1997.

"Reduced Growth Rate in Military Expenditure Will Not Hinder National Defense Construction," *Wen Wei Po*, March 9, 2003.

Ren Jian and Chen Mo. "Review and Reflections of the Third-Line Construction," *JSLS*, No. 1, 2001.

Ren Yujun. "Inside Information on the Sino-American Negotiations in Beijing for [the Solution of the] Air Collision," *Dazhong Wang* [Masses' Internet], www.dzdaily.com.cn/xinwen/200104200216.htm.

Research Section, General Office of the Standing Committee, National People's Congress, ed. *Renmin Daibiao Dahui Zhidu Jianshe Sishi Nian* [The Construction of the People's Congress System over the Past Forty Years]. Beijing, 1991.

"Review Sino-Soviet Relations at the Most Tense Moments," excerpt from Yao Jianping, *Zhu De de Zuihou Suiyue* [Zhu De's Last Years]. Beijing, 2002, http://news.eastday.com/epublish/gb/paper148/20020809/class014800023/hwz737187.htm.

"Revision of Some Articles of the Constitution of the Communist Party of China" (November 1, 1987), *Peking Review*, Vol. 30, No. 46 (November 16–22, 1987).

Robinson, Thomas W. "The Sino-Soviet Border Dispute: Background, Development and the March 1969 Clashes," *American Political Science Review*, Vol. 66, No. 4 (December 1972).

"Russia and China to Ink SU-30MK Supply Contract?" http://english.pravda.ru/diplomatic/2002/07/30/33488.html.

Sagan, Scott D., and Jeremi Suri. "The Madman Nuclear Alert: Secrecy, Signaling, and Safety in October 1969," *International Security*, Vol. 27, No. 4 (Spring 2003).

Sagan, Scott D., and Kenneth N. Waltz. *The Spread of Nuclear Weapons: A Debate*. New York, 1995.

Saiget, Robert J. "PRC Defense Budget Increase Earmarked for Developing Missiles," AFP (Hong Kong), March 7, 2003.

Scientific Research Department, National Defense University, ed. *Mao Zedong Junshi Sixiang zai Zhongguo de Shengli yu Fazhan* [The Victory and Development of Mao Zedong's Military Thought in China]. Beijing, 1994.

Scobell, Andrew. *China's Use of Military Force: Beyond the Great Wall and the Long March*. New York, 2003.

———, ed. *The Costs of Conflict: The Impact on China of a Future War*. Carlisle, Penn., 2001.

Second Artillery Team of the Arms Teaching and Research Section, National Defense University. "The Iron Fist of the Army Frightens the Enemy," *GFDXXB*, Nos. 8–9, 1997.

Segal, Gerald. *Defending China*. Oxford, England, 1985.

Sha Li and Min Li, eds. *Zhongguo Jiu Ci Da Fabing* [China's Nine Major Armed Conflicts]. Chengdu, 1992.

Shambaugh, David. *Modernizing China's Military: Progress, Problems, and Prospects*. Berkeley, Calif., 2002.

Shan Lan. *Hong Qiang Nei de Mishu Men* [The Secretaries inside the Red Wall (of Zhongnanhai)]. Yanji, 1998, Vols. 1, 2.

Shang Jinsuo et al., eds. *Mao Zedong Junshi Sixiang yu Gao Jishu Tiaojian xia Jubu Zhanzheng* [Mao Zedong's Military Thought and Local War under High-Tech Conditions]. Beijing, 2002.

Shang Lin. "Strategic Nuclear Counteroffensive Campaign," *JCZS*, No. 9, 2004.

Shao Zhenting et al. "Theoretical Thinking on Deng Xiaoping's Views on the Buildup of the Air Force and the Reform of Operational Arts," *ZGJSKX*, No. 4, 1996.

She Shui and Xiao Yue. "Selection of Papers Submitted to China's First International Symposium on 'Sun Tzu's Art of War,'" *JSSL*, No. 5, 1989.

Shi Baodong. "A Preliminary Investigation of the Cooperative Security Model," *Guojia Anquan Tongxun*, No. 1, 2000.

Shi Dongbing. *Duanzan de Chunqiu Hua Guofeng Xiatai Neimu* [An Inside Story: The Short Period of the Good Times before Hua Guofeng Was Driven from Office]. Hong Kong, 1995.

———. *Feng Zou Jingdu* [A Sudden Gale Struck Beijing (A Series of Records of Actual Events in the Great Cultural Revolution, No. 2)]. Hong Kong, 1992.

———. *Fengbao yu Niliu* [The Storm and an Adverse Current (A Series of Records of Actual Events in the Great Cultural Revolution, Vol. 3)]. Hong Kong, 1992.

———. *Huairen Tang Zhengbian* [A Coup d'état at Huairen Hall (in Zhongnanhai)], Vol. 3. Hong Kong, 1999.

———. *Lushan Zhen Mianmu* [The True Face of Lushan]. Hong Kong, 1997.

————. *Xumu cong Diaoyutai Lakai* [The Prologue (to the Cultural Revolution) Initiated at the Diaoyutai]. Hong Kong, 1992.

Shi Yan. "My Impressions of Du Ping's Memoir 'At the CPV's Headquarters,'" *RMRB*, July 19, 1990.

"Shortcomings of the Security in Chinese Metropolises in the Eyes of a Japanese Security Specialist," www.chinanews.com.cn/n/2004-01-30/26/396172.html.

Shu Yun. "Huang, Wu, Li, and Qiu on the Day before the 913 Incident," www.cnd.org/hxwxz/zk05/zk472.gb.html.

Shui Gong. *Zhongguo Yuanshuai He Long* [Chinese Marshal He Long]. Beijing, 1995.

Si Yanwen. "Naval Military Academic Research Plays an Increasingly Dynamic Role," *JFJB*, Sept. 21, 1989.

"Some Assumptions on the Number of Our Country's Nuclear Warheads," a reprinted article from *Hsiang-kang Shang Pao*, www.81force.com/nuclear/guess_no.htm.

Song Shilun, chief ed. *Zhongguo Dabaike Quanshu Junshi* [Chinese Encyclopedia (Military Affairs)], Vols. 1, 2. Beijing, 1989.

Song Yichang. "The Startup of China's Modern Aviation Industry and Reflections on It," *Zhanlüe yu Guanli* [Strategy and Management], No. 4, 1996.

Song Zhixia and Wang Shiqing. "Two Magical 'Briefcases': A True Description of a Portable Device for Psychological Testing and Training," *Zhongguo Guofang Bao*, January 29, 2002.

Stokes, Mark A. *China's Strategic Modernization: Implications for the United States.* Carlisle, Penn., 1999.

"Strategic Changes in the Guiding Principle for Building up China's Army in the 1990s," *Qiao Bao*, July 31, 1997.

"Strategic Research Is a Key Link in the Successful Realization of the Strategic Change [in the guiding ideology for our army building]," *JFJB*, May 16, 1986.

"Struggle to Smash the Counterrevolutionary Coup D'etat of the Lin Piao Anti-Party Clique" (Top Secret Document *Zhongfa* 1972, No. 24), in Michael Y. M. Kau, ed., *The Lin Piao Affair*. White Plains, New York, 1975.

Su Bei. "Why Does Bush Introduce Changes into Military Strategy? Lifting the Veil from the New U.S. Strategy of Resorting to 'Preemptive Attack,'" *JFJB*, June 4, 2002.

Su Caiqing. "On Lin Biao's No. 1 Order," *Huaxia Wenzhai*, supplementary issue (No. 326), www.cnd.org/HXWZ/ZK03/zk326.gb.html.

Su Ha. *Zhonggong Danei Zongguan Zeng Qinhong de Quanli zhi Lu* [Zeng Qinhong's Path to Power, A Big Manager of the CCP Center]. Hong Kong, 2001.

Su Kuoshan. "The Birth of Instrumentation Ships, Distant Observer," *Xin Guancha* [New Observation], No. 17, 1988.

Su Xin et al. "Probe China's Contingency Mechanism in Foreign Affairs," excerpt of an article in *Ershi Yi Shiji Jingji Daobao* [The Twenty-first Century

Economic Monitor], March 11, 2003, www7.chinesenewsnet.com/gb/Main-News/Forums/BackStage/2003_3_12_8_22_3_716.html.

"SU-27/J-11 Fighter Aircraft," www.sinodefence.com/airforce/aircraft/fighter/su27.asp.

"SU-27/SU-30/J-11," www.globalsecurity.org/military/world/china/su-30.htm.

Sun Daluo. *Mao Zedong Quanshu Shi* [How Mao Zedong Played Politics]. Hong Kong, 2001.

Sun Jianguo and Song Dongjun. "The 'Nerve Center' of the Strategic Missile Forces," *Liaowang*, No. 39, 1988.

Sun Kaitai. "The Military Thinking of Wu Qi," *Hunan Shifan Daxue Shehui Kexue Xuebao* [Hunan Normal University Journal of Social Science] (Changsha), No. 2, 1986.

Sun Yamin. "Gaining Some Ideas from the Afghanistan War for Our Preparations for Military Struggle," *Junshi Wenzhai*, No. 7, 2002.

Sun Zhenjiang. "Exploration of the Factors Restricting Command in Joint Operations," *GFDXXB*, No. 6, 2000.

Suo Li Weng. "An Analysis of Vice-Chairman Lin's No. 1 Order," http://bbs.omnitalk.org/military/messages/22010.html.

"A Support System Set Up in China Allowing Military Aircraft to Land on Freeways," *Qiao Bao*, May 31, 1996.

Swaine, Michael D. *The Role of the Chinese Military in National Security Policymaking*. Santa Monica, Calif., 1998.

Taiwan Affairs Office and the Information Office of the State Council. "The One-China Principle and the Taiwan Issue" (February 21, 2000), Xinhua, February 21, 2000.

"The Taiwan Affairs Office of CPC Central Committee and Taiwan Affairs Office of State Council Are Authorized to Issue a Statement on Current Cross-Straits Relations," Xinhua, May 17, 2004.

"Taiwan's Defense Minister Flatly Admits: 'The Nationalist Army Can at Most Resist an Attack [from Mainland China] for Two Weeks,'" www7.chinesenewsnet.com/gb/mainnews/inonews/Taiwan/2005_3_9_14_13_11_513.html.

Tan Jingqiao, chief ed. *KangMei YuanChao Zhanzheng* [The War to Resist America and Aid Korea]. Beijing, 1990.

Tan Ren. "A Rough Opinion on Exercising Command over Joint Operations," in Wen and Fang, 1998.

Tang Chaobo and Wu Xudong. "A Certain Communications Regiment of the Second Artillery Enhanced Capabilities for Ensuring Communications in Field Operations," *JFJB*, July 12, 2001.

Tang Fuquan. "Recognition of Our Country's Maritime Strategy," *JFJB*, Sept. 15, 1989.

Tao Dazhao. *Dongfang Shen Lü lai zi Zhongguo Daodan Budui de Baogao* [A Magical Army in the East: A Report from China's Missile Forces]. Beijing, 1996.

Tao Hanzhang. *Sun Tzu's Art of War: The Modern Chinese Interpretation.* New York, 1987.

Teng Lianfu and Jiang Fusheng. *Kongjun Zuozhan Yanjiu* [Studies on Air Force Operations]. Beijing, 1990.

"Three Purposes of the Military Maneuvers at Dongshan Island," *RMRB* (Internet version), July 19, 2004.

Tian Jingmei. *The Bush Administration's Nuclear Strategy and Its Implications for China's Security.* Stanford, Calif., Center for International Security and Cooperation, 2003.

Tian Yi. "Will China Engage in TMD?" *Junshi Wenzhai*, No. 5, 2000.

Tretiak, Daniel. "China's Vietnam War and Its Consequences," *China Quarterly*, No. 80 (December 1979).

2001 Chung-kung Nien-pao [Yearbook on Communist China 2001]. Taipei, 2001.

Tyler, Patrick. *A Great Wall: Six Presidents and China.* New York, 1999.

"'Unification Law' Is the Legal Framework for Maintaining Cross-Strait Stability," *Zhongguo Xinwen She*, October 26, 2004.

"A Unit under the Second Artillery Vigorously Does a Good Job of Military Security . . . ," *JFJB*, April 19, 2001.

"The United States Also Sells Weapons," *U.S. News & World Report*, May 27, 1991.

United States, Central Intelligence Agency, National Intelligence Council. *Foreign Missile Developments and the Ballistic Missile Threat through 2015.* Washington, D.C., December 2001.

———, Congress, House of Representatives. *Report of the Select Committee on U.S. National Security and Military/Commercial Concerns with the People's Republic Of China*, Vol 1. Washington, D.C., 1999.

———, Department of Defense. *Annual Report on the Military Power of the People's Republic of China.* Submitted to Congress on May 28, 2004. Washington, D.C., 2004.

———, *Nuclear Posture Review.* Submitted to Congress December 31, 2001. Washington, D.C., 2002.

———, Department of State. *Foreign Relations of the United States, 1969–1976.* Washington, D.C.: Internet online edition, www.state.gov/r/pa/ho/frus/nixon/i/.

———, White House. *The National Security Strategy of the United States of America.* Washington, D.C., September 2002.

Wang Chao-chün. *Shui Sha le Lin Piao* [Who Killed Lin Biao?]. Taipei, 1996.

Wang Dinglie, chief ed. *Dangdai Zhongguo Kongjun* [Contemporary China's Air Force]. Beijing, 1989

Wang Dongxing. *Wang Dongxing Huiyi Mao Zedong yu Lin Biao Fan'geming Jituan de Douzhen* [Wang Dongxing's Recollections of the Struggle between Mao Zedong and the Lin Biao Counterrevolutionary Clique]. Beijing, 1997.

Wang Fa'an and Zhang Jie. "Faced with Breakthroughs and Leaps: A Review of the Construction and Reform of the Army in the Ninth Five-Year Period," *JSLS*, No. 4, 2001.

Wang Fan. "Former Deputy Commander of the Central Guards Regiment Wu Jicheng Asks: 'Why Did Premier Zhou Want to See Me before His Death?'" www.shuku.net:8080/novels/zhuanji/phizwrnbjf/ycxx42.html.

———. *Muji Lishi Guanyu Dangdai Zhongguo Dashi Weiren de Koushu Shilu* [Oral Records of Those Who Witnessed China's Major Events and Great Men]. Changsha, 1998.

Wang Fulin. "People's Guerilla War under High-Tech Conditions," *Yunnan Guofang* [Yunnan National Defense] (Kunming), No. 1, 1998.

"Wang Gang: A Person Trusted by Hu Jintao, Wen Jiabao, and Zeng Qinhong," www.secretchina.com/news/articles/5/2/19/86071.html.

Wang Guozhong. "The Summary Report of the Symposium on State Security Strategy," in Ba Zhongtan, *Guojia Anquan.*

Wang Hai and Zhu Guang. "Consolidate Air Force Pilots' Training with Combat Capabilities as a Criterion," in Wang Runsheng, *Kongjun Huiyi Shiliao.*

Wang Houqing and Zhang Xingye, chief eds. *Zhanyi Xue* [Military Campaign Studies]. Beijing, 2001.

Wang Jianghuai. "Probing the Problem of Establishing Our Army's Command-and-Control System in Joint Operations," *GFDXXB*, Nos. 2–3, 1997.

Wang Jianyun. "A Visit to Major General Li Deyi, an Academician of the China Academy of Engineering," *Zhongguo Kongjun*, No. 2, 2001.

Wang Kexue. "Did (General) Tan Furen Force Zhou Enlai's Special Airplane to Land?" *Bainian Chao*, No. 6, 2003.

Wang Li. *Wang Li Fansi Lu* [Wang Li's Reflections], Vols. 1, 2. Hong Kong, 2001.

Wang Min. "The Evolution of China's Military Establishment," *Junshi Wenzhai*, No. 8, 1999.

Wang Nianyi. "Materials on the 'Adverse Current in February [1967],'" in Party History Research Section of the Chinese Revolutionary Museum, ed., *Gongheguo Zhongda Lishi Shijian Shushi* [A True Description of Major Historical Events in the Republic]. Beijing, 1999.

Wang Qiang and He Tianjin. "More Than 1,000 Veteran Soldiers from a Certain Base of the Second Artillery Carried 'Security Regulations' to Their Hometowns," *JFJB*, December 3, 2004.

Wang Runsheng, chief ed. *Kongjun Huiyi Shiliao* [The Air Force: Historical Materials on Recollections]. Beijing, 1972.

Wang Shangrong. "Several Major Battles after the Founding of the New China," in Oral Accounts.

Wang Shanhe and Chen Hanzhong. "'Attack' at Dawn," *JFJB*, August 15, 2001.

Wang Te-Chun. "Central Government Fully Accepts Good Proposal on Unification of Motherland," *Ta Kung Pao* (Internet version), May 13, 2004.

Wang Wenjie. "Jiang Zemin Solemnly Announces That the Party Central Leadership and the CMC Have Decided to Cut Down Our Army by 200,000," *JFJB*, September 2, 2003.

Wang Wenrong, chief ed. *Zhanlüe Xue* [Studies of Strategy]. Beijing, 1999.

Wang Xiaohua and Sun Zhenjiang. "The Major Theoretical and Practical Differences between China and the United States Concerning Joint Operations," *GFDXXB*, No. 7, 2000.

Wang Xiaojun and Xia Hongqing. "A Certain Brigade of the Second Artillery Introduces Psychological Testing into the Training Field," *JFJB*, August 21, 2002.

Wang Yufang. "Inspired by Their Assignments: A Description of Assignment Management at a Certain Technical Regiment of the Second Artillery," *JFJB*, December 19, 1997.

Wang Yusheng. "Reconsidering China's Strategy of 'Keeping a Low Posture,'" a reprint from *Huanqiu* [The World], www.cas.ac.cn/html/Dir/2004/07/08/4141.htm.

Wang Yuxiang et al. "The Guiding Role of Mao Zedong's Military Thinking for Local Wars," *Mao Zedong Sixiang Yanjiu* [Studies on Mao Zedong's Thought] (Chengdu), No. 3, 1988.

Wang Zhenping. "The Requirement for the Construction of the Second Artillery Is Determined by the Development of the Military Situation in the Asian-Pacific Region," in China Forum.

Wang Zhicheng. "Understand Rules and Undertake Practice to Probe into a New Path for Training for Joint Operations," *GFDXXB*, No. 5, 1999.

Wang Zhuo and Cui Xianghua. "[Develop] Science and Technology to Strengthen the Army," in Li Dianren, chief ed., *Wen Tu Bing Shuo Zhongguo Renmin Jiefangjun Dashi Jujiao* [Focusing on the Major Events of the Chinese People's Liberation Army in Both Written and Pictorial Sources]. Beijing, 2002.

Wei Chuan. "Contemplation after the March 14 Sea Battle," *Haiyang Shijie* [Marine World], No. 3, 1989.

Wen An. "From Acting in Collusion to Irreconcilability: The Lin Biao and Jiang Qing Cliques in the 'Cultural Revolution,'" *Dangshi Bocai* [Encyclopedic Knowledge of the Party's History] (Shijiazhuang), No. 1, 2001.

Wen Feng. *Shentan Xia de Lin Biao* [The Lin Biao Who Came Down from the Altar]. Beijing: 1993.

Wen Honghai and Fang Min, chief eds. *Zhongguo Dangdai Guofang Wenku* [A Collection of Essays on Contemporary China's Defense], Vol. 1. Beijing, 1998.

Wen Tao. "PLA Bent on Seizing 'Information Control,'" *Ching Pao* [The Mirror] (Hong Kong), No. 6, 2002.

Wen Zhi. "The Mysterious Espionage Confrontation Across the Strait," *Guangjiaojing*, No. 2, 2004.

"What Problems Exist in Our Country's Aviation Industry for the Development of Military Aircraft?" http://bbs.xilu.com/cgi-bin/bbs/view?forum=aerofield& message=6650.

"What Should the 'Second Artillery Corps' Do in the Face of 'Nuclear Encirclement?'" *Xizang Wenxue* [Tibetan Literature], supplementary issue, No. 4, 1998.

Whiting, Allen S. *The Chinese Calculus of Deterrence: India and Indochina.* Ann Arbor, 1975.

"Why Does China Belatedly Develop Its New-Type Military Aircraft?" http://jings.3322.org/mymemo/military/airforce/201.htm.

"Why Should You Xigui Be Promoted to General When Deng Xiaoping's Chief Bodyguard Zhang Baozhong Was Only a Lieutenant General?" published by *Yazhou Shibao* [Asia Times], www.kanzhongguo.com/news/articles/4/8/23/70739.html.

"Will the U.S. Really Intervene Militarily in the Taiwan Strait?" *Renmin Haijun* [People's Navy], August 21, 2004.

Wortzel, Larry M., ed. *The Chinese Armed Forces in the Twenty-first Century.* Carlisle, Penn., 1999.

Wu Chunqiu. "The Iraq War: [U.S. Officials] Mistakenly Recite 'Sun Tzu's Art of War,'" *Guofang Bao*, April 27, 2004.

———. *Zhanlüe Yanjiu yu Xiandai Guofang* [Strategic Studies and Modern Defense]. Shanghai, 1988.

Wu Chunqiu and Dong Lingyun. "Defense Strategy," a special report, 1986, excerpts of this report reprinted in *Zhanzheng yu Zhanlüe Lilun Jicui* [The Essence of Theories on War and Strategy]. Beijing, 1989.

Wu De. "The Lushan Conference and the Lin Biao Incident," in Oral Accounts.

Wu Donghai and Wang Guangxian. "Try to Use Mao Zedong's Methodology for Ascertaining the Trends of War and Peace to Analyze the Developing Trends of War and Peace in the Transition from an Old World Pattern to a New World Pattern," in Scientific Research Department.

Wu Jianhua. "Chairman Mao Meticulously Cultivated His Bodyguards," *Bainian Chao*, No. 10, 2003.

Wu Jicheng and Wang Fan. *Hongse Jingwei: Zhongyang Jingwei Ju Yuan Fu Juzhang Wu Jicheng Huiyilu* [Red Guards: Memoir of Wu Jicheng, Former Deputy Director of the Central Guards Bureau]. www.bookdns.com/zhuanji/jzzhuanji/hsejwei/hsejwei.html.

Wu Jiulong, chief ed. *Sun Zi Jiao Yi* [Checked and Translated (Text of) Sun Tzu (on the Art of War)]. Beijing, 1990.

Wu Ke. "Concerned about PLA's Military Exercise, Taiwan Mobilizes Troops Urgently," *Renmin Wang*, June 8, 2001.

Wu Lengxi. *Yi Mao Zhuxi: Wo Qinshen Jingli de Ruogan Zhongda Lishi Shijian Pianduan* [Cherish the Memory of Chairman Mao: Fragments of Those Major Events I Myself Have Experienced]. Beijing, 1995.

Wu Miaofa. *Waijiao Caizi Qiao Guanhua* [Gifted Diplomat Qiao Guanhua]. Shenzhen, 1998.

Wu Qingli and Xie Jingsheng. "Analysis of Global Force Readjustment by the U.S. Military," *JFJB*, September 1, 2004.

Wu Xiangting and Han Xuejing. *Gensui Mao Zedong Jishi* [Accounts of Events That Occurred When We Followed behind Mao Zedong]. Taiyuan, 1991.

Wu Xudong et al. "A Description of Zhang Junxiang, the Commander of a Certain Regiment of the Second Artillery," *Guofang* [National Defense], No. 9, 1999.

Wu Xujun. "Mao Zedong's Five-Step Wise Strategy: The Whole Story of Opening the Door for Sino-American Relations," in Lin Ke et al., *Lishi de Zhenshi* [The Truth of History]. Beijing, 1998.

Xi Wang. "Landing Operations and Meteorology under Nuclear Conditions," *JCZS*, No. 3, 2004.

Xiao Sike. *Chaoji Shenpan Tu Men Jiangjun Canyu Shenli Lin Biao Fan'geming Jituan Qinli Ji* [The Super Trial: General Tu Men's Personal Experience Participating in the Trial of Lin Biao's Counterrevolutionary Clique], www.boxun.com/hero/linbiao/43_1.shtml.

Xiao Xinli, chief ed. *Mao Zedong yu Gongheguo Zhongda Lishi Shijian* [Mao Zedong and the Republic's Major Historical Events]. Beijing, 2001.

Xiao Yiping and Shi Yousong. "A Review of the Party's Collective Leadership in the Democratic Revolutionary Period," *Zhonggong Dangshi Yanjiu* [Studies on the History of the CCP], No. 5, 1988.

Xiao Yusheng. "Stride Forward toward the New Century: The Newest Development of Chinese Military Might," *Jiefangjun Shi Jia Hexin Qikan* [The Liberation Army's Ten Best Periodicals], No. 3, 1998.

Xie Guang, chief ed. *Dangdai Zhongguo de Guofang Keji Shiye* [Contemporary China's Defense Science and Technology Cause]. Beijing, 1992, Vol. 2.

Xie Guoliang. "Studies on the Thought of 'Sun Tzu's Art of War,'" *JSSL*, Nos. 1, 2, 3, 4, 5, 1986.

Xin Si. "When Can China Possess an Aircraft Carrier?" *Haiyang Shijie*, No. 3, 1989.

Xiong Lei. "Mao Zedong around the 'September 13 Incident' (of 1971)," in Wang Dongxing et al., *Lin Biao Taowang Zhenxiang* [The Actual Facts of Lin Biao's Escape (from China)]. Hong Kong, 2001.

———. "[Recollection of] an Event Prior to the September 13 Incident," in Xiong Xianghui, *Wo de Qingbao*.

Xiong Xianghui. "Mao Zedong's 'Unexpected' Victory: Recollections of the Recovery of Our Country's Seat in the United Nations," in Xiong Xianghui, *Wo de Qingbao*.

———. "The Prelude to the Opening of Sino-American Relations: The Judgment and Proposals of Four Senior Marshals Regarding the International Situation in 1969," in CCP Central Party History Research Section, *Zhonggong Dangshi Ziliao*, Vol. 42, 1992.

————. *Wo de Qingbao yu Waijiao Shengya* [My Intelligence and Diplomatic Career]. Beijing, 1999.

Xiong Yuxiang. "[The U.S.] Still Attempts to Seek Hegemony in Strategic Readjustment," *Huanqiu Junshi Banyuekan*, first half of March 2002.

Xu Feng and Sha Zhiliang. "President Jiang Zemin Is Concerned about the Modernization of the PLA Naval Air Force," *Xinhua*, September 16, 2002.

Xu Jian. *Daguo Changjian: Zhongguo Zhanlüe Daodan Budui Jishi* [The Long Sword of a Great Power: A Description of China's Strategic Missile Force]. Beijing, 1995.

Xu Jingyue, "Defense Strategic Research Is Now Ascendant," *RMRB* (Overseas ed.), July 26, 1987.

Xu Kui. "Rationally Recognize and Consider the Nationwide Massive War Preparations," *JSLS*, No. 5, 2002.

Xu Minjie. "How to Subdue the Enemy in a Future War," Parts 1, 2, *Zhongguo Kongjun*, Nos. 1, 2, 2003.

Xu Ping. "The Evolution of the PLA's Greater Military Regions after the Founding of the PRC (Part 2)," *JSSL*, No. 6, 2004.

Xue Xinglin, chief ed. *Zhanyi Lilun Xuexi Zhinan* [A Study Guide to Operational Theory]. Beijing, 2002.

Yan Fangming. "A Review of Third-Line Construction," *Dangshi Yanjiu* [Studies on the Party's History], No. 4, 1987.

Yan Jingtang. "A Brief Introduction to the Evolution of the Central Military Commission," *Dangshi Yanjiu*, No. 2, 1983.

Yan Mingzai. "The Process of Issuing the 'No. 1 Order' in 1969," excerpt of an article published by the author in *Dangshi Xinxi Bao* [Party History Information Newspaper]. http://202.96.224.197/dabl/zjjm/200305290009.html.

Yang Baoshun. "PLA Second Artillery Engineering Unit Is Undertaking Dozens of Large Defense Emplacement Projects," *JFJB*, September 5, 2001.

Yang Chengwu. "A Call on Chairman Mao," *Dangshi Yanjiu yu Jiaoxue*, No. 5, 1990.

Yang Dezhi. "Command and Control of the Armed Forces," in Song Shilun, Vol. 1.

Yang Guihua and Chen Chuangang, eds. *Gongheguo Jundui Huimou Zhongda Shijian Juece he Jingguo Xieshi* [Review of the Republic's Army: The Decision-making Process and True Record of Major Events]. Beijing, 1999.

Yang Guoliang. "The Third-Generation Leadership of the Party and the Qualitative Construction of the Second Artillery," *ZGJSKX*, No. 3, 1997.

Yang Guoyu, chief ed. *Dangdai Zhongguo Haijun* [Contemporary China's Navy]. Beijing, 1987.

Yang Hong and Zhou Men. "The Beijing Greater Military Region Command Has Successfully Organized a Networking Confrontation Exercise between [Two Group Armies Stationed in] Remote Places," *JSSL*, Nos. 2–3, 2000.

Yang Jinhua and Huang Bin, chief eds. *Zuozhan Zhihui Gailun* [An Introduction to Operational Command]. Beijing, 2001.

Yang Kuisong. *Mao Zedong yu Mosike de En En Yuan Yuan* [The Feeling of Gratitude and Resentment between Mao Zedong and Moscow]. Nanchang, 1999.

Yang Qinhua. "The History of Contacts between Deng Xiaoping and Mao Zedong," *Sichuan Dangshi* [Party History (Sichuan)] (Chengdu), No. 4, 1994.

Yang Shangkun. *Yang Shangkun Huiyilu* [Yang Shangkun's Memoirs], www.kanzhongguo.com/news/articles/2/8/8/22617.html.

Yang Yinlu. *Wo Gei Jiang Qing Dang Mishu* [(Reminiscence of The Years When) I Was Jiang Qing's Secretary]. Hong Kong, 2000.

Yang Yongmei. "Principles Shaping the Command System for Joint Operations," *GFDXXB*, No. 8, 2001.

Yang Zanyu. "Chinese Students Shed Blood at Red Square in Moscow," *Bainian Chao*, No. 3, 1998.

Yao Jianping. *Zhu De de Zuihou Suiyue* [Zhu De's Last Years], www.shuku.net:8082/novels/zhuanji/zddzhsy/zddzhsy24.html.

Yao Jun. "The Scientific Research Work of the Air Force," in Wang Runsheng, *Kongjun Huiyi Shiliao.*

Yi Ming. "Xiao Jingguang and Su Zhenhua Who Had Staged a Comeback," Supplementary issue (No. 366), www.cnd.org/GB/HXWZ/ZK04/zk366.gb.html.

Yin Weixing. "The Weight That Shapes a Global Balance," *Zhongguo Qingnian* [China Youth], No. 1–2, 1987.

Ying. "The Roles of the 'JH-7' and 'J-10' in the PLAAF," www.chilicity.com/publishhtml/1/2003-09-18/20030918102723.html.

Yu Guangyuan. "Thirty-six Days That Changed the Course of Chinese History," *Bainian Chao*, No. 6, 1998.

Yu Guantang, chief ed. *Kongjun Zhanlüe Yanjiu* [On Air Strategy]. Beijing, 1991.

Yu Huating and Liu Guoyu, chief eds. *Gao Jishu Zhanzheng yu Jundui Zhiliang Jianshe* [High-Tech Wars and the Army's Qualitative Construction]. Beijing, 1994.

Yu Qifen, chief ed. *Guoji Zhanlüe Lun* [On International Strategy]. Beijing, 1998.

Yu Ruxin. "A Face-to-Face Talk with Qi Benyu," *Huaxia Wenzhai*, supplementary issue (No. 366), www.cnd.org/GB/HXWZ/ZK04/zk366.gb.html.

Yu Shusheng. "An Elementary Introduction to the Coordination between Ground Forces and the Air Force in Joint Operations," *GFDXXB*, No. 5, 1999.

Yu Yongbo, ed. *China Today: Defense Science and Technology*, Vol. 1. Beijing, 1993.

Yu Zemin. "Sun Tzu's Cautions Thought of Fighting a War and Our Country's Security Strategy," *GFDXXB*, No. 4, 2001.

Yuan Jiaxin. "Pondering the Strategic Shift of the Guiding Ideology for Our Army's Construction," *JSSL*, No. 4, 1987.

Yuan Jin. "Opinions on Strengthening Our Army's Information Warfare Capabilities," *GFDXXB*, No. 9, 2001.

Yuan Jun. "The Applicable Development of the Key Early-Warning Technologies of Ballistic Missiles," www.bbs.xilu.com/cgi-bin/bbs/view?forum=bqlt&emssage=114032.

Yuan Wei, chief ed. *Mao Zedong Junshi Huodong Jishi* [A Record of Mao Zedong's Military Activities]. Beijing, 1994.

Yuan Wenxian. "Challenges Facing the Construction and Development of the Commands in the New Situation," *GFDXXB*, No. 1, 2000.

————. "Several Salient Characteristics of the Regulations Regarding Our Army's Commands," *GFDXXB*, No. 1, 1997.

Yuan Zhengling. "On the Thinking and Practice of Conventional Deterrence after the Founding of the New China," *JSLS*, No. 1, 2002.

Yue Siping and Chou Baoshan. "The Formation and Conclusion of the CCP First-Generation Central Collective Leadership," *JSLS*, No. 3, 2001.

Yun Hai. "Assaults by Tank and Armored Forces in Nuclear Contaminated Areas in an Amphibious Campaign," *JCZS*, No. 4, 2004.

Yun Zhen. "Three Nuclear Submarines Launched Guided Missiles to Accurately Hit Targets; Our Army's Exercises at Dongshan Island Ended Spectacularly; China's Submarines Become Focus of World Attention," *Renmin Wang*, August 31, 2001.

Zeng Tai. "Special Operations in an Amphibious Campaign under Nuclear Conditions," *JCZS*, No. 8, 2004.

Zeng Youqing. "The Creator of the Mysterious 'Communication of Last Resort': A Description of Military Scientist Situ Mengtian," *Mingren Zhuanji* [Biographies of Famous Persons], No. 1, 2000.

Zhan Ping and Zhao Fengyun. "The Second Artillery Standardizes All Its Equipment," *JFJB*, December 31, 2001.

Zhan Xuexi. "The Strategic Features of a Modern Campaign," *GFDXXB*, No. 11, 1997.

Zhang Aiping. "A Speech at a Conference Attended by Leading Cadres from Aviation Industrial Enterprises (March 6, 1981)," in *Zhang Aiping Junshi Wenxuan* [Selected Military Writings of Zhang Aiping]. Beijing, 1994.

————, chief ed. *Zhongguo Renmin Jiefangjun* [The Chinese People's Liberation Army]. Beijing, 1994, Vol. 2.

Zhang Changzhi. "Air Deterrence and National Resolve," *Zhonguo Kongjun*, No. 1, 1997.

Zhang Chengang et al. "A Tentative Study on Some Questions about the Strategy for Our Army Building in Peacetime," *Weilai yu Fazhan* [Future and Development], No. 3, 1987.

Zhang Huairui and Zhu Hengxing. "Resist the Enemy's Surprise Attacks on Our Country's Coastal Areas by Employing the Integrated Combat Capabilities of the Army, Navy, and Air Force," *GFDXXB*, No. 7, 1987.

Zhang Jiajun. *Jueqi de Zhanlüe Daodan Buluo Qun* [Strategic Missile Bases Have Suddenly Appeared]. Beijing, 1991.

Zhang Jiechuan. "Several Questions about the Air Force's Combat Employment in Joint Operations," *GFDXXB*, Nos. 2–3, 1998.

Zhang Junben and He Tianjin. "A Description of Zhang Jincheng, Director of the On-Site Equipment Installation Teaching and Research Section of the Second Artillery's Command Academy," *JFJB*, May 9, 2002.

Zhang Lianchao and Ma Sancheng. "A True Description of the Efforts Made by the Lanzhou Military Region Command to Train Communication Officers Needed for a High-Tech War," *JFJB*, December 11, 1997.

Zhang Lianyin. "The Impact of the New Corps-Brigade-Battalion System on the Management and Education of Armed Forces and Its Countermeasures," *GFDXXB*, No. 8, 1999.

Zhang Lijun and Liao Yanling. "On Jiang Zemin's Strategic Thinking of Strengthening the Army through Science and Technology," *GFDXXB*, No. 7, 2002.

Zhang Peigao, chief ed. *Lianhe Zhanyi Zhihui Jiaocheng* [Teaching Materials on the Command of Joint Operations]. Beijing, 2001.

———. "A Summary of Several Major Issues Concerning the Command and Control of Armed Forces," *GFDXXB*, No. 7, 1999.

Zhang Qinsheng et al. "Research on and Exploration of the Local War Theory," *Liaowang* (Overseas ed.), September 15, 1986.

Zhang Tingfa and Gao Houliang. "The Construction of the Air Force Has Entered a New Historical Stage after Bringing Order out of Chaos," in Wang Runsheng, *Kongjun Huiyi Shiliao*.

Zhang Wannian, chief ed. *Dangdai Shijie Junshi yu Zhongguo Guofang* [Contemporary Military Affairs of the World and China's National Defense]. Beijing, 1999.

Zhang Weiping, chief ed. *Zhongguo Tese de Guofang Xiandaihua zhi Lu* [The Path to Defense Modernization with Chinese Characteristics]. Beijing, 1997.

Zhang Xiaogang. "A Brief Account of Mao Zedong's Notion of Third-Line Construction," *JSLS*, No. 2, 2001.

Zhang Xiaojun and Xu Jia. "The Iraq War and the U.S. Military Reform," *JFJB*, April 23, 2003.

Zhang Yunsheng. *Maojiawan Jishi Lin Biao Mishu Huiyilu* [What I Saw and Heard in Maojiawan: The Memoirs of a Secretary of Lin Biao]. Beijing, 1988.

———. "Talk about Lin Biao's 'No. 1 Order,'" *Huaxia Wenzhai*, supplementary issue (No. 323), www.cnd.org/HXWZ/zk03/zk323.gb.html.

Zhang Zhen. "Several Questions about the Development of Operational Arts for Our Army," *GFDXXB*, No. 2, 1986.

———. *Zhang Zhen Huiyilu* [Zhang Zhen's Memoirs], Vols. 1, 2. Beijing, 2003.

Zhang Zongxun. *Zhang Zongxun Huiyilu* [Memoirs of Zhang Zongxun]. Beijing, 1990.

Zhao Dexin, chief ed. *Zhonghua Renmin Gongheguo Jingji Zhuanti Dashiji (1967–1984)* [Specialized Chronology on the Economy of the People's Republic of China (1967–1984)]. Zhengzhou, 1989.

Zhao Guoqiang and Wang Xuejin. "Ideas on Establishing Our Country's Combined Missile Offensive and Defensive Systems," *GFDXXB*, No. 3, 2000.

Zhao Li. "Globalization and China's Sea Power," *Junshi Wenzhai*, No. 10, 2002.

Zheng Qian. "The National War Preparedness around the Time of the CCP Ninth Congress," in CCP Central Party History Research Section, *Zhonggong Dangshi Ziliao*, Vol. 41, 1992.

Zheng Qian and Han Gang. *Mao Zedong zhi Lu Wannian Suiyue (4)* [The Road of Mao Zedong: His Remaining Years (Vol. 4)]. Beijing, 1994.

Zheng Shengxia. "Importance Should Be Attached to Certain Issues Concerning the Employment of the Air Force in Joint Operations," *GFDXXB*, No. 1, 1997.

Zheng Shengxia and Zhang Changzhi. "On the Development of the Modern Air Force and the Change in Military Strategy," *ZGJSKX*, No. 2, 1996.

Zheng Wenhan. "Chief Peng's Great Contributions to the Building of Our Army in the 1950s," *JSLS*, No. 6, 1988.

———, chief ed. *Junshi Da Cidian* [Large Military Dictionary]. Shanghai, 1993.

Zhi Shaozeng. "Essentials of the Evolution of the Central Military Commission," *JSLS*, No. 6, 1989.

Zhong Min. "China Displays the Power of a New Long-Range Strategic Missile," *Zhongguo Tongxun She*, August 3, 1999.

Zhou Baoyi. "The Threat of a High-Tech Local War to Command Organs and Its Countermeasures," in Wen and Fang, 1998.

Zhou Deli. *Yige Gaoji Canmouzhang de Zishu* [An Account of a Senior Chief of the Staff in His Own Words]. Nanjing, 1992.

Zhou Enlai. "Several Philosophical Thoughts of the Chinese People on Managing Foreign Affairs (April 4, 1963)," in PRC Ministry of Foreign Affairs and the CCP Central Documentation Research Section, chief eds., *Zhou Enlai Waijiao Wenxuan* [A Collection of Zhou Enlai's Speeches and Articles on Foreign Affairs]. Beijing, 2000.

———. "We Will Win Progress and Win Peace (May 21, 1965)," in the CCP Central Document Research Section and the PLA Academy of Military Science, eds., *Zhou Enlai Junshi Wenxian* [Documents on Zhou Enlai's Military Work], Vol. 4. Beijing, 1997.

———. "Zhou Enlai's Talk at a Meeting of the Chinese Delegation Attending the Sino-Soviet Border Negotiation (Excerpt) (7 October 1969)," in *Cold War Bulletin*, No. 11 (Winter 1998).

Zhou Enlai and Luo Ruiqing. "Strengthen Construction and War Preparedness in the Rear of the First- and Second-Line Regions," note 1, in the CCP Central Document Research Section and the PLA Academy of Military Science, eds., *Zhou Enlai Junshi Wenxian* [Documents on Zhou Enlai's Military Work], Vol. 4. Beijing, 1997.

Zhou Jianguo. "The Nuclear Strategy of the Bush Administration Is Moving Gradually from Deterrence to Actual Combat," *JFJB*, March 18, 2002.

Zhu Fei. "How to Destroy the Future Operational Command System of the Taiwanese Military," *JCZS*, No. 5, 2004.

Zhu Hongsheng. "'*Shashoujian*' or '*Sashoujian*'?" *Guofang*, No. 8, 2004.

Zhu Qiangguo. "U.S. Seeks Absolute Military Superiority," *China Daily*, March 13, 2002 (Internet version).

Zhu Rongchang, chief ed. *Kongjun Da Cidian* [Air Force Big Dictionary]. Shanghai, 1996.

Zhu Songchun. "Chinese Scholars Are Probing into the Developmental Strategy for National Defense for the Year 2000," *Liaowang* (Overseas ed.), July 21, 1986.

Zhu Wenyi. "An Arena of Rivalry between Groups of Secretaries in China," www .ncn.org/zwginfo/da.asp?ID=17339&ad=6/1/2002.

Zhu Yu et al. *Nijing zhong de Weiren Li Xiannian* [Li Xiannian, A Great Man in Adverse Circumstances]. Beijing, n.d. http://news.eastday.com/epublish/gh/ paper148/20010814/class014800023/hwz461728.html.

Zhu Zhongli. *Jifeng Zhi Jingcao Mao Zedong yu Wang Jiaxiang* [Strength of Character Is Tested in a Crisis: Mao Zedong and Wang Jiaxiang]. Beijing, 1999.

ZT. "Our Army's Early Warning Aircraft Can Be Used in Actual Battles," http://mil .eastday.com/eastday/mil/node3039/node3173/node3176/userobject1ai730996 .html.

Zuo Ying. "Cherish the Memory of Comrade Liu Peishan," *Fujian Dangshi Yuekan* [Party History Monthly (Fujian)], No. 7, 1987.

Index

Page references to illustrations and captions are bold-faced.